Lilian M Quiller-Couch

Reminiscences of Oxford

Lilian M Quiller-Couch

Reminiscences of Oxford

ISBN/EAN: 9783742855282

Manufactured in Europe, USA, Canada, Australia, Japa

Cover: Foto ©Andreas Hilbeck / pixelio.de

Manufactured and distributed by brebook publishing software (www.brebook.com)

Lilian M Quiller-Couch

Reminiscences of Oxford

Reminiscences of Oxford

by Oxford Men

1559—1850

SELECTED AND EDITED

BY

LILIAN M. QUILLER COUCH

Oxford
PRINTED FOR THE OXFORD HISTORICAL SOCIETY
AT THE CLARENDON PRESS
1892

PREFACE.

IT seems expedient to say a word or two in preface on the scope and limitations of this volume. To begin with, it is a selection, and a selection strictly of Reminiscences of Oxford Men,—the writer of each extract being an *alumnus* of Oxford who, looking back, has described, judged and commented upon its collegiate life by the light of later years and a larger knowledge of the world. No room has been found for diaries, nor for any record of immediate impressions; the case of Evelyn being but a seeming relaxation of this rule, since internal evidence abounds in his 'Diary' to show that it was not posted from day to day, but often, indeed, written up long after the events which it chronicles.

These Reminiscences, therefore, may be described as the outside views of men who have been inside the University. Their interest, too, is distinct from the interest of memoirs which treat elaborately of academic politics and intrigue or trace the progress of renowned movements and high events. They are written for the most part by men who came to Oxford to seek an education, though at different periods and with very various notions of what that education ought to be; for the list extends from Elizabethan times to our own, and includes men of pleasure and country squires as well as statesmen, scholars and theologians. And in the following pages each tells us what he found and what he missed, straightly and, in most cases, with no conscious adornment. This complete ruggedness of truth, which is apt unwittingly to take a certain polish when an Englishman attempts to transfer it from his own language to another, seems the more ensured by the exclusion of all Reminiscences written in Latin. There is ample material for another volume of the same nature as this; and sufficient for many future volumes of a separate but kindred type may be gleaned from diaries, outsiders' views, impressions of Oxford by visitors, and Latin Reminiscences; but the admission of any of these into this selection would have given it a different character.

The sentiment with which Oxford haunts her sons has elsewhere found frequent and lofty utterance. These are plainer confessions, and in more than one case relentless enough, the voice of no submissive son. None the less, since that sentiment is a fact, as much as anything else, some residuum of it will be found, together with a certain unity of truth, even after reading the judgments of men so diverse as Laud and Hobbes, Amhurst and Whitefield, Gibbon and Shelley and George Colman the younger. And possibly the writer who touches it most surely is honest old Stephen Penton, of the 'rambling head,' as he tells how, with many misgivings, he brought up his son to the old University; how the mother and sisters came too; of their interview with the tutor, and how the young ladies 'called him the *merest* scholar, and if this were your *Oxford* breeding, they had rather he should go to Constantinople to learn manners'; and of the public bowling-green, where 'coming in, I saw half a score of the finest youths the sun, I think, ever shined upon.' Records such as these, though, perhaps, not strictly speaking *history*, yet help to vivify our understanding of history.

It is sometimes said that there is no first-rate novel founded on University life (for *Verdant Green* is a humorous sketch rather than a novel: and opinions differ upon *Tom Brown at Oxford*), and the conclusion is drawn that the elements of profound human interest are wanting in it. Is this so? In spite of the character given to Oxford of being a city of short memories and abruptly ended friendships, in spite of the inchoative qualities of youths of eighteen or twenty, especially in respect to the 'ruling passion' so dear to novelists, yet surely in the three or four years spent at Oxford by an incredible company of young students 'fresh from public schools, and not yet tossed about and hardened in the storms of life'—as the author of *My Oxford Days* writes—some of them Penton's 'finest youths,' some obviously otherwise—there must be, one would think, abundance of romantic incident awaiting its Thackeray or its Meredith. For how many have these years been the turning point of a life, as they were at the sister University for Charles Kingsley? Truly there is more at Oxford than 'Mild *monastic faces in quiet collegiate cloisters*': and greater battles than Waterloo are fought and won on these sterner playing fields, battles 'before which,' as another writer says, 'the name of Marathon shall fade away.'

The Reminiscences are arranged, so far as is possible, chronologically according to the date of birth of each author. The notes are restricted to what is necessary to elucidate the text, and to a large extent are primary facts about the University life of persons mentioned, so that they may fit into their proper places in the narrative. For these facts Mr. Foster's *Alumni Oxonienses* has been largely drawn upon.

viii   *PREFACE.*

Grateful thanks are due to many friends for valuable suggestions during the preparation of this volume, and particularly to Mr. F. Madan, M.A., of the Bodleian Library, for his untiring help, also to the editors of several modern magazines[1]—in some cases to the authors also (see footnote) for permission to reproduce their articles.

L. M. QUILLER COUCH.

[1] The Editors or present representatives of *The Month* (No. xxvi), *London Society* (No. xxvii), *Boys' Own Volume* (No. xxviii), *National Review* (No. xxix, revised by Mr. Kebbel), and *Time* (Nos. xxx and xxxi, the former revised by Mr. Bedford, the latter inserted by permission of Lord Brabourne).

ERRATA, ETC.

On page 1 *for* from [thence London] *read* from thence [London]
,,   3 *for* Bodlelan *read* Bodleian
,,   39 *for* 1659 *read* 1661
,,   93 line 8 *for* statuterequires *read* statute requires
,,   97 *for* 1736 *read* 1763
,, 115 note, *for* 1864 *read* 1684
,, 128 note, *for* codicil to his will *read* codicil to his will,
,, 178 note 5, *for* B.A. 1780 *read* B.A. 1784
,, 202 *for* John Hamilton Thorn, *read* John Hamilton Thom
,, 338 line 20 *for* undegraduate *read* undergraduate
,, 366 line 6 *for* Elizabethian *read* Elizabethan
,, 377 Robert Smith Surtees, author of *Handley Cross*, etc., was never at B.N.C.

CONTENTS.

I.
                                                                                                  PAGES

BODLEY, SIR THOMAS ($1544/6$—1609 : *in residence* 1559—76, etc.)   1–3
Probationer and Fellow of Merton, 1.—Undertakes the reading of a Greek lecture in the College Hall, 1.—Stands for Proctorship, 2.—Leaves England, 1576, 2.—Returns to Oxford and devotes himself to its library, 3.

II.

LAUD, WILLIAM (1573—$164\frac{2}{3}$: *in res.* 1590—1601, etc.)   .   4–12
Letter to Walter Curle, Bishop of Winchester, respecting the reading of *Calvin's Institutions* at New College, 4.—Letter to Richard Baylie, Vice-Chancellor, respecting 'Mr. Crofts and his great horses,' 5.—Extract from a letter to Christopher Potter, Vice-Chancellor, concerning the Christmas-day sermon and communion in College Chapels, 6.—Extract from Laud's answer to the speech of Lord Say and Sele, 7.—Letter to Sir Robert Cotton, desiring the return of an ancient volume of Beda, lent from St. John's College library, 10.

III.

HOBBES, THOMAS (1588—1679 : *in res.* 1602—8, etc.)   .   13–7
His birth and early education, 14.—Admitted into Magdalen Hall, 14.—Hobbes' studies at Oxford, 16.—Tutor in the Cavendish family, 16.

IV.

EVELYN, JOHN (1620–1706 : *in res.* 1637—40, etc.)   .   .   18–34
Admitted a fellow commoner at Balliol, 18.—Coffee houses in England, 19.—Evelyn's gift to his College library, 20.—Learns dancing, vaulting, and the rudiments of music, 20.—Leaves Oxford to reside in the Middle Temple, 20.—Visits Oxford in 1654, 21.—Visits Oxford in 1664, 25.—The building of the Sheldonian Theatre, 26.—Evelyn obtains the Arundel Marbles from Mr. Henry Howard, as a gift to the University of Oxford, 26.—Receives the thanks of the University, 27.—Visits Oxford in 1669, 29.—The Encænia of the new Theatre, 29.—Honorary degree of D.C.L. is conferred on Evelyn, 32.—Visits Oxford in 1675, 33.

CONTENTS.

V.

SHAFTESBURY, ANTHONY ASHLEY COOPER, first Earl of (1621—
1683: *in res.* 1637—8) 35–8
Enters at Exeter College, 35.—Keeps horses and servants at Oxford, 35.
—Coursing in the Schools, 36.—Attempt to alter the college beer, 37.—
The abolition in Exeter College of 'tucking freshmen,' 37.

VI.

PENTON, STEPHEN (1640—1706: *in res.* 1659—6$\frac{9}{70}$, etc.) . 39–52
Entered at Oxford during the 'King and Parliament' difficulties, 39.—
Enthusiasm and disappointment, 40.—Indecision as to the education of his second son, 41.—Decides to take him to Oxford, 42.—Converses with the Proctor, 42.—Interviews the tutor, 43.—The tutor's advice to Penton, 44.—That his son observe the College rules, 44.—That he reside the whole year, 45.—That he 'frequent not publick places,' 46.—That he discharge all debts quarterly, 46.—That he keep no horse, 47.—That he attend the University Church, 47.—That his allowance should go through his tutor's hands, 48.—On the subject of his friends, 48.—Invitation to a Commons with the tutor, 50.—Penton visits the bowling-green, 50.—Becomes more satisfied with the University, 51.

VII.

POTENGER, JOHN (1647—1733: *in res.* 1663—9) . . 53–6
Gains a scholarship at Corpus, 53.—His studies, 54.—Reads in the College Hall, 55.—Receives his B.A. degree, 55.—Performs a portion of the exercises for M.A. degree, 56.

VIII.

NEWTON, RICHARD (1676—1753: reminiscences referring to
1723) 57–67
Opposition of Exeter College to the Incorporation of Hart Hall, 57.—
Rebellion among the Commoners, 57.—An attempt to obtain the complete evacuation of the Hall, 58.—Case of Joseph Somaster, 59.—Tutor at Hart Hall, 60.—Expenses at Hart Hall, 63.—Somaster's scholarship at Balliol unfairly gained, 67.

IX.

TERRÆ FILIUS, i. e. N. AMHURST (1697—1742: *in res.* 1716—
19) 68–96
Admission and Matriculation, 68.—Loyalty at Oxford, 70.—Letter from Wadham College concerning neglectful lecturers, 71.—Method of disputation, 72.—The case of Richard Meadowcourt, 75.—Method of acquiring University degrees, 90.

X.

SHENSTONE, WILLIAM (1714—1763: *in res.* 1732—about 1735) 97–103
Commoner at Pembroke College, 97.—Richard Graves at Pembroke College, 97.—College society, 97.—Shenstone's intercourse with Graves and Whistler, 99.—His studies, 100.—His personal appearance, 101.—Visits Mr. Jago privately on account of his being a servitor, 101.—Leaves Oxford without taking a degree, 103.—His house at the Leasowes, 103.

XI.

WHITEFIELD, GEORGE (1714—1770: *in res.* 1732—6, etc.)   104–12
Servitor at Pembroke College, 104.—Expenses at the University, 105.—Attends St. Aldate's Church, and St. George's in the Castle, 105.—Meets Charles Wesley, 106.—Becomes a Methodist, 106.—Threatened with expulsion for visiting the poor, 107.—Inability to perform the College exercises, 108.—Becomes ill, 109.—Acquaintance with the Bishop of Gloucester, 110.—Is ordained, 111.—Sir John Phillips, his benefactor, 111.—Whitefield labours at Oxford, 111.

XII.

GIBBON, EDWARD (1737—1794: *in res.* 1752—3) .   .   113–29
Matriculates at Magdalen College, 113.—Comparison of English and foreign Universities, 113.—First introduction to the University, 114.—Bishop Lowth's description of his academical life, 114.—John Locke's expulsion from Christ Church, 115.—Condemnation of 'the schools of Oxford and Cambridge,' 116.—Condemnation of the Professors, 117.—Description of Magdalen College, 119.—Description of the Fellows, 119.—Lax discipline of his College, 120.—Inefficient tutors, 121.—Gibbon's neglectful behaviour, 122.—Writes an essay on 'The Age of Sesostris,' 123.—His second tutor, 123.—Absences from College, 123.—Conversion to the Church of Rome, 124.—Expulsion from Magdalen, 126.—Later opinion of the University, 127.—Lord Clarendon's bequest applied to the establishment of a Riding-school, 128.

XIII.

VINDICATION OF MAGDALEN COLLEGE (by the Rev. James
    Hurdis, 1767—1801: Fellow of Magdalen, 1788—1800) 130–48
Early matriculation of Gibbon, 130.—His short residence at the University, 132.—Expulsion from Magdalen, 134.—Custom of declaiming continued at Magdalen, 135.—Terminal exercises, 136.—Public exercise by B.A.'s, 138.—The 'manufactures of the monks of Magdalen,' 143.—Vindication of the Professors, 146.—Dr. White's Bampton Lectures, 148.

XIV.

SHELBURNE, WILLIAM FITZMAURICE, second Earl of (1737—
    1805 : *in res.* 1755—about 1757)   .   .   .   149-51
Falls under a narrow-minded tutor at Christ Church, 149.—Is introduced
to Lord Chesterfield and Lord Granville, 149.—His reading, 150.—The
anti-Westminsters an unfashionable portion of the undergraduates, 150.—
Low state of the House intellectually, 151.

XV.

EDGEWORTH, RICHARD LOVELL (1744—1817: *in res.* 1761—4)   152-6
Enters at Corpus, 152.—Attends a fencing school, 152.—Foul play
during the fencing, 153.—Dr. Randolph, the President, 153.—Gentleman
commoners not obliged to attend early Chapel regularly, 154.—Interview
with the President, 154.—Attends the Assizes, 155.

XVI.

MALMESBURY, JAMES HARRIS, first Earl of (1746—1820 : *in
    res.* 1763—5)   157-8
Spends six months in London, 157.—Lax discipline at the University,
158.—Distinguished members of Merton College, 158.

XVII.

KNOX, VICESIMUS (1752—1821 : *in res.* 1771—5, etc.)   .   159-67
'On the necessity of an attention to things as well as books,' 159.—
Respect paid to a Senior Fellow, 159.—'On some parts of the discipline
in our English Universities,' 160.—Exercises for degrees, 161.—' Doing
generals,' 161.—'Answering under bachelor,' 162.—' Determining, doing
quodlibets, doing austins,' 164.—The lectures called ' *Wall* lectures,'
165.

XVIII.

COLMAN, GEORGE, THE YOUNGER (1762—1836: *in res.* 1780—1) 168-82
His dress when presented for matriculation, 168.—Courtesy shown to
Eton and Westminster boys, 169.—Becomes involved in a money trans-
action, 170.—Trials of a Freshman, 173.—Description of a Scout and a
Bedmaker, 174.—A sleepless night, 176.—Distinguished members of
Christ Church, 178.—The Poet Harding, 180.—Lord Wellesley's declama-
tions, 180.—Colman is sent to Aberdeen, 182.

XIX.

LETTERS FROM OXFORD (probably by John Skinner, 1772—
    1839: *in res.* 1790—4)   183-201
Rooms in College, 183.—Academical dress, 184.—Impositions written
for undergraduates by the barber, 185.—The Public Schools, 185.—

Description of a day spent in College, 185.—Morning Chapel, 187.—Breakfast in College, 188.—Skating on Christ Church meadows, 189.—Description of dinner in Hall, 190.—Speaking the *narrare*, 191.—A jovial evening in Trinity College, 193.—A sober evening, 195.—A sail in the 'Hobby-horse,' 199.—A row on the Cherwell, 200.

XX.

WHITE, JOSEPH BLANCO (1775—1841 : *in res.* 1826—32, etc.)   202–11
Establishes himself at Oxford, 202.—His friends there, 202.—Tutor at Holland House, 203.—Hebdomadal Board proposes to confer on him an M.A. degree by diploma, 204.—Opposition to this proposal, 204.—Admitted into Oriel College, 206.—White's ideal College, 207.—Unorthodoxy, 208.—Supposed jealousy of the University in neglecting to give him employment, 209.—The setting up of the *London Review*, 209.—The Peel contest, 209.—White's right of voting examined, 210.—Separation from the Church, 210.

XXI.

DIBDIN, THOMAS FROGNALL (1776—1847 : *in res.* 1793—7)   212–27
Matriculates at St. John's College, 212.—On the election of President, St. John's College goes to do homage to Christ Church, 213.—College life, 214.—The Society for Scientific and Literary Disquisition, 218.—A deputation of members of the Society wait upon the Vice-Chancellor, 219.—The Society is carried on privately, 220.—Its members named 'Lunatics,' 221.—Encænia of the Duke of Portland, 222.—Illumination in honour of Earl Howe's victory, 224.—'Paradise,' 226.

XXII.

CLINTON, HENRY FYNES (1781—1852 : *in res.* 1799—1806)   228–39
Introduced to Dr. Cyril Jackson at Christ Church, 228.—Love of literature and book collecting, 229.—John Symmons and John Conybeare, 230.—Clinton is examined under the new system, with Class Lists, 232.—Becomes a student of Christ Church, 232.—Takes his B.A. degree, 232.—Tutor to Lord Gower, 232.—Appointed to the commemoration speech and receives the first Bachelor's prize, 233.—Isaac Gardiner makes Clinton his heir, 234.—Begins to compose the tragedy of 'Solyman,' 234.—Takes his M.A. degree, 234.—Death of Mr. Pitt, 235.—Clinton becomes M.P. for Aldborough, 235.—Declares his classical knowledge to be most limited, 236.—List of Greek writers possessed on leaving Oxford, 237.—The study of the Greek language at Oxford, 238.

XXIII.

HEBER, REGINALD (1783—1826 : *in res.* 1800—4, etc.)   .   240–6
Letter to E. D. Davenport concerning changes at Oxford, 240.—Letter to John Thornton concerning the All Souls' Mallard Feast, 242.—Early

rising and a course of mathematics, 243.—Verses sung at the Mallard Feast, 244.—Original air to which they were sung, 245.

XXIV.

COLERIDGE, JOHN TAYLOR (1790—1876: *in res.* 1809—13)   247–53

Is an undergraduate at Corpus with Thomas Arnold, 247.—Writes for the Latin verse prize, 247.—Description of Corpus, 248.—Description of Arnold, 250.—The Attic Society, 252.—Freedom of Oxford from religious controversies, 252.

XXV.

SHELLEY, PERCY BYSSHE (1792—1822: *in res.* 1810—11)   254–300

First meeting with T. J. Hogg at dinner, 255.—A discussion on German and Italian writings, 256.—Shelley's discordant voice, 256.—He attends a lecture on mineralogy, 257.—Discourses on chemistry, 258.—His rooms at University College, 260.—Electrical experiments, 263.—Companionship with Hogg, 264.—Practice of pistol-shooting, 266.—Country walks, 268.—Happy life at the University, 273.—Shelley regrets the limited period of residence, 275.—The 'oak,' 275.—Shelley's opinion of his instructors, 277.—The Long Vacation, 279.—Latin verses of Shelley, 281.—Feuds consequent on the election of Chancellor, 283.—Political divisions in the University, 284.—Lax state of the University, 285.—Shelley begins to print, 286.—The case of W. Attfield, 286.—Shelley's pamphlet on 'Atheism,' 287.—He is expelled, 289.—T. J. Hogg expelled also, 292.—Easy discipline at University College, 296.—Anecdote respecting the University of Oxford, 297.

XXVI.

OAKELEY, FREDERICK (1802—1880: *in res.* 1820—37)   .   301–45

(I.) Christ Church under Dean Hall, 301.—Unhappy recollections of his undergraduate life, 302.—His life with a private tutor, 304.—He is taken to the Sheldonian Theatre at Commemoration, 304.—Sent home from College owing to want of space, 307.—Description of wine-parties, 307.—'Gown and Town' rows, 309.—Distinguished men at Christ Church, 309.—Oakeley writes for prizes, 310.—College authorities at Christ Church, 311.—Oakeley gains a College prize, 313.—His rooms at Christ Church, 317.—Disappointing result of his examination, 319.—(II.) Christ Church under Dean Smith, 319.—Careless bestowal of studentships, servitorships, and choristerships, 319.—Oakeley resolves upon reading for a fellowship, 322.—Becomes a candidate for the Oriel fellowship, 323.—Attends Lloyd's divinity lectures, 324.—Moral and religious state of Christ Church, 329.—Establishment of the Union Debating Society, 331.—(III.) Balliol under Dr. Jenkyns, 332.—Scholarships on the foundation thrown open to competition, 334.—Election of Archibald Campbell Tait, 335.—Oakeley placed on the foundation as

Fellow and College Chaplain, 337.—Distinguished additions to the
society of Balliol, 339.—Tractarianism at Balliol, 340.—Resignation of
Mr. Ward, 341.—Moral tone of Balliol, 342.

XXVII.

ST. ALBAN HALL, OXFORD (by the Rev. Henry Robinson,
    D.D., 1821—1887: *in res.* 1838—42, etc.) .   346–55
St. Alban Hall merged into Merton, 346.—Number of members, 346.—
St. Edmund, Magdalen, and New Inn, Halls, 348.—Scholars of Merton
live at Beam Hall, 349.—Sociability at St. Alban Hall, 350.—Popular
'coaches,' 350.—College tutors, 351.—Condemnation of Newman's
Tract, 352.—Distinguished men, 353.—Fellows of All Souls, 355.

XXVIII.

TOURNAMENTS HOLDEN AT OXFORD (about 1850—60) .   356–65
Arm-chair races round the 'quad,' 356.—'Tilting' becomes fashionable,
358.—The 'gate-bill,' 360.—'Knocking in,' 361.—Noisy proceedings
after a wine-party, 362.—Magnanimous behaviour of the Dean, 363.

XXIX.

OLD AND NEW OXFORD (by T. E. Kebbel, 1827: *in res.*
    1845—9, etc.) 366–76
Changes at Oxford, 367.—Shooting at Eynsham, 368.—Altered style of
dress, 369.—Changes in undergraduate life, 370.—Insufficient intercourse
between Dons and undergraduates in former days, 371.—Alteration in the
status of the Fellows, 374.—The Long Vacation, 375.

XXX.

THE O. D. A. (by the Rev. William K. R. Bedford, 1827:
    in res. 1844—8) 377–85
Brasenose, about 1845, 377.—Fancy dress ball in College, 378.—'Sitting
in the Schools,' 378.—Suggested theatricals, 379.—*Macbeth Travestie*
acted at Henley, 379.—Second performance at Henley, 382.—Unfortunate
reception of the Mayor of Henley, 383.—The O. D. A. take *The Royalty*
theatre for the night of the University Boat Race, 1849, 384.—Last performance of the O. D. A., 385.

XXXI.

MY OXFORD DAYS (by the Rt. Hon. E. H. Knatchbull-
    Hugessen, M.P., now Lord Brabourne: *in res.*
    1847—50) 386–401
Gentlemen commoners at Magdalen, 388.—Account of Dr. Routh, President of Magdalen, 389.—Anecdotes of Dr. Routh, 390.—Notable Fellows

at Magdalen, 391.—Lax discipline exercised over gentlemen commoners, 392.—Drinking toasts to a chorus, 393.—Arm-chair races in the cloisters, 395.—Death of a Demy of Magdalen, 396.—The Magdalen cook, 398.—Pleasant memories of Oxford, 400.

APPENDIX.

LETTER FROM ROBERT SOUTHEY (1774—1843: *in res.* 1792—4)   403–8

Coach drive to Oxford, 403.—Loses his purse, 404.—Recovers it again, 406.—Interviews John Davy, Master of Balliol, 406.—Is matriculated, 407.—His rooms and furniture, 407.—Attends service at the University Church, 407.

INDEX   .   409–30

I.

SIR THOMAS BODLEY.

[*Born* March 2, 1544-5, at Exeter: *died* Jan. 28, 1612-3. Studied Hebrew, Greek and Divinity as a refugee at the University of Geneva, 1556-8. This autobiography is dated Dec. 1609.]

The Life of Sir Thomas Bodley . . . Written by Himselfe. Oxford, 1647.

I.

' I was sent away from [thence London] to the University [1] of *Oxford*, recommended to the teaching and tuition of Doctour *Humfrey* [2], who was shortly after chosen the chiefe reader in divinity, and President of *Magdalen* Colledge; there I followed my studies till I tooke the degree of Batchelour of Arts, which was in the yeare 1563, within which yeare I was also chosen probationer of *Merton* Colledge, and the next yeare ensuing admitted Fellow. Afterwards, to wit in the yeare 1565, by speciall perswasion of some of my fellowes, and for my private exercise, I undertooke the publique reading of a Greeke lecture, in the same Colledge Hall, without requiring or expecting any stipend for it. Neverthelesse it pleased the Fellowship of their owne accord to allow me soone after foure markes by the ' yeare, and ever since to continue that lecture to the Colledge. In the yeare of our Lord 1566 I proceeded Master of Arts, and read for that yeare in the Schoole-streets naturall philosophy; after which time, within lesse than three yeares space, I was wonne by intreaty of my best affected friends, to stand for the Proctour-

---
[1] About 1559.
[2] Lawrence Humphrey; President of Magdalen Coll., 1561-90.

ship, to which I and my colleague, Master *Bearblocke* of *Exeter* Colledge, were quietly elected in the yeare 1569, without any competition or countersuite of any other. After this, for a long time I supplyed the office of the University Oratour, and bestowed my time in the study of sundry faculties, without any inclination to professe any one above the rest, insomuch as at last I waxed desirous to travell beyond the seas, for attaining to the knowledge of some speciall moderne tongues, and for the encrease of my experience in the managing of affaires, being wholly then addicted to employ my selfe, and all my cares, in the publique service of the State. My resolution fully taken I departed out of *England* Anno 1576. . . .

II.

P. 14. . . . | I fell to discourse and debate in my mind, that although I might find it fittest for me to keep out of the throng of Court contentions, and addresse my thoughts and deeds to such ends altogether as I my selfe could best affect; yet withall I was to think, that my duty towards God, the expectation of the world, my naturall inclination, and very morality, did require that I should not wholly so hide those little abilities that I had, but that in some measure, in one

P. 15. kind or other, | I should doe the true part of a profitable member in the State: Whereupon, examining exactly for the rest of my life, what course I might take, and having sought (as I thought, all the waies to the wood) to select the most proper, I concluded at the last to set up my staffe[1] at the library doore in *Oxford*; being thoroughly perswaded that in my solitude and surcease from the Common-wealth affaires, I could not busy my selfe to better purpose than by reducing that place (which then in every part lay ruined and wast) to the publique use of students; for the effecting whereof, I found my selfe furnished in a competent proportion, of such foure kindes of aides, as unlesse I had them all, there was no

[1] About 1598.

hope of good successe. For without some kinde of knowledge, as well in the learned and moderne tongues as in sundry other sorts of scholasticall literature, without some purse-ability to goe through with the charge, without very great store of honourable friends to further the designe, and without speciall good leisure to follow such a worke, it could but have proved a vaine attempt, and inconsiderate. But how well I have sped in all my endeavours, and how full provision I have made for the benefit and ease [1] of all frequenters of the P. 16. library, that which I have already performed in sight, that besides which I have given for the maintenance of it, and that which hereafter I purpose to adde, by way of enlargement to that place (for the project is cast, and whether I live or dye it shall be, God willing, put in full execution) will testifie so truly and aboundantly for me, as I need not be the publisher of the dignity and worth of mine owne institution [1].

[1] The early history of Sir Thomas Bodley's noble foundation is best studied in the Rev. W. D. Macray's *Annals of the Bodleian Library*, 2nd edition. Oxford, 1890.

II.

WILLIAM LAUD,
ARCHBISHOP OF CANTERBURY.

[*Born* Oct. 7, 1573: *executed* Jan. 10, 164$\frac{4}{5}$. Laud was born at Reading and educated at the free-school there. In 1590 he became scholar of St. John's College, Oxford, and was made fellow in 1593, president in 1611, chancellor of the University in 1630, archbishop in 1633.]

Laud's Works, 8 vols. *Library of Anglo-Catholic Theology.* Oxford, 1847–60.

I.

[LETTER TO THE BISHOP OF WINCHESTER [1].]

Another business there is, which I think may be very well worthy your consideration; and if you do not give it remedy (as I think it abundantly deserves) I do not know who either can or will. I have often wondered why so many good scholars came from Winchester to New College, and yet so few of them afterwards prove eminent men: and while I lived in Oxford I thought upon divers things that might be causes of it, and I believe true ones, but I have lately heard of another, which I think hath done and doth the college a great deal of harm, in the breeding of their young men. When they come from Winchester they are to be probationers two years and then fellows. A man would think those two years, and some years after, should be allowed to logic, philosophy, mathematics, and the like grounds of learning, the better to enable them to study divinity with judgment: but I am of

[1] Walter Curle, D.D. of Cambridge, Bishop of Winchester, 1632.

late accidentally come to know, that when the probationers stand for their fellowships, and are to be examined how they have profited, one chief thing in which they are examined is, how diligently they have read Calvin's Institutions; and are more strictly held to it, how they have profited in that, than almost in any kind of learning besides. I do not deny but that Calvin's Institutions may profitably be read, and as one of their first books for divinity, when they are well grounded in other learning; but to begin with it so soon, I am afraid doth not only hinder them from all grounds of judicious learning, but also too much possess their judgments before they are able to judge, and makes many of them humourous in, if not against the Church. For so many of them have proved in this latter age, since my own memory in that university. Your lordship is visitor there, and I think you cannot do a better deed, than to advise on a way, how to break this business with the warden [1], who is a learned and discreet man, and then think upon some remedy for it. For I am verily persuaded it doth that college a great deal of harm. I do not hold it fit that your lordship should fall upon this business too suddenly. When the warden comes next to the election may be a fit time; nor would I have you let it be known that you have received this information from me; but sure I am 'tis true, and needs a remedy.

W. CANT.

February 2, 1635 (163⅘).

II.

[LETTER TO THE VICE-CHANCELLOR[2].]

SIR,

For Mr. Crofts and his great horses [3], he may carry them back if he please, as he brought them. For certainly it

---

[1] Robert Pinke, Warden of New College, 1617.
[2] Richard Baylie, Dean of Salisbury, and President of St. John's College.
[3] For 'riding the great horse,' see Collectanea, Vol. I (Oxf. Hist. Soc. V, 1885), pp. 272-7, 284-5.

cannot be fit for the university, though the exercise in itself be exceeding commendable: for the gentlemen there are most part too young, and not strong enough; besides you cannot put that charge upon their parents, without their particular leave and directions; but this especially is considerable, that where ever this place of riding shall be, where one scholar learns, you shall have twenty or forty to look on, and there lose their time, so that upon the whole matter, that place shall be fuller of scholars, than either schools or library. Therefore I pray give Mr. Crofts thanks fairly for his good intentions; but as thus advised, I cannot give way to his staying there to the purpose he intends; nor is it altogether inconsiderable, that you should suffer scholars to fall into the old humour of going up and down in boots and spurs, and then have their excuse ready, that they are going to the riding house; and I doubt not, but other inconveniences may be thought on, therefore I pray no admittance of him.

W. CANT.

Lambeth,
June 23, 1637.

III.

[EXTRACT FROM LETTER TO THE VICE-CHANCELLOR[1].]

It is true, you write that most colleges have upon Christmas day a sermon and a communion in their private chapels, and by that means cannot come to the public sermon of the university at Christ Church. And whereas you write farther, that some have wished, that in regard of this the morning sermon for the university might be put off to the afternoon (as it is upon Easter-day for the like occasion), I for my part think the motion very good, it being a day of solemn

---

[1] Christopher Potter, Dean of Worcester, and Provost of Queen's College.

observation. Yet I would have it proposed to the heads, and then that which you shall do by public consent shall very well satisfy me.

W. CANT.

*Lambeth,
Dec. 4, 1640.*

IV.

[EXTRACT FROM LAUD'S ANSWER TO THE SPEECH OF THE LORD SAY AND SEAL TOUCHING THE LITURGY.]

(*Dec.* 3, 1641.)

... *My Lord of Canterbury! a man of mean birth, bred up in a College, (and that too frequently falls out to be in a faction,) whose narrow comprehension extended itself no further than to carry on a side in a College, or canvass for a Proctor's place in the University.* Vol. VI. P. 86.

.. To my birth, his Lordship adds that I was bred up in a College. That's true. But 'tis as true that his Lordship was bred up in a College[1] also, and of the same University; and therefore, so far he speaks as much against himself as me. But I hope he intends not to charge being bred in a College, as a fault upon either of us; and though 'it too frequently falls out that Colleges be in a faction,' (for that also is too truly observed by his Lordship,) yet that is no fault in any man who neither causes nor nourishes the faction. But that which his Lordship charges next upon me is both a ¹ weakness and a fault, if true: weakness, that 'my comprehensions are narrow;' and a fault, because 'they extended no further than to carry on a side in the College, or a canvass for a Proctor's place in the University.' P. 87. P. 88.

For the weakness first. My comprehensions, as narrow as they are, are yet as large as God hath been pleased to make them, and as large as my hard study, accompanied with His grace, hath been able to stretch them; and so large I am sure

[1] New College.

they are, as that I have ever looked carefully upon the whole Catholic Church of Christ, spread upon the face of the whole earth.

And therefore certainly my comprehensions are not so narrow as theirs, whose largest cannot, or will not, look upon one entire national Church; nay, a parochial is too big for them, and a conventicle big enough. Nor did my 'narrow comprehensions' ever reject that great body, the Catholic Church, out of the Creed, as some of late have done, whose comprehensions are not, for all that, censured by his Lordship for their narrowness.

Next for the fault. That's twofold. First, my comprehensions went no further (says my Lord) than 'to carry on a side in a College.' Here my Lord is either utterly mistaken, or, which is worse, in a wilful error; for, while I was Fellow of St. John Baptist's College, where I was bred, it is well known I never made nor held up any side. Indeed, when I was chosen President of that College, there was a bitter faction both raised and countenanced against me (I will forbear to relate how and by whom). But this is certain, I made no party then; for four being in nomination for that headship, I lay then so sick at London, that I was neither able to go down, nor so much as write to my friends about it. Yet, after much tumble, a major part of the votes made choice of me. Thus I was chosen President, May 10, 1611. After this my election was quarrelled at, and great means made against me, insomuch that the most gracious king, King James, sat to hear the cause himself, for the space of full three hours, Aug. 28, at Tichburn in Hampshire, as he returned out of the western progress. Upon this hearing, his Majesty approved my election, and commanded my settlement;[1] which was done accordingly at Michaelmas following. But the faction in the College finding such props above, as they had, continued very eager and bitter against me. The audit of the College, for the year's accounts, and choice of new officers, followed in November; there so God blessed me with patience and moderation in the choice of all offices, that I made all quiet in the College. And for all the narrowness of my comprehensions, I governed that College in peace, without so much as the show of a faction, all my time, which was near upon eleven years. And the truth of all this is notoriously known, and many yet living, of great worth in the Church, able and ready to avow it. And this, I hope, was not to lead on a side.

Secondly, my Lord charges my narrow comprehensions as reaching no further than 'a canvass for a Proctor's place.' I was (with thanks to their love that thought me worthy) chose Proctor[1] of the University, so soon as by statute I was capable of it; but I never meddled in the managing of the canvass for it for myself, nor afterwards for any other, while I continued Fellow of the College. When I was chosen President, I continued so for two years, and meddled not in that business; and this I did, because in some things I did utterly dislike that canvass, and the carriage of it. At last some of the senior Fellows came to me, and told me that the College had been many years without the credit of a Proctor, and that the Fellows began to take it ill at my hands that I would not show myself, and try my credit and my friends in that business. Upon this, rather than I would lose the love of my companions, I did settle myself in an honest and fair way to right the College as much as I could; and by God's blessing it succeeded beyond expectation. But when we were at the strongest, I made this fair offer more than once and again, that if the greater Colleges would submit to take their turns in order, and not seek to carry all from the lesser, we would agree to any indifferent course in Convocation, and allow the greater Colleges their full proportion according to their number. This would not be hearkened unto; whereupon things continued some years.

[1] After this, by his Majesty's grace and favour, I was made Bishop of St. David's[2]; and after that of Bath and Wells[3].

[1] In 1603. [2] In 1621. [3] In 1626.

When I was thus gone out of the University, the election of the Proctors grew more and more tumultuous, till at the last the peace of the University was like to be utterly broken; and the divided parties brought up a complaint to the Council-table. The Lords were much troubled at it, especially the right honourable William, Earl of Pembroke, Lord Steward, and their honourable Chancellor. I had by that time, and by the great grace of his now Majesty, the honour to be a Councillor, and was present. There I acquainted the Lords what offers I had made, during my time in the University, which I did conceive would settle all differences, and make peace for ever. The Lords approved the way; and after the Council was risen, my very honourable Lord the Earl of Pembroke desired me to put the whole business in writing, that he might see and consider of it. I did so: his Lordship approved of it, and sent it to the University, with all freedom to accept or refuse, as they saw cause. The University approved all, only desired the addition of a year or two more to the circle; which would add a turn or two more, to content some of the greater Colleges. This that honourable Lord yielded unto; and that form of election of their Proctors was by unanimous consent made a statute in Convocation, and hath continued the University in peace ever since. And this is all 'the carrying on of a canvass for a Proctor's place' which any truth can challenge me withal. And it may be, my Lord is pleased to impute 'narrow comprehensions' to me, because my advice enclosed the choice of the Proctors within a circle . . . .

V.

[TO SIR ROBERT COTTON.]

Sir,—After long deliberation, I am bold to impart a business unto you which troubles me. It is not long since I was President of St. John's College, in Oxon; and during the time I was in that place, Sir William Paddye (a worthy benefactor[1] to that poor College) importuned the lending of an ancient volume of Beda[2] to you, which the Statutes of that house could not well bear; but that it was thought at that time unfit to distaste a man that had done so much good for the College, and intended much more. The cause which he alleged was, that you had use of it for some things that concerned your house and inheritance.

Upon my coming away from that headship, there began (as there uses in such societies) a faction about the choice of a new governor. The heat that was then struck is not yet quenched in the losing party; and out of an opinion that I had some hand in the business for him that obtained[3], they have been so angry with me, that they have not only been content to forget all the service I did that College, (which I can without vanity say was some,) but have picked all the occasions they could to detract from me.

That which they have most colour for against me, is the lending of this part of Beda out of the library; and though at that time when it was done, their consents were more forward than other honester men's, yet now they are over bold with my reputation, and charge all the guilt of the action upon me, and more too.

Sir, if it please you to think me worth the having, you have now an opportunity to bind me to you; and if it please you to let me have this book to send back to the College, and to take off that which troubles my own mind, and gives some unadvised men too much occasion to be bold with me, you shall in lieu of it have my continual service; and if any thing

[1] Sir William Paddy by will in 1634 provided the salary of the organist of St. John's College, and endowed the choral service; in addition to previous benefactions.

[2] Sir Robert Cotton seldom relaxed his grasp of any MS. which came into his hands: the Bede does not now appear to be at St. John's, although both Sir William Paddy and Laud himself presented old MSS. of Bede to that College, partly perhaps in reparation.

[3] William Juxon, elected in 1621, afterwards Bishop of London, and Archbishop of Canterbury.

of worth in like kind come to my hands, in any place, where
God shall send me to live, I will freely give it in recompence.
This hath been the occasion which hath kept me from
begging your acquaintance; and because I find that I suffer
at the College every day more than other for it, (though the
President and some of the Seniors, out of their due respect to
Sir William Paddy, forbear,) I am very desirous to do two
things at once; namely, to quit that business, and to make
myself both known and a debtor to you, both at once. I will
hope you will refuse me in neither. And so for this time
I leave you to the grace of God, and shall be ready to show
myself both to you and to your worth,

Your very loving Friend,
GUIL. MENEVEN.

Durham House,
November 22, 1623.

III.

THOMAS HOBBES.

THOMAS HOBBESIUS.

[*Born* 1588, at Westport, close to Malmesbury; educated at Malmesbury School; matric. at Magd. Hall, Oxford, 1602; B.A. Feb. 5, 160⅜; *died* Dec. 4, 1679. See Wood's *Ath. Oxon.* ed. Bliss, iii. 1204, and *Dict. of National Biography*.]

Thomæ Hobbesii Malmesburiensis Vita. Authore seipso. Lond. 1679.

P. 1.   Natus erat noster Servator Homo-Deus annos
　　　　Mille & quingentos, octo quoq; undecies.
　　　Stabat & Hispanis in portubus inclyta Classis
　　　　Hostilis, nostro mox peritura mari:
　　　Primo Vere, dies & quintus inibat Aprilis,
　　　　Illo vermiculus tempore nascor ego,
　　　In *Malmesburiâ*; Baptisma à [1]Patre Ministro
　　　　Accepi, & nomen mî dedit ille suum.

　　　　　　　　.　　.

P. 2.   Disco loqui quatuor, totidem legere, & numerare,
　　　　Non bene præterea fingere literulas.
　　　Sex annis ad verba steti *Græcæ* atque *Latinæ*,
　　　　Et decimo quarto mittor ad *Oxonium.*
　　　Huc *Magdalenæ* veniens admittor in Aulam,
　　　　Inque imâ *Logicæ* classe locatus eram.
　　　Et Prælectori cum primis sedulus adsum;
　　　　Is licet imberbis cum gravitate legit,
　　　Barbara, Celarent, Darii, Ferio, Baralypton,
　　　　Hos (dicebat) habet prima Figura Modos.

[1] Hobbes's father was Vicar of Charlton and Westport.

THOMAS HOBBES.

The Life of Mr. Thomas Hobbes of Malmesbury, Written by himself in a Latine Poem. And now translated into English. Lond. 1680. (The doggrel verse must be excused for the sake of the subject.)

In Fifteen hundred eighty eight, Old Style,   P. 1.
When that Armada did invade our Isle,
Call'd the *Invincible*; whose Freight was then,
Nothing but Murd'ring Steel, and Murd'ring Men;
Most of which Navy was disperst, or lost,
And had the Fate to Perish on our Coast:
April the fifth (though now with Age outworn)
I' th' early Spring, I, a poor worm, was born.
In *Malmesbury* Baptiz'd, and Named there
By my own Father, then a Minister.

.   .

Did Learn to speak Four Languages, to write   P. 2.
And read them too, which was my sole delight.
Six years i' th' *Greek* and *Latin* Tongue I spent,
And at Fourteen I was to *Oxford* sent;
And there of *Magd'len*-Hall admitted, I
Myself to *Logick* first did then apply,
And sedulously I my Tutor heard,
Who gravely Read, althou' he had no Beard.
Barbara, Celarent, Darii, Ferio, Baralypton,   P. 3.
These Modes hath the first Figure; then goes on

Cæsare, Camestres, Festino, Baroco, Darapti,
    Hæc etiam totidem stat variata Modis.
Felapton, Disamis, Datici, Bocardo, Ferison,
    Sunt rursus totidem legitimique Modi.
Quos tardè disco, disco tamen, abjicióque
    Admittórque meo quæque probare modo.
Admoveor *Physicæ*, conflatáque cuncta Magister
    Materia & Forma, ut partibus esse docet;
Résque procul positos volitando per aera, Formas
    Reddi visibiles, audibilésque facit.
Multos Effectus tribuit *Syn* & *Antipathiæ*,
    Et supra captum talia multa meum.
Ergo ad amœna magis me verto, librósque revolvo
    Quos prius edoctus, non bene doctus eram.
Pascebámque animum chartis imitantibus Orbem,
    Telluris faciem, & Sydera picta videns.
Gaudebam Soli comes ire, & cernere cunctis
    Terricolis justos quâ facit arte dies.
Quoque *Dracus* filo *Neptunum* [1] *Candisiúsque*
    Cinxerunt medium, quæque adiere loca;
Atque hominum exiguos, si possem, cernere nidos,
    Et picta ignotis Monstra videre locis.
Sunt sua *Geographis* etiam pleromata Doctum.
    Commendat vacuus nullus in orbe locus.
Tempore sed justo cum Baccalaureus Artis
    Essem (namque hic est primus in Arte gradus)
Oxonium linquo, servitum me fero in amplam
    Gentis [2] *Candisiæ* conspicuámque domum;
[3] Rectorisque Aulæ commendat Epistola nostræ,
    Accipior, placitâ conditione steti:

---

[1] Thomas Cavendish, the third circumnavigator of the globe, in 1586-88: Ferdinand Magellan being the first, in 1519-22, although he did not live to return with his ship; and Sir Francis Drake the second, in 1577-80.

[2] Hobbes was tutor to the son of William Cavendish, baron of Hardwick.

[3] Dr. John Wilkinson, Principal of Magdalen Hall, 1605.

Cæsare, Camestres, Festino, Baroco, Darapti,
This hath of Modes the same variety.
Felapton, Disamis, Datisi, Bocardo, Ferison,
These just so many Modes are look'd upon.
Which I, tho' slowly Learn, and then dispense
With them, and prove things after my own sense.
Then *Physicks* read, and my Tutor display'd,
How all Things were of Form and Matter made.
The Aëry Particles which make forms we see,
Both Visible and Audible, to be
Th' Effects of Sympathy, Antipathy.
And many things above my reach Taught me.
Therefore more pleasant studies I then sought,
Which I was formerly, tho' not well Taught.
My Phancie and my Mind divert I do,
With Maps Celestial and Terrestrial too.
Rejoyce t' accompany *Sol* cloath'd with Rays,
Know by what Art he measures out our Days;
How *Drake* and *Cavendish* a girdle made
Quite round the World, what Climates they survey'd;
And strive to find the smaller Cells of Men
And painted Monsters in their unknown Den.
Nay there's a Fulness in Geography;   P. 4.
For Nature e'r abhor'd Vacuity.
Thus in due time took I my first Degree
Of Batchelor i' th' University.
Then *Oxford* left; serv'd *Ca'ndish* known to be
A Noble and Conspicuous Family.
Our College-Rector did me Recommend,
Where I most pleasantly my Days did spend.

IV.

JOHN EVELYN.

[*Born* 31 Oct. 1620; educated at the free-school, Southover, near Lewes; Balliol Coll. Oxford, matr. 29 May, 1637; author of 'Sylva' and many other works; *died* 27 Feb. 1706.]

The Diary of John Evelyn, Esq., F.R.S. Edited by William Bray, Esq., Lond. n.d. (Chandos Classics).

I.

3d April, 1637. I left schoole, where, till about the last yeare, I had been extreamely remisse in my studies, so as I went to the Universitie rather out of shame of abiding longer at schoole, than for any fitnesse, as by sad experience I found, which put me to re-learne all that I had neglected, or but perfunctorily gain'd.

10 May. I was admitted a fellow communer of Baliol College, Oxford, and on the 29th I was matriculated in the Vestry at St. Marie's, where I subscribed the Articles and took the oaths, Dr. Baily[1], head of St. John's, being Vice Chancelor, afterwards Bp. The Fellow Communers in Balliol were no more exempt from exercise than the meanest scholars there, and my Father sent me thither to one Mr. Geo. Bradshaw[2] (*nomen invisum!* yet the son of an excellent father, beneficed—Rector of Ockham—in Surrey.) I ever thought my

---

[1] Richard Baylie, Pres. of St. John's, 1633-48, when he was ejected by the Parliament delegates and became Dean of Salisbury; he was restored in 1660; Vice-Chancellor 1636-8; died at Salisbury in 1667. He never became a bishop.

[2] George Bradshaw, Master of Balliol, 1648-51.

Tutor had parts enough, but as his ambition made him much suspected of the College, so his grudge to Dr. Lawrence[1], the governor of it (whom he afterwards supplanted) tooke up so much of his tyme, that he seldom or never had the opportunity to discharge his duty to his scholars. This I perceiving, associated myself with one Mr. Jas. Thicknesse (then a young man of the Foundation, afterwards a Fellow of the House,) by whose learned and friendly conversation I received great advantage. At my first arrival, Dr. Parkhurst[2] was Master; and after his discease, Dr. Lawrence, a chaplaine of his Ma'ties and Margaret Professor, succeeded, an accute and learned person; nor do I much reproch his severity, considering that the extraordinary remissenesse of discipline had (til his coming) much detracted from the reputation of that Colledg.

There came in my tyme to the Coll: one Nathaniel Conopios out of Greece, from Cyrill the Patriarch of Constantinople, who returning many years after, was made (as I understand) Bishop of Smyrna. He was the first I ever saw drink coffee, which custom came not into England till 30 years after[3].

After I was somewhat settled there in my formalities (for then was the University exceedingly regular, under the exact discipline of William Lawd, Abp. of Canterbury, then Chan-

[1] Thomas Lawrence, Master of Balliol, 1637-48.
[2] John Parkhurst, Master of Balliol, 1617-37.
[3] Anthony à Wood in his Life (autobiography) writes under the year 1650: 'This yeare Jacob a Jew opened a coffey house at the Angel in the parish of S. Peter in the East, Oxon. and there it was by some, who delighted in noveltie, drank. When he left Oxon. he sold it in Old Southampton buildings in Holborne neare London, and was living there in 1671.' In 1654 he mentions that 'Cirques Jobson, a Jew and Jacobite, borne neare Mount Libanus, sold coffey in Oxon. in an house between Edmund Hall and Queen coll. corner.' And again in 1655 that 'In this yeare Arth. Tillyard, apothecary and great royallist, sold coffey publickly in his house against All-soules coll. He was encouraged so to do by som royallists, now living in Oxon. and by others who esteam'd themselves either virtuosi or wits ... This coffey house continued till his majestie's returne and after, and then they became more frequent, and had an excise set upon coffee.'

celor,) I added, as benefactor to the Library of the Coll. these books:

Zanchii Opera, vols. 1, 2, 3. *Granado in Thomam Aquinatem*, vols. 1, 2, 3. *Novarini Electa sacra*, and *Cresolii Anthologia sacra*, authors (it seems) desired by the students of Divinity there.

1637. At Christmas the Gentlemen of Exeter College presented a Comedy to the University.

I was admitted into the dauncing and vaulting Schole, of which late activity one Stokes, the Master, set forth a *pretty book*, which was publish'd with many witty elogies before it[1].

1638. My Father order'd that I should begin to manage myne owne expenses, which till then my Tutor had done; at which I was much satisfied.

1639. I began to look on the rudiments of musick, in which I afterwards ariv'd to some formal knowledge, though to small perfection of hand, because I was so frequently diverted by inclinations to newer trifles.

20 May. Accompany'd with one Mr. Jo. Crafford, (who afterwards being my fellow-traveller in Italy there chang'd his religion,) I tooke a journey of pleasure to see the Sumersetshire Bathes, Bristoll, Cirencester, Malmesbury, Abington, and divers other townes of lesser note, and returned the 25th.

1640. Came my bro. Richard from schole to be my chamber-fellow at the University. He was admitted the next day, and matriculated the 31st....

27 April. I went to London to be resident in the Middle

---

[1] The original note in Bray's edition of Evelyn's Diary, concerning this book, is as follows: 'It being now become extremely scarce, the title of it is here given: "The Vaulting Master, or the Art of Vaulting Reduced to a method comprized under certain Rules. Illustrated by examples, and now primarily set forth by Will. Stokes. Printed for Rich. Davis in Oxon. 1655." A small oblong quarto, with the author's portrait prefixed, and a number of plates beautifully engraved (most probably by Glover) representing feats of activity on horseback that appear extraordinary ones at this time of day.' The copy in the Bodleian Library has no portrait prefixed, but is of an earlier date, being 'Imprinted at *London* by J. Okes. 1641.'

Temple. My being at the University, in regard of these avocations, was of very small benefit to me.

II.

[1654. July] 6. I went early to London, and the next day met my wife and company at Oxford, the eve of the Act.

8. Was spent in hearing several exercises in the scholes, and after dinner the Proctor[1] opened the Act at St. Marie's (according to custome) and the Prevaricators their drolery. Then the Doctors disputed. We supp'd at Wadham College.

9. Dr. French[2] preach'd at St. Marie's on 12 Matt. 42. advising the Students to search after true wisdome, not to be had in the bookes of Philosophers, but in the Scriptures alone. In the afternoone the famous Independent, Dr. Owen[3], perstringing Episcopacy. He was now Cromwell's Vice-Chancelor. We din'd with Dr. Ward[4], Mathematical Professor (since Bp. of Sarum), and at night supped in Balliol Coll. Hall, where I had once ben Student and Fellow Commoner, and where they made me extraordinarily welcome.

10. On Monday I went againe to the Scholes to heare the severall Faculties, and in the afternoone tarried out the whole Act in St. Marie's, the long speeches of the Proctors, the Vice-Chancellor, the severall Professors, creation of Doctors by the cap, ring, kisse, &c., those antient ceremonies and institution being as yet not wholy abolish'd[5]. Dr. Kendal,

---

[1] Thomas Cracroft, Magdalen.

[2] Probably Peter French, preb. of Oxford 1651, by the donation of Oliver Cromwell, whose sister he married; died 1655.

[3] John Owen, Dean of Ch. Ch., Vice-Chan. 1652-7.

[4] Seth Ward: sometime Fellow of Sidney-Sussex Coll., Camb.; Bp. of Exeter, 1662; Savilian prof. of astron., 1648; President of Trinity, 1659-1660; Bp. of Salisbury, 1667.

[5] A. Clark, M.A., in his *Register of the University of Oxford*, says: 'After the disputations, the Inceptors were presented to the Vice-Chancellor, who gave them a book, placed the Master's hood round their neck, put their cap on, and kissed them on the cheek, as appears by this "formula creationis Magistri":—"en tibi insignia honoris tui, en librum, en cucullum, en pileum, en denique amoris mei pignus osculum in nomine Patris et Filii et Spiritus Sancti." This ceremony has gone altogether out of our University fashion.' Vol. ii. pt. 1, p. 84.

now Inceptor amongst others, performing his Act incomparably well, concluded it with an excellent oration, abating his Presbyterian animosities, which he witheld not even against that learned and pious divine Dr. Hammond. The Act was closed with the speech of the Vice-Chancellor, there being but 4 in Theologie, 3 in Medicine, which was thought a considerable matter, the times consider'd. I din'd at one Monsieur Fiat's[1], a Student at Exeter College, and supp'd at a magnificent entertainment in Wadham Hall, invited by my deare and excellent friend Dr. Wilkins[2], then Warden (afterwards the Bishop of Chester.)

11. Was the Latin sermon, which I could not be at, tho' invited, being taken up at All Souls, where we had music, voices, and theorbos, perform'd by some ingenious scholars. After dinner I visited that miracle of a youth Mr. Christopher Wren[3], nephew of the Bishop of Ely. Then Mr. Barlow[4] (since Bishop of Lincoln) Bibliothecarius of the Bodleian Library, my most learned friend. He shew'd us the rarities of that most famous place, manuscripts, medails, and other curiosities. Amongst the MSS. an old English Bible, wherein the Eunuch mentioned to be baptized by Philip is called the Gelding: 'and Philip and the Gelding went down into the water,' &c. The original Acts of the Council of Basil 900 yeares since, with the bulla or leaden affix, which has a silken cord passing thro' every parchment; a MS. of Venerable Bede of 800 yeares antiquity; the old Ritual *secundum usum Sarum*, exceeding voluminous; then amongst the nicer curiosities, the Proverbs

---

[1] Peter Fiat or Fiott, of the Isle of Jersey: matr. 13 Feb. 1645; see Boase's *Registrum Collegii Exoniensis*, pp. xxxi, 70.

[2] John Wilkins, Warden of Wadham, 1648, in the place of John Pytt, who was deprived by the Parliament delegates; resigned 1659, and became Master of Trin. Coll., Camb.; Bp. of Chester, 1668.

[3] Christopher Wren entered Wadham in 1646, and took his B.A. degree 1650, his M.A. 1653; afterwards a fellow of All Souls; in 1657 he was made Savilian professor of astronomy; died 1723, and was buried under the choir of St. Paul's; he was a nephew of Matthew Wren, successively Bishop of Hereford, Norwich, and Ely.

[4] Thomas Barlow, Provost of Queen's, 1657; Bp. of Linc. 1675.

of Solomon written in French by a Lady[1], every chapter of a severall character or hand the most exquisite imaginable; an hieroglyphical table or carta folded up like a map, I suppose it painted on asses hide, extremely rare; but what is most illustrious, there were no less than 1000 MSS. in 19 languages, especialy Oriental, furnishing that new part of the Library built by Abp. Lawd from a designe of Sir Kenelme Digby and the Earle of Pembrook. In the closet of the Tower they shew some Indian weapons, urnes, lamps, &c. but the rarest is the whole Alcoran written on one large sheet of calico, which is made up in a priest's vesture or cope, after the Turkish and Arabic character, so exquisitely written as no printed letter comes neere it; also a roll of magical charms, divers talismans, and some medails.

Then I led my wife into the Convocation House, finely wainscoted; the Divinity Schole and Gotic carv'd roofe; the Physick or Anatomie Schole, adorn'd with some rarities of natural things, but nothing extraordinary save the skin of a jaccall, a rarely colour'd jacatoo or prodigious large parrot, 2 humming birds not much bigger than our humble bee, which I had not seene before, that I remember.

12. We went to St. John's, saw the Library and the 2 skeletons which are finely cleans'd and put together; observable is here also the store of mathematical instruments, cheifely given by the late Abp. Lawd, who built here an handsome quadrangle.

Thence we went to New College, where the Chapel was in its ancient garb, notwithstanding the scrupulositie of the times. Thence to Christ's Church, in whose library was shew'd us an Office of Hen. 8, the writing miniatures, and gilding whereof is equal if not surpassing any curiosity I had

---

[1] Esther Inglis or English, a Frenchwoman by birth, who lived in the time of Queen Elizabeth and James the First. Several books written by her are in the Bodleian Library; she was married to a Scotchman named Bartholomew Kello. See Laing in *Proceedings of Antiquaries of Scotland*, vol. vi. pp. 284-309, and Ballard's *Memoirs of British Ladies*.

scene of that kind; it was given by their founder, Cardinal Wolsey. The glasse windows of the Cathedrall (famous in my time), I found much abus'd. The ample Hall and columne that spreads its capital to sustaine the roofe as one goes up the stayres is a very remarkable structure.

Next we walked to Magdalen College, where we saw the Library and Chapell, which was likewise in pontifical order, the altar onely I think turn'd table-wise, and there was still the double organ, which abominations (as now esteem'd) were almost universaly demolish'd; Mr. Gibbon[1], that famous musitian, giving us a taste of his skill and talents on that instrument.

Hence we went to the Physick Garden, where the sensitive plant was shew'd us for a greate wonder. There grew canes, olive-trees, rhubarb, but no extraordinary curiosities, besides very good fruit, which when the ladys had tasted, we returned in our coach to our lodgings.

13. We all din'd at that most obliging and universally-curious Dr. Wilkins's, at Wadham College. He was the first who shew'd me the transparent apiaries, which he had built like castles and palaces, and so order'd them one upon another as to take the hony without destroying the bees. These were adorn'd with a variety of dials, little statues, vanes, &c. and he was so aboundantly civil, as finding me pleas'd with them, to present me with one of the hives which he had empty, and which I afterwards had in my garden at Sayes Court[2], where it continu'd many years. and which his Majestie came on purpose to see and contemplate with much satisfaction. He had also contriv'd an hollow statue which gave a voice and utter'd words, by a long conceal'd pipe that went to its mouth, whilst one speaks through it at a good

---

[1] Probably Christopher Gibbons, musical composer and organist, 1615–76; he was one of the organists of the Chapel Royal in the time of Charles I; also organist of Westminster Abbey, and private organist to Charles II. Died Oct. 20, 1676, and was buried in the cloisters of Westminster Abbey.

[2] The house of Evelyn's father-in-law, Sir Richard Brown, at Deptford, in Kent, afterwards belonging to Evelyn, and once the abode of Peter the Great for three months.

distance. He had above in his lodgings and gallery variety of shadows, dyals, perspectives, and many other artificial, mathematical, and magical curiosities, a way-wiser, a thermometer, a monstrous magnet, conic and other sections, a ballance on a demi-circle, most of them of his owne and that prodigious young scholar Mr. Chr. Wren, who presented me with a piece of white marble, which he had stain'd with a lively red very deepe, as beautiful as if it had ben natural.

Thus satisfied with the civilities of Oxford, we left it, dining at Faringdon, a towne which had ben newly fir'd during the warrs; and passing neere the seat of Sir Wal. Pie, we came to Cadenham. . . .

III.

[1664. Oct.] 24. We din'd at Sir Tim. Tyrill's[1] at Shotover. This gentleman married the daughter and heyre of Dr. James Usher, Abp. of Armagh, that learned Prelate. There is here in the grove a fountaine of the coldest water I ever felt, and very cleere. His plantation of oakes, &c. is very commendable. We went in the evening to Oxford, lay at Dr. Hide's, Principal of Magdalen Hall (related to the Lo. Chancellor) brother to the Lord Ch. Justice, and that Sir Hen. Hide who lost his head for his loyalty. We were handsomely entertain'd two dayes. The Vice Chancellor[2], who with Dr. Fell, Deane of Christ Church, the learned Dr. Barlow, Warden of Queenes, and severall heads of houses, came to visite Lord Cornebury (his father being now Chancellor of the University), and next day invited us all to dinner. I went to visite Mr. Boyle[3] (now here), whom I found with Dr. Wallis[4], and Dr. Christopher Wren in the Tower of the Scholes, with an

---

[1] Sir Timothy Tyrrell, of Oakley, Bucks, and Shotover, in the county of Oxford; he was of the Privy Chamber to King Charles I, and held the rank of colonel in the royal army. See Burke's *Extinct and Dormant Baronetcies.*

[2] Robert Say, Provost of Oriel; Vice-Chancellor.

[3] Hon. Robert Boyle, 1627–91, natural philosopher and chemist; he settled at Oxford from 1654–68.

[4] John Wallis, D.D., of Exeter, sometime Fellow of Queen's Coll., Camb.; Savilian professor of geometry, 1649–1704.

inverted tube or telescope, observing the discus of the Sunn for the passing of Mercury that day before it, but the latitude was so great that nothing appeared; so we went to see the rarities in the Library, where the keepers shewed me my name among the benefactors. They have a cabinet of some medails, and pictures of the muscular parts of a man's body. Thence to the new Theater[1], now building at an exceeding and royal expence by the Lo. Abp. of Canterbury [Sheldon], to keepe the Acts in for the future, till now being in St. Mary's church. The foundation had ben newly laied and the whole design'd by that incomparable genius my worthy friend Dr. Christopher Wren, who shewed me the model, not disdaining my advice in some particulars. Thence to see the picture on the wall over the Altar at All Soules, being the largest piece of fresco painting (or rather in imitation of it, for it is in oil of turpentine) in England, not ill design'd by the hand of one Fuller; yet I feare it will not hold long. It seems too full of nakeds for a chapell.

Thence to New College, and the painting of Magdalen Chapel, which is on blew cloth in *chiaro oscuro*, by one Greenborow, being a *Coena Domini*, and a *Last Judgment* on the wall by Fuller, as is the other, but somewhat varied.

Next to Wadham, and the Physick Garden, where were two large locust trees, and as many platana, and some rare plants under the culture of old Bobart[2].

IV.

[1667. Sept.] 19. To London with Mr. Hen. Howard[3] of Norfolk, of whom I obtain'd the gift of his Arundelian Marbles, those celebrated and famous inscriptions Greeke and Latine, gather'd

---

[1] The first stone of the Sheldonian Theatre was laid July 26, 1664, and the building was opened July 9, 1669, at the cost of £15,000. Below p. 29, Sir Chris. Wren says £25,000.

[2] Jacob Bobart, a German, was appointed the first keeper of the Physic Garden at Oxford (*Bray*).

[3] Henry, afterwards sixth Duke of Norfolk, died 1683. The Arundel marbles are still among the greatest treasures of the University.

with so much cost and industrie from Greece, by his illustrious grandfather the magnificent Earle of Arundel, my noble friend whilst he liv'd. When I saw these precious monuments miserably neglected and scatter'd up and downe about the garden, and other parts of Arundel House, and how exceedingly the corrosive aire of London impair'd them, I procur'd him to bestow them on the University of Oxford. This he was pleas'd to grant me, and now gave me the key of the gallery, with leave to mark all those stones, urns, altars, &c. and whatever I found had inscriptions on them, that were not statues. This I did, and getting them remov'd and pil'd together, with those which were incrusted in the garden-walls, I sent immediately letters to the Vice-Chancellor of what I had procur'd, and that if they esteem'd it a service to the University (of which I had ben a member) they should take order for their transportation. . . .

8 Oct. Came to dine with me Dr. Bathurst[1], Deane of Wells, President of Trinity Coll. sent by the Vice-Chancelor of Oxford, in the name both of him and the whole University, to thank me for procuring the Inscriptions, and to receive my directions what was to be don to shew their gratitude to Mr. Howard. . . .

17. Came Dr. Barlow, Provost of Queen's Colledge and Protobibliothecarius of the Bodleian Library, to take order about the transportation of the Arundel Marbles.

25. There were delivered to me two letters from the Vice-Chancelor of Oxford with the Decree of the Convocation attested by the Publick Notary, ordering four Doctors of Divinity and Law to acknowledge the obligation the University had to me for procuring the *Marmora Arundeliana*, which was solemnly don by Dr. Barlow, Dr. Jenkins[2], Judge of the Admiralty, Dr. Lloyd, and Obadiah Walker[3] of

---

[1] Ralph Bathurst, President of Trinity, 1664-1704; Dean of Wells, 1670.

[2] Afterwards Sir Leoline Jenkins, Principal of Jesus Coll., 1661; resigned in 1673; Secretary of State and Judge of the High Court of Admiralty; died 1685.

[3] Obadiah Walker, Master of University, 1676-89.

University Coll. who having made me a large compliment from the University, deliver'd me the Decree fairly written:

Gesta venerabili domo Convocationis Universitatis Oxon; .. 17. 1667. Quo die retulit ad Senatum Academicum Dominus Vicecancellarius, quantum Universitas deberet singulari benevolentiæ Johannis Evelini Armigeri, qui pro eâ pietate quâ Almam Matrem prosequitur non solum Suasu et Concilio apud inclytum Heroem Henricum Howard, Ducis Norfolciæ hæredem, intercessit ut Universitati pretiosissimum eruditæ antiquitatis thesaurum Marmora Arundeliana largiretur; sed egregius insuper in ijs colligendis asservandisq; navavit operam: Quapropter unanimi suffragio Venerabilis Domus decretum est ut eidem publicæ gratiæ per delegatos ad Honoratissimum Dominum Henricum Howard propediem mittendos, solemnitèr reddantur.

Concordat superscripta cum originali collatione facta per me Ben. Cooper Notarium Publicum et Registrarium Universitat. Oxon.

'SIR,

'We intend also a noble inscription, in which also honorable mention shall be made of yourselfe; but Mr. Vice-Chancellor commands me to tell you that that was not sufficient for your merits, but that if your occasions would permit you to come down at the Act (when we intend a dedication of our new Theater), some other testimonie should be given both of your owne worth and affection to this your old Mother; for we are all very sensible of this greate addition of learning and reputation to the University is due as well to your industrious care for the Universitie, and interest with my Lord Howard, as to his greate noblenesse and generositie of spirit.

'I am, Sir. your most humble servant,
'OBADIAH WALKER, Univ. Coll.'

The Vice-Chancellor's letter to the same effect were too vaine glorious to insert, with divers copies of verses that were also sent me. Their mentioning me in the inscription I totally declin'd when I directed the titles of Mr. Howard, now made Lord upon his ambassage to Morocco.

These fower Doctors having made me this compliment, desir'd me to carry and introduce them to Mr. Howard at Arundel House: which I did, Dr. Barlow (Provost of Queenes) after a short speech, delivering a larger letter of the University's thankes, which was written in Latine, expressing the greate sense they had of the honour don them. After this compliment handsomely perform'd, and as nobly receiv'd, Mr Howard accompanied the Doctors to their coach. That evening I supp'd with them.

V.

[1669.] 7 July. I went towards Oxford; lay at Little Wycomb.—8. Arrived at Oxford.

9. In the morning was celebrated the Encenia of the New Theater, so magnificently built by the munificence of Dr. Gilbert Sheldon, Abp. of Canterbury, in which was spent £25,000, as Sir Christopher Wren, the architect, (as I remember) told me; and yet it was never seene by the benefactor, my Lord Abp. having told me that he never did nor ever would see it. It is in truth a fabrick comparable to any of this kind of former ages, and doubtless exceeding any of the present, as this University does for Colledges, Librairies, Scholes, Students, and order, all the Universities in the world. To the Theater is added the famous Sheldonian Printing-house. This being at the Act and the first time of opening the Theater (Acts being formerly kept in St. Mary's church, which might be thought indecent, that being a place set apart for the immediate worship of God, and was the inducement for building this noble pile) it was now resolv'd to keep the present Act in it, and celebrate its dedication with the greatest splendor and formalitie that might be, and therefore drew a world of strangers and other companie to the University from all parts of the nation.

The Vice Chancellor, Heads of Houses, and Doctors, being seated ¹ in magisterial seates, the Vice Chancellor's chaire and deske, Proctors, &c. cover'd with Brocatall (a kind of brocade) and cloth of gold; the Universitie Register read the founder's grant and gift of it to the Universitie for their scolastic exercises upon these solemn occasions. Then follow'd Dr. South, the Universitie's Orator, in an eloquent speech, which was very long, and not without some malicious and indecent reflections on the Royal Society, as underminers of the University, which was very foolish and untrue, as well as unseasonable. But, to let that pass from an ill natur'd man, the rest was in praise of the Archbishop and the ingenious architect. This ended, after loud musiq from the corridor above, where an organ was plac'd, there follow'd divers panegyric speeches both in prose and verse, interchangeably pronounc'd by the young students plac'd in the rostrums. in Pindarics, Eclogues, Heroics, &c. mingled with excellent musiq, vocal and instrumental, to entertain the ladies and the rest of the company. A speech was then made in praise of academical learning. This lasted from 11 in the morning till 7 at night, which was concluded with ringing of bells and universal joy and feasting.

10. The next day began the more solemn Lectures in all the Faculties, which were perform'd in their several scholes, where all the Inceptor Doctors did their exercises, the Professors having first ended their reading. The assembly now return'd to the Theater, where the *Terræ filius* (the *Universitie Buffoone*) entertain'd the auditorie with a tedious, abusive, sarcastical rhapsodie, most unbecoming the gravity of the Universitie, and that so grossly, that unlesse it be suppress'd, it will be of ill consequence, as I afterwards plainly express'd my sense of it both to the Vice Chancellor and severall heads of houses, who were perfectly asham'd of it, and resolv'd to take care of it in future. The old facetious way of raillying upon the questions was left off, falling wholy upon persons, so that 'twas rather licentious lyeing and railing

than genuine and noble witt. In my life I was never witnesse of so shamefull entertainment. After this ribauldry, the Proctors made their speeches. Then began the Musick Act, vocal and instrumental, above in the ballustrade corridore opposite to the Vice Chancellor's seate. Then Dr. Wallis, the Mathematical Professor, made his Oration, and created one Doctor of Musiq according to the usual ceremonies of gowne (which was of white damask), cap, ring, kisse, &c. Next follow'd the Disputations of the Inceptor Doctors in Medicine, the Speech of their Professor Dr. Hyde, and so in course their respective creations. Then disputed Inceptors of Law, the Speech of their Professor, and creation. Lastly, Inceptors in Theologie; Dr. Compton (brother to the Earle of Northampton) being junior, began with greate modesty and applause; so the rest. After which Dr. Tillotson, Dr. Sprat, &c. and then Dr. Allestree's speech, the King's Professor, and their respective creations. Last of all the Vice Chancellor, shutting up the whole in a panegyrical oration celebrating their benefactor and the rest, apposite to the occasion.

Thus was the Theater dedicated by the scholastic exercises in all the Faculties with greate solemnity; and the night, as the former, entertaining the new Doctors friends in feasting and musiq. I was invited by Dr. Barlow, the worthy and learned Provost of Queene's Coll.

11. The Act Sermon was this forenoon preach'd by Dr. Hall in St. Maries in an honest practical discourse against Atheisme. In the afternoone the Church was so crowded, that not coming early I could not approach to heare.

12 Mon. Was held the Divinity Act in the Theater againe, when proceeded 17 Doctors, in all Faculties some.

13. I din'd at the Vice-Chancellor's, and spent the afternoone in seeing the rarities of the publick libraries, and visiting the noble marbles and inscriptions, now inserted in the walles that compasse the area of the Theater, which were 150 of the most ancient and worthy treasures of that kind in the learned world. Now observing that people approching

them too neere, some idle persons began to scratch and injure them, I advis'd that an hedge of holly should be planted at the foot of the wall, to be kept breast-high onely, to protect them, which the Vice-Chancellor promis'd to do the next season.

14. Dr. Fell, Dean of Christ-church and Vice-Chancellor, with Dr. Allestree Professor, with Beadles and Maces before them, came to visite me at my lodging.—I went to visite Lord Howard's sons at Magdalen College.

15. Having two daies before had notice that the University intended me the honour of Doctor-ship, I was this morning attended by the Beadles belonging to the Law, who conducted me to the Theater, where I found the Duke of Ormond[1] (now Chancellor of the Universitie) with the Earl of Chesterfield and Mr. Spencer (brother to the late Earl of Sunderland). Thence we march'd to the Convocation House, a Convocation having been call'd on purpose; here, being all of us rob'd in the Porch in scarlett with caps and hoods, we were led in by the Professor of Laws and presented respectively by name, with a short eulogie, to the Vice-Chancellor, who sate in the chaire, with all the Doctors and Heads of Houses and Masters about the roome, which was exceeding full. Then began the Publiq Orator his speech, directed chiefly to the Duke of Ormond the Chancellor, but in which I had my compliment in course. This ended, we were call'd up and created Doctors according to the forme, and seated by the Vice-Chancellor amongst the Doctors on his right hand; then the Vice-Chancellor made a short speech, and so saluting our brother Doctors, the pageantry concluded, and the Convocation was dissolved. So formal a creation of Honorarie Doctors had seldome ben scene, that a Convocation should be call'd on purpose and speeches made by the Orator; but they could do no lesse, their Chancellor being to receive, or rather do them, this honour. I should have ben

---

[1] James Butler, first Duke of Ormond, Chancellor of the University, 1669-88.

made Doctor with the rest at the Publiq Act, but their expectation of their Chancellor made them defer it. I was then led with my brother Doctors to an extraordinary entertainment at Dr. Mewes, Head of St. John's College, and after aboundance of feasting and compliments, having visited the Vice Chancellor and other Doctors, and given them thanks for the honour done me, I went towards home the sixteenth, and got as far as Windsor, and to my house the next day....

VI.

[1675. 8 July.] ... Next day, dining at Shotover, at Sir Tim. Tyrill's, a sweete place, we lay at Oxford, where it was the time of the Act. Mr. Robert Spencer, unkle to the Earle of Sunderland and my old acquaintance in France, entertain'd us at his apartment in Christ Church, with exceeding generosity.—The 10th, the Vice-Chancellor, Dr. Bathurst (who had formerly taken particular care of my sonn), President of Trinity Colledge, invited me to dinner, and did me greate honour all the time of my stay. The next day he invited me and all my company, tho' strangers to him, to a very noble feast. I was at all the academic exercises.—Sonday, at St. Maries, preach'd a Fellow of Brazen-nose, not a little magnifying the dignity of Churchmen.—The 11th, we heard the speeches, and saw the ceremonie of creating Doctors in Divinity, Law, and Physic. I had early in the morning heard Dr. Morison, Botanic Professor, reade on divers plants in the Physic Garden; and saw that rare collection of natural curiosities of Dr. Plot's[1], of Magdalen Hall, author of 'The Natural History of Oxfordshire,' all of them collected in that Shire, and indeede extraordinary, that in one County there should be found such varietie of plants, shells, stones, minerals, marcasites[2], fouls, insects,

---

[1] Robert Plot, of Magdalen Hall, afterwards of University; Keeper of the Ashmolean, 1683-90.

[2] Formerly this name was used for all crystallized and radiated pyrites. They were much used as ornamental stones, were usually small in size, faceted, and highly polished. In modern times the name 'marcasite' is only applied to the forms of native bisulphide of iron which crystallize in the orthorhombic system.

models of works, chrystals, achates, and marbles. He was now intending to visite Staffordshire, and as he had of Oxfordshire, to give us the natural, topical, political, and mechanical history. Pitty it is that more of this industrious man's genius were not employ'd so to describe every County of England; it would have been one of the most usefull and illustrious workes that was ever produced in any age or nation.

I visited also the Bodleian Library, and my old friend the learned Obadiah Walker, head of University Coll. which he had now almost rebuilt or repair'd. . . .

V.

ANTHONY ASHLEY COOPER,
FIRST EARL OF SHAFTESBURY.

[*Born* July 22, 1621: *died* January 21, 1683.]

Life of Anthony Ashley Cooper, First Earl of Shaftesbury. By W. D. Christie, M.A. London and New York, 1871, 8vo. Vol. I. Appendix I.

I.

IN the year 1637, I went to Oxford to Exeter College, under the immediate tuition of Dr. Prideaux[1].

During my residing with my uncle and my being at Oxford, my business often called me to London in the terms, where I was entered of Lincoln's Inn. Thus the condition of my affairs gave me better education than any steady, designed course could have done: my business called me early to the thoughts and considerations of a man, my studies enabled me better to master those thoughts and try to understand my learning, and my intermixed pleasures supported me and kept my mind from being dulled with the cares of one or the intentness I had for the other.

I kept both horses and servants in Oxford, and was allowed what expense or recreation I desired, which liberty I never much abused; but it gave me the opportunity of obliging by entertainments the better sort and supporting divers of the activest of the lower rank with giving them leave to eat when in distress upon my expense, it being no small honour amongst those sort of men, that my name in the buttery book

[1] John Prideaux, Rector of Exeter College, 1612.

willingly owned twice the expense of any in the University. This expense, my quality, proficiency in learning, and natural affability easily not only obtained the good-will of the wiser and older sort, but made me the leader even of all the rough young men of that college, famous for the courage and strength of tall, raw-boned Cornish and Devonshire gentlemen, which in great numbers yearly came to that college, and did then maintain in the schools coursing against Christ Church, the largest and most numerous college in the University. This coursing[1] was in older times, I believe, intended for a fair trial of learning and skill in logic, metaphysics, and school divinity, but for some ages that had been the least part of it, the dispute quickly ending in affronts, confusion, and very often blows, when they went most gravely to work. They forbore striking, but making a great noise with their feet, they hissed and shoved with their shoulders, and the stronger in that disorderly order drove the other out before them, and, if the schools were above stairs, with all violence hurrying the contrary party down, the proctors were forced either to give way to their violence or suffer in the throng. Nay, the Vice-Chancellor, though it seldom has begun when he was present, yet being begun, he has sometimes unfortunately been so near as to be called in, and has been overcome in their fury once up in these adventures. I was often one of the disputants, and gave the sign and order for their beginning, but being not strong of body was always guarded from violence by two or three of the sturdiest youths, as their chief and one who always relieved them when in prison and procured their release, and very often was forced to pay the neighbouring farmers, when they of our party that wanted money were taken in the fact, for more geese, turkeys, and

[1] Walker, in his *Oxoniana*, vol. i. p. 61, states that 'Dr. Fell, when Vice-Chancellor (1646-7), reformed several abuses in the schools, and "because *coursing* in the time of *Lent*, that is, the endeavours of one party to run down and confute another in disputation, did commonly end in blows, and domestic quarrels (the refuge of the vanquished side) he did by his authority annul that custom."—*Ath. Oxon.*, vol. ii. p. 796.'

poultry than either they had stole or he had lost, it being very fair dealing if he made the scholar when taken pay no more than he had lost since his last reimbursement.

Two things I had also a principal hand in when I was at the college. The one, I caused that ill custom of tucking freshmen to be left off; the other, when the senior fellows designed to alter the beer of the college, which was stronger than other colleges, I hindered their design. This had put all the younger sort into a mutiny; they resorting to me, I advised all those were intended by their friends to get their livelihood by their studies to rest quiet and not appear, and that myself and all the others that were elder brothers or unconcerned in their angers should go in a body and strike our names out of the buttery book, which was accordingly done, and had the effect that the senior fellows, seeing their pupils going that yielded them most profit, presently struck sail and articled with us never to alter the size of our beer, which remains so to this day.

The first was a harder work, it having been a foolish custom of great antiquity that one of the seniors in the evening called the freshmen (which are such as came since that time twelvemonth) to the fire and made them hold out their chin, and they with the nail of their right thumb, left long for that purpose, grate off all the skin from the lip to the chin, and then cause them to drink a beer glass of water and salt. The time approaching when I should be thus used, I considered that it had happened in that year more and lustier young gentlemen had come to the college than had done in several years before, so that the freshmen were a very strong body. Upon this I consulted my two cousin-germans, the Tookers[1], my aunt's sons, both freshmen, both stout and very strong, and several others, and at last the whole party were cheerfully engaged to stand stoutly to defence of their chins. We all appeared at the fires in the hall,

[1] Martha, 3rd daughter of John Cooper, Esq., married Edward Tooker, Esq., of Madington, Wilts.

P. xiii.

and my Lord of Pembroke's[1] son calling me first, as we knew by custom it would begin with me, I according to agreement gave the signal, striking him a box on the ear, and immediately the freshmen fell on, and we easily cleared the buttery and the hall, but bachelors and young masters coming in to assist the seniors, we were compelled to retreat to a ground chamber in the quadrangle. They pressing at the door, some of the stoutest and strongest of our freshmen, giant-like boys, opened the doors, let in as many as they pleased, and shut the door by main strength against the rest; those let in they fell upon and had beaten very severely, but that my authority with them stopped them, some of them being considerable enough to make terms for us, which they did, for Dr. Prideaux being called out to suppress the mutiny, the old Doctor, always favourable to youth offending out of courage, wishing with the fears of those we had within, gave us articles of pardon for what had passed, and an utter abolition in that college of that foolish custom. . . .

II.

APPENDIX II.

P. xxvi.

. . . Then, being sixteen years old, he went to Oxford, where he was of Exeter College; Dr. Prideaux, then rector of the College and doctor of the chapel, since Bishop of Worcester, being his tutor, and Mr. Hussey, since minister of Hinton Martin, being his servitor. . . .

---

[1] Probably Philip, 2nd son of Philip, fourth Earl of Pembroke, and afterwards his successor, Charles, the eldest son, having died during his father's lifetime.

VI.

STEPHEN PENTON.

[Born and educated at Winchester, Fellow of New Coll., Oxford, 1659; Principal of St. Edmund Hall, 1675–83; *died* 1706. According to Wood's *Ath. Oxon.* he had 'a rambling head.']

The Guardians Instruction ... Lond. 1688.

'You will wonder how I should come to be an advocate for *Oxford*, who have railed at it for above forty years together, and perhaps upon better grounds than most men do.

I was entred there when the first great difficulties arose betwixt the old King and Parliament, and as much care was taken as was usual in the choice of a tutour; but, as I came to understand, there was a certain Master of Arts who was to be the next tutour of course, and so the next gentleman who entred was to be recommended to him in his turn; it happened I was the man, who came with tolerable parts and learning at the rate of a gentleman. I had a great reverence for the person who was to be my guide, and a strong opinion to be made very wise.

It happened that my tutour was a great philosopher, which made me proud to hear of, expecting in some short time to be so too. He began at first *gloriously* with me, to magnifie the advantages of a good education; how the greatest conditions of *honour* and *trust* were supplied from the University; what a disgrace it was to the nation, and what an injury to government of Church and State, that when other countries, *France, Poland, Scotland, &c.* are studious to discipline their nobility and gentry into *good manners, politicks,* and *religion,* here, eldest sons are generally condemned to hawks and hounds, and wisedom left the patrimony of *younger* brothers onely, and *poor* men's sons; that the mutual lustre of a diamond beset with gold was a mean *comparison* to wisedom in the breast of such a man as I. This ravished my rustick modesty, and made me proud with the thoughts of what I should hereafter be. I out-waked the bell, and scorned to be called to my duty. I attended every motion of his eye for a summons to philosophy, and thought every minute an hour till I was entred into that course of study, which was to make me and all my relations happy. But, alas! the fame of his parts and learning had gained him acquaintance whose company was dearer than mine; so that a lecture now and then was a great *condescention,* and I, most days in the week, when others were carefully looked after, left naked to infinite temptations of doing nothing, or worse. But God's *grace,* the good *example* of my parents and a *natural* love of vertue, secured me so far as to leave *Oxford* (the troubles coming on) though not much more learned, yet not much worse than I came thither. I must in justice say in favour of the University in general, that the growing *disturbances* in Church and State, and some disputes in the University, may well be supposed an unhappy occasion of slackening the *discipline* there at that time.

But this infinite *disappointment* did so afflict me, that when I came to have children, I did almost *swear* them in their childhood never to be friends with *Oxford.* This peevishness of mine was much increased by a chaplain of my sister's, who was made a Fellow of a college in the late times, and turned out upon the Restauration of the King. He sought occasions continually to rail at the University for ignorance, debauchery, and irreligion, insomuch that I sent my eldest son abroad, to try what improvement might be gained by travelling. . . .

... ¹ It became no small concern of mine to take better care for the *second son,* who had smarted for a better share of learning somewhat than his brother, at a *greater school*. Him therefore I was resolved not to *condemn* (as gentlemen phrase it) but to prefer to a *profession*. But what course to take I was at a loss; *Cambridge* was so far off, I could not ¹ have any eye upon him; *Oxford* I was *angry* with.

There was in the neighbourhood an old grave learned divine, (a rigid Churchman) and therefore thought me not zealous enough; but yet the great integrity and simplicity of his life, and the inoffensiveness of a free converse in matters of indifferency, was reason enough to me of standing by his *judgment* in this great *confusion* of mine own thoughts. I desired his advice in the choice of a profession. . . .

¹ At last I *plainly* owned that the Common Law was my design. . . . ¹ And when I objected my prejudice against *Oxford* from my own experience formerly, and from the suggestions of my sister's chaplain just before and after the King came in; the first he could not answer for, the latter he confessed in part was true at the time it points out.

For of all places the University being *fast* to the monarchy, suffering most and being most weary of the usurpation; when *Oliver* was dead and *Richard* dismounted, they saw through a maze of changes that in little time the nation would be fond of that government which twenty years before they hated. The hopes of this made the scholars talk aloud, drink healths, and curse *Meroz* in the very streets. Insomuch that when the King came in, nay, when the King was but *voted* in, they were not onely like them that dream, but like them who ¹ are out of their wits, mad, stark, staring mad. To study was *fanaticism*, to be moderate was downright *rebellion*, and thus it continued for a twelve-month; and thus it would have continued till this time, if it had not pleased God to raise up some Vice-Chancellours who stemmed the torrent which carried so much filth with it, and in defiance of the loyal zeal of the *learned*, the drunken zeal of *dunces*, and the great amazement of *young gentlemen* who really knew not what they would have but yet made the greatest noise, reduced the Uníversity to that temperament that a man might study and not be thought a *dullard*, might be sober and yet a *conformist*, a scholar and yet a *Church of England-man*. And from that time the University became sober, modest, and studious as perhaps any *University* in *Europe*.

And if after all this I thought well of an University, he advised me not to *avoid* this or that House, because a vicious, debauch'd person came thence; not to be *fond* of an House because I myself was of it, or because the head thereof was a fam'd man. These (said he) many times prove very fallacious measures. The onely sure method to proceed by was the known *integrity* and *prudence* of a *tutour*, who would improve him if he were regular, if not would certainly tell me it. Such an one he told me he knew, and would write unto.

Now, full of instruction, I was not long in getting on horseback, but an *unhappy accident* at *Oxford* had almost spoil'd all; for at ten of the clock in the inn there was such a roaring and singing that my hair stood on end, and my former prejudices were so heightned that I resolved to lose the journey and carry back my son again, presuming that no noise in *Oxford* could be made but *scholars* must doe it; but the proctour coming thither and sending two young, pert townsmen to the prison for the riot, relieved my fears, and quickly came to my chamber, and perceiving my boy designed for a gown, told me that it was for the preservation of such *fine youths* as he, that the proctors made so bold with gentlemen's *lodgings*. He was a man of presence and sutable address, and upon my request sate down. I told him I was glad to see authority *discountenance* the publick-houses, because it is an incredible *scandal* the University labours under from the account that countrey gentlemen (who come and lodge in *Oxford*) give of ranting in inns and taverns, as if there was no sleeping in that town for scholars. He civily replied, that things might *be better*, but he thanked God they were *no worse*; that scholars did often bear the blame of *countrey gentlemen* and the *townsmen's* guilt; and that absolutely to keep young men from publick-houses was impossible but by *parents* injunction to their children, by *tutours* observing the conversation of their pupils, and every Head of an House commanding home in time all the *junior* part at least of their societies.

As for the *prejudices* we suffer under in the countrey, he said there were many reasons of that. The constant *declamations* against us of those intruding members who were turned out again in 60, the *hatred* all enemies of King and Church shew against us for being presumed parties; and the *envy* the gentry bear us upon a false supposition of our *ease, luxury*, and *prosperity*; to which we ourselves (said he) do foolishly contribute by treating friends in our chambers as splendidly as if we were worth *thousands*, when, perhaps, half a Fellowship would not pay for two such *dinners* as are made upon a [1] slight occasion. And of all men living the *gentry* ought not to be against us or envy our *moderate* fortunes, whose whole employment is taken up in serving them by *breeding* their sons here, and *serving* their cures hereafter. Perhaps it will be said the sons of some of them miscarry; it is a great *pity* any one should; but I am sure that person ought to vindicate us whose son goes off *vertuously bred;* they do not know the *care* is taken to secure their children, and make them happy. I could willingly have heard him longer but that he was to go his *rounds*. It was pleasant to see how my son trembled to see the proctour come in without knocking at his father's chamber door.

The next morning I carried my neighbour's letter to the *tutour*, who express'd a just deference to the hand, but did not seem *fond* of the employment. I thought to have found him mightily *pleased* with the opinion we had of his conduct, and the credit of having a gentleman's son under his charge, and the father with his cap in hand. Instead of all this he talked at a rate as if the gentry were *obliged* to tutours more than tutours to them. And when I asked him whether he thought

P. 48.

me a man who did not know | how to be *gratefull?* No, said he, (with somewhat of sharpness) I never met with a gentleman backward in that in my life; and to tell you a great truth, if I were of a *craving temper*, I would not take half the care I do. For many mothers (I would say fathers too were it not for shame) are so wise as to think that man much more accomplished for a tutour, who can cringe solemnly, tattle in their way, lead them handsomely over a gutter, and kiss their hands with a good grace than a man of less *fashion* and *ceremony*, who instead of flattering parents and humouring the son, sets carefully to work, and lets the youth know what he comes up for. Though in the mean time I do not think *clownishness* a vertue, but *plain dealing* was always thought so; and some parents have not wit enough to distinguish these two, especially when they are a little proudish. As for *ingratitude* in gentlemen, I never had any reason to complain, nay, I have often refused presents when I thought my pains over-valued; though, I believe, (*generally*) an honest tutour sells his hours cheaper than the fencer or dancing-master will. That which I value is the great success and satisfaction I have had in the towardliness | and proficiency of a great many young gentlemen who at this day doe the University *credit*, and the places where they live, *good*, by their excellent example. But to be in earnest, the *care* is infinite, and the fear they should miscarry is very *afflicting*. And yet after all this, if the divine you came from told you that he thought I would undertake your son for his sake, then I must doe it, and your son shall know before your own face what he must *trust* to. I do not see any lines of *disobedience* in his countenance, but I must desire you to lay your *commands* upon him.

—That he observe the duties of the House for prayers, exercise, etc. as if he were the son of a *beggar*; for when a young boy is plumed up with a *new suit*, he is apt to fancie himself a fine thing. Because he hath a peny commons more than the rest, therefore he ought to be abated a peny-worth of duty, learning, and wisedom. Whereas the gentlemen in the

University ought to doe *more exercise* than others, for they stay but little time there, and ought to be accomplished in *haste*, because their quality and the national concern make them men *apace*. And truly if men may be heard in their own cause, the gentry are too severe in condemning the Universities for not sending home their sons furnish'd with *ethicks, politicks, rhetorick, history*, the necessary learning of a gentleman, *logick*, and *philosophy*, etc. and other *usefull parts*; when they send up their sons for two, perhaps three years onely, and suffer them to trifle away half that time too. It is an ungratefull task to the tutour always to be *chiding*, the father must command *greater strictness*; otherwise, when the young man who hath been long in *durance*, and here finds his shackles knocked off, and the gate wide open, he will *ramble* everlastingly, and make it work more than enough for us to keep him sober: whereas, if they will take care that he be furnish'd *early* at school with Latin, come up hither young and *pliable*, stay here and study hard for *five years*, then if he prove not able to doe the king and his countrey service, I am content it should be *our fault*.

—That he writes no letter to come home for the first *whole year*[1]. It is a common and a very great inconvenience, that soon after a young gentleman is settled, and but *beginning to begin* to study, we have a tedious ill spell'd letter from a dear sister, who languishes and longs to see him as much almost as she doth for a husband. And this, together with rising to prayers at six a clock in the morning, softens the lazy youth into a fond desire of seeing them too. Then all on the sudden up *posts* the livery-man and the led horse, enquires for the college where the young *squire* lives, finds my young master with his boots and spurs on *beforehand*, quarrelling the poor man for not coming sooner. The next news of him is at

---

[1] It seems to have been a general custom to reside the whole year at the University, probably on account of the expense and difficulty of travelling. Wesley in 1776 writes: 'In the English colleges every one may reside all the year, as all my pupils did; and I should have thought myself little better than a highwayman if I had not lectured them every day in the year but Sundays.'—*Wesley's Journal*, 1827, vol. iv. p. 75. See *Oxford City Documents* (O. H. S. vol. xviii), p. 78.

home; within a day or two he is invited to a *hunting match*, and the sickly youth, who was scarce able to rise to prayers, can now rise at four of the clock to a fox-chase; then must he be treated at an ale-house with a rump of beef seven miles from home, hear an uncle, cousin, or neighbour rant and swear; and after such a sort of *education* for six or eight weeks, full of tears and melancholy, the sad soul returns to *Oxford*; his brains have been so *shogged*, he cannot think in a fortnight; and after all this, if the young man prove debauch'd, the University must be blam'd. . . .

P. 53. — ¹ That he frequent not *publick places*, such as are bowling green, racket court, etc. for beside the danger of firing his bloud by a *fever*, heightning passion into *cursing* and *swearing*, he must unavoidably grow acquainted with *promiscuous* company, whether they are or are not *vertuous*. Nay, were his new acquaintance all very good, and of the strictest house, the certainty of making him idle by receiving and paying *treats* and *visits* is dangerous. . . .

P. 54. — ¹ Be sure that he discharge all dues *quarterly*, and not learn to run into debt, this will make him gain credit and buy cheaper. Whatever he saves of your allowance let it be his own gain, perhaps that may teach him *thrift*; and if I were fit to be your tutour, I would advise you to *double* it; for prodigality is a little more catching than niggardliness with *young gentlemen*. I know a person in the world who lived with as much credit in *Oxford* as any man, always genteel in habit, and where entertainments were becoming, always generous; and yet carried away with him a good sum of money saved out

P. 55. of his father's *allowance*, and if ¹ he would give me leave I would propose him as an *example* to the gentry of the university.

—Whatever letters of *complaints* he writes home I desire you to send me a copy; for ill-natured, untoward boys, when they find discipline sit hard upon them, they then will learn to lie, complain, and rail against the university, the college, and the tutour, and with a *whining* letter, make the mother, *make the father*, believe all that he can invent, when all this while his main design is to leave the university and go home again to spanning farthings[1].

—I understand by one of your daughters that you have brought him up a *fine padd* to keep here for his health's sake; now I will tell you the use of an horse in *Oxford*, and then do as you think fit. The horse must be kept at an *ale-house* or an *inn*, and he must have leave to go once *every day* to see him eat oats, because the master's eye makes him fat; and it will not be *genteel* to go often to an house and spend nothing; and then there may be some danger of the horse growing *resty* if he be not used often, so that you must give him leave to go to *Abingdon* once every week to look out of the tavern window, and see the maids sell turnips; and in one month or two come home with a surfeit of poisoned wine, and save any *farther charges* by dying, and then you will be troubled to send for your horse again. This was the unhappiness of a delicate youth, whose great misfortune it was to be worth two thousand a year before he was *one and twenty*.

—That he go constantly to the *university church* on Sundays. Before I came to be a tutour, curiosity and a natural share of thoughtfulness made me observe the *tempers* of the youth of the university, such as either *necessity* or *accident* had brought me acquainted with, and I found one too common an humour, which from the beginning I did lament, foreseeing even then a very unhappy consequence of it. You should see young gentlemen mighty forward to hasten to *St. Mary's*, and happy the man who could get the foremost place in the *gallery*; but if the preacher who came up did not please either with his *looks*, his *voice*, his *text*, or any *whimsey* else, immediately a great bustling to get out; neighbours of each side dis-

P. 56.

---

[1] Spanning farthings was probably the same game as that mentioned in Halliwell's *Dict. of Archaic Words* under the name of 'Span-counter,' where it is described as 'A game thus played. One throws a counter on the ground, and another tries to hit it with his counter, or to get it near enough for him to span the space between them and touch both the counters. In either case, he wins; if not, his counter remains where it lay, and becomes a mark for the first player, and so alternately till the game be won.'

P. 57. turbed to make the gentleman room, (who sometimes [1] drags half a score along with him) especially if he had a *pointed band*, and a *silk suit*, and kept a *brace of geldings*. Well, when they had *fought* their way out into the streets, they were for *venturing* their fortunes at another church; but there the minister was *practical, dull* and *plain*, and being uncertain what to doe, it being not yet *dinner* time, they resolved to stumble in at one holy threshold more, and what with staring about on the auditours, talking aloud of, and censuring the preacher, they made a hard shift to hold out till the little greezy bells began to ring to veal and mutton, and then by the *modest admonition* of going out, put the minister in the mind of being civil to the rest of the hearers. Coming home they talk as big as bull beef of each man they heard, though if you ask the very text, (alas!) he talked so low they could never remember that.

At last I perceived that this *ambulatory roving* carelessness of humour, begat an indifference of going to *any church* at all; and so prepared the young gentry when they should come to be let loose into the wide world, to be no great opposers of *Atheism.* . . .

P. 60. — [1] As for your allowance and moderate pocket money, it must be at your *discretion*; onely I desire that it may go through my hands, at least the whole first year, till I can take some measures of his *discretion*. I would not have him allowed too little, that he may live like a *gentleman*; and I would not have him allowed too much, lest he should set up for *nothing else*.

P. 61. — [1] That he grow intimate with none but such as I shall recommend to his acquaintance. Necessity, good-manners, and the customary respect which is usually paid strangers, will command a friendly *correspondency* with the members of the same college: but it is of very ill-consequence, for an unexperienced, easie-natured person of quality (*the better natur'd the sooner undone*) to make himself fond of every man who shall court a constant familiarity, with all the civility of address and friendship.

For if he be a man of *great acquaintance*, so must you. If he be *idle*, then by frequent avocations he will by degrees lessen the *practice* of your duty, and jest you out of the *opinion* of it. Then *prayers* shall be call'd loss of time; *disputations*, school-play; and *lectures*, pedantry; then the tutour's presence will become frightfull, advice useless, and commands provoking.

—You must leave him wholly to me for the *method* of his study and the books he must reade; and expect an account from me of his abilities and inclinations in order to a course of life hereafter. . . .

| It was very comical to hear the *differing* apprehensions and the rest of the company had of this discourse; for the women long'd to go and see the *college* and the *tutour*. And when he was gone out of the room I asked how they liked the person and his converse. My *boy* clung about his mother and cry'd to go home again, and she had no more *wit* than to be of the same mind; she thought him too weakly to undergo so much hardship | as she foresaw was to be expected. My daughters (who instead of catechism and Lady's-Calling[1]) had been used to reade nothing but speeches in *romances*, and hearing nothing of *Love* and *Honour* in all the talk, fell into downright *scolding* at him; call'd him the *merest* scholar; and if this were your *Oxford* breeding, they had rather he should go to *Constantinople* to learn manners. But I, who was *older* and understood the language, call'd them all great fools, and told them that there was so much plain, *practicable truth* in what he had said, that if every gentleman would *effectually* take such a course, it were impossible for one child in forty to miscarry. . . .

| I heartily thanked him, [the tutour] and finding it late, I invited him to dinner with me at the *inn*, but he refused, saying that such houses were not built for *gownmen*, and | made me leave my son to dine with him, having (said he) observed

---

[1] The first edition of the *Lady's Calling* (probably by Dr. Richard Allestree) was issued at Oxford in 1673.

the great *improvidence* of the gentry, who when they come to enter a son, (which is commonly at the *Act*[1], that solemn season of *luxury*) bring *wife* and *daughters* to shew them the university: there's mighty feasting and drinking for a week, every tavern examin'd, and all this with the company of a child, forsooth, sent up hither for *sobriety* and *industry*.

After this he invited us the next day to a Commons; and according to his *humour* before, I expected to have been *starved* in his chamber, and the girles drank chocolette at no rate in the morning for fear of the *worst*.

It was very pleasant to see when we came, the *constrain'd* artifice of an unaccustomed complement; silver tankards heaped upon one another; napkins, some twenty years younger than the rest; glasses fit for a *Dutchman* at an *East-India Return*.

And at last came an entertainment big enough for ten *members* of the house. I was asham'd, but would not disoblige him, considering with myself that I should put this man to such a charge of forty shillings at least, to entertain me, [1] when for all his honest care and pains he is to have but forty or fifty shillings a quarter; so that for one whole quarter he must doe the drudgery to my son for nothing.

After dinner I went to the publick *bowling-green*, it being the onely recreation I can affect. Coming in, I saw half a score of the finest youths the sun, I think, ever shined upon. They walked to and fro, with their hands in their pockets, to see a match played by some scholars and some gentlemen fam'd for their skill. I gaped also and stared as a man in his way would doe; but a country ruff gentleman, being like to *lose*, did swear at such a rate that my heart did grieve that those fine young men should *hear* it, and know there was such a thing as *swearing* in the kingdom. Coming to my lodging,

---

[1] The *Act* was properly a solemn season for the conclusion of academical exercises and for full admission to degrees, but was accompanied by much gaiety and hospitality. It was held on the first Tuesday in July, in the University Church, until the opening of the Sheldonian Theatre in 1669.

I charged my son never to go to such publick places unless he resolved to quarrel with me.

Having *settled* my son and left my commands with him, we all made haste home again, in earnest much better satisfied with the *government* of the university than I was before; for all this while I had as critically observed all miscarriages as a *prejudiced* man may be imagined to doe.

¹ And (to say more) when we were summon'd thither while before to sit in *parliament*¹, I was resolved narrowly to scan the carriage of the university towards the *members*, to understand the temper and opinion, as far as the free converse in *coffee-houses* (where every man's *religion* and *politicks* are quickly seen) could discover.

The plainness and freedom *young masters* us'd was odd at the first, but afterwards very pleasant, when it appeared to be a kind of *trade*, not policy; for being used all the week long to dispute paradoxes, the disputacity reached afterwards to matter of *religion* and *state*. But in fine I perceived there was nothing of design or malice in all this, but a *road* of converse, arising partly out of hatred to *fanaticks*, and want of *experience* and conversation in the world, which teaches men to be more cautious in promiscuous discourse.

As for their *civility* to the members, we must own it; we had their lodgings (as good as they were) for nothing, with civility and respect whereever they met us *agreeable*; when at the same time the *townsmen* put Dutch rates upon their houses that under five or six pound a ¹ week a Whig could not have *room enough* to speak treason in. I could not perceive but they both talked and preached against popery as much as any men, though in the business of succession² they

---

¹ The last Parliament was held at Oxford in March, 1681; the House of Lords sitting in Christ Church Hall, the Commons in the Gallery of the Schools and the Sheldonian Theatre. Perhaps Penton was at Oxford at that time in attendance on the Earl of Aylesbury, whose Chaplain he was.

² The question of succession in 1681 chiefly turned on the eligibility of the Duke of York (afterwards King James II) to succeed King Charles II.

still favoured the duke. I walk'd the streets as late as most people, and never in ten days time ever saw any scholar rude or disordered: so that as I grow old, and more engaged to speak the *truth*, I do repent of the *ill opinion* I have had of that place, and hope to be farther obliged by a very good *account* of my son.

VII.

JOHN POTENGER.

[*Born* July 21, 1647: *died* December 18, 1733. Educated at Winchester.]

Private Memoirs of John Potenger, Esq. Edited by C. W. Bingham, M.A. London, 1841.

WHEN I had spent so much time at school, as had carried me up to be the senior of the fifth book, I was between sixteen and seventeen years of age; my mother, by the advice of friends, resolved to remove me to Oxford. A Hantshire place in Corpus Christi college in Oxford being then void, they all proposed my standing for it, which I was willing to do, that I might be freed from the bondage of a school: but I was very doubtfull of my ability for such an adventure, having two school-fellows my competitors for the same place, both my seniors, and both better scholars: so that I had nothing but my age, which gave me any advantage of them, being some years younger, a circumstance much considered by the electors. I had likewise the good fortune on the day of election, to have such places in Horace and Lucius Florus put to us, who were candidates, to construe, which I understood much better than they. And Dr. Morley[1], the then bishop of Winchester, gave me his letter to recommend me to the college, so that by favour and good fortune, I was elected into the foundation, my youth commuting for my slender proficiency in the Greek tongue. It was a great victory considering with what force it was obtained. I was mightily pleased, but not in the least puft up, being conscious of my own weakness.

[1] George Morley, Bishop of Winchester, 1662–84.

Now to repair these defects, great care was taken by my friends, to provide me such a tutor as might improve my skill in the Latin and Greek tongues. I had the good fortune to be put to Mr. John Roswell, a man, eminent for learning and piety, whose care and diligence ought gratefully to be remembered by me as long as I live. I think he preserved me from ruin, at my first setting out into the world. He did not only endeavour to make his pupils good scholars, but good men. He narrowly watched my conversation; knowing I had too many acquaintance in the university that I was fond of, though they were not fit for me. Those he disliked he would not let me converse with, which I regretted much, ¹thinking that, now I was come from school, I was to manage myself as I pleased, which occasioned many differences between us for the first two years, which ended in an entire friendship on both sides.

I did not immediately enter upon logick and philosophy, but was kept for a full year to the reading of classical authors, and making of theams in prose and verse. I was forced to manage myself with great circumspection, that my fellows might not find out my blind side, though they shrewdly ghessed at it. In discourse I seldom offered at anything I did not understand. At dinner and supper, it being the custom to speak latin¹, my words were few, till I came to a tollerable proficiency in colloquial latin. My tutor, Mr. Roswell, was so pleased with several of my performances in latin, and english verse, that he gave me several books for an encouragement. I acquired just logick and philosophy enough, to dispute in my turn in the hall, for I was addicted most to poetry, and making of declamations, two exercises I desired to excell in. My talent in declaiming, was beyond being safe, though I dare not say I reached an excellence. I was never ¹ nimble in composing, my invention

---

¹ Latin dropped out of colloquial use at the Universities before the Restoration, but was required for disputations and other prescribed exercises throughout the 18th century and in a few cases even later than 1850.

being slow, and my judgment doubtfull in chusing. My head would not bear long thinking, so that I was forced to relieve myself with some diversion, or another employment. I hated to have a subject imposed upon me, loving to have a free choice, which enlivened my fancy, and fired me with an ambition of doing something extraordinary, for I was always covetous of a tollerable reputation.

Being about twenty years of age, the time drew nigh for me to go out Bachelour of Arts, and in order to that, I did my publick exercises in the schools, and my private in the college. If I was safe in the rest, 'twas well, for I remember but one, which I did performe to my own or others liking; which was, my reading in the college hall upon Horace. I opened my lectures with a speech, which I thought pleased the auditors, as well as myself.

Being Bachelour of Arts, I was free from the government of a tutor, and wholly left to my own management and freedom, as far as it was consistent with the college and university discipline. 'Tis with horror and amazement, I look back upon these eleven ensuing years: though I commenced vicious at Oxford, London completed the sinner, which I visited several times before I left the university. I must confess I was tinctured with all the vices of the age, though I was not totally possessed by them; neither was I so hard as to be without any secret stings of conscience; but they served only to make me sad, and not to mend, till God, by his grace, in some measure rescued me from destruction. It has often been the subject of a thankfull meditation, my not being cut off in the midst of these many sins I have committed, and taken away whilst I was in a course of iniquities. Though I was so highly criminal, yet I was not so notorious as to incurr the censure of the governors of the college, or the university, but for sleeping out morning prayer, for which I was frequently punished. The two last years I stayed in the university, I was Bachelour of Arts, and I spent most of my time in reading books, which were not very common, as

Milton's Works, Hobbs his Leviathan; but they never had the power to subvert the principles which I had received, of a good christian, and a ' good subject. Now I was to determine what profession I would be of. My mother, and others of my relations, were mightily inclined to my being a divine; but I, who understood my own licentious temper, and my ignorance of the greek tongue, thought I should dishonour that calling by my life, or by my ignorance, proposed my being a lawyer, which at last prevailed; I was entered of the Inner Temple, some time before I left Oxford. But, some of my friends surmising that my inclination to the law proceeded from my unwillingness to do my exercises for my Master of Arts degree, to take off all suspicion of that nature, I performed the greatest and most difficult part of them before I quitted the college.

VIII.
RICHARD NEWTON.

[Of Christ Church, B.A. 1698, M.A. 1701, D.D. 1710; Principal of Hart Hall, 1710–40, and of the new foundation of Hertford Coll. 1740 to his death, 21 April, 1753. He was an Oxford reformer a century before his time.]

University Education ... By R. Newton, D.D. Lond. 1726. 8º.

I.

ONE of my Tutors, whilst I was attending the grievous opposition given by *Exeter College* to the Incorporation of my *Hall*[1], had undertaken to be the Publick Lecturer, in my absence, and in my stead; and, for proper reasons, had alter'd the hour of the Lecture, as I my self have often done, from *Two* in the afternoon till *Four*; and had given early notice of it to those who were concern'd. A certain *Leader*, who assum'd to himself to be the Protector of the Commoners in their privileges, that nothing of hardship might be impos'd upon them by their Tutors, took the liberty to expostulate with the Reader of the Lecture (tho' not himself subject to it,) about the alteration of the hour, in so unbecoming a manner, and with such improper insinuations, as could not but have very ill effects upon the Society. Accordingly, many of them enter'd into a conspiracy not to submit to the Lecturer's injunction, and the rule of the House in that particular. They came not to Lecture; they were impos'd. They refused to make their impo-

P. 70.

[1] In 1740, at the recommendation of Dr. Newton, Hart Hall was converted by George II into a college for students and called Hertford College, but the endowments proving insufficient the college was dissolved in 1805. In 1822 the premises were occupied by the Principal and members of Magdalen Hall, who received the residue of the property formerly held by Hertford College. In 1874 Magdalen Hall was dissolved and Hertford College reconstituted.

P. 71. sitions; they were put out of Commons. They ¹ broke open doors to come at the provisions; they were sconc'd. They hissed the Tutors of the Society, and shew'd other marks of insolence and contempt, and went in a body to offer themselves to be admitted into another House. They were rejected, return'd home, cool'd in a day or two, came to themselves, were asham'd and confounded at what they had been doing, begg'd pardon in proper epistles, made their impositions, and were receiv'd again into favour, their pecuniary penalties were remitted, the *Hall* for the present, was exposed, but the *Discipline* of it, as I apprehended, most effectually established. . . .

II.

P. 128.
P. 129. Those, who had been push'd away from my Society in *Act Term* 1723, for having been *Ring-leaders* in the late ¹ *Rebellion*, presently conceiv'd hopes, they might at once lighten their disgrace and gratify their resentment, if they could be so happy as to draw a good many *Others* after them; and that, if they succeeded, the *Rest* would not be fond of living in a *Desert*; and so flatter'd themselves that, in three or four months' time, they should be able to triumph in the *Evacuation* of *Hart Hall*; and imagin'd the present opportunity to be the most favourable to their Design, for that the Principal's attention was, at this time, unhappily diverted from the immediate care of his Society by the grievous opposition given to the intended Incorporation of it by *Exeter College*. To this end, many of the young Scholars were instructed to solicit their Parents (in *Personal Conferences*, if they should go into the Country, now the *Long Vacation* was approaching; or by *Letters* from the *Hall*, if they should not;) that they might have liberty to enter themselves in what Houses of Learning they pleas'd, before *Michaelmas* next. But, whether having had time to reflect, that they had already been spirited up into

P. 130. a wicked Rebellion without ¹ any manner of provocation to it; or whether, having escap'd with little or no punishment, they were glad to come off so, without engaging in a fresh conspiracy, for no other reason than to abett the virulence of their baffled *Leaders*; or whether they mistrusted the force of their arguments, and were aware they must at once relate things *Incredible* and be *Believ'd* before they could succeed; or whether they were thoroughly convinc'd of their error, and asham'd of it, as they all seem'd to be, and, I am confident, most of them were; they certainly did not try their Friends, or tried them in vain. For, as I had early notice of what was concerted, so I gave early advice of it where-ever I had the least suspicion there would be any attempt, in order to prevent the ill effects of any misrepresentations; and was presently assur'd, that the Young Men had *Themselves* condemn'd their own conduct; and I found, upon their return, that their behaviour was agreeable thereto. But one, however, of whom I had no *Suspicion*, nor indeed *Reason* to have any, the *Faction* did get from me, by a *Stratagem* against which [1] there was hardly any Fence. His P. 131. name *Joseph Somaster*[1]; his Father an Officer of the *Excise* in the West of *England*. He was enter'd a little before the Rebellion in *Hart-Hall*; and, within a *Day* or *Two* after his Admission, was appriz'd by his Tutor, that possibly some attempts might be made upon him by the Disaffected to disincline him to the *Officers* of the *House*, and even to *Himself*. To which he answer'd, 'That he was too sensible of that *already*.' He was caution'd not to be discourag'd; for that he would find things very different from what the *Malevolent* should represent them. As yet he was *not* discourag'd; he liv'd regularly; he studied hard; he was very sober; he seem'd not to be offended either with his *Governor*, or any of the *Officers*; for, having incurr'd no penalty, he had suffer'd none; and, having often deserv'd commendation, he had as often receiv'd it. He was pleas'd with his Tutor, and his Tutor so well pleas'd with him, and so careful of him, as, in half a year's time, to have improv'd him considerably in the two Languages of *Greek* and *Latin* which he I brought along with him to the UNIVERSITY; P. 132.

[1] Joseph Somaster; Hart Hall, matr. April 1723, aged 18; B.A. from Balliol Coll. 1726; M.A. 1729.

and to have made a good progress with him in a third, the *Hebrew* Language also.

A little before *Michaelmas,* this Young Man came to me, and desir'd a *Discessit*; and produc'd a *Letter* from his Father signifying *His Concurrence*; and, that he might the better conceal his having been invited to *Baliol College,* tho' he was in haste to be gone, seem'd undetermined whither he should go. 'He had *Recommendations,* he said, both to *Exeter,* and to *Baliol*; and, when he should be provided with my *Instrument* of *Leave* to go from *Hart-Hall,* he would soon make his choice.' I was surpris'd. He shook his head, and said, 'A great many *Others,* I should find, would *go* as well as *Himself.*' I was no longer surpris'd. I recollected what had been concerted. I refus'd him the desir'd *Instrument* of *Leave.* I writ to the Father. I was a great deal too late. He was prepossess'd. This Young Man, it seems, had been *School-Fellow* to the chief supporter of the Faction, who was most ¹ intimate with the intended Tutor in *Baliol,* who was most intimate with the *Father,* who, not having been bred at any UNIVERSITY, was wholly ignorant of our Rules; and not the less so, for the *Informations* he had receiv'd from those who *had* been bred at the UNIVERSITY; and, in short, so *Prejudic'd,* as not to be *capable* of being undeceiv'd, tho', otherwise, a Man of a good understanding.

The *Reasons* given to me for the removal of this Scholar were these three.

1. That, in *Baliol* he had the promise of a Tutor *for nothing.*

2. That he could live *Cheaper* there than at *Hart-Hall.*

3. That a *Scholarship* in that *House,* value 3*l.* 2*s.* 6*d.* a year, would be conferr'd upon him soon after his arrival.

I shall consider *These Reasons* in their order.

¹ With regard to the *First* of them, it may be observ'd, that the UNIVERSITY doth *Allow* Tutors to *Receive* a consideration for their care of the Youth intrusted to them; that, as this is very *Reasonable* in itself, so hath it ever been the

Practice of Tutors to *Receive* a consideration for such their care; that the consideration they have receiv'd, not being limited by any *Statute*, hath *varied*, and is, at this day, *Different* in different Houses of Education within the UNIVERSITY: that the Tutor's *Demand* being *known*, and not objected to *before* a Scholar is enter'd under his care, the *same*, upon entrance, becomes the consideration that is *agreed* to be paid *for* his care. That the Labourer is *Worthy* of his *Hire;* that *some Hire* is both a better *Encouragement* to a Tutor, and a greater *Obligation* upon him to take a due care, than *no Hire;* that the *greatest Hire*, of which any Tutor in the UNIVERSITY is, at this day, thought worthy, compar'd with the *Expence* he hath been at, and the *Pains* he hath taken, and the *years* he hath spent in order to *Qualifie* ¹ himself for this trust, and also, with the *further Labour* and *Time* he must employ in *discharging* it faithfully, is very *small*, for each Scholar to be educated by him, and that he can the *less afford* to be depriv'd of any *part* of it by invitations given to his Scholars to desert him; and a *Tutor* of *Hart-Hall* much *less* than any *other Tutor*, because he is *limited* to a small number of pupils falling under his care within a limited time, and cannot, after his Class is compleat, fill up the vacancies which shall happen by defections from him. That unless Learning be the very *lowest* of all *attainments*, and the Education of Youth the very *worst* of all *Professions*, *Thirty Shillings* a Quarter, for near *three times as many Lectures*, is not so extravagant a demand, as that even he who *pays* it, should do it with an *unwilling* hand. Much less that any one, who hath *Himself* been a *Tutor*, and who hath experienc'd a faithful Tutor's *trouble* and *anxiety*, should think it *too much* for any of his *Fellow-Labourers* in the same Vocation, altho' their circumstances should happen to be so affluent that they need not any reward, ¹ or their Friendship so particular that they do not desire it. That, therefore, if the promise of being a Tutor *for nothing* had been a proper inducement to this Young Man to have enter'd himself in *Baliol College*, when he first came to the UNIVERSITY, it will not, I conceive, be allow'd to be so justifiable a motive to his leaving *Hart-Hall*, of which Society he, at that time, chose to be a member. That, if this practice should prevail, and Tutors thus *defrauded* of their *Pupils* should be dispos'd to make *Reprisals*, it would bring the UNIVERSITY into confusion, and not much tend to the advancement of Learning. For, it is a known discouragement to *Industry* and *Ingenuity* in some Countries, that a man cannot be secure of possessing the estate he shall raise by his *Labour* and *Skill*; and the same will a Tutor be under to improve his Pupils, if, afterwards, they may be so easily taken from him, and perhaps, so much the sooner, by how much the better they are improv'd.

P. 137.   Thus much I submit to the Judgment of the UNIVERSITY; and one thing I would ¹ also suggest to *Parents*. That I never had anything done for me *for nothing*, which did not, in the end, stand me in much more than the full value; and that, for the most part, that which costs little is worth less. I do not say this to derogate from the Character of the gentleman who hath so cheaply offer'd his services, because he hath the Reputation of a *Scholar* and of a *Man* of *Parts*, and, I believe, deservedly; but the more worthy he is to be *prais'd* on the account of his *Abilities* as a *Tutor*, the more I *blame* him, if, whilst he was *himself* unhurt, he hath not doubted to interest himself in the unjust resentments of his *Friend*; and whilst he was a Member of so *flourishing* a *Society*, and had so *acceptable* a *Character* as might entitle him to as *many Pupils* as he pleas'd out of the wide World, he hath submitted to so mean an Art, upon so unworthy a motive, in order to increase his *large Flock* out of my *small Fold*.

The *Second Reason* offer'd to me by *Joseph Somaster* for his removal, was, that he could live *cheaper* in *Balliol College*.

P. 138.   ¹ The Father, when he enter'd him in *Hart-Hall*, told the Young Man's Tutor, that he therefore enter'd him in *Hart-Hall*, and not in *Baliol College*, because he already had a son¹

¹ William Somaster, Ball. Coll., matr. Dec. 1718, aged 16; B.A. 1722, M.A. 1729.

of *Baliol College* who had spent him too much money; and, I own, I could not help being surpris'd that the House of Education he had *chosen* for the *suppos'd frugality* of it, should have prov'd more *chargeable* to him, than even that which he had *avoided* for the *tried expence* thereof. I beg I may not be misunderstood. I do not hereby insinuate, that *Baliol College* is a more expensive House of Education than *Hart-Hall*, for *their Oeconomy* I do not know, and I do know there have been Young Men in *Hart-Hall* who have spent their Fathers too much money. I am moreover very willing, that *Baliol College* should be esteem'd as *cheap* a House of Learning, as any in either UNIVERSITY; but I am not willing, that either *Baliol*, or any *other College* whatsoever, should be thought a *cheaper* place to live [1] in than *Hart-Hall*, P. 139. because I do not think it possible.

I will not be a Judge in my own Cause; the World shall judge between us, so far as I can enable them to do it.

The following is an exact account of *Joseph Somaster's* expences in *Hart-Hall*, for that Quarter, wherein he apply'd to me for a *Discessit* to go to *Baliol College*, in order to live *cheaper* there, being *Michaelmas* Quarter *One Thousand Seven Hundred and Twenty Three*, beginning, in the UNIVERSITY, on the Twenty First of *June*, and ending on the *Twenty Seventh* of *September*. To the best of my memory, the Account then given in to *Joseph Somaster* by the Butler, was *less* than this now given in by me, by about *Eight Pence*. The error was Butler's, in detriment to the *House*; and the Account, in proportion, less exceptionable to the Commoner.

[1] *A Particular of the said* Commoner's *Expences in the said* P. 140. Mich. *Quarter* :—

	l.	*s.*	*d.*
Chamber-Rent	01	00	00
Tuition and Officers Stipends [1] . .	02	05	00

[1] To the *Tutor* 1*l.* 10*s.* To the *Publick Lecturer* 5*s.* To the *Vice-Principal, Chaplain, Catechist,* and *Moderator* 2*s.* 6*d.* each. *Stipends* somewhat different from those allow'd to these Officers in other Houses, and some small matter larger than

	l.	*s.*	*d.*
[1] University Dues	00	01	03
[2] Charter	00	00	06
Bedmaker's Wages	00	06	06
Domus	00	00	03
[3] Decrements	00	04	02
Servitor	00	02	06
Commons and Battels (*Cook* and *Butler's* Salaries *included*[4])	03	16	11
	07	17	01

P. 141. [1] A View of *Each Week's* Expence for *Commons*, and *Battels*, in the said Quarter, exclusive of the Cook and Butler's Salaries.

	l.	*s.*	*d.*
June 28.	00	04	04½
July 5.	00	04	05½
12.	00	04	06½
19.	00	04	05½
26.	00	04	08
Aug. 2.	00	04	05½
9.	00	05	09
16.	00	05	03
23.	00	04	11

have formerly been paid in this; but of late *demanded* here, in consideration that, the Society being limited to a small number, the Tutors and Officers of the House would have room to deserve this augmentation, and wou'd not have sufficient encouragement without it; and likewise, that the Young Men oblig'd to *this* additional charge, for the first *four* Years of their Education, are *therefore* exempted from *many other expences*, to which their Predecessors had been subject, no ways *necessary* or *proper*; and, in *seven* years time, amounting to very near an equivalent. [*Orig. note.*]

[1] To the *Readers* of the *Unendow'd Lectures* 6d. To the *Bedell* of *Arts* 2d., call'd *Culet*, i. e. *Collecta*. To the Keeper of the Galleries at St. *Mary's* 6d. To the Clerk of St. *Mary's* 1d. [*Orig. note.*]

[2] Paid to the *University*, at *Michaelmas* and *Lady-Day* only, for the defence of their *Privileges*. [*Orig. note.*]

[3] Each Scholar's proportion for *Fuel, Candles, Salt*, and other *common* necessaries: originally *so* call'd as so much did, on these accounts, *decrescere*, or was *discounted* from a Scholar's Endowment. [*Orig. note.*]

[4] 4d. a week to *each* of *those Servants* from every Commoner of the Society, in lieu of all Fees and Perquisites before receiv'd by them. [*Orig. note.*]

							l.	*s.*	*d.*
Aug. 30.	.	.	.	.	.	.	00	04	10½
Sept. 6.	.	.	.	.	.	.	00	05	01½
13.	.	.	.		.	.	00	04	11½
20.	.	.	.	.	.	.	00	04	09½
27.	.	.	.	.	.	.	00	04	11½
							03	07	07

¶ The Peruser of this account may be pleas'd to take notice, that this was a Quarter in which there were *fourteen* weeks, and of which the Commoner was not absent from the Hall *one* day, and that the pure *Commons* and *Battels* of this whole Quarter amount to no more than—

l. 3   07   07

Add to this:

	l.	*s.*	*d.*
The Cook and Butler's *Salaries* for *fourteen* weeks	00	09	04
The *Decrements*	00	04	02
The Allowance to *Domus* . . .	00	00	03
The Allowance to the *Servitor* for Waiting	00	02	06
The Whole Expence of Eating and Drinking and of the Accommodations and Attendance and Service relating thereto, comes but to . . .	04	03	10

Which (*three halfpence* over) is 5*s.* 11*d.* ¾ *per* Week, or 10*d.* ¼ *per* Day.

¶ After this manner did *this Commoner* live in *Hart-Hall*; and after this manner, within a trifle over or under, (and, if an instance be produc'd to the contrary, I will be bound to give a satisfactory reason for it) have *other Commoners* liv'd, and do still live in *Hart-Hall*; and after this manner, whenever my Family are not with me, which sometimes they are not for a Fortnight or three Weeks together, do I *myself* live in *Hart-Hall*. Upon these occasions I hardly ever dine or sup out of the common Refectory; I neither *vary* the meat, nor *exceed* the proportion that is set before the *lowest* Commoner. *Ten-pence* a Day hath paid for my Breakfast, Dinner, and

Supper, even when there was *Ale* in the Society, which now there is not. I have, I thank God, as good *Health* as any Man in *England*; and as good an *appetite* as any Member of the Community; and, for a constancy, had rather live in this manner in *Hart-Hall*, so far as relates to *Eating* and *Drinking*, than at any Nobleman's table in *Europe*. If young Scholars can live *cheaper* in *Baliol College*, I must [1] submit, for I do not pretend that they can live *cheaper* in *Hart-Hall*. If they cannot, this Young Man hath only given the World an opportunity to remark his *Disingenuity* towards the *Society* he had a mind to *disgrace* by *leaving* it; and his *Unskilfulness* in expressing his *Good Will* to that *College* he was impatient to *honour* with his *Presence*.

But tho' I dislik'd the *First Reason* for removing as *improper* to have been given tho' *true*; and the *Second*, as not being *true*, at least not believ'd by *me*, nor explain'd by *Joseph Somaster* to be so, yet the *Third*, with some reluctance I comply'd with. For, tho' a *Scholarship* of £3 2s. 6d. a year, was but a *small matter* to induce this Commoner to change the place of his Education; tho', small as it was, a pretty deal of *expence* was antecedently necessary to the enjoyment of it; tho' it was afterwards to *decrease* in its value in proportion to the time he should not *Reside* upon it; and did not lead to any *future advantage* in the *House* he was going to be a Member of; yet, whilst [1] I labour'd under the grievous opposition given by *Exeter College* to the Incorporation of my Society, and the Favourers of my Design withheld their intended Benefactions, until the same might be firmly establish'd by the *Charter* his Majesty was graciously dispos'd to grant me; I consider'd, *this* was more than I could then give him; and, therefore, being assured by the Master of *Baliol*[1], that *Joseph Somaster* would be admitted into the said *Scholarship* so soon as he should leave *Hart-Hall*, I let him go. But I must not let him go, without

---

[1] Joseph Hunt, Master of Balliol Coll., 1723-6.

intreating the very worthy *Master* of that flourishing Society, whom I Love and Honour for his Learning, and for his care of the youth committed to his charge, to enquire, whether he hath not been impos'd upon by a false *Certificate* of this Young Man's *Age*, in order to his obtaining a *Scholarship* in that *College*, of which, by the *Statutes* thereof, he was not *capable*. For, I am *credibly inform'd*, that a Person having exceeded the *Eighteenth* Year of his Age, tho' but a Day, is not *Capable of*[1] *this Scholarship*; and I *certainly know Jos.* P. 146. *Somaster* was between *Eighteen* and *Nineteen* when he was *Matriculated* in the UNIVERSITY[1]; and above *Nineteen* when he was admitted a *Scholar* of that *College*[2]. And, if so, he is eating the bread of some poor Youth *duly Qualified* for this Scholarship, when he is not; and having a *Right* to it, when he hath none. And then, of the *Three* weighty Arguments produc'd for leaving his former Society, he is left without *One*.

[1] *Joseph*, the son of *Joseph Somaster*, and of *Julian* his Wife, was Baptiz'd Dec. 5, 1704. See the *Reg.* of *Modbury*, in *Devon* [altered to *Reg.* of *Kingsbridge*, in *Devon*, in the 2nd edition of 1733]. He was *matriculated* Apr. 2. 1723, and then writ himself 18 Years of Age. *Univ. Matric.* [*Orig. note.*]

[2] He was not admitted Scholar of *Balliol College*, till after the 14th of *December*, 1723, having Battel'd upon his own Name in the *Buttery* Book of *Hart Hall* on that Day. [*Orig. note.*]

IX.

TERRÆ FILIUS.

[By Nicholas Amhurst, *b.* 16 Oct. 1697, at Marden, in Kent; educated at Merchant Taylors' School; Scholar of St. John's Coll., Oxford, 1716; was expelled 29 June, 1719; *d.* April 12, 1742, at Twickenham.]

Terræ Filius ... By N. Amhurst, of St. John's Coll. 3rd edition. Lond. 1754.

I.

No. III. JANUARY 21. [172$\frac{0}{1}$.]

... To give a just account of the state of the university of Oxford, I must begin where every freshman begins, with admission and matriculation ; for it so happens, that the first thing a young man has to do there, is to prostitute his conscience and enter himself into perjury, at the same time that he enters himself into the university.

If he comes elected from any public school, as from Westminster, Winchester, or Merchant-Taylors, to be admitted upon the foundation of any college, he swears to a great volume of statutes, which he never read, and to observe a thousand customs, rights and privileges, which he knows nothing of, and with which, if he did, he could not perhaps honestly comply.

He takes one oath, for example, 'that he has not an estate in land of inheritance, nor a perpetual pension of five pounds *per annum*,' though perhaps he has an estate of ten times that value; being taught that it is mere matter of form, and may be very conscientiously complied with, notwithstanding the seeming perjury it includes.

To evade the force of this oath, several persons have made their estates over in trust to a friend, and sometimes to a bed-maker; as a gentleman at Oxford did, who lock'd her up in his closet, till he had taken the oath, and then dispossess'd the poor old woman of her imaginary estate, and cancell'd the writings. . . .

. . . ¹ Within fifteen days after his admission into any college, he is obliged to be matriculated, or admitted a member of the university; at which time he subscribes the thirty-nine articles of religion, though often without knowing what he is doing, being order'd to write his name in a book, without mentioning upon what account; for which he pays ten shillings and sixpence. [P. 12.]

At the same time he takes the oaths of allegiance and supremacy, which he is prætaught to evade, or think null: some have thought themselves sufficiently absolved from them by kissing their thumbs, instead of the book; others, in the croud, or by the favour of an honest beadle, have not had the book given them at all.

He also swears to another volume of statutes, which he knows no more of than of his private college-statutes, and which contradict one another in many instances, and demand unjust compliances in many others; all which he swallows ignorantly, and in the dark, without any wicked design. . . .

¹ But I have not mention'd the most absurd thing in matriculation yet. The statute says, if the person to be matriculated is sixteen years of age, he must subscribe the thirty-nine articles, and take the oaths of allegiance and supremacy, as also an oath of fidelity to the university: but, if the person is not sixteen years of age, and above twelve, then he is only to subscribe the thirty-nine articles. [P. 14.]

What a pack of conjurors were our forefathers! to disqualify a person to make a plain simple promise ¹ to obey his King, until he is sixteen years of age, which a child of six is able to do; and at the same time suppose him capable, at twelve years of age, to subscribe thirty-nine articles of religion, which a man of threescore, with all his experience, learning, and application, finds so hard to understand!—I wonder they did [P. 15.]

not command us to teach our children logic and mathematics, before they have learn'd to read.

It is hardly worth mentioning, amongst all these absurdities, that by this statute many persons avoid taking the oaths of allegiance and supremacy at all; for being, or pretending to be, under sixteen when they are matriculated, they are excused from it at that time; and I never heard that anybody was ever call'd upon afterwards to take them, unless they take a degree; but how many are there, who stay many years at Oxford, without taking any degree? . . .

II.

No. VI. FEBRUARY 1, 1721.

P. 28. [1] . . . It is plain that they are the loyalest lads alive at Oxford. . . . During the reign of the late queen Anne, their loyalty had several turns and fetches; but toward the latter end of her life, it discover'd itself firmly settled in her interest, by openly espousing the cause of her rival.

Their conduct, since the accession of his present majesty, is so fresh in everybody's memory, that, I fear, it will be thought impertinent to repeat some instances of it.

It is well known, that Owen, the rebel, and his companions, were entertain'd publicly by most of the heads of colleges; that they walk'd about the streets, at noon-day, with the mob at their heels, huzzaing King James and the duke of Ormond for ever, and no usurpers, in defiance of the government and the friends of the government[1]; that the few friends it had there

P. 29. went every day in danger of their lives from [1] them and their abettors; that they actually besieged Oriel college, and demanded out of it two gentlemen, remarkable for their zeal for the protestant succession, to sacrifice to the mob; that they inlisted great numbers of students and others in the pretender's cause; that they mark'd all the horses there fit for service, and waited only for the news of the duke of Ormond's landing in the west; upon the first reception of which, they design'd

[1] On Aug. 15.

to fly off in a body to join him; I need not mention that the pretender's health was drunk openly and unreservedly in all places; and that a gentleman of Merton college was put into the black book for drinking King George's health, and obliged to plead the benefit of the act of grace to get his degree, after he had been kept out of it two years for that heinous offence[1]; that all sermons, public speeches, and declamations were stuff'd with reproaches and insults upon the king and his ministry; that they presented a known promoter of the pretender's cause in Ireland with a doctor's degree, upon the very day of the king's coronation[2]; and that, at last, a regiment of dragoons march'd into Oxford, sword in hand, to prevent their rising in open rebellion. . . .

III.

Wadham-college, Jan. 22, 1720-21.

To the Author of TERRÆ-FILIUS.

'Sir,

'I hope you intend to acquaint the world, amongst other abuses, in what manner the pious designs of those good men, who left us all our public lectures, are answer'd. Yesterday morning at nine o'clock the bell went as usually for lecture; whether for a rhetorical or logical one, I cannot tell; but I went to the schools, big with hopes of being instructed in one or the other, and having saunter'd a pretty while along the quadrangle, impatient of the lecturer's delay, I ask'd the major (who is an officer [1] belonging to the schools) whether it was usual now and then to slip a lecture or so; his answer was, that he had not seen the face of any lecturer in any faculty, except in poetry and music, for three years past; that all lectures besides were entirely neglected: both of great consequence! especially the first, as it is perform'd by so ingenious and accomplish'd a proficient [3].

'Every Thursday morning in term time there ought to be a

---

[1] Richard Meadowcourt, see pp. 75-90.
[2] Constantinus Phipps, Chancellor of Ireland, 1710; D.C.L. Oct. 20, 1714.
[3] Thomas Warton, Professor of Poetry, 1718-28.

divinity lecture in the divinity school: two gentlemen of our house went one day to hear what the learned professor had to say upon that subject; these two were join'd by another master of arts, who without arrogance might think they understood divinity enough to be his auditors; and that consequently his lecture would not have been lost upon them: but the doctor thought otherwise, who came at last, and was very much surprized to find that there was an audience. He took two or three turns about the school, and then said, *magistri, vos non estis idonei auditores; præterea, juxta legis doctorem Boucher, tres non faciunt collegium—valete;* and so went away.

'Now it is monstrous, that notwithstanding these public lectures are so much neglected, we are all of us, when we take our degrees, charged with and punish'd for non-appearance at the reading of many of them; a formal dispensation is read by our respective deans, at the time our grace is proposed, for our non-appearance at these lectures, and it is with difficulty that some grave ones of the congregation are induced to grant it. Strange order! that each lecturer should have his fifty, his hundred, or two hundred pounds a year for doing nothing; and that we (the young fry) should be obliged to pay money for not hearing such lectures as were never read, nor ever composed.

'PRAY, Mr. TERRÆ-FILIUS be so kind as to insert this as soon as it will suit with your convenience, and oblige

'Your constant reader, and unknown friend.

'P.S. The Vice-chancellor has prohibited all our coffee-houses to take in your paper, under pain of being discommon'd.'

IV.

No. XX. MARCH 24.

... 'This art of chopping logick (as it is properly call'd) is the easiest art in the world; for it requires neither natural parts, nor acquired learning, to make any one a compleat master of it; a good memory is the only one thing necessary to arrive at a perfection in it; and even that may upon occasion be dispensed with; as by the following account of the method of their disputations at Oxford will appear.

The persons of this argumentative drama are three, viz. the Opponent, the Respondent, and the Moderator.

The Opponent is the person, who always begins the attack, and is sure of losing the day, being always (as they call it) on the wrong side of the question; tho' oftentimes that side is palpably the right side, according to our modern philosophy and discoveries. [P. 103.

The Respondent sits over against the opponent, and is prepared to deny whatever he affirms, and always comes off with flying colours; which must needs make him enter the lists with great fortitude and intrepidity.

The Moderator is the hero, or principal character of the drama, and is not much unlike the goddess Victoria, as described by the poets, hovering between two armies in an engagement, and with an arbitrary nod, deciding the fate of the field. There is this difference, indeed, between the military combatants and our school combatants, that the latter know the issue of their conflict before they begin, which the former do not.

This Moderator struts about between the two wordy champions, during the time of action, to see that they do not wander from the question in debate; and when he perceives them deviating from it, to cut them short, and put them into the right road again; for which purpose he is provided with a great quantity of subtle terms and phrases of art, such as, *quoad hoc, & quoad illud, formaliter & materialiter, prædicamentaliter & transcendaliter, actualiter & potentialiter, directè & per se, reductivè & per accidens, entitativè and quiditativè*, *etc.* all which I would explain to my English reader with all my heart, if I could.

Having described the persons of this *ethico-logico-physico-metaphysico-theological* drama, I will now give some account of the drama itself, or rather of the method of conducting it.

Academical disputations are two-fold, ordinary and extraordinary: ordinary disputations are those which are privately perform'd in colleges every day, or twice or thrice a week (according to different customs or statutes) in term-time; extraordinary disputations I call those which are perform'd in the public schools of the university, as requisite qualifications for ¹ degrees: the method of both is the same, and equally arduous is the performance. But I will confine my account to the public disputations, because more solemn and important than the other.

When any person is to come up in the schools to dispute (*pro formâ*) for his degree, he is obliged by statute to fix a paper upon both the gates of the schools, before eight o'clock in the morning, signifying that he is to dispute in the afternoon upon such a question (which is to be approved of by the master of the schools) with his own name, and the name of the college or hall to which he belongs.

All students in the university, who are above one year's standing, and have not taken their batchelor (of arts) degree, are required by a statute to be present at this awful solemnity, which is design'd for a public proof of the progress he has made in the art of reasoning; tho' in fact, it is no more than a formal repetition of a set of syllogisms upon some ridiculous question in logick, which they get by rote, or, perhaps, only read out of their caps, which lie before them with their notes in them. These commodious sets of syllogisms are call'd strings, and descend from undergraduate to undergraduate, in a regular succession; so that, when any candidate for a degree, is to exercise his talent in argumentation, he has nothing else to do, but to enquire amongst his friends for a string upon such or such a question, and to get it by heart, or read it over in his cap, as aforesaid. I have in my custody a book of strings upon most or all of the questions discussed in a certain college, very famous for their ratiocinative faculty; on the first leaf of which are these words,

Ex dono Richardi P———e primæ classi benefactoris munificentissimi.

From whence it appears, that this Richard P——e was a great string-maker, and by his beneficent [1] labours had furnish'd his successors, in the first class, with a sufficient inheritance of syllogisms, to be as good logicians as himself, without taking any pains.

Behold, loving reader, the whole art and mystery of logick, as it is taught in the most famous university in the world; and judge for thyself, whether sir Richard Steele has not described it very justly in his dedication to the pope[1], thus:—

'This method may be call'd the art of wrangling, as long as the moderator of the dispute is at leisure; and may well enough be supposed to be a game at learned racket. The question is the ball of contention; and he wins, who shews himself able to keep up the ball longest. A syllogism strikes it to the respondent: and a negation, or lucky distinction returns it back to the opponent: and so, it flies over the heads of those, who have time to sit under it, till the judge of the game strikes it down, with authority, into rest and silence.'

V.

No. XXII. MARCH 31.

[1] Being inform'd, that what I have cursorily said in one of my papers concerning a gentleman (Mr. Meadowcourt[2]) of Merton-college, viz. that he was put into the black book for drinking King George's health, and obliged to plead the benefit of his majesty's act of grace to get his degree, after he had been kept out of it two years for that heinous offence: I say, being inform'd that this charge has been sturdily deny'd as a falsehood at Oxford, I will give the reader a true account of the whole matter, from beginning to end.

I confess it does not displease me to find the gowned gentlemen so willing to conceal or evade this insolent and almost incredible transaction: it looks as if they had some modesty left, and were ashamed to own what they cannot possibly justify.

---

[1] At the beginning of his *Account of the State of the Roman Catholic Religion throughout the World.*

[2] Richard Meadowcourt, of Merton, B.A. 1714; M.A. 1718.

As this affair was occasion'd by a society of gentlemen, called the CONSTITUTIONAL CLUB[1], it may be expected that I should give an account of that society; . . . at present I will content myself with premising in general, that this society took its rise from the iniquity of the times, and was intended to promote and cultivate friendship between all such persons as favour'd our present happy constitution: they thought themselves obliged openly and publicly to avow their loyalty, and manifest their sincere affection to king George upon all proper and becoming occasions, and to check, as much as in them lay, the vast torrent of treason and disaffection which overflow'd the university. They thought it their duty to shew all possible marks of respect to those faithful officers, who were so seasonably sent to that place, by the favour of the government, to protect the quiet part of the king's subjects, and to suppress the tumultuary practices of the profess'd enemies to his majesty's person and government; and for constantly adhering to what they thought their duty in these points; and for no other cause, that they can apprehend, they have been so unfortunate as to become obnoxious to the university, and to feel, many of them, the severe effects of their resentments.

This short account of the constitution club is sufficient for our present purpose, to which I now proceed;

On the 29th of May, 1716, in the evening, the constitution club, and several officers in colonel Handyside's regiment, met together at a tavern. Whilst they were drinking the king's and other loyal healths, several squibs were thrown in at the window, which burnt some of their cloaths, and fill'd the room with fire and smoak. Besides this, they were continually insulted with loud peals of hisses and conclamations of 'down with the roundheads,' from the gownmen, and other disorderly people in the street; of which they took no notice. They continued together till about eleven o'clock, or not quite so late, when Mr. Holt, of Maudlin college, sub-proctor at

[1] See Chr. Wordsworth's *Social Life*, p. 42, &c.

that time[1], came, and making up to Mr. Meadowcourt (who happen'd to be steward of the club that night) demanded of him the reason of their being at the tavern. Mr. Meadowcourt rose up, and told him, that they were ¹ met together to P. 113. commemorate the restoration of king Charles the second, and to drink king George's health; *and that they should be obliged to him if he would be pleased to drink king GEORGE'S health with them;* which the proctor, after some intreaties, comply'd with. After which, one of the captains went to him, and desired him to excuse the scholars that were there, promising that he would take care that no harm or disorder should be committed, and then waited upon the proctor down stairs.

The next day Mr. Meadowcourt was sent for by Mr. Holt; who, when he came to him, told him, that he had spoken words to him the night before, that were affronting and improper to be spoken to a proctor; that, however, he would not insist upon the affront, nor take any advantage of him for words which he attributed to the effects of wine, but that his brother proctor Mr. White of Christ-church college (though the words were not spoken to him, nor in his presence) was very angry with him, and had desired that the power of taking cognizance of, and proceeding against all that was done that night, might be transferr'd into his hands; that he was therefore no longer a party concern'd in this affair, but advised him as a friend to go to Mr. White, and, in submissive terms, to make his peace with him. Mr. Meadowcourt answer'd, that he knew no occasion which he had given Mr. White to be angry with him; that for any improper words which he might speak the night before, he begg'd his [Mr. Holt's] pardon, and assured him that whatever he spoke, it was not with any design to affront him; and desired him that, since Mr. White did not take him at the tavern, and since he himself was the only person, whom he had any way

---

¹ Charles Holt, matr. 13 Oct. 1699; B.A. 1703; Senior Proctor, not 'Sub-Proctor,' in 1716. The Junior Proctor was John White, of Christ Church; B.A. 1704, M.A. 1707.

offended, he would be pleased not to deliver him up to Mr. White, but inflict upon him what punishment he thought fit, which he would willingly submit to. He press'd him, as far as was proper, to consent to this, but was not able to prevail.

¹ The reader cannot help remarking that these affronting and improper words, about which all this stir was made, were only those which are printed in Italic characters, desiring the 'proctor to drink king George's health with the company.' They may, for aught I know, be improper; and I don't in the least doubt, but that they were affronting: but yet, methinks the submission which Mr. Meadowcourt made was enough to appease an ordinary resentment.

The day following, Mr. Meadowcourt waited upon Mr. White, to whom he was now assign'd over by Mr. Holt: I will not believe so unchristian a thing of Mr. White, as to suppose that he desir'd the prosecution of Mr. Meadowcourt, in order to gratify an old grudge against him; though by his being so very officious in such an ill-natured office (which most people would rather avoid than seek) he has given occasion to such an uncharitable reflection.

Mr. Meadowcourt, the first time he waited upon Mr. White, found him in a most ungovernable passion, insomuch that he often brandished his arm at him, and told him, that the members of the constitution club were the most profligate fellows in the university, and all deserved to be expell'd, for pretending to have more loyalty (very profligate indeed!) than the rest of the university; he wonder'd how they, who were but an handful of men, could have the impudence to oppose themselves to such a majority; and declared, that there were ten tories in the university to one whig. He said, that Mr. Meadowcourt had been notoriously guilty of keeping company with officers; that he was a miscreant, and had committed the most flagrant crimes that ever any person had done before; that he made it his business to oppose the university; that he had been guilty of rebellion against the university, and much more to the same purpose; telling him, that the honour of the university, the authority of magistrates, and his own conscience (good man!) obliged him to proceed against him with the utmost rigour and severity.

¹ On the morrow he went to him again, as he had order'd him, to pay him forty shillings, the mulct imposed by the statute, for being found out of his college after nine o'clock at night; though, by the way it is very rarely insisted upon, unless from poor roundheads.

P. 115.

He told him, when he had paid this money, that he must not expect that this would be all the punishment that would be inflicted on him, though it was not yet determined after what manner he should be proceeded against; that there would be a very strict scrutiny made into his character and actions; and that if any of those facts, which had been charged against him, could be found out, he might depend upon being expell'd.

In this mild and gentle manner was Mr. Meadowcourt treated; and in the same mild and gentle manner must every one expect to be treated, till things are alter'd, who discovers the same zeal for the present government, and the protestant succession.

Several persons of note in the University interceded with Mr. White in behalf of Mr. Meadowcourt, and desired him to be reconciled to him; amongst whom were a most noble duke and marquis, who were pleased to use pressing instances to Mr. White in this matter. I have heard (but do not aver the truth of it) that Mr. White gave their lordships his word, that he would put all up, and proceed no farther; though, soon after this, Mr. Meadowcourt heard that he had put him into the black book, and sentenced him to be kept back from his degree for two years.

The black book is a register of the university, kept by the proctor, in which he records any person who affronts him, or the university; and no person, who is so recorded, can proceed to his degree, till he has given the proctor, who put him in, satisfaction; which must be enter'd accordingly in that book.

VI.

No. XXIII. April 4.

P. 116.   ' Mr. Meadowcourt finding Mr. White thus inexorable and unrelenting, had but small hopes that any intercession would prevail with him, after two noble lords had been so unhandsomely dealt by; and therefore he submitted to his burthen, resting contented without his degree, and without knowing for what reasons he was detain'd from it 'till the two years were almost expired. He then thought it time to be let into the secret of his crimes, that he might be able to make a defence against them, and therefore he waited upon the then proctor, Mr. Steed (of All-souls-college[1]) the day on which he laid down his office, and desired leave to transcribe a copy of what Mr. White had laid to his charge, and register'd in the black book; which Mr. Steed readily consented to, and received him with much kindness and humanity.

When he look'd into that dreadful and gloomy volume, it surprized him to find himself made answerable, not only for a charge of crimes placed to his own name, but also for a charge of crimes placed to another gentleman's name: both which charges, I will make public, lest the jealous reader should

P. 117.   ' suspect them to be worse than they are, or that I stifle the worst part of them.

They are drawn up in Latin, but I will insert them in English, for the use of all my readers.

June 28, 1716.

Let Mr. Carty of University-college[2] be kept from the degree, which he stands for next, for the space of one whole year.

I. For prophaning, with mad intemperance, that day, on which he ought, with sober chearfulness, to have commemorated the restoration of king Charles the second and the royal family, nay, of monarchy itself, and the church of England.

---

[1] John Stead, B.A. from Balliol, 1705; M.A. (All Souls), 1709; Senior Proctor, 1717.

[2] Basil Carty; he took his B.A. degree June 5, 1713, but no other subsequently.

II. For drinking in company with those persons, who insolently boast of their loyalty to king George, and endeavour to render almost all the university, besides themselves, suspected of disaffection.

III. For calling together a great mob of people, as if to see a shew, and drinking impious execrations, out of the tavern window, against several worthy persons, who are the best friends to the church and the king; by this means provoking the beholders to return them the same abuses; from whence follow'd a detestable breach of the peace.

IV. For refusing to go home to his college after nine o'clock at night, though he was more than once commanded to do it, by the junior proctor, who came thither to quell the riot.

V. For being catch'd at the same place again by the senior proctor, and pretending, as he was admonish'd by him, to go home; but with a design to drink again.

Let Mr. Meadowcourt of Merton-college be kept back from the degree which he stands for next, for the space of two years; nor be admitted to supplicate for his grace, until he confesses his manifold crimes, and asks pardon upon his knees.

[1] VI. Not only for being an accomplice with Mr. Carty in P. 118. all his faults (or rather crimes), but also,

VII. For being not only a companion, but likewise a remarkable abetter of certain officers, who ran up and down the high-street with their swords drawn, to the great terror of the townsmen and scholars.

VIII. For breaking out to that degree of impudence, (when the proctor admonish'd him to go home from the tavern at an unseasonable hour) as to command all the company, with a loud voice, to drink king George's health.

JOH. W. proc. jun.

Of all these pompous articles, Mr. Meadowcourt owns himself guilty only of the last, viz. that he was caught out of his college at an unstatutable hour, (for which he paid forty shillings, which is the penalty annex'd to that crime by the statute) and that he did drink king George's health in the presence of the proctor; which being deem'd an affront, he ask'd his pardon for it, and offer'd to make him any other honourable satisfaction.

But, as to all the other articles, he utterly denies himself to be guilty of any of them, having many undeniable testimonies to vindicate his innocence, whenever he should have an opportunity; particularly, in answer to what is alledged against him in the seventh article [which relates to him singly] Mr. Meadowcourt solemnly declares, that he was so far from being an abbetter and encourager of any such officers, as are mention'd to run up and down the high-street with drawn swords in their hands, to the great terror of the townsmen and scholars, that he was not even an eye-witness of them; and he challenges any of those magnanimous townsmen or scholars, who were frighten'd at the sight of these naked swords, to say that they saw him either as an encourager or a companion of those officers, in whatever was done by them in the street, which, no doubt they would have ¹ done, if they could, after he had put them into such bodily fear.

In this, and every other particular (except those two before-mention'd) he could undeniably have purged himself from the guilt laid to his charge.—But proving and disproving are not academical methods of proceeding; the dull forms of Westminster-hall being too tedious for the literati to observe. If you would be acquitted by them, you must plead guilty, and submit.

Upon the expiration of the two years, Mr. Meadowcourt made application to the then proctor for leave to supplicate for his grace, and proceed to his (master of arts) degree. The proctor's answer was; that he thought it reasonable he should have leave; but that he could not grant it him, without Mr. White's consent; and that he would go himself to Mr. White, and speak to him in his behalf; accordingly he went the same day to Mr. White, who told him, that he was very willing Mr. Meadowcourt should now proceed to his degree; but that it was necessary first to consult Mr. Holt (to whom the king's health was drank) about it, to know whether he would concur with him; and that he would write to Mr. Holt, (who was then at the Bath), and acquaint him with his answer.

Some time after this, Mr. Holt return'd to Oxford, and having received a letter from Mr. Meadowcourt concerning this affair, sent for him to his chamber, and assured him, that he had resolved from the beginning not to make himself a party in this affair; that he had resign'd it entirely into Mr. White's hands, and therefore could not resume it, without seeming to withdraw that confidence which he had before placed in Mr. White; that for his own part, he required no satisfaction to be given to him; that his consent went along with Mr. White's consent; and that it was imply'd in whatsoever Mr. White should think fit to act. Mr. Meadowcourt, however, begg'd of him, that since Mr. White insisted upon it, he would be pleased¹ to speak to him, and let him know P. 120. that he had received satisfaction, and was willing to let Mr. Meadowcourt have his degree; which Mr. Holt promised, and took his leave of him at that time.

To make short of the story; they neither of them intended that Mr. Meadowcourt should have his degree; Mr. White could not do it without Mr. Holt's consent; and Mr. Holt had left it entirely to Mr. White, who, for all that, would not concern himself without Mr. Holt, who had from the beginning resolved to be no party in this affair. Thus did they bandy it about, sending Mr. Meadowcourt backward and forward upon sleeveless errands; till, at last, having jumbled their learned noddles together, they sent him a paper containing the following articles, which they insisted upon to be read by Mr. Meadowcourt in the convocation-house, before he should proceed to his degree.

I. I do acknowledge all the crimes laid to my charge in

the black book; and that I deserved the punishment imposed on me.

II. I do acknowledge that the story of my being punish'd on account of my affection to king George, and his illustrious house, is unjust and injurious, not only to the reputation of the proctor, but of the whole university.

III. I do profess sincerely, that I do not believe that I was punish'd on that account.

IV. I am very thankful for the clemency of the university, in remitting the ignominious part of the punishment, viz. begging pardon upon my knees.

V. I beg pardon of Almighty God, of the proctor, and all the masters, for the offences which I have committed respectively against them; and I promise that I will, by my future behaviour, make the best amends I can, for having offended by the worst of examples.

Modest! reasonable! candid! and honourable gentlemen! I stand astonish'd at Mr. Meadowcourt's [1] obstinacy and perverseness, that he should refuse to comply with such fair and equitable terms! alas! it is now too evident that he has, indeed, play'd the rebel against the university; and been notoriously guilty of keeping company with officers.

Bold and contumacious wretch! how easy would it have been for him (according to academical custom) to confess himself guilty of crimes, of which he knew and could prove himself to be guiltless?

To allow the justice of a punishment which he was convinced was unjust and arbitrary?

To declare, in the face of the convocation, that a story was false and scandalous, which was notorious and demonstrable?

To acknowledge clemency, where he had experienced nothing but cruelty; and to beg pardon of those, whom he was not conscious of having offended?

How easy, I say, would all this have been to any one, that had lived seven or eight years within the sound of Christchurch Tom, and under the tuition of so good a woman?

But matriculation, like divers other good things, is quite thrown away upon some people.

Mr. Meadowcourt having rejected this submission, desponded for some time of ever obtaining his degree; but duly weighing the heinousness of his offences, and the time when they were committed, since which his majesty has been pleased to publish an act of grace, he was advised that he was included in it; and that amongst his fellow-subjects in iniquity, who had talk'd treason, drunk treason, plotted and rebell'd against his majesty, he might also hope to find mercy from it, for insolently boasting of his loyalty to his majesty, and audaciously drinking his majesty's health to one of his majesty's viceregents.

This method therefore he resolved to try; but meeting with new difficulties upon this occasion, I must refer the particulars to my next; which will close this subject.

VII.

No. XXIV. April 7.

' In pursuance of the advice given to Mr. Meadowcourt by his friends, to plead his majesty's act of grace in the vice-chancellor's court, which they inform'd him extended to those pretended crimes, which were register'd against him in the black book; he went to one B——r, a proctor of the court, (not a proctor of the university, who is a quite different officer) and retain'd him with a fee, giving him the following instructions:

That he should cite the two proctors (of the university) to give their reasons in the court for continuing his name in the black book; and, upon giving their reasons, he should plead the act of grace in his behalf, and petition the court to decree, that his name might be blotted out. He at first scrupled to cite the proctors into the court, and required to be allow'd a great deal of time to consider of this nice and ticklish affair, (as he call'd it) but, upon Mr. Meadowcourt's refusing to agree to any delay, and pressing him to proceed with all possible expedition, he promised to follow his instructions.

P. 123.   ¹ When the day came, on which Mr. Meadowcourt design'd his cause should be brought into the court, he went to B——r, whom he had retain'd, to know whether he had cited the two proctors; he told him that he had not, that he (Mr. Meadowcourt) was too hasty, and would do his cause harm by going on so fast; that he had been with the vice-chancellor[1], and inform'd him of the whole case; that the vice-chancellor had promised to consider of it; and that he could not, by any means, proceed, till he had known the vice-chancellor's thoughts of the matter.

Finding his business was likely to be carried on but slowly, under B——r's management, Mr. Meadowcourt went from him to one Pl——ll, another proctor of the court, and told him what he wanted to have done, without mentioning anything of his intention to plead the act of grace: he seem'd very ready to undertake the cause; but said, that it was too late to send a citation to the proctors that day; and that he would not fail to do it the next week.

From him Mr. Meadowcourt return'd to B——r, and told him, that his business would not admit of any delay; and therefore hoped that he would not take it ill, if he try'd whether it was possible for another proctor to bring it sooner into the court, than he found he was inclined to do. To this B——r gave Mr. Meadowcourt a civil answer, and left him.

In the afternoon Pl——ll came to him, and said, that he had talk'd with the assessor of the court; that his was a very ticklish business; that he did not know what to say to it; that it was never known that the proctors had been put into the court; that it was a dangerous thing; that he must take time to consider whether any thing could be done in it, or not; and that, in fine, he had much better make some acknowledgement to Mr. White, and beg pardon.

[1] Robert Shippen, Principal of Brasenose.

All that Mr. Meadowcourt was able to say to him now could not prevail with him to undertake his cause; and he found, by what he said, that he had been terrify'd and discouraged both by B——r, and by the assessor

[1] Upon this, Mr. Meadowcourt resolved to offer his cause to the rest of the proctors, and try whether they would all reject it: wherefore, the next morning he went to A——n, of Allsouls college, Br——n,[1] of New-inn hall, and I——m, of Maudlin college.

The first of these told him, that he was going out of town, and should not return again before the end of the term.

Br——n said, that it was a ticklish case; that he should be glad to serve Mr. Meadowcourt, but was afraid of bringing himself into a scrape, and of disobliging the university.

And I——m was of opinion too, that it was a very nice case, and begg'd that he might be excused from being concern'd in it.

Thus was his cause rejected by all the proctors; the vice-chancellor's court was shut against him; he was precluded from all access to justice, and injuriously with-held from claiming the benefit of a law, to which these very men, perhaps, owed the power they enjoy'd to do him this injury.

He then waited upon the vice-chancellor, and told him, that he had a cause to be brought into his court; that he had apply'd himself to all the proctors of the court, that none of them would undertake it; and that therefore he begg'd the favour of him to assign him a proctor, and to oblige him to bring his cause into the court. Sir, said the vice-chancellor, what is your cause? he answer'd, that he would have the two proctors of the university cited to give their reasons in the court for continuing his name in the black book. This, said the vice-chancellor, is such a cause as none of the proctors (of the court) thought it safe to appear in; that it had not been known that the proctors (of the university) were ever cited to

---

[1] John Brabourne, New Inn Hall, matr. 6 March, 1710–11, aged 14; B.A. 1714, M.A. 1717, died 1729.

appear in the court; and that his name was continued in the black book, because he had not given Mr. White satisfaction. Mr. Meadowcourt told him, that he desired the proctors might give their reasons in the court. Your business, said the vice-chancellor, is not with the present proctors, ¹ but with Mr. White, who put you into the black book, and you are to make up the matter with him. Mr. Meadowcourt answer'd, that he did not think that he had any thing to do with Mr. White; that his complaint lay against the proctors in office; that he was directed by his friends to proceed against them; and that he thought himself obliged to follow their direction.

Then, said the vice-chancellor, you are ill-directed; that he would advise him to go to Mr. White, and desire him to take his name out of the black book, and to enter his *satisfecit.* Mr. Meadowcourt told him, that he had waited upon Mr. White often enough already; that he insisted upon unreasonable terms of satisfaction; that he had been very ill used by Mr. White, and that he would not concern himself with him, nor speak to him any more about it; but that he would proceed in the court, if he (the vice-chancellor) would give him leave; that if he would not give him leave, he had no more to say, and must rest satisfy'd.—Upon this Mr. Meadowcourt was going away; when the vice-chancellor said, sir, I do not say that I will not give you leave; I will consider of it, and you shall hear from me in a day or two's time.

I forgot to mention, that B——r, when Mr. Meadowcourt went to him first, said, that he thought that he had a right to plead the act of grace; and that he afterwards intimated to Mr. Meadowcourt, that the assessor and the vice-chancellor were of the same opinion.

I cannot therefore but ascribe this dilatory and evasive conduct of the vice-chancellor, as well as the combination of the assessor and proctors of the court, to a consciousness that Mr. Meadowcourt was entitled to the act of grace, which they fear'd would relieve him from the injuries he had long lain under, and deprive the university of their promised triumph and revenge, from the hopes they had of forcing him at last to comply with a base and scandalous form of submission.

When the vice-chancellor found that Mr. Meadowcourt was resolved to plead the act of grace, and not submit to Mr. White, his next artifice was to make him plead it privately to him and Mr. White, and not in the court; being asham'd, I suppose, to have it known that he obliged a gentleman to plead the benefit of such an act upon such an occasion: but Mr. Meadowcourt insisted upon pleading it in the court, which he was advised was the only legal way; and told the vice-chancellor that if he would not give him leave to proceed in his court, he should look upon it that his court was shut up against him, and that he was deny'd a privilege which every member of the university had a right to.

At length the vice-chancellor assign'd him a proctor, whom he order'd to cite the two proctors of the university into the court; as soon as the proctor had done this, the vice-chancellor order'd him to uncite them; and then, after much ado, order'd him to cite them again, and sent Mr. Mcadowcourt word that he had agreed to let his cause be brought into the court on such a day.

Accordingly Mr. Meadowcourt went to the court, and one of the proctors of the university appear'd and left the black book with the assessor; upon reading over the pretended charge of crimes register'd in it, and Mr. Meadowcourt's plea, the assessor decreed that his crimes were wiped off by the act of grace, and that his name should be put out of the black book.

The next congregation (which is a meeting of the members of the university to grant degrees) he stood for his grace, which was deny'd (as was suspected) by Mr. White.

The second time he stood for his grace, he was deny'd (as it was supposed) by a master of arts of Jesus-college.

But the person, who denies any body his grace, being obliged to give his reasons for it the third time, and having nothing to alledge against Mr. Meadowcourt, since the act, of which he pleaded the benefit, took place, his grace was granted the third time he stood for it; and the next congregation he was presented to his degree[1].

Thus did he at length escape out of the hands of his merciless enemies and persecutors, who, by this one instance, in every step they took, seem'd desirous to convince people what hardships, injuries, oppressions and discouragements, they keep in store for those men, who insolently dare to affront the university, by honouring king George and the protestant succession.

I have pursued this affair through all its various scenes of partiality, corruption, and prevarication, fairly and honestly, without concealing anything which was urged against Mr. Meadowcourt, or charging the officers of the university with any method (however seemingly unjust and arbitrary) which they did not take upon this occasion: and I now leave the world to judge, whether I have not made my charge good, that Mr. Meadowcourt suffer'd all this for his affection to king George, and was obliged to plead his majesty's act of grace for drinking his majesty's health; the chief article against him in the black book, and on which (even there) the greatest stress is laid, being, 'that he proceeded so far in impudence as to command all the company with a loud voice, to drink king George's health.'

VIII.

No. XLII. June 8.

P. 218.   'As university degrees are supposed to be the badges of learning and merit, there ought to be some qualifications requisite to wear them, besides perjury, and treason, and paying a multitude of fees; which seem to be the three principal things insisted upon in our universities.

P. 219.   'Indeed, they have long, tedious forms, which they call exercises, through which every candidate for a degree must pass, before he is invested in the convocation-house:

[1] May 13, 1714.

but, by the same rule that the vulgar esteem him a deep scholar, who has gone through these forms, they may esteem the city buff-coats, who took Lisle in Bunhill-fields, gallant soldiers and experienced leaders.

These scholastic exercises may be divided into four branches, viz. disputations, frequenting public lectures, examinations, and determinations.

I have explain'd the manner of their disputations in a former paper, and have shewn them to be nothing but the repetition of long strings of threadbare syllogisms upon some ridiculous, obsolete, and unedifying questions in logic, metaphysics, and school divinity, which a fresh-man can do as well as the oldest doctor in the university.

It is also required, by statute, of all candidates, that they have been constant hearers of the public lectures in those faculties, in which they stand for degrees; for instance, every candidate for the degree of bachelor of arts is obliged for one whole year, from his first entrance into the university, to be present at the grammar lecture twice every week, viz. on tuesdays and fridays; and at the rhetorical lecture on mondays and thursdays; after the end of the first year, 'till he is presented to his degree, he is obliged to attend the logical lecture every monday and thursday; and the moral-philosophy lecture every tuesday and friday; and from the end of his second year, until one whole year after he has taken his bachelor's degree, he is obliged, according to the Savilian statutes, to attend the geometry lecture every wednesday and saturday.

In other degrees, the same attendance is required at the public lectures in other faculties; for all which, particular places are appointed by the statutes of the university.

I doubt not my reader will be surprised at this, after I have complain'd that no qualifications for degrees [1] are required as to the learning of the candidates; and will readily ask what more prudential method could possibly be taken to exclude all unqualify'd persons, than this is? But his astonishment will abate, when he finds that the candidates are so far from

P. 220.

attending, as is strictly required by statute, upon these lectures, that there are no such lectures read in any of the faculties, except music and poetry, as hath been observed in a former paper.

And yet, before any person can obtain his degree, he is obliged to supplicate (by the person who proposes his grace) for a dispensation for his non-attendance at these lectures; such is the modesty of the dons, that they neglect their duty, and oblige the fellows to ask pardon, and pay for it.

It cannot therefore be argued any where, but in the convocation-house at Oxford, that a person deserves his degree, because he ought to deserve it; the best laws, when they become dead letters, are no laws; and a qualification, which is dispensed with, is no qualification.

Examination is the next test required of every candidate; let us therefore see whether there is anything more in this, than in the others.

The statute, which enjoins this ceremony, begins with this preamble, 'That the congregation of regent-masters may be the better apprised of the learning and proficiency in good letters of all persons who take degrees in arts; it is enacted, that every one, before he is admitted to supplicate for his grace, shall undergo the examination of a regent-master.'

The person to be examined is obliged, the day before his examination, to affix a *programma* on several public places in the university, signifying his name, what college he belongs to, and what degree he stands for.

P. 221. ¹ The place appointed for these examinations is the natural-philosophy school, (one of the most public places in the university), the hour from nine 'till eleven in the morning, during all which time the candidate is obliged to stay there; and again from one in the afternoon, if the examiner thinks fit, as long as he pleases.

The arts or sciences, in which the candidate is to be examined, are those in which, according to the statutes of the university, he is obliged to hear public lectures: besides which, he is to be examined in the classics, and to return all his answers as fluently and properly in Latin, as he could in his mother tongue.

These examiners are (or ought to be) appointed by the senior proctor, who administers an oath to them to this effect.

'That they will either examine, or hear examined, all candidates that fall to their lot, in those arts and sciences, and in such manner as the statute requires.

'Likewise, that they will not be prevail'd upon by intreaties or bribes, or hatred or friendship, or hope or fear, to grant any one a *testimonium*, who does not deserve it, or to deny it to any one that does.'

Now this, again, looks all very fair and satisfactory: but let us examine the practice, not the theory; the execution of the statutes, and not the statutes themselves.

The meaning of the statute in ordering the candidates to be examined in those arts and sciences, in which they were obliged to attend public lectures, was (I suppose) to see whether they had attended them diligently or not; for, if those lectures were duly kept up, and the young students frequented them, their examination would be an easy task, tho' perform'd with the utmost rigour, which the statutes require: but as these lectures are laid aside, as very few tutors take care to instruct their pupils in any thing but a little humdrum logic, and as very few young fellows are disposed to study more than they are obliged to do, they have found out a new method of performing this public exercise with great fluency, and very little pains.

As I told my reader, that for disputations they have ready-made strings of syllogisms; so for examination, they have the skeletons of all the arts or sciences, in which they are to be examined, containing all the questions in each of them, which are usually ask'd upon this occasion, and the common answers that are given to them; which in a week or a fortnight they may get at their tongue's end.—But is this a sufficient mark of intrinsic learning? Is this a proper qualification for university degrees? Many a school-boy has done more than this for his breaking-up task!

Several ingenuous candidates have confess'd to me, that they never studied an hour, nor look'd into any system of the sciences, 'till a month before they were examined.

How well the examiners perform their duty, I leave to God and their own consciences; tho' my shallow apprehension cannot reconcile their taking a solemn oath, 'that they will not be prevail'd upon by entreaties, or bribes, or friendship, etc.' with their actually receiving bribes, and frequently granting testimoniums to unworthy candidates, out of personal friendship and bottle acquaintance.

It is a notorious truth that most candidates get leave of the proctor, by paying his man a crown, (which is call'd his perquisite) to chuse their own examiners, who never fail to be their old cronies and toping companions. The question therefore is, whether it may not be strongly presumed from hence, that the candidates expect more favour from these men, than from strangers; because otherwise it would be throwing away a crown to no purpose: and if they do meet with favour from them, *quære*, whether the examiner is not prevail'd upon by intreaties or friendship?

It is also well-known to be the custom for the candidates either to present their examiners with a piece of gold, or to give them an handsome entertainment, [1] and make them drunk; which they commonly do the night before examination, and sometimes keep them till morning, and so adjourn, cheek by joul. from their drinking room to the school, where they are to be examined.—*Quære*, whether it would not be very ungrateful of the examiner to refuse any candidate a testimonium, who has treated him so splendidly over night? and whether he is not, in this case, prevail'd upon by bribes?

When these and some more trifling exercises are perform'd, any person is intitled to his bachelor of arts degree, provided he has been four years (or sixteen terms) a member of any college or hall; and has not, by his morals, render'd himself obnoxious to the university. . . .

But though a candidate obtains his grace, and is presented to his bachelor's (in arts) degree, and wears the habit suitable to it; yet he is not properly a compleat graduate until the Lent following, when he is obliged to perform certain other exercises, called his determinations, under the penalty, that if he neglects this, the grace before granted him shall be revoked, unless he meets with some impediment, which the vice-chancellor and proctors shall approve of; in which case his determination may be defer'd to the Lent following, under the like penalty. For this reason I have placed determination amongst the exercises requisite for a bachelor of arts degree.

The manner of this determination is as follows.

All persons, that have taken their bachelor of arts degree since the Lent preceding, are obliged to dispute twice in one of the public schools, which the collectors (whom I will presently describe) shall appoint, and go to prayers at St. Mary's church every saturday morning; these disputations, which are just like other disputations, are so order'd, that they last all Lent-time.

The collectors (who are two in number) are chosen out of the determining bachelors by the two proctors, each proctor chusing one; and their business is to divide ¹ the determiners into certain classes, and to appoint to every one what school he shall dispute in; which he is to dispose in such a manner, that some of them may come up in all the schools every monday, tuesday, wednesday, thursday, and friday, (excepting holidays) from the beginning of Lent to the end of the term.

For this purpose they draw a scheme (which is printed and sent to every college) in which the names of all determiners are placed in several columns; and over against them, in other columns, the days when, and the schools where they are to respond.

Some of these days are call'd gracious days, because upon them the respondent is not obliged to stay in the schools above

P. 224.

half the time, which respondents upon other days are; and some of the schools are esteem'd better than other, because more private; but the first column and the last column in the scheme (which contain the names of those who are to come up the first day and the last day, and which is call'd posting and dogging) are esteem'd very scandalous.

The collectors therefore, having it in their power to dispose of all the schools and days in what manner they please, are very considerable persons and great application is made to them for gracious days and good schools; but especially to avoid being posted or dogg'd, which commonly happens to be their lot, who have no money in their pockets.

The statute indeed forbids the collectors to receive any presents, or to give any treats; but the common practice is known to be directly against the statute; every determiner (that can afford it) values himself upon presenting one of the collectors with a broad (piece) or half a broad; and Mr. collector, in return entertains his benefactors with a good supper, and as much wine as they can drink, besides gracious days and commodious schools.

I have heard that some collectors have made four score or an hundred guineas of this place.

P. 225. ¹ This to me seems the great business of determination; to pay money, and get drunk.

Thus I have given the reader some account of the exercises requisite to a bachelor of arts degree; in other degrees the corruptions are the same, and the exercises requisite to taking them equally neglected, or equally insignificant.

To conclude: I hope nobody will be, for the future, surprised, when they read many empty and stupid volumes, dignified in the title pages with these illustrious letters, A.B., A.M., L.L.B., L.L.D., B.D., S.T.P.¹, etc.

¹ =*Sanctae Theologiae Professor*, the Latin equivalent of D.D., as A.B., A.M. is of B.A., M.A. L.L.B., L.L.D. should of course be LL.B., LL.D.

X.
WILLIAM SHENSTONE
[*born* Nov. 18, 1714; *died* Feb. 11, 1736]

AND

RICHARD GRAVES[1].

Recollections of some particulars in the life of the late William Shenstone. [By the Rev. Richard Graves.] Lond. 1788. 8º.

MR. SHENSTONE was entered a commoner at Pembroke college in Oxford, in the year 1732, where I first became acquainted with him, though not till some months after I went to reside there[1].

The young people of the college, at that time (as I believe is the case in most colleges) were divided into different small associations, according to their different tastes and pursuits.

Having been elected from a public school in the vicinity of Oxford, and brought with me the character of a tolerably good Grecian, I was invited, by a very worthy person now living, to a very sober little party, who amused themselves in the evening with reading Greek and drinking water. Here I continued six months, and we read over Theophrastus, Epictetus, Phalaris's Epistles, and such other Greek authors as are seldom read at school. But I was at length seduced from this mortified symposium to a very different party; a set of jolly, sprightly young fellows, most of them west-country lads; who drank ale, smoked tobacco, punned, and

---

[1] Richard Graves, of Pembroke Coll., matr. Nov. 7, 1732; Fellow of All Souls; died 1805; author of several popular works. To be distinguished from the divine of the same name, 1763-1829.

H

sung bacchanalian catches the whole evening: our 'pious orgies' generally began with,

> 'Let's be jovial, fill our glasses,
> Madness 'tis for us to think,
> How the world is rul'd by asses,
> And the wisest sway'd by chink.'

I own, with shame, that, being then not seventeen, I was so far captivated with the social disposition of these young people (many of whom were ingenious lads and good scholars) that I began to think *them* the only wise men; and to have a contempt for every degree of temperance and sobriety.

P. 16. Some gentlemen commoners, however, [1] who were my countrymen (amongst whom were the two late successive lords Ch—d—th[1]) and who considered the above-mentioned as very *low* company, (chiefly on account of the liquor they drank) good-naturedly invited me to their party: they treated me with port-wine and arrack-punch; and now and then, when they had drank so much, as hardly to distinguish wine from water, they would conclude with a bottle or two of claret. They kept late hours, drank their favourite toasts on their knees, and, in short, were what were then called 'bucks of the first head.' This was deemed good company and high life; but it neither suited my taste, my fortune, or my constitution.

P. 17. [1] There was, besides, a sort of flying squadron of plain, sensible, matter-of-fact men, confined to no club, but associating occasionally with each party. They anxiously enquired after the news of the day, and the politics of the times. They had come to the university in their way to the Temple, or to get a slight smattering of the sciences before they settled in the country. They were a good sort of young people, and perhaps the most rational of the college: but neither with these was I destined to associate.

[1] Probably *Chedworth*, sons of John Howe, created Baron of Chedworth in 1741. John (Thynne) Howe (afterwards second Lord Chedworth, *d.* 1762), and his brother Henry (Frederick) Howe (afterwards third Lord, *d.* 1781), matr. at Pembroke Coll., 25 Nov., 1731, aged 17 and 16.

In each of the above-mentioned parties, except the water-drinkers, I had once or twice met Mr. Shenstone, and another young man, a Mr. Whistler[1], of a gentleman's family, and born to a genteel estate in Oxfordshire. Neither Mr. Shenstone or Mr. Whistler, however, seemed quite in their element, amidst those sons of Comus, the politer votaries of Bacchus, or with the matter-of-fact society; not from any opinion of superior understanding, but from a difference of taste and pursuits.

Our more familiar acquaintance commenced by an invitation from Mr. Shenstone to breakfast at his chambers, which we accepted; and which, according to the sociable disposition of most young people, was protracted to a late hour; during which, Mr. Shenstone, I remember, in order to detain us, produced Cotton's Virgil Travestie, which he had lately met with; and which, though full of indelicacies and low humour, is certainly a most laughable performance. I displayed my slender stock of critical knowledge by applauding, as a work of *equal humour*, Echard's 'Causes of the Contempt of the Clergy.' Mr. Whistler, who was a year or two older than either of us, I believe, and had finished his school-education at Eton, preferred Pope's 'Rape of the Lock,' as a higher species of humour, than any thing we had produced.

In short, this morning's lounge, which seemed mutually agreeable, was succeeded by frequent repetitions of them; and, at length, by our meeting likewise, almost every evening, at each other's chambers the whole summer; where we read plays and poetry, Spectators or Tatlers, and other works of easy digestion, and sipped Florence wine. This commencement of our acquaintance grew into an intimacy, which, with very slight interruptions, terminated but with the lives of Mr. Whistler and Mr. Shenstone.

As people, however, who seclude themselves from the rest of their neighbours, generally become the subject of

---

[1] Of Whitchurch, Oxfordshire. Anthony Whistler, Pembroke Coll.; matr. Oct. 21, 1732.

invidious speculation, and excite jealous suspicions in the minds of their equals, we began to be considered as a dangerous triumvirate, and as meditating some design of unfriendly import: to which a very trifling incident added 'confirmation strong as proof of holy writ.'

As I was a scholar of the house, and had some dry studies prescribed to me, which I thought it necessary to pursue with regularity and strict attention the whole morning, I did not like to be interrupted. Mr. Shenstone one day came into my room, and, as I could not listen to any conversation, he took up a pen, and said, ' he would write my character; this (at least what he called such) he wrote impromptu, and left it on my table; which an impertinent fellow, coming in soon after, saw and read, without knowing who was the subject of it; and immediately retired unnoticed. And now it was discovered, that we three, Mr. Shenstone, Mr. Whistler, and myself, shut up ourselves to write the characters of the whole society; and we were thenceforth, for some time, considered in no very favourable light by the rest of the college.

' Dr. Johnson says, that Mr. Shenstone *employed* himself at Oxford in the study of English poetry. But, at Oxford, Mr. Shenstone only *amused* himself occasionally with English poetry; and *employed* himself in the study of the mathematics, logic, natural and moral philosophy, and the other sciences usually taught in the university: he made a considerable progress in them, and seemed fond of them: of which the frequent allusions to those sciences in his writings are a sufficient proof.

Mr. Shenstone made but few acquaintance ' in the university. A degree of bashfulness, from his confined education, joined with a consciousness of his own real abilities, made him not inclined to make advances to strangers: indeed, though those that knew him highly loved and esteemed him, yet the singularity of his appearance rather prejudiced some people against him. Dr. Johnson represents it as his opinion, ' that fashion ought to be *no rule* of dress,' and ' that every man was to suit his appearance to his natural form.' These were not precisely his sentiments; though he thought, justly enough, that every one should, in some degree, consult his particular shape and complexion in adjusting his dress; and that no fashion ought to | sanctify what was ungraceful, absurd, or really deformed.

According to the unnatural taste which then prevailed, every school-boy, as soon as he was entered at the university, cut off his hair, whatever it was; and, without any regard to his complexion, put on a wig, black, white, brown, or grizzle, as 'lawless fancy' suggested. This fashion, no consideration could at that time have induced Mr. Shenstone to comply with. He wore his hair, however, almost in the graceful manner which has since generally prevailed: but, as his person was rather large for so | young a man, and his hair coarse, it often exposed him to the ill-natured remarks of people who had not half his sense; insomuch, that his friends were often in pain for the unfavourable opinion which strangers sometimes expressed of him, and were under a necessity of vindicating him, as Horace is *supposed* to have done Virgil, by allowing his foibles, and balancing them with his more valuable good qualities.

> '—Rideri possit—
> —at est bonus—at ingenium ingens
> Inculto latet hoc sub corpore—.' [1]

> 'Yet, underneath this rough disguise,
> A genius and uncommon merit lies.'

| Mr. Shenstone had one ingenious and much-valued friend in Oxford, Mr. Jago[2], his school-fellow, whom he could only visit in private, as he wore a servitor's gown; it being then deemed a great disparagement for a commoner to appear in public with one in that situation; which by the way, would make one wish, with Dr. Johnson, that there were no young

---

[1] Horace, *Sat.* I. 3. 30–34.
[2] Richard Jago of University Coll., matr. Oct. 30, 1732. Author of *Edge Hill*, a poem in four books.

people admitted, in that servile state, in a place of liberal education.

P. 28.   ¹ Servitors, or sizers as they are called in Cambridge, were probably appointed when colleges were first established, and when there was a scarcity of fit persons to supply the learned professions, that a greater number might have the advantage of literary instruction, by the poorer waiting on the more affluent students.

But what good end can it answer in these times, when every genteel profession is over-stocked, to rob our agriculture or our manufactures of so many useful hands, by encouraging every substantial farmer or mechanical tradesman to breed his son to the church?

If now and then a very uncommon genius, in those walks of
P. 29.   life, discovers itself, there seldom are wanting gentlemen ¹ in the neighbourhood who are proud of calling forth, and, if *necessary*, of supporting by a subscription, such extraordinary talents.

Mr. Jago, however, who was the son of a clergyman in Warwickshire, with a large family, and who could not otherwise have given his son a liberal education, may be thought an instance in favour of this institution.

But I make no doubt, that a respectable clergyman, as Mr. Jago's father was, might, by a very slight application to the head or fellows of almost any college, have procured some scholarship or exhibition for a youth of genius and properly qualified; which, with a very small additional expence, might
P. 30.   have supported him in the university, ¹ without placing him in so humiliating a situation; which, in some future period of his life (when perhaps his parts might have raised him to some eminence in the world) might put it in the power of any purse-proud fellow-collegian to boast, that he had waited on him in the college; though, perhaps, all the obligation he had lain under to such a patron, was the receiving sixpence a week, not as an act of generosity, but as a tribute imposed on him by the standing rules of the society.

[1] Though Mr. Shenstone obtained no academical honours, nor took any degree in the university, he did not, like many young coxcombs of more parts perhaps than application, or who, from too large an allowance from wealthy parents, have bid defiance to the established discipline, speak contemptuously of the fruit, to which he was too indolent to climb up. On the contrary, he was fond of an academical life, and greatly approved of its institution; and, as his fortune was a very sufficient foundation for a genteel profession, he intended [1] to have taken his degrees, and to have proceeded in the study of physic. But being now of age, and coming into possession of his estate at the Leasowes[1], and also to a moiety of the estate at Harborough, which fell to him by the unexpected death of his maternal uncle—as his house at the Leasowes was inhabited by the tenant, instead of boarding there, or in the neighbourhood, as he might have done, he rather prematurely began to keep house at Harborough, which he found furnished to his hands. . . .

[1] In this retirement, in which Mr. Shenstone invited me to accompany him, being his own master, and feeling [1] himself much at his ease, he prolonged his stay in the country beyond what the business of the college regularly admitted. And having once neglected to return to the university at the *proper* season, he deferred it from time to time, till at length he felt a reluctance to returning at all; so that, although he kept his name in the college books, and changed his commoner's gown for that of a civilian[2], yet he had now, I believe, no thoughts of proceeding to any degree; and seldom resided in college any more.

---

[1] In the parish of Hales-Owen, Worcestershire.
[2] I. e. a Student of Civil Law.

XI.

GEORGE WHITEFIELD.

[*Born* at Gloucester Dec. 16, 1714; educated at St. Mary de Crypt school in that city; *died* in America Sept. 30, 1770.]

A Short Account of God's Dealings with the Rev. George Whitefield. Lond. 1740.

P. 23. BEING now near eighteen years old, it was judged proper for me to go to the University. God had [sweetly [1]] prepared my way. The friends before applied to, recommended me to the Master [2] of *Pembroke College*. Another friend took up ten pounds upon bond, (which I have since repaid,) to defray
P. 24. the first expence of entring [3]; and the [1] Master, contrary to all expectations, admitted me servitor immediately.

Soon after my admission I went and resided, and found my having been used to a publick-house [4] was now of service to me. For many of the servitors being sick at my first coming up, by my diligent and ready attendance I ingratiated myself into the gentlemen's favour so far, that many, who had it in their power, chose me to be their servitor.

This much lessened my expence; and, indeed, God was so

---

[1] All notes enclosed in square brackets were omitted in the edition published by Whitefield in 1756.

[2] Matthew Panting, Master, 1714–1728.

[3] Whitefield matr. as 'pleb. fil.' on Nov. 7, 1732; B.A. July 6, 1736. A servitor ranked even below a batteller: for the degradation attaching to the position, see Chr. Wordsworth's *Social Life at the English Universities* (1874), p. 101, &c.; and for notes of expenses at Oxford, *ibid.* p. 413.

[4] The Bell Inn at Gloucester, of which his father was landlord, and in which he himself had been drawer.

gracious, that, with the profits of my place, and some little presents made me by my kind tutor, for almost the first three years I did not put all my relations together to above 24*l*. expence. [And it has often grieved my soul to see so many young students spending their substance in extravagant living, and thereby entirely unfitting themselves for the prosecution of their proper studies.]

I had not been long at the University before I found the benefit of the foundation I had laid in the country for a holy life. I was quickly sollicited to joyn in their excess of riot with several who lay in the same room. God, in answer to prayers before put up, gave me grace to withstand them; and once, in particular, it being cold, my limbs were so benummed by sitting alone in my study, because I would not go out amongst them, that I could scarce sleep all night. But I soon found the benefit of not yielding; for when they perceived they could not prevail, they let me alone as a singular, odd fellow. . . .

P. 25.

I now began to pray and sing psalms thrice every day, besides morning and evening, and to fast every *Friday*, and to receive the Sacrament at a parish church near our college, and at the Castle[1], where the despised Methodists used to receive once a month.

P. 26.

The young men so called, were then much talked of at *Oxford*. I had heard of, and loved them before I came to the University; and so strenuously defended them when I heard them reviled by the students, that they began to think that I also in time should be one of them.

For above a twelvemonth my soul longed to be acquainted with some of them, and I was strongly pressed to follow their good example, when I saw them go through a ridiculing crowd to receive the Holy Eucharist at *St. Mary's*. At length, God was pleased to open a door. It happened that a poor woman in one of the workhouses had attempted to cut her throat, but

---

[1] St. Aldate's, and St. George's in the Castle.

P. 27.

P. 29.

P. 30.

P. 33.

P. 34.

was happily prevented. Upon hearing of this, and knowing that both the Mr. *Wesleys* [1] were ready to every good work, I sent a poor aged apple-woman of our college to inform Mr. *Charles Wesley* of it, charging her not to discover who sent her. She went; but, [1] contrary to my orders, told my name. He having heard of my coming to the Castle and a parish-church Sacrament, and having met me frequently walking by myself, followed the woman when she was gone away, and sent an invitation to me by her, to come to breakfast with him the next morning....

From time to time Mr. *Wesley* permitted me to come unto him, and instructed me as I was able to bear it. By degrees, he introduced me to the rest of his Christian brethren....

I now began, like them, to live by rule, and to pick up the very fragments of my time, that not a moment of it might be lost. ... Like them, having no weekly Sacrament, (although the rubrick required it,) at our own college, I received every *Sunday* at *Christ Church*. I joined with them in [keeping the stations by] fasting *Wednesdays* and *Fridays*....

The course of my studies I soon intirely changed. Whereas, before I was busied in studying the dry sciences, and books that went no farther than the surface, I now resolved to read only such as entered into the heart of religion....

The first thing I was called to give up for God, was what the world calls my fair reputation. I had no sooner received the Sacrament publickly on a week-day at *St. Mary's*, but I was set up as a mark for all the polite students that knew me to shoot at. [By this they knew that I was commenced Methodist; for though there is a Sacrament at the beginning of every term, at which all, especially the seniors, are, by statute, obliged to be present, yet so dreadfully has that once faithful city played the harlot, that very [1] few masters, no undergraduates (but the Methodists) attended upon it.

---

[1] John Wesley, of Christ Church; matr. 18 July, 1720, aged 16; B.A. 1724; Fellow of Lincoln Coll., 1725; M.A. 172$\frac{8}{9}$. Charles Wesley, of Christ Church; matr. 13 June, 1726, aged 18; B.A. 1730; M.A. March 12, 173$\frac{2}{3}$.

Mr. *Charles Wesley* (whom I must always mention with the greatest *deference* and respect,) walked with me, (in order to confirm me,) from the church even to the college. I confess, to my shame, I would gladly have excused him; and the next day, going to his room, one of our Fellows passing by, I was ashamed to be seen to knock at his door. . . .

Soon after this, I incurred the displeasure of the Master of the college, who frequently chid, and once threatened to expel me, if ever I visited the poor again. Being surprized by this treatment, and overawed by his authority, I spake unadvisedly with my lips, and said, if it displeased him, I would not. My conscience soon pricked me for this ¹ sinful compliance. I P. 35. immediately repented, and visited the poor the first opportunity. . . . My tutor, being a moderate man, did not oppose me [much, but thought, I believe, that I went a little too far. He lent me books, gave me money, visited me, and furnished me with a physician when sick. In short he behaved in all respects like a father. . . .]

. . . I daily underwent some contempt at college. Some have thrown dirt at me; others, by degrees, took away their pay from me; and two friends that were dear unto me, grew shy of, and forsook me. . . .

. . . [At this time *Satan* used to terrify me much, and P. 37. threatened to punish me if I discovered his wiles. It being my duty, as servitor, in my turn to knock at ¹ the gentlemen's P. 38. rooms by ten at night, to see who were in their rooms, I thought the devil would appear to me every stair I went up. . . .]

¹ . . . By degrees, I began to leave off eating fruits and such P. 39. like, and gave the money I usually spent in that way to the poor. Afterward, I always chose the worst sort of food, tho' my place furnished me with variety. I fasted twice a week. My apparel was mean. I thought it unbecoming a penitent to have his hair powdered. I wore woollen gloves, a patched gown, and dirty shoes. . . .

The devil also sadly imposed upon me in the matter of my P. 41.

college exercises. Whenever I endeavoured to compose my theme, I had no power to write a word, nor so much as tell my Christian friends of my inability to do it. *Saturday* being come, (which is the day the students give up their compositions,) it was suggested to me that I must go down into the hall, and confess I could not make a theme, and so publickly suffer, as if it were for my Master's sake. When the bell rung to call us, I went to open the door to go downstairs, but feeling something give me a violent inward check, I entered my study, and continued instant in prayer, waiting the event. For this my tutor fined me half a crown. The next week *Satan* served me in like manner again; but having now got more strength, and perceiving no inward check, I went into the hall. My name being called, I stood up, and told my tutor I could not make a theme. I think he fined me a second time; but, imagining that I would not willingly neglect my exercise, he afterwards called me into the common room, and kindly enquired whether any misfortune had befallen me, or what was the reason I could not make a theme? I burst into tears, and assured him that it was not out of contempt of authority, but that I could not act otherwise. Then, at length, he said he believed I could not; and, when he left me, told a friend, (as he very well might,) that he took me to be really mad. . . .

. . . It was now suggested to me that *Jesus Christ* was amongst the wild beasts when He was tempted, and that I ought to follow His example; and being willing, as I thought, to imitate *Jesus Christ*, after supper I went into *Christ Church* walk, near our college, and continued in silent prayer under one of the trees [for near two hours, sometimes lying flat on my face, sometimes] kneeling upon my knees, [all the while filled with fear and concern lest some of my brethren should be overwhelmed with pride. The night being stormy, it gave me awful thoughts of the day of judgment. I continued I think,] till the great bell rung for retirement to the college, not without finding some reluctance in the natural man against staying so long in the cold.

[The next night I repeated the same exercise at the same place. But the hour of extremity being now come, God was pleased to make an open shew of those diabolical devices by which I had been deceived.] . . .

Soon after this, [the holy season of] *Lent* came on, which P. 47. our friends kept very strictly, eating no flesh during the six weeks, except on *Saturdays* and *Sundays*. I abstained frequently on *Saturdays* also, and ate nothing on the other days, (except on *Sunday*) but sage-tea without sugar, and coarse bread. I constantly walked out in the cold mornings till part of one of my hands was quite black. This, with my continued abstinence and inward conflicts, at length so emaciated my body, that, at Passion-week, finding I could scarce creep upstairs, I was obliged to inform my kind tutor of my condition, who immediately sent for a physician to me.

¹ This caused no small triumph amongst the collegians, who P. 48. began to cry out, 'What is his fasting come to now?' . . .

As fast as I got strength after my sickness, my tutor, P. 50. physician, and some others were still urging me to go into the country, hoping thereby to divert me, as they thought, from a too intense application to religion. [I had, for some time, been aware of their design, and wrote letters beseeching my mother, if she valued my soul, not to lay her commands on me to come down. She was pleased to leave me to my choice; but,] finding at last it was necessary for my health, and many other providential circumstances pointing out my way, after earnest prayer for support, by the advice of my friends, I left my sweet retirement at *Oxford*, and went to *Gloucester*, the place of my nativity. . . .

[. . . When I came from *Oxford*, on account of my sick- P. 53. ness ¹ and other extraordinary and unavoidable expenses, P. 54. I owed, I think, about twelve or thirteen pounds. . . . This, I bless God, did not dishearten me; but I continued pleading the promises in the name of *Christ*; and, soon after my coming to *Bristol*, I received an answer. For, a brother of mine coming from sea, God inclined him to give me four guineas and some other necessaries. . . .]

P. 59.
P. 60.
[. . . Fresh supplies came from unexpected hands to defray my | expences at the University; and, at the end of nine months, I returned thither, to the mutual joy and comfort of my friends, till I was called to enter into Holy Orders. . . .

From the time I first entered at the University, especially from the time I knew what was true and undefiled Christianity, I entertained high thoughts of the importance of the ministerial office, and was not sollicitous what place should be prepared for me, but how I should be prepared for a place.] . . . And that first question of our excellent ordination office, 'Do you trust that you are *inwardly moved* by the Holy Ghost to take upon you this office and administration?' used even to make me tremble whenever I thought of entering

P. 61.
into the ministry. [The shyness that *Moses* and some other prophets expressed, when God sent them out in a publick capacity, I thought was sufficient to teach me not to run till I was called. . . .]

To my prayers I added my endeavours, and wrote letters to my friends at *Oxford*, beseeching them to pray to God to disappoint the designs of my country friends, who were for my taking orders as soon as possible. Their answer was,

P. 62.
'Pray we the | Lord of the harvest to send thee and many more labourers into His harvest.' . . . All this did not satisfy me. I still continued instant in prayer against going into holy orders, and was not thoroughly convinced it was the Divine will, till God, by His providence, brought me acquainted

P. 63.
with the present Bishop of *Gloucester*[1]. . . . ' The Bishop told me he had heard of my character, liked my behaviour at church, and, enquiring my age, 'Notwithstanding,' says he, 'I have declared I would not ordain any one under three and twenty, yet I shall think it my duty to ordain you when-

---

[1] Martin Benson, D.D., Bp. of Gloucester, 1734–5; died 1752.

ever ¹ you come for holy orders.' [He then made me a present of five guineas to buy me a book....]

... I then began to think myself, 'That if I held out any longer, I should fight against God.' At length, I came to a resolution, by God's leave, to offer myself for holy orders the next Ember days [1].

The only thing now in dispute was into what part of my Lord's vineyard I should be sent to labour first. God had given me much success in *Gloucester*; and my friends being desirous of having me near them, I ¹ had thoughts of settling amongst them. But, when I came to *Oxford*, my friends urged several reasons for my continuing at the University. 'The Mr. *Wesleys* had not long been gone abroad, and now no one was left to take care of the prison affairs, etc.' They further urged, 'That God had blessed my endeavours *there*, as well as at *Gloucester*; that the University was the fountain-head; that every gownsman's name was legion; and that if I should be made instrumental in converting one of *them*, it would be as much as converting a whole parish.' At the same time, (unknown to me), some of them sent to that great and good man, the late Sir *John Phillips*[2], who was a great encourager of the *Oxford* Methodists; and, tho' he had never seen, but only heard of me, yet he sent word he would allow me thirty pounds a year, if I would continue at the University. Upon this, finding the care of the prisoners would be no more than, under God, I could undertake with pleasure, and knowing the University was the best place to prosecute my studies, I resolved, God willing, to wait at *Oxford* a blessing on the first fruits of my ministerial labours. . . .

[¹ Oh, the unspeakable benefit of reading to the poor, and exercising our talents while students at the University! Such previous acts are very proper to prepare us for the work of our Lord, and make us not unapt to teach in a

---

[1] He was ordained June, 1736.
[2] Sir John Philipps, Bart., of Picton Castle, Pembrokeshire; died Jan. 5, 1737.

more publick manner. It is remarkable that our Lord sent out His Apostles on short missions, before they were so solemnly authorized at the day of *Pentecost.* Would the Heads and Tutors of our Universities follow His example, and, instead of discouraging their pupils from doing any thing of this nature, send them to visit the sick and the prisoners, and to pray with, and read practical books of religion to the poor, they would find such exercises of more service to *them*, and to the *Church* of God, than *all* their private and publick *lectures* put together.

 Thus God dealt with my soul. At the same time, by His gracious providence, He supplied me with all things needful for my body also. For He inclined the Bishop's heart to give me five guineas more; and, by this time, a quarter's allowance was due to me from Sir *John Phillips*; both which sums put together fully served to defray the ' expences of my ordination, and taking my batchelor's degree, which was conferred on me at *Oxford* the week after my being ordained, when I was about one and twenty years of age. . . .]

XII.
EDWARD GIBBON.

[*Born* at Putney April 27, 1737; educated at Kingston and Westminster School; *died* Jan. 16, 1794.]

Miscellaneous Works of Edward Gibbon ... Vol. I. Lond., 1796, 4to.

I WAS matriculated in the university as a gentleman com- P. 29. moner of Magdalen College, before I had accomplished the fifteenth year of my age (April 3, 1752) .... I arrived at P. 31. Oxford with a stock of erudition, that might have puzzled a doctor, and a degree of ignorance, of which a school-boy would have been ashamed....

A traveller, who visits Oxford or Cambridge, is surprised P. 32. and edified by the apparent order and tranquillity that prevail in the seats of the English muses. In the most celebrated universities of Holland, Germany, and Italy, the students, who swarm from different countries, are loosely dispersed in private lodgings at the houses of the burghers: they dress according to their fancy and fortune; and in the intemperate quarrels of youth and wine, their *swords*, though less frequently than of old, are sometimes stained with each other's blood. The use of arms is banished from our English universities; the uniform habit of the academics, the square cap, and black gown, is adapted to the civil and even clerical profession; and from the doctor in divinity to the undergraduate, the degrees of learning and age are externally distinguished. Instead of being scattered in a town, the students of Oxford and Cambridge are united in colleges; their maintenance is provided at their own expence, or that of the founders; and the stated hours of the hall and chapel represent the discipline of a regular, and, as it were, a religious community. The eyes of the traveller are attracted by the size or beauty of the public edifices; and the principal colleges appear to be so many palaces, which a liberal nation has erected and endowed for the habitation of science. My own introduction to the university of Oxford forms a new æra in my life; and at the distance of forty years I still remember my first emotions of surprise and satisfaction. In my fifteenth year I felt myself suddenly raised from a boy to a man: the persons, whom I respected as my superiors in age and academical rank, entertained me with every mark of attention and civility; and my vanity was flattered by the velvet cap and silk gown, which distinguish a gentleman commoner from a plebeian student. A decent allowance, more money than a school-boy had ever seen, was at my own disposal; and I might command, among the tradesmen of Oxford, an indefinite and dangerous latitude of credit. A key was delivered into my hands, which gave me the free use of a numerous and learned library; my apartment consisted of three elegant and well-furnished rooms in the new building[1], a stately pile, of Magdalen College; and the adjacent walks, had they been frequented by Plato's disciples, might have been compared to the Attic shade on the banks of the Ilissus. Such was the fair prospect of my entrance (April 3, 1752) into the university of Oxford.

A venerable prelate, whose taste and erudition must reflect honour on the society in which they were formed, has drawn a very interesting picture of his academical life. 'I was educated (says Bishop Lowth[2]) in the UNIVERSITY OF OXFORD. I enjoyed all the advantages, both public and private, which that famous seat of learning so largely affords. I spent many years in that illustrious society, in a well-regulated course of useful discipline and studies, and in the

[1] Still called the 'New Buildings,' though the foundation-stone was laid in 1733.
[2] Robert Lowth, Bp. of St. David's, 1766; of Oxford, 1766-77; of London, 1777-87; was Fellow of New College. (Matric. 26 Mar. 1729).

agreeable and improving commerce of gentlemen and of scholars; in a society where emulation without envy, ambition without jealousy, contention without animosity, incited industry, and awakened genius; where a liberal pursuit of knowledge, and a genuine freedom of thought, was raised, encouraged, and pushed forward by example, by commendation, and by authority. I breathed the same atmosphere that the HOOKERS, the CHILLINGWORTHS, and the LOCKES had breathed before; whose benevolence and humanity were as extensive as their vast genius and comprehensive knowledge; who always treated their adversaries with civility and respect; who made candour, moderation, and liberal judgment as much the rule and law as the subject of their discourse. And do you reproach me with my education in this place, and with my relation to this most respectable body, which I shall always esteem my greatest advantage and my highest honour?' I transcribe with pleasure this eloquent passage, without examining what benefits or what rewards were derived by Hooker, or Chillingworth, or Locke, from their academical institution; without inquiring, whether in this P. 34. angry controversy the spirit of Lowth himself is purified from the intolerant zeal, which Warburton had ascribed to the genius of the place. It may indeed be observed, that the atmosphere of Oxford did not agree with Mr. Locke's constitution; and that the philosopher justly despised the academical bigots, who expelled his person and condemned his principles [1]. The expression of gratitude is a virtue and a pleasure: a liberal mind will delight to cherish and celebrate the memory of its parents; and the teachers of science are the parents of the mind. I applaud the filial piety, which it is impossible for me to imitate; since I must not confess an imaginary debt, to assume the merit of a just or generous retribution.

To the university of Oxford *I* acknowledge no obligation; and she will as cheerfully renounce me for a son, as I am

[1] John Locke was expelled from Christ Church under the King's warrant dated 12 Nov. 1864.

willing to disclaim her for a mother. I spent fourteen months at Magdalen College; they proved the fourteen months the most idle and unprofitable of my whole life: the reader will pronounce between the school and the scholar; but I cannot affect to believe that Nature had disqualified me for all literary pursuits. The specious and ready excuse of my tender age, imperfect preparation, and hasty departure, may doubtless be alleged; nor do I wish to defraud such excuses of their proper weight. Yet in my sixteenth year I was not devoid of capacity or application; even my childish reading had displayed an early though blind propensity for books; and the shallow flood might have been taught to flow in a deep channel and a clear stream. In the discipline of a well-constituted academy, under the guidance of skilful and vigilant professors, I should gradually have risen from translations to originals, from the Latin to the Greek classics, from dead languages to living science: my hours would have been occupied by useful and agreeable studies, the wanderings of fancy would have been restrained, and I should have escaped the temptations of idleness, which finally precipitated my departure from Oxford.

P. 35. Perhaps in a separate annotation I may coolly examine the fabulous and real antiquities of our sister universities, a question which has kindled such fierce and foolish disputes among their fanatic sons. In the meanwhile it will be acknowledged that these venerable bodies are sufficiently old to partake of all the prejudices and infirmities of age.

The schools of Oxford and Cambridge were founded in a dark age of false and barbarous science; and they are still tainted with the vices of their origin. Their primitive discipline was adapted to the education of priests and monks; and the government still remains in the hands of the clergy, an order of men whose manners are remote from the present world, and whose eyes are dazzled by the light of philosophy. The legal incorporation of these societies by the charters of popes and kings, had given them a monopoly of the public instruction; and the spirit of monopolists is narrow, lazy, and oppressive; their work is more costly and less productive than that of independent artists; and the new improvements so eagerly grasped by the competition of freedom, are admitted with slow and sullen reluctance in those proud corporations, above the fear of a rival, and below the confession of an error. We may scarcely hope that any reformation will be a voluntary act; and so deeply are they rooted in law and prejudice, that even the omnipotence of parliament would shrink from an inquiry into the state and abuses of the two universities.

The use of academical degrees, as old as the thirteenth century [1], is visibly borrowed from the mechanic corporations; in which an apprentice, after serving his time, obtains a testimonial of his skill, and a licence to practice his trade and mystery. It is not my design to depreciate those honours, which could never gratify or disappoint my ambition; and I should applaud the institution, if the degrees of bachelor or licentiate were bestowed as the reward of manly and successful study: if the name and rank of doctor or master were strictly reserved for the professors of science, who have approved their title to the public esteem.

P. 36.

In all the universities of Europe, excepting our own, the languages and sciences are distributed among a numerous list of effective professors: the students, according to their taste, their calling, and their diligence, apply themselves to the proper masters; and in the annual repetition of public and private lectures, these masters are assiduously employed. Our curiosity may inquire what number of professors has been instituted at Oxford? (for I shall now confine myself to my own university;) by whom are they appointed, and what may be the probable chances of merit or incapacity? how many are stationed to the three faculties, and how many are left for the liberal arts? what is the form, and what the

---

[1] Gibbon might have said the twelfth.

substance, of their lessons? But all these questions are silenced by one short and singular answer, 'That in the university of Oxford, the greater part of the public professors have for these many years given up altogether even the pretence of teaching.' Incredible as the fact may appear, I must rest my belief on the positive and impartial evidence of a master of moral and political wisdom, who had himself resided at Oxford. Dr. Adam Smith assigns as the cause of their indolence, that, instead of being paid by voluntary contributions, which would urge them to increase the number, and to deserve the gratitude of their pupils, the Oxford professors are secure in the enjoyment of a fixed stipend, without the necessity of labour, or the apprehension of controul.

It has indeed been observed, nor is the observation absurd, that excepting in experimental sciences, which demand a costly apparatus and a dexterous hand, the many valuable treatises, that have been published on every subject of learning, may now supersede the ancient mode of oral instruction. Were this principle true in its utmost latitude, I should only infer that the offices and salaries, which are become useless, ought without delay to be abolished. But there still remains a material ¹ difference between a book and a professor; the hour of the lecture enforces attendance; attention is fixed by the presence, the voice, and the occasional questions of the teacher; the most idle will carry something away; and the more diligent will compare the instructions, which they have heard in the school, with the volumes, which they peruse in their chamber. The advice of a skilful professor will adapt a course of reading to every mind and every situation; his authority will discover, admonish, and at last chastise the negligence of his disciples; and his vigilant inquiries will ascertain the steps of their literary progress. Whatever science he professes, he may illustrate in a series of discourses, composed in the leisure of his closet, pronounced on public occasions, and finally delivered to the press. I observe with pleasure, that in the university of Oxford, Dr. Lowth, with equal eloquence and erudition, has executed this task in his incomparable *Prælections* on the Poetry of the Hebrews[1].

The college of St. Mary Magdalen was founded in the fifteenth century by Wainfleet, bishop of Winchester; and now consists of a president, forty fellows, and a number of inferior students. It is esteemed one of the largest and most wealthy of our academical corporations, which may be compared to the Benedictine abbeys of Catholic countries; and I have loosely heard that the estates belonging to Magdalen College, which are leased by those indulgent landlords at small quit-rents and occasional fines, might be raised, in the hands of private avarice, to an annual revenue of nearly thirty thousand pounds. Our colleges are supposed to be schools of science, as well as of education; nor is it unreasonable to expect that a body of literary men, devoted to a life of celibacy, exempt from the care of their own subsistence, and amply provided with books, should devote their leisure to the prosecution of study, and that some effects of their studies should be manifested to the world. The shelves of their library groan under the weight of the Benedictine folios, of the editions of the fathers, and the collections of the middle ages, which have issued from the single abbey of St. Germain de Préz at Paris. A composition of genius must be the offspring of one mind; but such works of industry, as may be divided among many hands, and must be continued during many years, are the peculiar province of a laborious community. If I inquire into the manufactures of the monks of Magdalen[2], if I extend the inquiry to the other colleges of Oxford and Cambridge, a silent blush, or a scornful frown, will be the only reply. The fellows or monks of my time were decent easy men, who supinely enjoyed the gifts of the founder; their days were filled by a series of uniform employments; the chapel and the hall, the coffee house and the

P. 38.

---

[1] First published in 1753.
[2] One is reminded of Clough's 'Mild monastic faces in quiet collegiate cloisters.'

common room, till they retired, weary and well satisfied, to a long slumber. From the toil of reading, or thinking, or writing, they had absolved their conscience; and the first shoots of learning and ingenuity withered on the ground, without yielding any fruits to the owners or the public. As a gentleman commoner, I was admitted to the society of the fellows, and fondly expected that some questions of literature would be the amusing and instructive topics of their discourse. Their conversation stagnated in a round of college business, Tory politics, personal anecdotes, and private scandal: their dull and deep potations excused the brisk intemperance of youth; and their constitutional toasts were not expressive of the most lively loyalty for the house of Hanover. A general election was now approaching[1]: the great Oxfordshire contest already blazed with all the malevolence of party-zeal. Magdalen College was devoutly attached to the old interest! and the names of Wenman and Dashwood were more frequently pronounced, than those of Cicero and Chrysostom. The example of the senior fellows could not inspire the undergraduates with a liberal spirit or studious emulation; and I cannot describe, as I never knew, the discipline of college. Some duties may possibly have been imposed on the poor scholars, whose ambition aspired to the peaceful honours of a fellowship (*ascribi* [1] *quietis ordinibus . . . Deorum*[2]); but no independent members were admitted below the rank of a gentleman commoner, and our velvet cap was the cap of

---

[1] This remarkable contest, still known as the Great Oxfordshire Election, took place in April, 1754; and probably no county contest ever excited more interest. Sir James Dashwood, of Northbrook, Kirtlington, Baronet; and Viscount Wenman, a Peer of Ireland, were the candidates in the 'Old Interest (Jacobitism);' their rivals, in the 'New Interest,' being Sir Edward Turner, of Ambrosden, Baronet; and Viscount Parker, son of the Earl of Macclesfield. After six days polling the numbers were found to be for Wenman 2,033; Dashwood 2,014; Parker 1,929; Turner 1,890. The High Sheriff, however, hesitated to return Wenman and Dashwood, and finally made a double return of all four candidates; this was instantly appealed against and a scrutiny was ordered, which after a lapse of twelve months resulted in the election of Lord Parker and Sir Edward Turner by a large majority.

[2] Hor. *Odes*, iii. 3. 35.

liberty. A tradition prevailed that some of our predecessors had spoken Latin declamations in the hall; but of this ancient custom no vestige remained: the obvious methods of public exercises and examinations were totally unknown; and I have never heard that either the president or the society interfered in the private œconomy of the tutors and their pupils.

The silence of the Oxford professors, which deprives the youth of public instruction, is imperfectly supplied by the tutors, as they are styled, of the several colleges. Instead of confining themselves to a single science, which had satisfied the ambition of Burman or Bernouilli, they teach, or promise to teach, either history or mathematics, or ancient literature, or moral philosophy; and as it is possible that they may be defective in all, it is highly probable that of some they will be ignorant. They are paid, indeed, by private contributions; but their appointment depends on the head of the house: their diligence is voluntary, and will consequently be languid, while the pupils themselves, or their parents, are not indulged in the liberty of choice or change. The first tutor into whose hands I was resigned appears to have been one of the best of the tribe: Dr. Waldegrave [1] was a learned and pious man, of a mild disposition, strict morals, and abstemious life, who seldom mingled in the politics or the jollity of the college. But his knowledge of the world was confined to the university; his learning was of the last, rather than of the present age; his temper was indolent; his faculties, which were not of the first rate, had been relaxed by the climate, and he was satisfied, like his fellows, with the slight and superficial discharge of an important trust. As soon as my tutor had sounded the insufficiency of his disciple in school-learning, he proposed that we should read every morning from ten to eleven the comedies of Terence. ¹ The sum of my improvement in the university of Oxford is confined to three or four Latin plays; and even the study of an

P. 40.

---

[1] Thomas Waldgrave, matric. at Lincoln, 11 July 1728.

elegant classic, which might have been illustrated by a comparison of ancient and modern theatres, was reduced to a dry and literal interpretation of the author's text. During the first weeks I constantly attended these lessons in my tutor's room; but as they appeared equally devoid of profit and pleasure, I was once tempted to try the experiment of a formal apology. The apology was accepted with a smile. I repeated the offence with less ceremony; the excuse was admitted with the same indulgence: the slightest motive of laziness or indisposition, the most trifling avocation at home or abroad, was allowed as a worthy impediment; nor did my tutor appear conscious of my absence or neglect. Had the hour of lecture been constantly filled, a single hour was a small portion of my academic leisure. No plan of study was recommended for my use; no exercises were prescribed for his inspection; and, at the most precious season of youth, whole days and weeks were suffered to elapse without labour or amusement, without advice or account. I should have listened to the voice of reason and of my tutor; his mild behaviour had gained my confidence. I preferred his society to that of the younger students; and in our evening walks to the top of Heddington-hill, we freely conversed on a variety of subjects. Since the days of Pocock and Hyde, Oriental learning has always been the pride of Oxford, and I once expressed an inclination to study Arabic. His prudence discouraged this childish fancy; but he neglected the fair occasion of directing the ardour of a curious mind. During my absence in the summer vacation, Dr. Waldegrave accepted a college living at Washington in Sussex, and on my return I no longer found him at Oxford. From that time I have lost sight of my first tutor; but at the end of thirty years (1781) he was still alive; and the practice of exercise and temperance had entitled him to a healthy old age.

P. 41.   ¹ The long recess between the Trinity and Michaelmas terms empties the colleges of Oxford, as well as the courts of Westminster. I spent, at my father's house at Buriton in

Hampshire, the two months of August and September. It is whimsical enough, that as soon as I left Magdalen College, my taste for books began to revive; but it was the same blind and boyish taste for the pursuit of exotic history. ... [In his Vacation Gibbon wrote an essay on the Age of Sesostris, but burnt it in 1772.]

¹ After the departure of Dr. Waldgrave, I was transferred, P. 42. with his other pupils, to his academical heir, whose literary character did not command the respect of the college. Dr. —— well remembered that he had a salary to receive, and only forgot that he had a duty to perform. Instead of guiding the studies, and watching over the behaviour of his disciple, I was never summoned to attend even the ceremony of a lecture; and, excepting one voluntary visit to his rooms, during the eight months of his titular office, the tutor and pupil lived in the same college as strangers to each other. The want of experience, of advice, and of occupation, soon betrayed me into some improprieties of conduct, ill-chosen company, late hours, and inconsiderate expence. My growing debts might be secret; but my frequent absence was visible and scandalous; and a tour to Bath, a visit into Buckinghamshire, and four excursions to London in the same winter, were costly and dangerous frolics. They were, indeed, without a meaning, as without an excuse. The irksomeness of a cloistered life repeatedly tempted me to wander; but my chief pleasure was that of travelling; and I was too young and bashful to enjoy, like a Manly Oxonian in Town, the pleasures of London. In all these excursions I eloped from Oxford; I returned to college; in a few days I eloped again, as if I had been an independent stranger in a ¹ hired lodging, without P. 43. once hearing the voice of admonition, without once feeling the hand of control. Yet my time was lost, my expences were multiplied, my behaviour abroad was unknown ; folly as well as vice should have awakened the attention of my superiors, and my tender years would have justified a more than ordinary degree of restraint and discipline.

It might at least be expected, that an ecclesiastical school should inculcate the orthodox principles of religion. But our venerable mother had contrived to unite the opposite extremes of bigotry and indifference: an heretic, or unbeliever, was a monster in her eyes; but she was always, or often, or sometimes, remiss in the spiritual education of her own children. According to the statutes of the university, every student, before he is matriculated, must subscribe his assent to the thirty-nine articles of the church of England, which are signed by more than read, and read by more than believe them. My insufficient age excused me, however, from the immediate performance of this legal ceremony; and the vice-chancellor directed me to return, as soon as I should have accomplished my fifteenth year; recommending me in the meanwhile to the instruction of my college. My college forgot to instruct: I forgot to return, and was myself forgotten by the first magistrate of the university. Without a single lecture, either public or private, either christian or protestant, without any academical subscription, without any episcopal confirmation, I was left by the dim light of my catechism to grope my way to the chapel and communion table, where I was admitted, without a question, how far, or by what means, I might be qualified to receive the sacrament. Such almost incredible neglect was productive of the worst mischiefs. From my childhood I had been fond of religious disputation; ... nor had the elastic spring been totally broken by the weight of the atmosphere of Oxford. The blind activity of idleness urged me to advance without armour into the dangerous [1] mazes of controversy; and at the age of sixteen, I bewildered myself in the errors of the church of Rome.

The progress of my conversion may tend to illustrate, at least, the history of my own mind. It was not long since Dr. Middleton's free inquiry had sounded an alarm in the theological world: much ink and much gall had been spilt in the defence of the primitive miracles; and the two dullest of their champions were crowned with academic honours by the university of Oxford¹. The name of Middleton was unpopular; and his proscription very naturally led me to peruse his writings, and those of his antagonists. His bold criticism, which approaches the precipice of infidelity, produced on my mind a singular effect; and had I persevered in the communion of Rome, I should now apply to my own fortune the prediction of the Sibyl,

> Via prima salutis,
> Quod minimè reris, Graiâ pandetur ab urbe².

The elegance of style and freedom of argument were repelled by a shield of prejudice. I still revered the character, or rather the names, of the saints and fathers whom Dr. Middleton exposes; nor could he destroy my implicit belief, that the gift of miraculous powers was continued in the church, during the first four or five centuries of christianity. But I was unable to resist the weight of historical evidence, that within the same period most of the leading doctrines of popery were already introduced in theory and practice.

... ¹ In these dispositions, and already more than half a P. 45. convert, I formed an unlucky intimacy with a young gentleman of our college, whose name I shall spare. With a character less resolute, Mr. —— had imbibed the same religious opinions; and some Popish books, I know not through what channel, were conveyed into his possession. I read, I applauded, I believed....

No sooner had I settled my new religion than I resolved to P. 46. profess myself a catholic. Youth is sincere and impetuous; and a momentary glow of enthusiasm had raised me above all temporal considerations.

By the keen protestants, who would gladly retaliate the

---

¹ The reference seems to be to (1) Thomas Church; matric. at Brasenose Coll. 3 July, 1722, aged 18; B.A. 1726; M.A. 1731; D.D. by diploma 23 Feb. 1749-50; then preb. of St. Paul's.

(2) William Dodwell, matric. Trinity College, March 23, 1725-6, aged 15; B.A. 1729; M.A. 1732; D.D. by diploma Feb. 23, 1749-50; then preb. of Sarum.

² Virg. *Aen.* 6. 97.

example of persecution, a clamour is raised of the increase of popery: and they are always loud to declaim against the toleration of priests and jesuits, who pervert so many of his majesty's subjects from their religion and allegiance. On the present occasion, the fall of one or more of her sons directed this clamour against the university; and it was confidently affirmed that popish missionaries were suffered, under various disguises, to introduce themselves into the colleges of Oxford. But justice obliges me to declare, that, as far as relates to myself, this assertion is false; and that I never conversed with a priest, or even with a papist, till my resolution from books was absolutely fixed. . . .

P. 47. ' My father was neither a bigot nor a philosopher; but his affection deplored the loss of an only son; and his good sense was astonished at my strange departure from the religion of my country. In the first sally of passion he divulged a secret which prudence might have suppressed, and the gates of Magdalen College were for ever shut against my return.

Many years afterwards, when the name of Gibbon was become as notorious as that of Middleton, it was industriously whispered at Oxford, that the historian had formerly 'turned papist'; my character stood exposed to the reproach of inconstancy; and this invidious topic would have been handled without mercy by my opponents, could they have separated my cause from that of the university. For my own part I am proud of an honest sacrifice of interest to conscience. I can never blush, if my tender mind was entangled in the sophistry that seduced the acute and manly understandings of CHILLINGWORTH and BAYLE, who afterwards emerged from superstition to scepticism. . . .

P. 51. ' The academical resentment, which I may possibly have provoked, will prudently spare this plain narrative of my studies, or rather of my idleness; and of the unfortunate event which shortened the term of my residence at Oxford. But it may be suggested, that my father was unlucky in the choice of a society, and the chance of a tutor. It will perhaps be asserted, that in the lapse of forty years many improvements have taken place in the college and in the university. I am not unwilling to believe, that some tutors might have been found more active than Dr. Waldgrave, and less contemptible than Dr. ——. About the same time, and in the same walk, a Bentham was still treading in the footsteps of a Burton, whose maxims he had adopted, and whose life he had published. The biographer indeed preferred the school-logic to the new philosophy, Burgursdicius to Locke; and the hero appears, in his own writings, a stiff and conceited pedant. Yet even these men, according to the measure of their capacity, might be diligent and useful; and it is recorded of Burton, that he taught his pupils what he knew; some Latin, some Greek, some ethics and metaphysics; referring them to proper masters for the languages and sciences of which he was ignorant. At a more recent period, many students have been attracted by the merit and reputation of Sir William Scott[1], then a tutor in University College, and now conspicuous in the profession of the civil law: my personal acquaintance with that gentleman has inspired me with a just esteem for his abilities and knowledge; and I am assured that his lectures on history would compose, were they given to the public, a most valuable treatise. Under the auspices of the present Archbishop of York, Dr. Markham, P. 52. himself an eminent scholar, a more regular discipline has been introduced, as I am told, at Christ Church[2]; a course of

[1] Afterwards Lord Stowell, d. 1836.
[2] This was written on the information Mr. Gibbon had received, and the ob- P. 52. servation he had made, previous to his late residence at Lausanne. During his last visit to England, he had an opportunity of seeing at Sheffield-place some young men of the college above alluded to; he had great satisfaction in conversing with them, made many inquiries respecting their course of study, applauded the discipline of Christ Church, and the liberal attention shown by the Dean to those whose only recommendation was their merit. Had Mr. Gibbon lived to revise this work, I am sure he would have mentioned the name of Dr. Jackson with the highest commendation. There are other colleges at Oxford, with whose discipline my friend was unacquainted, to which, without doubt, he would willingly have allowed their due praise, particularly Brazen Nose and Oriel Colleges; the

classical and philosophical studies is proposed, and even pursued, in that numerous seminary: learning has been made a duty, a pleasure, and even a fashion; and several young gentlemen do honour to the college in which they have been educated. According to the will of the donor, the profit of the second part of Lord Clarendon's History has been applied to the establishment of a riding-school, that the polite exercises might be taught, I know not with what success, in the university[1]. The Vinerian professorship is of far more serious importance; the laws of his country are the first science of an Englishman [l] of rank and fortune, who is called to be a

former under the care of Dr. Cleaver, bishop of Chester, the latter under that of Dr. Eveleigh. It is still greatly to be wished that the general expence, or rather extravagance, of young men at our English universities may be more effectually restrained. The expence, in which they are permitted to indulge, is inconsistent not only with a necessary degree of study, but with those habits of morality which should be promoted, by all means possible, at an early period of life. An academical education in England is at present an object of alarm and terror to every thinking parent of moderate fortune. It is the apprehension of the expence, of the dissipation, and other evil consequences, which arise from the want of proper restraint at our own universities, that forces a number of our English youths to those of Scotland, and utterly excludes many from any sort of academical instruction. If a charge be true, which I have heard insisted on, that the heads of our colleges in Oxford and Cambridge are vain of having under their care chiefly men of opulence, who may be supposed exempt from the necessity of œconomical controul, they are indeed highly censurable; since the mischief of allowing early habits of expence and dissipation is great, in various respects, even to those possessed of large property; and the most serious evil from this indulgence must happen to youths of humbler fortune, who certainly form the majority of students both at Oxford and Cambridge.—S.

[1] Henry, Viscount Cornbury, afterwards Lord Hyde, in the lifetime of his father, Henry, Earl of Rochester, by a codicil to his will left divers MSS. of his great-grandfather Edward, Earl of Clarendon, to Trustees, with a direction that the money to arise from the sale or publication thereof should be employed *as a beginning of a fund for supporting a Manage or Academy for riding and other useful exercises in Oxford.* Lord Cornbury dying before his father, this bequest did not take effect. But Catherine, a daughter of the Earl of Rochester, whose property these MSS. became, afterwards by deed gave them, with all money which had arisen or might arise from the sale or publication of them, to three Trustees, upon trust, for the purposes expressed by Lord Hyde in his codicil. In 1860 the available sum in the hands of the Trustees of the Clarendon Bequest amounted to £10,000. The University no longer needed a riding-school, and the claims of Physical Science being urgent, the Clarendon Trustees added, in 1872, an additional wing to the University Museum, containing the lecture rooms and laboratories of the department of Experimental Philosophy. [See Oxf. Hist. Soc. Collectanea, vol. i. p. 305.]

magistrate, and may hope to be a legislator. This judicious institution was coldly entertained by the graver doctors, who complained (I have heard the complaint) that it would take the young people from their books: but Mr. Viner's benefaction is not unprofitable, since it has at least produced the excellent commentaries of Sir William Blackstone.

XIII.

VINDICATION OF MAGDALEN COLLEGE.

A word or two in vindication of the University of Oxford and of Magdalen College in particular, from the posthumous aspersions of Mr. Gibbon. [By the Rev. James Hurdis.] [*Printed at the author's private press at Bishopstone*, about 1800.]

I was matriculated, says the Historian, *as a Gentleman-commoner of Magdalen College, before I had accomplished the fifteenth year of my age*[1]. He frankly confesses it was *a singular and a desperate measure*. Matriculations and admissions not less early have happened within the recollection of the Author of this Vindication. Nothing, however, can excuse the imprudence of sending boys so hastily into the society of men, but unusual sobriety and discernment on their part, united to a more than common proportion of attainments, and a well-settled habit of application. Without these requisites there is as little hope of a youth being steady in his conduct, as there is of the mariner being able to cross the Atlantic in his bark, who puts to sea without ballast or lading, and without knowledge of the art of navigation. If, before he was possessed of any of these qualifications, Mr. Gibbon was launched into the world, every consequent imprudence ought to be imputed to his friends and to himself, and not to the waves which overwhelmed and wrecked him. Possessed, as he was, at best, of a slight knowledge of a few odes of Horace and episodes of Virgil, a stranger to the *beauties* of the Latin, and ignorant even of the *rudiments* of the Greek tongue, a reader merely of *Pope's Homer* and *Dryden's Virgil*, of the *concise, terse*, and *sententious* Phaedrus, or of the *copious brevity* of Cornelius Nepos—what could his ill-judging parent expect

[1] [p. 113, above.]

from committing so shallow a novice to the boisterous element of a public University? To plunge a child so miserably deficient into a vast academy where (to say the worst of academical merit) there could not be even a choirister of ¹his own years so destitute of knowledge as himself, was to expose him without chance of preservation to the seduction of the idle and profligate, and to the contempt of the better informed. The father who is weak enough to send his child at so unseasonable a period to a public seminary of young men of riper years, ought to ensure his good conduct, by the appointment of a private tutor or superintendent, who should regulate his expences and his studies. Mr. Gibbon was manifestly, from his own account, incapable of self-management when sent to the University, and if no male instructor could have been found, he ought at least to have been followed by his *dear and excellent aunt*. Could it be expected that one who was, speaking most strictly, *an infant* at fourteen, should conduct himself with even tolerable propriety, where so many dangers surrounded him? To place such a boy suddenly in the society of men, to give him the management of his purse and pursuits, to grant him an allowance ¹ which was larger than necessary, and to trust him at the same time with the power of commanding an *indefinite latitude of credit*¹, were dangerous experiments, the mischievous result of which might have been easily calculated. In fourteen months his academical career is finished, and furnishes us with a narrative, such as we might have expected, truly vexatious to his friends and inglorious to himself. Instead of employing the *key* delivered to him when admitted into Magdalen College, by which he might have enjoyed the use of *a numerous and learned library*, he scorns the occupation of a *plebeian* student, evades his tutor's lectures under frivolous pretences which he denominates *apologies*, and elopes frequently from college—clandestinely perhaps, and without leave. If from the *fourteen* months of his academical existence, we deduct about *five* months of vacation which

¹ [p. 114, above.]

must necessarily have happened in that period, we discover that in *nine* months this gay libertine made no less than *six* excursions, one [1] to Bath, one into Bucks, and four to London. That each of these philosophical perambulations was of considerable duration, is manifest when he adds, *I eloped from Oxford, I returned to College, in a few days I eloped again, as if I had been an independent stranger in a hired lodging*[1]. Being thus constantly absent upon some idle pretence or other which cannot now be recollected, or perhaps without even the formality of a pretence, and certainly without the formality of permission, how was it possible that he should *once hear the voice of admonition*, or *once feel the hand of controul?* In a large college the *absence* of an individual, especially of Mr. Gibbon's dimensions, might not have been *visible*, as he incorrectly asserts it must have been. The Fellows of Magdalen College are unacquainted with any miracle of philosophy, by which non-entity and vacuum can be made discernible. That his irregular behaviour, however, was *observed*, is manifest, and that it was *resented* is as plain, when he informs [1] us that the College very readily embraced, at the fourteen months' end, an opportunity of for ever shutting their gates against his return. Whatever he may assert of the inattention of his superiors, he has clearly proved by recording this fact, that there was not that absolute want of restraint and discipline of which he has so loudly complained.

The whole of Mr. Gibbon's residence in the University was composed of those few intervening days which fell between his different elopements. If we suppose he had *philosophy* enough to endure *the irksomeness of a cloistered life* for a *week* at least in each of these intervals of repose (and he allows himself that they were composed only of *a few days* each), we shall perceive that the whole of his actual residence in Oxford might have been *six weeks* in nine months. But not to confine him too strictly to his own words, let us grant that he resided *six months*. In *six months'* time then was this juvenile

[1] [p. 123, above.]

and incompetent idler able to take a complete survey of the discipline of a great University which consists of *five and twenty* several societies. In *six months* was he able to decide upon the merits and demerits of all its members, Tutors and Professors, at a time when his own knowledge did not extend farther than the Greek Alphabet, Phaedrus' Fables, Cornelius Nepos, a few odes in Horace, and a few episodes in Virgil. It will be needless to spend time in arguing that a youth so ignorant was not capable of forming a just estimate of the proficiency of his own companions, nor even of the choirister who waited at his table; much less could he measure by his childish standard the abilities of Tutors and Professors. It is wonderful that in penning his opinions of our English University the Historian should not have recollected that they were the opinions of a boy, who, by his own confession, was not sufficiently improved to be able to judge of matters so important. Though he might at his matriculation have *puzzled* even *a Doctor* with that heterogeneous mixture of scraps from the alms-basket of learning, which he had accidentally picked up, and which he fondly stiles *erudition*, has he not himself informed us that with respect to the knowledge infused at the public school and the University, he was in a state of *ignorance of which a school-boy would have been ashamed*[1]? At a more advanced period of life, and of literary improvement, when introduced to some young men of Christ Church, he formed a more favourable opinion of the discipline of that society, of the utility of its exercises, and of the ability of its officers. Being then better able to wield matters of such important magnitude, and to poise them in the ponderous balance of justice, immoveable to the sinews of a child, he declared them *not wanting*. Had he extended his investigations still farther before he wrote his Memoirs, had he sought for the whole truth and not sacrificed the small part of it thus acquired to the angry conclusions of *fifteen*, he would in the end without doubt have pronounced an eulogium, a reluctant

---

[1] [p. 113, above.]

P. 9.   one perhaps, even on his own College. How much soever he may have laboured to injure that society in the eyes of his countrymen, it ought always to be remembered that the discipline of that house, feeble as he represents it, was the immediate cause of his preservation. His *expulsion* from the gates of Magdalen College was the occasion of his being placed in a situation better suited to correct his extravagances and follies. It was Magdalen College which returned him into the hands of his friends, as fitter for the society of the School than that of the College. It was Magdalen College which placed him under a vigilant preceptor, abridged him of the dangerous powers which had been committed to him, and gave the management of his pursuits and his expences to a wiser head. It was Magdalen College which compelled him to exchange *elegant apartments* for a *small chamber ill-contrived and ill-furnished*, banished him for a time from his

P. 10.   country and his friends, and made him fly from the stately edifices of Oxford to an *old inconvenient tenement* in Lausanne, in *a narrow gloomy street the most unfrequented of an unhandsome town*. Whatever application, sobriety, and literary desert were consequent, must be referred to this salutary though severe proof of discipline still alive and still endued with energy in Magdalen College. Had the Historian been ingenuous and *Christian*, had he possessed even the humanity of the *Philosopher*, he would have suffered those vindictive heartburnings which this spirited measure excited in his infant bosom, to have been softened down by the recollection of the benefits which it ultimately produced. He would at a more informed period have felt even gratitude to a society which intercepted him in his precipitate career at so momentous a crisis, and compelled his friends to adopt measures better calculated to correct his mischievous propensities, and less likely to terminate in his ruin. Carefully to treasure up in

P. 11.   his mind for more than forty years this imaginary insult, to use the strength of manhood to revenge the correction of infancy, and to assault the mother who disgraced him for the best proof she could give him of her regard, a timely and determined use of severity, betrays a heart, however philosophical, at least unfilial and unmanly. To extend hatred to all ecclesiastics because a clerical society had thus corrected him, to revile indiscriminately both Universities, to contemn a whole Church foreign as well as national, to war with religion itself, and speak with aversion of its ministers wherever situated and however amiable (if such acts were the consequences of his expulsion from Oxford), will add no dignity to his present or future character. They will only serve to convince the more liberal part of mankind, that there are opaque spots, and spots of no common magnitude, even within the luminous disc of Gibbon.

Had the military Historian, when he resolved to open his batteries upon Magdalen [1] College, contented himself with fairly P. 12. thundering out the *truth*, his attack would have been feeble however laboured, and however ardent with the blaze of metaphorical phosphorus. The majestic foppery of the well-turned period could not alone have injured the reputation of his College, nor have excited indignation in the breast of any one who belongs to it. But so little was the attention which the author paid, during the short intervals of his residence, to collegial concerns, that he represents the discipline of his house to have been such as it *never* was, and very much unlike what it now is. A boy of fourteen hurrying from Bath to Oxford, from Oxford to London, from London into Bucks, with little or no respite or cessation, may know something of post-chaises, stage-coaches, whips and horses, ostlers and postilions, but will not upon any public road hear much of College exercises. It is not wonderful that to a youth so engaged, the Latin declamation in the Hall was only [1] a *prevailing tradition*, a P. 13. flying rumour, a very distant report. To the more steady part of the society it was better known; for to the present moment is that custom of *declaiming* continued, of the cessation of which the inaccurate Historian has complained. All young men of three years' standing, whether Gentlemen-commoners or dependent members, who belong to Magdalen College, are still called upon in their turns to discharge this useful exercise, before the whole College, immediately after dinner, while the society and their visitants are yet sitting at their respective tables. Neither is the Gentleman-commoner exempted from any other exercise which the College requires of its dependent members. *Plebeian* and *patrician* student are subject alike to the literary and religious regulations of the house, and both are compelled to keep the full Term.

After declaring the *declamation* to have become extinct, Mr. Gibbon adds that *the obvious methods of public exercises* [1] *and examinations are totally unknown* [1] in Magdalen College. The existence of the declamation in its full force, at once dismisses as untrue the former part of this charge. The remaining accusation that there are no *public examinations*, will be best refuted by taking a view of the terminal exercises of the College as they succeed to each other. At the end of every Term from his admission till he takes his first Degree, every individual Undergraduate of this College must appear at a *public examination* before the President, Vice-President, Deans, and whatever Fellows may please to attend; and cannot obtain leave to return to his friends in any Vacation, till he has properly acquitted himself according to the following scheme. In his *first* year he must make himself a proficient—

In the first Term, in Sallust and the Characters of Theophrastus.

In the second Term, in the first six books of Virgil's Aeneis, and the first three books of Xenophon's Anabasis.

[1] In the third Term, in the last six books of the Aeneis, and the last four books of the Anabasis.

In the fourth Term, in the Gospels of St. Matthew and St. Mark, on which sacred books, the persons examined are always called upon to produce a collection of observations from the best commentators.

[1] [p. 121, above.]

During his *second* year, the Undergraduate must make himself a proficient—

In the first Term, in Caesar's Commentaries, and the first six books of Homer's Iliad.

In the second Term, in Cicero de Oratore, and the second six books of the Iliad.

In the third Term, in Cicero de Officiis and Dion. Hal. de structurâ Orationis.

In the fourth Term, in the Gospels of St. Luke and St. John, producing a collection of observations from commentators, as at the end of the first year.

During his *third* year he must make himself a proficient—

¹ In the first Term, in the first six books of Livy, and Xenophon's Cyropaedia. P. 16.

In the second Term, in Xenophon's Memorabilia, and in Horace's Epistles and Art of Poetry.

In the third Term, in Cicero de naturâ Deorum, and in the first, third, eighth, tenth, thirteenth, and fourteenth of Juvenal's Satires.

In the fourth Term, in the first four Epistles of St. Paul, producing collections as before.

During his *fourth* and last year he must make himself a proficient—

In the first Term, in the first six books of the Annals of Tacitus, and in the Electra of Sophocles.

In the second Term, in Cicero's Orations against Catiline, and in those for Ligarius and Archias; and also in those Orations of Demosthenes which are contained in Mounteney's edition.

In the third Term, in the Dialogues of Plato published by Dr. Forster, ¹ and in the Georgics of Virgil. P. 17.

In the fourth Term, in the remaining ten Epistles of St. Paul, and the Epistles general, producing collections as before.

Let the reader carefully weigh in his own mind the above detail of the terminal exercises of Magdalen College, and then let him determine, if there be any justice or truth in Mr. Gibbon's assertion that *public exercises* and *examinations* are in this society *totally unknown*, and that *neither the President nor the society interfere in the private œconomy of the Tutors and their pupils*[1]. It may be true that the terminal exercises, upon their present plan, may not have been in force more than *thirty* years; yet ought a faithful and accurate Historian to have been apprised of their existence, and not to have fastened upon the society a calumny which (if it was *ever* applicable) could only affect the discipline of his own days.

The above exercises are imposed upon every student, of whatever denomination. [1] He has to attend besides, his Tutor's Lecture once a day, and must produce a theme or declamation once a week to the Dean.

There is yet remaining a *public exercise*, observed by the Bachelors of Arts previous to the degree of M.A. Every candidate for that degree is required by the Statutes of the University to read six Lectures in Natural and Moral Philosophy in the public schools. For time out of mind these Lectures have been unfrequented, and every individual who ascends the rostrum, spends the *major pars horæ* during which he is supposed to read, in silent but vain expectation of an audience. To preserve to this exercise its original utility, every Bachelor of Arts of Magdalen College, even though he may be impeded by a Cure at two or three hundred miles distance, is, previous to his Master's degree, called upon to read an equal number of Lectures, on separate days, before the President, Vice-President, [1] Dean, and all Bachelors of Arts and Undergraduates of his College, in the Antichapel, immediately after Morning Prayers. Unless he complies with this regulation he cannot be presented for his Degree. Whenever such Lectures are read, it is the business of all the junior part of the society to be present. They are also required to attend in the same place three distinct Lectures in every Term,

[1] [p. 121, above.]

that is twelve in a year, from three regular Lecturers appointed by the College from the body of the Fellows. They receive from these in turn four annual Lectures each, in Natural and Moral Philosophy, and in Divinity. Many excellent Lectures, especially in Divinity, has the author of this Vindication there heard, and has found himself improved by them, at years and in a state of mental improvement much more advanced than those of the Undergraduate Gibbon. Equal instruction might have been derived by the Historian from attendance on such occasions, had ¹ he not often been engaged in a frolic when he should have been fixed to a form. The persons employed in the reading of these Lectures have generally been Tutors of the College, men who *promised to teach*, and have taught every species of useful knowledge—men who might probably be ignorant of some sciences, but none who could be *defective in all*, according to the possibilities of Mr. Gibbon's calculation.

Mr. Gibbon was *fourteen months* in Oxford. He had in that time two Tutors. The first he pronounces to have been one of the best of the tribe, though unable at the time to judge of his attainments, or to form a just verdict by comparison of his relative merit. Of Dr. Waldegrave the memory is still grateful to those that knew him. Even his austere pupil, Mr. Gibbon, allows that he was *learned, pious, mild, moral*, and *abstemious*. Then follows the catalogue of his imperfections. His knowledge of the world was confined to the University, *his learning* ¹ *was of the last age*. The Doctor, it seems, thought *one page of Chillingworth's Religion of Protestants worth a library of Swiss divinity*¹. He was one of that *order of men whose eyes are* [*not*] *dazzled by the light of philosophy*, a man too intelligent to be deluded by an ignis fatuus. He disapproved of Swiss education. And what man of sense will not as readily disapprove of the modern practice of trusting young men of family and fortune in the hands of Swiss preceptors? That there may be pleasure and some

---

¹ Gibbon's *Miscellaneous Works*, vol. i. p. 417.

use in such a measure is not denied, but every nice observer must have noticed, that it never fails to undermine and shake the fabric of their religious persuasions, and to furnish them with the despicable cavils of the sceptic and atheist. Can it be urged that Mr. Gibbon himself was an exception? If he had contempt for religion, where did he acquire it? at Oxford or Lausanne?

But to return to Dr. Waldegrave and his imperfections. *His faculties were not* [1] *of the first rate*, that is, he despised Swiss divinity. *He was satisfied like his fellows with the slight and superficial discharge of an important task* [1]. Of what task? Of instructing Mr. Gibbon. Was it wonderful that any man, especially a scholar, should be disinclined to the laborious task of conducting a reader of Phaedrus through the labyrinths of literature? The patience of the Doctor, his good temper and condescension must have been of the finest quality, to have submitted for the sake of any remuneration to read Terence with a school-boy so miserably deficient. It was all he *could* perform; and if the sum of Mr. Gibbon's improvement under him be confined *to three or four Latin plays* [2], he cannot with any justice blame either the University or Dr. Waldegrave.

But let us examine the matter more accurately. Mr. Gibbon entered the University early in April, 1752. As Easter Day fell in that year on the 29th of March, he must have entered in the Vacation following, [1] and we can hardly suppose that the young men could be returned from their friends to their Tutor so as to commence lecture before April 15th. From that time to the summer vacation is three calendar months, or about thirteen weeks. If we deduct the short Whitsun-tide vacation which happened in the interval, we find that *ten weeks* will comprise the whole of Mr. Gibbon's attendance upon the lectures of Dr. Waldegrave. For he tells us that during his absence in the summer vacation, the Doctor accepted a college living, and *on my return*, says he,

[1] [p. 121, above.]   [2] [p. 121, above.]

I no longer found him in Oxford. His other Tutor he never attended at all. To Dr. Waldegrave *alone* then he was indebted for the three or four Latin plays which he read while at Oxford, and these must have been all read in the space of ten weeks. Four plays consist of twenty acts. Two acts therefore of Terence must have been read per week by Mr. Gibbon in his Tutor's apartment. Now if we [1] remember that the academical week never exceeds five days, and that Mr. Gibbon made many excursions, and framed many apologies for absence, one of these two important conclusions must follow; he has either given us an exaggerated account of his proficiency, or Dr. Waldegrave performed wonders. With such a pupil, a pupil who acknowledges *laziness* and *indisposition*, who could have done more? It is almost past credit that he should have been able to effect so much.

P. 24.

It seems necessary here to remark, that when young men appear in an English University, it is presumed that they are in the habit of application, and are old enough to continue their studies without compulsion, actuated by a knowledge of the expedience of research and a desire to comply with the wishes of their friends. Their attendance upon their Tutor continues for an hour only in every day; the time of their absence is the season in which they are to prepare [1] themselves for his next Lecture. Mr. Gibbon at such times ought to have been studying Terence, and to have himself illustrated that elegant classic *by comparison with ancient and modern theatres* in his closet. If only *a dry and literal interpretation of the Author's text* [1] filled up the whole hour of his Lecture, it so happened, because the pupil had not looked at the book till the Tutor opened it, and was only able to spell when he ought to have read off his lesson with fluency. The small salary which a college Tutor receives for his trouble, is doubly earned by a single hour of such daily perplexity. If Mr. Gibbon was so puny a scholar, that he was of necessity inactive as soon as his Tutor quitted the leading string, he

P. 25.

[1] [p 122, above.]

should, as we have before observed, have been furnished with a dry nurse or pædagogue.

In vindication of the person who succeeded Dr. Waldegrave in the care [1] of Mr. Gibbon, it is impossible to say anything. His name being suppressed, leaves it doubtful at whom the writer levels his censure, and justifies the conclusion, that when he wrote that character he felt himself to be penning a libel. He was perhaps conscious that he had overstrained the truth, as he did in another instance, when he asserted that as a Gentleman-commoner he was permitted to associate with the Fellows—a custom which never existed. That such a character as he has drawn might not have been found in the University, few will be so bold as to maintain; that any one, precisely of that description, was appointed to the office of a Tutor in Magdalen College, and tolerated in it, may be doubted. It is not impossible, it is highly improbable. In every society are to be found characters unworthy of it; characters that are useless, and sometimes characters that are vicious. A College, whatever qualifications it may [1] insist upon in those whom it elects into its vacancies, will always acquire and always wear the same variety of appearance as the world at large. It will comprehend the sportsman, the jockey, the toper, the quid-nunc, the idler, and the petit-maitre, as well as the student, so long as the dispositions and desires of men are different. . . . Such being the motley complexion of human society, whether viewed as a whole or contemplated in parts, it would be extremely unjust to judge of the whole of any profession or seminary by a particular sample. *Far be it from me or from any faithful Historian*, says Mr. Gibbon (speaking of the Universities in his Vindication) *to impute to respectable societies the faults of some individual members*[1]. And yet has this very Historian indiscriminately included [1] all persons, not only of his own College and University, but of Cambridge as well as Oxford, in the same pragmatical manifesto of incapacity. The members of

[1] *Miscellaneous Works*, vol. ii. p. 602.

Magdalen College are *monks* (it was well he did not stile them *monkeys*), and if he enquires into the manufactures of these monks, nay, if he extends the enquiry to other Colleges of Oxford or Cambridge, *a silent blush or a scornfull frown* is the only reply. He has heard of nothing performed by the monks of any College. May not the silent blush and scornful frown, steal over the cheek and dwell upon the brow of these societies in return, when they reflect that the self-sufficient Historian was so absorbed in writing his own vain Memoirs, as to be ignorant of all their performances? Who has peopled the page of the Reviewer? Shines the author of the Decline and Fall *alone* in the firmament of criticism? May it not boast of many a luminary of Oxonian and Cantabrigian [1] origin, whose brightness suffers no diminution by the proximity of the Historic star? May it not maintain that while the steady and pure beam of a host of useful planets is their's, his only is the pestilential glare of the comet?

The fellows or monks of my time (the Historian is still speaking of Magdalen College) *were decent easy men who supinely enjoyed the gifts of their Founder. From the toil of reading, or thinking, or writing, they had absolved their conscience*[1]. Not to insist upon the injustice of this assertion by producing every instance which may serve to disprove the truth of it, it shall only be observed, that one of the *decent, easy*, and *supine monks* thus stigmatised by Mr. Gibbon for their idleness and aversion to reading, thinking, and writing, was the late pious and excellent Bishop of Norwich, Dr. Horne. The chronological catalogue of the writings of this very idle monk of Magdalen College, which appears at the end of 'Jones's life of him, contains *one and thirty* distinct publications, besides a variety of inferior pieces. The first of these publications made its appearance in 1751, and as Mr. Gibbon did not enter the University till April 1752, he could not have been ignorant that there was at least one splendid instance to confute his assertion.

[1] [p. 119, above.]

Were it necessary to attempt a refutation of the charge of indolence as it affects the rest of the University, by calling to mind every studious contemporary of the Historian, the catalogue should begin with the name of Kennicott. But having mentioned this laborious and indefatigable collator, we may rest upon his Atlantaean shoulders the whole weight of our cause, and let him stand alone, an editor of mountainous desert, who lifts his head far above the reach of the thunders and luminous coruscations of Gibbon. Let us but compare the work of this writer, *quod humeri fere mille hominum ferre recusarent*, with the smaller labours ¹ of Gibbon, and what are they? Let us consider him as the publisher of a Hebrew Bible, which gives us at one view all the various readings of nearly *seven hundred* Manuscripts and Editions, preserved in all quarters of the world, and what are the six quartos of Gibbon, and all the researches which attended them? Can they boast of being the consequence of more labour and industry? can they claim the palm for superior utility? No—while the Colossus Kennicott literally *bestrides the world*, it is the inferior lot of Mr. Gibbon to be great only among us *petty men*, who

> Walk under his huge legs, and peep about
> To find ourselves dishonourable graves.

As a Gentleman-commoner I was admitted (says Mr. Gibbon erroneously) *to the society of the Fellows, and fondly expected that some questions of literature would be the amusing and instructing topics of their discourse* ¹. If admitted, he was admitted by favour only, and was not of such consequence as to be entitled to a ¹ chair in that room, with the conversation of which he was so much disappointed. But, if admitted, ought he not to have known, that questions of literature are seldom made the subject of discourse in any circle of recreation. Would not the student who should attempt to introduce a critical discussion of any kind, among the mixed company of a common-room, in the hour of free conversation, deservedly be ridiculed for a proof so ill-timed of his self-sufficiency? At

¹ [p. 120, above.]

such a season let Fellows of Colleges be permitted to discourse upon indifferent subjects, without the unmanly and unmannerly imputation of being absorbed in *port* and *prejudice*, and let the fountain of erudition be sealed, or only referred to as modesty and the occasion may warrant. If conversation chance to light upon the trite topics of *college business* and *politics*, if it even descend to *personal anecdote* and *private scandal*, the school-boy indulged with a seat for the day, ought not to be angry [1] that no mention is made of *Phædrus* P. 33. or *Cornelius Nepos*, nor should the accomplished Historian be offended, that he finds no room for a question from *Baronius* or *Tillemont*. Whatever the juvenile taste of Mr. Gibbon might disdain in the conversation of that room, it was, at the time in which he found it so disagreeable, enlivened by the pleasantry and good humour of Horne, and is well remembered to have been frequently resorted to by Lowth, then in the zenith of his abilities. Can it be supposed that the one entered it to pick up hints for his *Commentary on the Psalms?* or the other to gather materials for his *Hebrew Prælections?*

Whatever Mr. Gibbon may have hastily asserted against Magdalen College, it is sufficiently clear from his Memoirs that the thought of having been expelled from it *sat heavy on his soul*, and was ever considered by him as an insurmountable disgrace. This is particularly evident [1] when he declares P. 34. of Mr. Locke, *The philosopher despised the academical bigots who expelled his person and condemned his principles* [1]. Here he supposes his reader will suffer him to escape from imputation, by allowing the two cases of Locke and Gibbon to be parallel. But nothing parallel is to be found in them. Mr. Locke was removed from his studentship of Christ Church upon a supposition of factious and disloyal behaviour. Mr. Gibbon was repulsed from Magdalen College for his irregularities and extravagances. Mr. Locke was dismissed, not by *the academical bigots* (a term which in Mr. Gibbon's vocabulary signifies *the University*) but by a special order of King

[1] [P. 115, above.]

Charles II, as Visitor of the College. His Majesty, at the instigation of Charles, Earl of Middleton, Secretary of State, applied to Dr. Fell, then Dean of Christ Church, and enforced his expulsion, by expressing astonishment that Locke should be suffered to retain any place of profit [1] in that Society. The philosopher then was expelled by the King, and not by his College; a conclusion easily to be maintained, when we remember that the College afterwards offered to admit him again as a supernumerary student, the vacancy occasioned by his dismission having been filled up. Mr. Gibbon, on the contrary, was not a martyr of party, he was expelled for indiscretions by the University itself, by Magdalen College—and *therefore* they are *academical bigots*, to be *despised* by every *philosopher*.

Let us now quit Magdalen College that we may bestow a few comments on a general charge of the Historian, which affects all parts of the University alike. *In the University of Oxford*, says Mr. Gibbon, *the greater part of the public Professors have for these many years given up altogether even the pretence of teaching* [1]. Let us reply with all possible nicety to this formidable accusation. There are in the University of Oxford twenty [1] Professorships. They shall all be mentioned in their turns, and some account shall be given of the duties performed by each Professor. The Regius Professor of Divinity reads his Lectures regularly, and (if the author mistakes not) no young man can take orders in the diocese of Oxford, without producing to the Bishop a certificate of his having attended them. The Margaret Professor of Divinity—reads a public Lecture once in every term. The Regius Professor of Hebrew, the Prælector in Anatomy, the Vinerian Professor, and the Prælector in Chemistry—read on certain days of every week during term. The Regius Professor of Modern History does the same, giving without interruption both public and private Lectures, in person for the most part, and by substitute when his impaired health confines him at home [2]

---

[1] [P. 118, above.]

[2] Thomas Nowell, D.D., Principal of St. Mary Hall, Reg. Prof. Modern Hist., 1771-1801.

The Professor of Geometry—reads in like manner, by 'self or deputy. The Professor of Astronomy, both in that capacity, and as [1] Professor of Natural History, delivers regularly, Lectures deservedly popular and much frequented. The late noble but unfortunate Professor of Civil Law [1], began his office with reading Lectures, and only desisted for want of an audience. The present, newly appointed, (the Author has heard it from the first authority) means to read. The late Professor of Botany [2] —*did* read, but Botany not being much in fashion among the younger members of either University, he, for want of pupils, employed the latter part of his life in collecting materials for a Flora Græca, the probable utility of which cannot be disputed. Dying in consequence of a disorder contracted in Greece, he bequeathed his work for completion to his able friend Dr. Wenman, then Professor of Civil Law, but who was soon afterwards drowned by accident in the river Cherwell. The Professor of Poetry—reads a public Lecture once in every term. The Professor of Music [1] gives also a public Lecture in each term. The Anglo-Saxon Professor—commences lecture-reading in the course of the next year, and the appointment being a new one, there cannot yet have been any omission in its duties.

If the reader will be at pains to compute the number of Professors who, according to the above statement, cannot be accused of any neglect, he will find that *fifteen* out of *twenty* are clearly exculpated from Mr. Gibbon's charge. The remaining *five* may possibly read their Lectures as punctually, the Author of this Vindication being unable to make any report of them, for want of knowledge respecting them. Mr. Gibbon himself has informed us, that Sir William Scott, when Cambden's Professor of History, wrote at least, and therefore probably read, Lectures on History, *which I am assured*, says he, *would compose, were they given to the public, a most valuable treatise* [3]. This assertion no one will be disposed

---

[1] Hon. Thomas Francis Wenman, D.C.L., Fellow of All Souls, and Keeper of the Archives, Reg. Prof. Civil Law, 1789-96.

[2] John Sibthorp, D.M., University, Prof. of Botany, 1784-96.

[3] [P. 127, above.]

P. 39. to question,[1] nor will any one deny that Warton the late Poet-Laureat, if he read not his lectures, filled the same office with eminent utility, as the Author of the History of Poetry. Nothing however is here pleaded in justification of the omission of lecture-reading, or to disguise the evident tendency of a precedent of this kind, to make the Professorship to which it belongs a mere sinecure. Archbishop Laud's Professor of Arabic, Dr. White, whether he reads Lectures in Arabic or not, has ably proved by his Bampton Lectures[1], that he is worthy of the office he holds, and of any honours which can be annexed to it, for the sake of learning, and of that religion of which he is so accomplished an advocate.

To Mr. Gibbon's unqualified assertion therefore, that the *greater part* of the Public Professors have for *these many years given up altogether even the pretence of teaching*, whether borrowed or fabricated in his own imagination, we may con-
P. 40. fidently [1] reply that it is *untrue*. We have seen that by far the *greater part*, a majority which nearly amounts to all, cannot fairly be impeached of wilful omission, or of any the slightest neglect. The places then are not become *useless*, according to Mr. Gibbon's ungenerous declaration, and when he argues, supposing them such, that they ought without delay to be abolished, he adopts those Gallic principles, which he has always sense enough to abhor, but when speaking of the University or Church. . . . The offices and salaries of the Professors indeed, so far from being useless, if carefully examined, are found to be conferred on persons who, for the most part, conscientiously discharge the duties of their
P. 41. situation, and are deserving of [1] the stations which they fill. The purpose of this short Vindication, has been only to expose the flagrant injustice of Mr. Gibbon, so far as relates to the University of Oxford and Magdalen College. His aspersions, as they affect the Church in general, the Author leaves to be refuted by some more able hand. . . .

[1] This is an unfortunate reference, like some others in this Vindication. It is beyond question that part of Dr. White's Bampton Lectures (in 1784) was really the work of Mr. Badcock, who received £500 for his share.

XIV.

WILLIAM FITZMAURICE, SECOND EARL OF SHELBURNE.

[*Born* May 20, 1737; matr. at Christ Church, 1753; Colonel in the Army, and distinguished statesman; created Marquis of Lansdowne in 1784; *died* May 7, 1805.]

Life of William, Earl of Shelburne. By Lord Edmond Fitzmaurice. Lond. 1875.

AT sixteen I went to Christ Church, where I had again the misfortune to fall under a narrow-minded tutor. He had, however, better parts, and knew more of the world, and I was more independent of him. It has by one or other accident been my fate through life always to fall in with clever but unpopular connections. I began to see my own situation, and to feel the necessity I was under of repairing lost time. I should mention that my father, before I left London, used to carry me when he made visits, and introduce me to several old people, telling me that they might be dead when I left Oxford, and I might hereafter be glad to have it to say that I had seen them. I saw by this means Lord Chesterfield[1] and Lord Granville, and was wonderfully struck with the difference of their manner. . . .

. . . My tutor Mr. Hollwell[2], was in strong opposition to the Westminsters, always the ruling party at Christ Church.

[1] Philip Dormer, fourth Earl, the celebrated Lord Chesterfield, Lord-Lieutenant of Ireland; died March, 1773.
[2] Probably William Holwell, of Christ Church; M.A., 1748; Proctor, 1758; Vicar of Thornbury, Gloucester.

He was not without learning, and certainly laid himself out to be serviceable to me in point of reading. I read with him a good deal of natural law, and the law of nations, some history, part of Livy, and translated some of the Orations of Demosthenes with tolerable care. I read by myself a great deal of religion. Surely it is [1] natural for a person of the least reflection, if they are taught to believe in the Bible, etc., to be restless till they know the sum of what it contains, and come to some decisive judgment upon a subject so interesting as their future existence and eternal welfare. The certainty of ninety-nine out of a hundred never bestowing a thought upon the subject tells a volume in regard to mankind, and opens a very extraordinary view of the world, accounting for a great deal of otherways unaccountable matter. I was afterwards much struck with Machiavel's Discourses on Livy, Demosthenes, and by the law of nature more than the law of nations. I attended Blackstone's lectures with great care, and profited considerably by them. I got little or no knowledge of the world however. I came full of prejudices. My tutor added to those prejudices by connecting me with the anti-Westminsters, who were far from the most fashionable part of the college, and a small minority.

Dr. Gregory[1] succeeded Dr. Conybeare, and was very kind to me, conversed familiarly and frequently with me, had kept good company, was a gentleman, though not a scholar, and gave me notions of people and things, which were afterwards useful to me. I likewise fell into habits with Dr. King[2], President of St. Mary Hall, a Tory and Jacobite, but a gentleman and an orator. He had a great [1] deal of historical knowledge, and of anecdote, having been intimately connected with the heads of the Tory party from the reign of Queen Anne.

I was likewise much connected during all the time I was at college with Mr. Hamilton Boyle[3], afterwards Earl of Cork.

---

[1] As Dean of Christ Church.
[2] William King, Principal of St. Mary Hall, 1719-64.
[3] Sixth Earl of Cork and Orrery, Christ Church; matr. June 14, 1748, aged 18; created D.C.L., 1763; then High Steward of the University; died Jan. 17, 1764.

As to the rest, the college was very low; a proof of it is, that no one who was there in my time has made much figure either as publick man, or man of letters. The Duke of Portland[1] is the only one I recollect to have his name come before the publick.

[1] William Henry Cavendish Bentinck, third Duke of Portland, Christ Church; matr. March 4, 1755; created M.A., 1757; D.C.L. by Diploma, 1792; Chancellor of the University; twice Prime Minister; died Oct. 30, 1809.

XV.

RICHARD LOVELL EDGEWORTH.

[*Born* at Bath in 1744; *died* June 13, 1817; educated at a school in Warwick, Drogheda School, and at Longford; also entered Trinity College, Dublin, in 1760.]

Memoirs of Richard Lovell Edgeworth, Esq. 2 vols. Lond. 1820.

Vol. I.
P. 77.
I ENTERED Corpus Christi as gentleman-commoner on the 10th of October, 1761. . . .

P. 91.
Having entered Corpus Christi College, Oxford, I applied assiduously not only to my studies, under my excellent tutor Mr. Russell[1], but also to the perusal of the best English writers, both in prose and verse. Scarcely a day passed without my having added to my stock of knowledge some new fact or idea; and I remember with satisfaction, the pleasure I then felt, from the consciousness of intellectual improvement.

I had the good fortune to make acquaintance with the young men, the most distinguishd at Corpus Christi for application, abilities, and good conduct. When I mention Sir James McDonald[2], and those with whom he lived, as my companions, I need add nothing more.

My acquaintance with Sir James commenced at the fencing school of Paniotti, a native of one of the Greek islands, a fine old

[1] John Russell, scholar of Corpus Christi; matr. 1755; B.A. 1759; M.A. 1763; died 1802.
[2] Sir James Macdonald, of Macdonald, eldest son of Sir Alexander Macdonald, of Slate, county Antrim, 'one of the greatest scholars and mathematicians of his time;' died while on his travels, at Rome, July 26, 1766.

Grecian, full of sentiments of honor and courage, and of a most independent spirit.

Mr. L., a young gentleman of a noble family and of abilities, but of overbearing manners, was our fellow pupil under Paniotti. At the same school we met a young man of small fortune, and in a subordinate situation at Maudlin. He fenced in a regular way, and much better than Mr. L., who, in revenge, would sometimes take a stiff foil that our master used for parrying, and pretending to fence, would thrust it with great violence against his antagonist. The young man submitted for some time to this foul play, but at last he appealed to Paniotti, and to such of his pupils as were present. Paniotti, though he had expectancies from the patronage of the father of his nobly born pupil, yet without hesitation condemned his conduct.

One day, in defiance of L.'s bullying pride, I proposed to fence with him, armed as he was with this unbending foil, on condition that he should not thrust at my face: but at the very first opportunity he drove the foil into my mouth. I went to the door, broke off the buttons of two foils, turned the key in the lock, and offered one of these extemporaneous swords to my antagonist, who very prudently declined the invitation.

This person afterwards shewed through life an unprincipled and cowardly disposition. The young man, who had at first borne with him with so much temper, distinguished himself in afterlife in the army. I mention the circumstance in which I was concerned, because I believe it contributed to my being well received at first among my fellow students at Oxford. I remember with gratitude, that I was liked by them, and I recollect with pleasure the delightful and profitable hours I passed at that University during three years of my life.

Doctor Randolph[1] was at that time president of Corpus Christi College. With great learning, and many excellent qualities, he had some singularities, which produced nothing

[1] Thomas Randolph, President 1748-83.

more injurious from his friends than a smile. He had the habit of muttering upon the most trivial occasions, '*Mors omnibus communis.*' One day his horse stumbled upon Maudlin bridge, and the resigned president let his bridle go, and drawing up the waistband of his breeches as he sat bolt upright, he exclaimed before a crowded audience, '*Mors omnibus communis!*' The same simplicity of character appeared in various instances, and it was mixed with a mildness of temper, that made him generally beloved by the young students. The worthy Doctor was indulgent to us all, but to me in particular upon one occasion, where I fear that I tried his temper more than I ought to have done. The gentlemen-commoners were not obliged to attend early chapel on any days but Sunday and Thursday; I had been too frequently absent, and the president was determined to rebuke me before my companions. 'Sir,' said he to me as we came out of chapel one Sunday, 'You *never* attend Thursday prayers.' 'I do *sometimes*, Sir,' I replied. 'I did not see you here last Thursday. And, Sir,' cried the president, rising into anger, 'I will have nobody in my college,' (ejaculating a certain customary guttural noise, something between a cough and the sound of a postman's horn,) 'Sir, I will have nobody in my college that does not attend chapel. I did not see you at chapel last Thursday.' 'Mr. President,' said I, with a most profound reverence, 'it was impossible that you should see me, for you were not there yourself.'

Instead of being more exasperated by my answer, the anger of the good old man fell immediately. He recollected and instantly acknowledged, that he had not been in chapel on that day. It was the only Thursday on which he had been absent for three years. Turning to me with great suavity, he invited me to drink tea that evening with him and his daughter. This indulgent president's good humour made more salutary impression on the young men he governed, than has been ever effected by the morose manners of any unrelenting disciplinarian.

During the assizes at Oxford, the gownsmen are or were permitted to seat themselves in the courts[1]. In most country courts there is a considerable share of noise and confusion ; but at Oxford the din and interruption were beyond anything I have ever witnessed ; the young men were not in the least solicitous to preserve decorum, and the judges were unwilling to be severe upon the students. A man was tried for some felony, the judge had charged the jury, and called on the foreman, who seemed to be a decent farmer, for a verdict. While the judge turned his head aside to speak to somebody, the foreman of the jury, who had not heard the evidence or the judge's charge, asked me, who was behind him, and whom he had observed to be attentive to the trial, what verdict he should give. Struck with the injustice and illegality of this procedure, I stood up and addressed the judges Wills and Smith. 'My Lords,' said I.—'Sit down, Sir,' said the judge.— 'My Lord, I request to be heard for one moment.'—The judge grew angry.—' Sir, your gown shall not protect you, I must punish you if you persist.'—By this time the eyes of the whole court were turned upon me ; but feeling that I was in the right I persevered. 'My Lord, I must lay a circumstance before you which has just happened.' The judge still imagining that I had some complaint to make relative to myself, ordered the sheriff to remove me.—'My Lord, you will commit me if you think proper, but in the meantime I must declare, that the foreman of this jury is going to deliver an

P. 96.

P. 97.

---

[1] 'Statutum est, quod nullus Scholaris cujuscunque conditionis ad publicos et generales Conventus Juridicos, vel Civitatis, vel Comitatus Oxoniensis (qui Sessiones aut Assisæ vocantur) nisi ex causa rationabili, per Vice-Cancellarium approbanda, accedat, vel iisdem interesse præsumat, sub pœna 10s. unicuique ibidem deprehenso infligenda ; et Incarcerationis etiam, omnibus et singulis per Vice-Cancellarium vel Procuratores inde recedere jussis, nec obtemperantibus : Cui adeundi carceris mandato, (quia grassanti incommodo alias commode occurri non potest) omnes et singuli, virtute juramenti Universitati præstiti, obedire teneantur. Juniores autem, Tyrones, et alii non Graduati (qui illuc spectatum maxime confluere solent) ibidem deprehensi, pro arbitrio Vice-Cancellarii aut Procuratorum, poenas dare teneantur.' *Corpus Statutorum Univ. Oxon.* (Oxon. 1768) Tit. xv. § 3 (*enacted in* 1636).

illegal verdict, for he has not heard the evidence, and he has asked me what verdict he ought to give.'

The judge from the bench made me an apology for his hastiness, and added a few words of strong approbation. This was of use to me, by tending to increase my self-possession in public, and my desire to take an active part in favor of justice.

XVI.

JAMES HARRIS,
FIRST EARL OF MALMESBURY.

[*Born* at Salisbury, April 21, 1746; educated at Salisbury Grammar School, and at Winchester; matr. at Merton, June 13, 1763; took no degree, but was created D.C.L., July 3, 1793; created Earl of Malmesbury, 1800; *died* Nov. 21, 1820.]

Diaries and Correspondence of James Harris, First Earl of Malmesbury. Lond. 1844. Vol. I. Introductory Memoir.

I LEFT Winchester in September 1762. ... My father[1], at that time in office and living in London, kept me with him for six months before he sent me to Oxford. I cannot even now decide whether this was a wrong or right step (I speak as to the result of my own conduct). I believe the seeing many of the leading men in Administration, hearing them converse on public business, contributed to form my mind to think on public affairs, and to give me an interest in them which, probably, otherwise I might never have acquired; but the mixing at that age (seventeen) and raw from school, in all the gaiety and dissipation of London, filled my mind at the same time with false objects of admiration, false notions of excellence, and gave me, in my own conceit, a knowledge of the world so much greater than I supposed my fellow-collegians could possibly possess, that I apprehend I carried to the University a considerable share of self-sufficiency, and no great propensity to attend lectures, and conform to college rules; and, in

[1] James Harris, M.P. for Christchurch, Hants; a Lord Commissioner of the Admiralty, 1763; Secretary and Comptroller to Queen Charlotte, 1774.

fact, the two years of my life I look back to as most unprofitably spent were those I passed at Merton. The discipline of the University happened also at this particular moment to be so lax, that a Gentleman Commoner was under no restraint, and never called upon to attend either lectures, or chapel, or hall. My tutor, an excellent and worthy man, according to the practice of all tutors at that moment, gave himself no concern about his pupils. I never saw him but during a fortnight, when I took into my head to be taught trigonometry. The set of men with whom I lived were very pleasant, but very idle fellows. Our life was an imitation of High Life in London; luckily drinking was not the fashion, but what we did drink was claret, and we had our regular round of evening card parties, to the great annoyance of our finances. It has often been a matter of surprise to me, how so many of us made our way so well in the world, and so creditably. Charles Fox[1], Lord Romney[2], North[3], Bishop of Winchester, Sir J. Stepney[4], Lord Robert Spencer[5], William Eden[6] (now Lord Auckland), and my good and ever-esteemed friend the last Lord Northington[7], were amongst the number. I left Oxford at the beginning of the long vacation 1765.

[1] Charles James Fox, son of Henry, Lord Holland, Hertford Coll.; matr. Oct. 23, 1764, aged 15; statesman and orator; died 1806.
[2] Charles Marsham, Christ Church; matr. Feb. 28, 1763, aged 18; third Baron Romney; created Viscount Marsham and Earl of Romney, 1801; died 1811.
[3] Brownlow North, son of the Earl of Guilford, Trin. Coll.; matr. 1760, aged 18; Bp. of Lichfield, 1771; Worcester, 1774; and Winchester, 1781-1820.
[4] Sir John Stepney, Christ Church; matr. Nov. 4, 1760, aged 17; seventh Baronet; Envoy Extraordinary at Dresden and Berlin; died 1811.
[5] Robert Spencer, son of Charles, Duke of Marlborough, Christ Church; matr. April 10, 1762, aged 14; created M.A. 1765; also D.C.L. 1773; died 1831.
[6] William Eden, Christ Church; matr. April 2, 1762, aged 17; B.A. 1765; M.A. 1768; Barrister-at-law; created Lord Auckland, 1789; died 1814.
[7] Robert Henley, Christ Church; matr. Oct. 24, 1763, aged 16; created M.A. 1766; second Earl of Northington; died July 5, 1786, and with him that peerage expired.

XVII.

VICESIMUS KNOX.

[*Born* in London, Dec. 8, 1752; matr. July 13, 1771, St. John's Coll.; B.A. 1775; M.A. 1779; Head Master of Tunbridge Grammar School, 1778-1811; *died* at Tunbridge, Sept. 6, 1821.]

Essays Moral and Literary, by Vicesimus Knox. Vol. I. Lond. 1782. 8º.

I.

[No. LXXV. ON THE NECESSITY OF AN ATTENTION TO THINGS AS WELL AS BOOKS, EXEMPLIFIED IN THE INSTANCE OF A FELLOW OF A COLLEGE. IN A LETTER.]

... I had been used for thirty years to scarcely any interruption, save the tinkling of the chapel and the dinner bell, and could not help being disgusted at the noise of servants, and the bustle of a family. Amid the din which was seldom interrupted, how often did I wish myself transported to the blissful region of the common room fire-side! Delightful retreat, where never female shewed her head since the days of the founder!

There was one circumstance attending my new situation, which, though only an imaginary evil, gave me at first a sensible mortification. As a senior fellow, I was a little monarch within the verge of my college. The statutes had required, that persons of the lower degrees should pass before me, nay, stand in the quadrangle whenever I was present, with heads uncovered. From this general obeisance, and from many other circumstances, I had been led to conceive myself a person of great importance. I was so, indeed, in the circumscribed limits of my society. But the misfortune was, that I could not easily free myself from the consciousness of it when no longer a member, and expected a similar degree of deference from all I met, which cannot be paid in the busy world without inconvenience. . . .

II.

[No. LXXVII. ON SOME PARTS OF THE DISCIPLINE IN OUR ENGLISH UNIVERSITIES.]

P. 331.   Our English universities are held in high esteem among foreigners; and, indeed, considering the number of great men, who have received a part of their education in them, and their opulent establishments of colleges and professorships, they are really respectable. I have therefore been the more disposed to lament, that the public exercises should be so futile and absurd, as to deserve not only the severity of censure, but the utmost poignancy of ridicule.

Reverence, it has been justly remarked, is always encreased by the distance of the object. The world at large, who hear of colleges like palaces devoted to learning, of princely estates bequeathed for the support of professors, of public libraries and schools for every science, are disposed to view the consecrated place in which they abound with peculiar veneration. Accidental visitors also, who behold the superb dining-halls, the painted chapels, the luxurious common rooms, the elegant chambers, and a race of mortals, in a peculiar dress, strutting through the streets with a solemn air of importance; when they see all the doctors, both the proctors, with all the heads of colleges and halls, in solemn procession, with their velvet sleeves, scarlet gowns, hoods, black, red, and purple—cannot but be struck with the appearance, and are naturally led to conclude, that here, at length, wisdom, science, learning, and whatever else is praiseworthy, for ever flourish and abound.

P. 332.   Without entering into an invidious and particular examination of the subject, we may cursorily observe, [1] that after all this pompous ostentation, and this profuse expence, the public has not, of late at least, been indebted for the greatest improvements in science and learning, to all the doctors, both the proctors, nor to all the heads of colleges and halls laid together. That populous university, London [1], and that region of literary labour, Scotland, have seized every palm of literary honour, and left the sons of Oxford and Cambridge to enjoy substantial comforts, in the smoke of the common or combination room. The bursar's books are the only manuscripts of any value produced in many colleges; and the sweets of pensions, exhibitions, fines, fellowships, and petty offices, the chief objects of academical pursuit.

If I were to enter into the many laughable absurdities of collegiate life and university institutions, as they now stand, I should exceed the limits of my paper. It is my intention at present only to acquaint the public with the exercises, which one celebrated seat of the Muses requires, of those who seek the envied honour of a Master of Arts degree. I speak not from displeasure or resentment; but voluntarily incur the odium of many persons attached by interest and connections to the universities, with no other motive than the desire of removing the disgrace of these noble establishments, by exposing the futility of the exercises to public animadversion.

The youth, whose heart pants for the honour of a Bachelor of Arts degree, must wait patiently till near four years have revolved. But this time is not to be spent idly. No; he is obliged, during this period, once to oppose, and once to respond, in disputations held in the public schools—a formidable sound, and a dreadful idea; but, on closer attention, the fear will vanish, and contempt supply its place.

This opposing and responding is termed, in the cant of the place, *doing generals* [2]. Two boys, or men, as they call them-

[1] London first became technically a University in 1836.

[2] 'A Soph was one who had passed the first set of disputations on the way to the B.A. degree, in or after the ninth Term. At the end of each day's disputations, those who had been disputing "pro formâ" were created "sophistae generales" (or briefly "generales"), a sort of quasi-degree "in logicalibus et grammaticalibus."'
Register of the University of Oxford, edited by A. Clark, vol. ii. part 1, p. 22.

selves, agree to *do generals* together. The first step in this mighty work is to procure arguments. These are always handed down, from generation to generation, on long slips of paper, and consist of foolish syllogisms on foolish subjects, of the formation or the signification of which, the respondent and [1] opponent seldom know more than an infant in swaddling cloaths. The next step is to go for a *liceat* to one of the petty officers, called the Regent-Master of the Schools, who subscribes his name to the questions, and receives sixpence as his fee. When the important day arrives, the two doubty disputants go into a large dusty room, full of dirt and cobwebs, with walls and wainscot decorated with the names of former disputants, who, to divert the tedious hours, cut out their names with their penknives, or wrote verses with a pencil. Here they sit in mean desks, opposite to each other, from one o'clock till three. Not once in a hundred times does any officer enter; and, if he does, he hears one syllogism or two, and then makes a bow, and departs, as he came and remained, in solemn silence. The disputants then return to the amusement of cutting the desks, carving their names, or reading Sterne's Sentimental Journey, or some other edifying novel. When this exercise is duly performed by both parties, they have a right to the title and insignia of *Sophs*[1]; but not before they have been formally *created* by one of the regent-masters, before whom they kneel, while he lays a volume of Aristotle's works on their heads, and puts on a hood, a piece of black crape, hanging from their necks, and down to their heels; which crape, it is expressly ordained by a statute[2] in this case made and provided, shall be plain, and unadorned either with wool or with fur.

And this work done, a great progress is made towards the wished-for honour of a bachelor's degree. There remain only one or two trifling forms, and another disputation almost exactly similar to *doing generals*, but called *answering under bachelor*, previous to the awful examination.

[1] See note p. 161.   [2] Statt. Univ. Oxon. Tit. vi. sect. 1, pt. 4.

Every candidate is obliged to be examined in the whole
circle of the sciences by three masters of arts, *of his own choice.*
The examination is to be held in one of the public schools,
and to continue from nine o'clock till eleven. The masters
take a most solemn oath, that they will examine properly and
impartially. Dreadful as all this appears, there is always found
to be more of appearance in it than reality; for the greatest
¹ dunce usually gets his *testimonium* signed with as much ease P. 334.
and credit as the finest genius. The manner of proceeding is
as follows: The poor young man to be examined in the
sciences often knows no more of them than his bedmaker, and
the masters who examine are sometimes equally unacquainted
with such mysteries. But *schemes,* as they are called, or little
books, containing forty or fifty questions on each science, are
handed down, from age to age, from one to another. The
candidate to be examined employs three or four days in
learning these by heart, and the examiners, having done the
same before him when they were examined, know what questions to ask, and so all goes on smoothly. When the candidate has displayed his universal knowledge of the sciences, he
is to display his skill in philology. One of the masters,
therefore, desires him to construe a passage in some Greek or
Latin classic, which he does with no interruption, just as he
pleases, and as well as he can. The statutes next require,
that he should translate familiar English phrases into Latin.
And now is the time when the masters shew their wit and
jocularity. Droll questions are put on any subject, and the
puzzled candidate furnishes diversion by his awkward embarrassment. I have known the questions on this occasion to
consist of an inquiry into the pedigree of a race-horse. And
it is a common question, after asking what is the *summum
bonum* of various sects of philosophers, to ask what is the
summum bonum, or chief good, among Oxonians; to which
the answer is such as Mimnermus would give. This familiarity, however, only takes place when the examiners are pot-
companions of the candidate, which indeed is usually the case;

for it is reckoned good management to get acquainted with two or three jolly young masters of arts, and supply them well with port, previously to the examination. If the vice-chancellor and proctors happen to enter the school, a very uncommon event, then a little solemnity is put on, very much to the confusion of the masters, as well as of the boy, who is sitting in the little box opposite to them. As neither the officer, nor anyone else, usually enters the room (for it is reckoned very *ungenteel*), the examiners [1] and the candidates often converse on the last drinking-bout, or on horses, or read the newspaper, or a novel, or divert themselves as well as they can in any manner, till the clock strikes eleven, when all parties descend, and the *testimonium* is signed by the masters. With this *testimonium* in his possession, the candidate is sure of success. The day in which the honour is to be conferred arrives; he appears in the Convocation house, he takes an abundance of oaths, pays a sum of money in fees, and, after kneeling down before the vice-chancellor, and whispering a lie, rises up a Bachelor of Arts.

And now, if he aspires at higher honours (and what emulous spirit can sit down without aspiring at them?) new labours and new difficulties are to be encountered during the space of three years. He must *determine*[1] in Lent, he must do *quodlibets*, he must do *austins*[2], he must declaim twice, he must read six solemn lectures, and he must be again examined in the sciences, before he can be promoted to the degree of Master of Arts.

None but the initiated can know what *determining, doing quodlibets,* and *doing austins* mean. I have not room to enter

---

[1] 'Determination—the last step in completing the B.A. degree—consisted of certain disputations which took place in Lent, generally the Lent following the admission to the B.A. degree.' *Register of the Univ. of Oxford,* vol. ii. pt. 1, p. 51.

[2] ' The Austin disputations are said to have derived their name from the house of the Augustinian monks, in which they had once been held. At a later time they took place in the Natural Philosophy School. But during this period they were held in the choir of St. Mary's Church, and hence are sometimes called "Marianae disputationes."' *Register of the Univ. of Oxford,* vol. ii. pt. 1, p. 74.

into a minute description of such contemptible *minutiæ*. Let it be sufficient to say, that these exercises consist of disputations, and the disputations of syllogisms, procured and uttered nearly in the same places, time, and manner, as we have already seen them in *doing generals*. There is, however, a great deal of trouble in little formalities, such as procuring sixpenny liceats, sticking up the names on the walls, sitting in large empty rooms by yourself, or with some poor wight as ill employed as yourself, without anything to say or do, wearing hoods, and a little piece of lambskin with the wool on it, and a variety of other particulars too tedious and too trifling to enumerate.

The declamations would be an useful exercise, if it were not always performed in a careless and evasive manner. The lectures are always called *Wall*[1] Lectures, because the lecturer has no other audience but the walls. Indeed, he usually steals a sheet or two of Latin out of some old book, no matter on what subject, though it ought to be on natural philosophy. ' These he keeps in his pocket, in order to take them out and read away, if a proctor should come in; but, otherwise, he sits by himself, and solaces himself with a book, not from the Bodleian but the circulating library.

P. 336.

The examination is performed exactly in the same manner as before described; and, though represented as very formidable, is such an one as a boy from a good school just entered, might go through as well as after a seven years' residence. Few, however, reside; for the majority are what are called *term-trotters*, that is, persons who only keep the terms for form-sake, or spend six or eight weeks in a year in the

[1] ' Dr. Fell, that he might as much as possible support the exercises of the University, did frequent examinations for degrees, hold the examiners up to it, and if they would, or could not do their duty, he would do it himself, to the pulling down of many. He did also sometimes repair to the Ordinaries (commonly called *Wall Lectures* from the paucity of auditors), and was frequently present at those exercises called *disputations in Austins*, where he would make the disputants begin precisely at one, and continue disputing till three of the clock in the afternoon ; so that upon his appearance more auditors were then present, than since have usually appeared at those exercises.' Wood's *Athenæ Oxon.* vol. ii. p. 796.

university, to qualify them for degrees, according to the letter of the statutes.

After all these important exercises and trials, and after again taking oaths by wholesale, and paying the fees, the academic is honoured with a Master's degree, and issues out into the world with this undeniable passport to carry him through it with credit.

Exercises of a nature equally silly and obsolete, are performed, in a similar manner, for the other degrees; but I have neither time nor patience to enter into the detail.

And now I seriously repeat, that what I have said proceeds from no other motive than a wish to see the glory of the universities unsullied by the disgrace of requiring, with ridiculous solemnity, a set of childish and useless exercises. They raise no emulation, they confer no honour, they promote no improvement. They give a great deal of trouble, they waste much time, and they render the university contemptible to its own members. I have the honour, such as it is, to be a member of the university of Oxford, and a master of arts in it. I know the advantages of the place; but I also know its more numerous and weighty disadvantages; and the confidence the public has already placed in me, makes it a duty to inform them of every thing, in which the general state of morals and literature is greatly concerned. I have done this duty; nor shall I regard the displeasure of all the doctors, both the proctors, nor of all the heads of colleges and halls, with their respective societies.

¹ 'As to the imprudence of this undertaking,' to use the words of an able but unfortunate writer, 'I confess it to be such, and that I have all along proceeded without a single view to my own interest, without any promise or expectation of the smallest reward, even that of being presented to a Doctor's degree by the university, in return for all my industry, and the pains which I have taken in its behalf.

'The worldly wise, and the prudent of this generation, consider things only as they respect their temporal interest and advantage, without any regard to right or wrong, truth or falsehood, any further than they conduce to their corrupt purposes and selfish aims. But it is the part of a scholar and an honest man to consider things intrinsically, and to make truth, reason, and equity, the standards of all his determinations.'

XVIII.

GEORGE COLMAN, THE YOUNGER.

[*Born* Oct. 21, 1762; educated at Westminster; matr. at Ch. Ch. Jan. 28, 1780; Lieutenant of the Yeomanry of the Guard, 1820; Licenser and Examiner of Plays; entered at Lincoln's Inn, 1789; *died* Oct. 17, 1836.]

Random Records, by George Colman, the Younger. Lond. 1830.

I.

Vol. I.
P. 261.

I WENT annually to Wynnstay[1], for three seasons,—beginning as a promising actor, and having greatly risen in my cast of parts, after the first year. At the end of the THIRD SEASON, 1779, my transition from the festivities of Wales to the austerities of a College was more violent than agreeable:—but my father, on his way to town, then dropp'd me

P. 262.

at Oxford, leaving me there, ¹ after having seen me matriculated, as a Member of Christ Church. . . .

P. 263.

¹ When I was an Oxonian, the hand of Time was forestall'd by the fingers of the Barber; and an english stripling, with his hair flowing over his shoulders, was, in the course of half an hour, metamorphosed into a man, by means of powder, pomatum, the comb, the curling irons, and a bit of black ribbon to make a pigtail. . . .

P. 264.

¹ On my entrance at Oxford, as a member of Christ Church, I was too foppish a follower of the prevailing fashions to be a reverential observer of academical dress :—in truth, I was an egregious little puppy:—and I was presented to the Vice-Chancellor, to be matriculated, in a grass-green coat, with the

---

The seat of Sir Watkin Williams Wynn, in Wales.

furiously be-powder'd pate of an ultra-coxcomb; both of which are proscribed, by the Statutes of the University[1].

[1] Much courtesy is shown, in the ceremony of matriculation, to the boys who come from Eton and Westminster; insomuch, that they are never examined in respect to their knowledge of the School Classicks;—their competency is consider'd as a matter of course:—but, in subscribing the articles of their matriculation oaths, they sign their *prænomen* in Latin; —I wrote, therefore, GEORGEIUS,—thus, alas! inserting a redundant *e*,—and, after a pause, said inquiringly to the Vice-Chancellor,—looking up in his face with perfect *naïveté*,— 'pray, sir, am I to add *Colmanus*?'

My Terentian father, who stood at my right elbow, blush'd at my ignorance;—the Tutor (a piece of sham marble) did not blush at all,—but gave a Sardonick grin, as if *scagliola*[2] had moved a muscle!

The good-natured *Vice*[3] drollingly answer'd me, that,—' the Surnames of certain *profound Authors*, whose comparatively modern works were extant, had been latinized;—but that a Roman termination tack'd to the patronymick of an english gentleman of my age, and appearance, would *rather* be a redundant formality.'

[1] There was too much delicacy in the worthy Doctor's satire for my green comprehension,—and I walk'd back, unconscious of it, to my college,—strutting along in the pride of my unstatutable curls and coat, and practically breaking my oath, the moment after I had taken it.

No character is more jealous of the 'Dignity of Man' (not excepting Colonel Bath, in Fielding's Novel of Amelia,) than

---

[1] 'Statutum est quod omnes Præfecti, etc. .., quodque alii omnes (exceptis filiis Baronum in superiore Parliamenti Domo suffragii jus habentium, necnon Baronum ex Gente Scoticâ et Hibernicâ,) vestibus coloris *nigri et subfusci* se assuefaciant; nec quæ fastum aut luxum præ se ferunt, imitentur; sed ab iis procul absint. . . . . Etiam in capillitio modus esto; nec *cincinnos*, aut *comamnimis promissam alant*.' *Parecbolæ, sive Excerpta, è Corpore Statut. Univers. Oxon.* (Colman's note.)

[2] This is probably a reference to marble or some composition having the appearance of marble.

[3] George Horne, D.D., President of Magdalen.

a lad who has just escaped from School-birch to College discipline.

This early Lord of the Creation is so inflated with the importance of virility, that his pretension to it is carefully kept up, in almost every sentence he utters.—He never mentions any one of his associates but as a *gentlemanly* or a pleasant *man*;—a studious man, a dashing man, a drinking man, etc., etc.;—and the *Homunculi Togati* of Sixteen always talk of themselves as Christ-Church *men*, Trinity, St. John's, Oriel, Brazen-Nose *men*, etc.,—according to their several colleges, of which Old Hens, they are the Chickens;—in short, there is no end to the colloquial *manhood* of these mannikins.—I recollect two of them upon the point of settling a ridiculous dispute by *gentlemanly satisfaction*, who had, scarcely six weeks¹ before, given each other a black eye, in a fair set-to with fists, at Westminster. . . .

¹ In those my days of academical precocity, a brother collegian of my own *non-age*, with whom I was very intimate, and who is now a Dignitary of the Church, frisk'd up to London, while I remain'd at Oxford.—During his short stay in Town, he made the young Oxonian's usual discovery of a vacuum in his pocket;—and his reflections upon it were not at all in unison with that contempt for riches manifested by Diogenes in¹ his tub;—looking at the question algebraically, he was of decided opinion that converting the *minus* of his finances into *plus* would be vastly agreeable:—

It occurr'd to him, therefore, that, being of an excellent family, though a younger brother, he might raise a good round sum, at once, for his present and future *menus plaisirs*;—and there were then in London, as there always will be, plenty of depredators, who profess to furnish pecuniary accommodation,—not merely for gentlemen come of age, but even for *infants* of good expectancy.

One morning, I received a letter from him,—he in London and I at College,—enclosing his draughts upon me for five hundred pounds, which he desired me to accept, *as a matter of course*, that he might complete a loan:—in the flush of youthful friendship, and ignorance of wordly business and cares, I subscribed the Bills, without hesitation, and sent them back by return of Post.

A few days afterwards, he sent me a second letter, containing further Bills to the same amount, for my acceptance;— stating that there was some informality in the first draughts, which were, therefore, useless.—I accepted *de novo*;—thus, the Notes for Five Hundred were *encored*, to the tune of a Thousand.

The reader need not be told that my friend, who was as unpractised in the world as myself, had fallen into the clutches of one of those low advertising scoundrels who call themselves money-scriveners, with whom the town swarms.—All the money advanced was a hundred, or a hundred and fifty pounds;—the first bills were not return'd, when the second were given; *all* of them were put into circulation, and brought against us, according to their dates, as they became due.

Here was the devil to pay!—or, rather, the bill-holders (confederates, most likely, with the original rascal,) were to be paid, or not paid, as it might happen.—The young pigeons had '*no assets*'; the rooks, therefore, attack'd the parent nests;—in other words, they attempted to bully our relations.

My father, on being apprized of what had occurr'd, was outrageous against me;—he forgot every line in his elegant version of parental lenity towards youthful delinquents[1];— far from being intimidated by the claimants, he swore that, instead of paying them a shilling, he would make a Bow-

---

[1] Terent. Adelph., Act 1, Scene 1. (Colman's Translation.)
'Tis this, then, is the duty of a father;
To make a son embrace a life of virtue
Rather from choice than terror or constraint.
Here lies the mighty difference between
A Father and a Master. He who knows not
How to do this, let him confess he knows not
How to rule children.' (Colman's note.)

street business of it, and take them all up, for a parcel of swindlers:—in respect to non-payment, he most religiously kept his oath.

I do not exactly remember how the affair was settled;— but it appear'd, upon investigation, that I had never received, or expected to receive, any money upon the bills;—my seeming prodigality, therefore, dwindled into the old story,— the imprudence of becoming 'bound for a friend.' My father, in consequence, as one of the consulting family elders, who met upon the occasion, declared himself *hors de combat*; and I believe that my friend's mother, who was a widow, and his near relative Sir —— ——, compromised the matter at some expense; which, upon principles of publick justice, should, perhaps, have been resisted; particularly as there was every reason to suspect that the bill-holders were not *bonâ fide* creditors.—But let me apostrophize my quondam associate, who was engaged with me in this transaction:—

Dear and worthy Doctor! My Condiscipulus of Westminster, and chief Companion at Christ Church,—who, in our Spring of Life did'st nourish with me those blossoms of regard which were blighted by vernal accidents, and have never come to fruit;—Bosom Friend of my Immaturity! . . . Should these Crudities fall in thy way, they will cause thee to ruminate awhile perhaps, and to philosophize upon this wild transaction of our 'Salad Days, when we were green in judgment.'—They may bring back to thy mind's eye the eight-feet square Study,—thy *Sanctum Sanctorum*, in Peckwater Quadrangle,—whither we were wont to retire, after our three o'clock dinner in the Hall;—and there, over a bottle of fiery Oxford Port, (worthless and pernicious, dear Doctor, as the draughts which I had accepted for thee!) compose letters to our angry relatives,—palliating, as ably as we could, the follies which had brought us into such a scrape.—Thou may'st recollect, too, (I can, if Thou can'st not,) thy ingenuous impulses of youthful honour, which made thee so anxious to take the whole blame upon thyself, and to clear me from the supposition of being an intended participator in the loan ;— P. 275. calling thyself the '*only responsible* MAN ; '—at which my father (to whom thy letter was address'd) would frequently laugh outright after his wrath against me had subsided ;—for much, indeed, did he chuckle at thy manly tone, and the ripe responsibility of thy pubescence. . . .

A FRESHMAN, as a young academician is call'd on his P. 293. admission at Oxford, is a forlorn animal.—It is awkward for an *old stager* in Life to be thrown into a large company of strangers, to make his way among them, as he can ;—but to the poor *Freshman* every thing is strange,—not only College society, but any society at all,—and he is solitary in the midst of a crowd.

If, indeed, he should happen to come to the University (particularly to Christ Church) from one of the great publick P. 294. schools, he finds some of his late school-fellows ; who, being in the same straggling situation with himself, abridge the period of his fireside loneliness, and of their own, by forming a familiar intercourse ;—otherwise he may mope for many a week ;—at all events, it is generally some time before he establishes himself in a *set* of acquaintance.

But the principal calamity of the Freshman,—by which, as I shall presently show, he smarts in purse, and suffers in person,—arises from his ignorance in œconomicks ;—from his utter helplessness in providing himself with the common articles of consumption, and comfort, requisite for the occupant of a lodging.

An outline of my own grievances, on my *début* as a Commoner, at Christ Church, may serve to describe the state of P. 295. almost all the new comers.

This flourishing College was, at least, full, if not overflowing ; and afforded me a very remote prospect of sitting down in regular apartments of my own ;—in the mean time, my Tutor stow'd me in the Rooms of one of his absent pupils, which were so much superior to those of most other undergraduates, that I did not at all relish the probability of being turn'd out of them, as soon as the owner arrived,—and he was daily expected.

This precarious tenure, however, was envied by several of my contemporaries; for the College was so completely cramm'd, that shelving garrets, and even unwholesome cellars, were inhabited by young gentlemen, in whose fathers' families the servants could not be less liberally accommodated.

I *drank wine*[1], one afternoon, in the little Canterbury Quadrangle, with a young friend,—a brother Westminster, of the name of Watkins[2],—who was stuff'd into one of these underground dogholes;—he was in a course of ancient and modern geographical research, and the maps of the learned Cellarius served him for the double purpose of reference and decorating the walls of his *Souterrain*. I half affronted him, though without any such intention, by calling him *Cellarius Watkins*, in allusion to his studies and his habitation. . . .

[1] The retainers in my establishment, at Oxford, were a Scout and a Bedmaker;—so that, including myself, I might have said with Gibbet,—'My Company is but small,—we are but three[3].' There was this difference, indeed, between Captain Gibbet and myself,—he insisted on dividing booty with his gang, but I submitted to be robb'd by my adherents.

My two mercenaries, having to do with a perfect *greenhorn*, laid in all the articles for me which I wanted,—wine, tea, sugar, coals, candles, bed and table linen,—with many useless *et cætera*, which they *told* me I wanted;—charging me for every thing full half more than they had paid, and then

---

[1] 'The Members of Christ Church all dine in the Hall at different tables, according to the degrees they have taken; and, as libations to Bacchus are not allow'd at the table of the undergraduates, they give invitations reciprocally to take wine and a dessert, in each other's rooms; whither they repair on quitting the Hall, as soon as they have dined.' (Colman's Note.)

[2] Thomas Watkins, matr. Dec. 17, 1779, aged 18; was afterwards in Holy Orders (Rector of Llandefailog in 1799, and Vicar of Llandefalley in 1800) until his death in 1829.

[3] Farquhar's '*Beaux' Stratagem*.' (Colman's Note.)

purloining from me full half of what they had sold.—Each of these worthy characters, who were upon a regular salary, introduced an assistant, (the first his wife, the second her husband,) upon no salary at all;—the auxiliaries demanding no further emolument than that which arose from their being the conjugal helpmates of the stipendiary despoilers.

Hence I soon discover'd the policy of always employing a married Scout, and Bedmaker, who are married to *each other* ; —for, since almost all the college menials are yoked in matrimony, this rule consolidates knavery, and reduces your *ménage* to a couple of pilferers, instead of four.

¹ *Your Scout*, it must be own'd is not an animal remarkable for sloth ;—and, when he considers the quantity of work he has to slur over, with small pay, among his multitude of masters, it serves, perhaps, as a salve to his conscience, for his petty larcenies.   P. 299.

He undergoes the double toil of Boots at a well-frequented Inn, and a Waiter at Vauxhall, in a successful season.—After coat-brushing, shoe-cleaning, and message-running, in the morning, he has, upon an average, half-a-dozen supper-parties to attend, in the same night, and at the same hour ;—shifting a plate here, drawing a cork there,—running to and fro, from one set of chambers to another,—and almost solving the Irishman's question of ' how can I be in two places at once, *unless I was a bird?* '

A good and really honest drudge of this description is a phænomenon at Christ Church ; and, even then, his services are scarcely worth the purchase ;—he is so split into shares, that each of his numerous employers obtains in him something like the sixteenth of a twenty-pound prize in a Lottery.

¹ The Bedmaker whom I originally employ'd was rather more rapacious than her sister harpies ; for, before she commenced the usual depredations upon me, she had the ingenuity to ' rob me of that which did not enrich *her*,' and made me very ' uncomfortable, indeed ! '—The article of which she contrived to despoil me was neither more nor less   P. 300.

than a *night's sleep*:—this aforesaid theft was committed, as the deponent hereby setteth forth, in manner and form following:—

My spirits had been flurried during the day, from the revolution in my state:—launch'd from the School-Dock, into the wide Ocean of a University; matriculated by the Vice-Chancellor, in the morning,—left by my father, at noon,—dining in the Hall, at three o'clock, unknowing, and almost unknown,—inform'd that I must be in the Chapel, next day, soon after sun-rise,—elated with my growing dignity,—depress'd by boyish *mauvaise honte*, among the *Sophs*,—dreading College discipline,—forestalling College jollity,—ye Gods! what a conflict of passions does all this create in a booby boy!

I was glad, on retiring early to rest, that I might ruminate, for five minutes, over the *important* events of the day, before I fell fast asleep.

I was not, then, in the habit of using a night-lamp, or burning a rush-light;—so, having dropt the extinguisher upon my candle, I got into bed; and found, to my dismay, that I was reclining in the dark, upon a surface very like that of a pond in a hard frost.—The jade of a Bedmaker had spread the spick and span new sheeting over the blankets, fresh from the linen-draper's shop;—unwash'd, uniron'd, unair'd, 'with all its imperfections on its head.'

Through the tedious hours of an inclement January night, I could not close my eyes;—my teeth chatter'd, my back shiver'd;—I thrust my head under the bolster,—drew up my knees to my chin;—it was all useless; I could not get warm; —I turn'd again and again; at every turn a hand or a foot touch'd upon some new cold place; and, at every turn, the chill glazy clothwork crepitated like iced buckram.—God forgive me, for having execrated the authoress of my calamity! but, I verily think, that the meekest of Christians who prays for his enemies, and for mercy upon all 'Jews, Turks, Infidels, and Hereticks,' would in his orisons, in such a night of misery, make a specifick exception against his Bedmaker.

I rose betimes,—languid and feverish,—hoping that the customary morning ablutions would somewhat refresh me;—but, on taking up a towel, I might have exclaim'd with Hamlet: 'Ay, there's the rub!'—it was just in the same stubborn state as the linen of the bed; and as uncompromising a piece of huckaback, of a yard long, and three quarters wide, (I give the usual dimensions) as ever presented its superficies to the skin of a gentleman.

Having wash'd and scrubb'd myself in the bed-chamber, till I was nearly flay'd with the friction, I proceeded to my sitting-room, where I found a blazing fire, and a breakfast very neatly laid out;—but again I encounter'd the same *rigour!* The tea equipage was placed upon a substance which was snow-white, but unyielding as a skin of new parchment from the Law Stationer;—it was the eternal unwash'd linen!—and I dreaded to sit down to hot rolls and butter, lest I should cut my shins against the edge of the table-cloth.

In short, I found upon enquiry that I was only undergoing the common lot,—the usual seasoning,— ' of almost every Freshman; whose fate it is to *crackle* through the first ten days, or fortnight, of his residence in College.—But the most formidable piece of drapery belonging to him is his new surplice; in which he attends Chapel, on certain days of the week;—it covers him from his chin to his feet, and seems to stand on end, in emulation of a full suit of armour.—Cased in this linen panoply, (the certain betrayer of an academical *débutant,*) the New-Comer is to be heard at several yards' distance, on his way across a quadrangle, cracking and bouncing like a dry faggot upon the fire;—and he never fails to command notice, in his repeated marches to prayer, till soap and water have silenced the noise of his arrival at Oxford.

Several of the Offspring with which Christ-Church teem'd, at the period I am recording, were destined to become eminent men. — Of embryo Statesmen, there were the Marquess of

P. 303.

Wellesley[1], Earl Bathurst[2], and Lord Grenville[3], (I mention them according to their present titles,) the last of whom is, now, Chancellor of the University.—There was, also, Lord Colchester[4], now Keeper of the Privy Seal in Ireland, who was ' Speaker of the House of Commons. Appended to these, as if by a foretaste of his attendance on the Lords, was the much respected Sir Thomas Tyrwhit[5]; whose gentle and unassuming manners, in his conspicuous office of Usher of the Black Rod, so well accord with the personal modesty of his perpendicular elevation above any surface parallel with the horizon.

There was, moreover, the late Mr. Samuel Whitbread[6]:—this honourable gentleman was not of the first-rate abilities; yet, after certain Whigs, far superior to him in talent, had dropp'd off, he did not rank meanly as a Wrangler in the Lower House. . . .

And why, in this enumeration, should I omit ! my honest, open-hearted, quondam friend, 'Jerry Curteis[7],' as we familiarly call'd him, at Westminster, and at Oxford? He is a joint representative of the County of Sussex,—less prepared, perhaps, to illustrate the doctrines of *Cicero de Oratore* than to comment upon the *Georgicks* and *Bucolicks* of Virgil;—but he is to be class'd among those plain-spoken independent Country Gentlemen whose voices are important in the

[1] Richard, second Earl of Mornington, Christ Church; matr. Dec. 24, 1778, aged 18; created Marquess Wellesley, Dec. 2, 1799; died 1842.

[2] Henry, Lord Apsley, third Earl Bathurst, Christ Church; matr. April 22, 1779, aged 17; died 1834.

[3] William Wyndham Grenville, of Wotton-under-Bernwood, second son of the Right Hon. George Grenville; Christ Church; matr. Dec. 14, 1776, aged 17; having attained a high reputation as an orator and statesman, he was created Baron Grenville, Nov. 25, 1790; Chancellor of the University 1809-34.

[4] Charles Abbot, Esq., Christ Church; matr. June 14, 1775, aged 17; created Lord Colchester, June 3, 1817; died 1829.

[5] Sir Thomas Tyrwhitt; matr. July 3, 1780, aged 17; B.A. 1780; M.A. 1787; Private Secretary of the Prince of Wales.

[6] Samuel Whitbread, Christ Church; matr. July, 1780, aged 16; M.P. for Bedford in six parliaments, 1790 until his death in 1815.

[7] (Edward) Jeremiah Curteis, Christ Church; matr. Dec. 13, 1779, aged 17; B.A. 1783, Oriel Coll.; M.A. 1787; of Windmill Hill, Sussex; M.P. 1820-30; Barrister-at-law; died 1835.

Senate, and who are, in part, bulwarks of the english constitution.

Among my youthful contemporaries, in so clerical a hot-bed as Christ Church, there could not fail to be plenty of future Parsons;—some of these have shot up to the height of Dignitaries, partaking in the honours and revenues of a Cathedral, or a Collegiate Church;—others have branch'd into the rank of Incumbents, with all the pastoral fruition of fat Benefices, glebe land, 'tythe pig, and mortuary guinea.'— The late Doctor Hall[1] was Dean, and Doctors Pett[2] (Archdeacon) and Dowdeswell[3], are Canons of Christ Church,— the College in which they were undergraduates; Doctor Webber[4] is an Archdeacon, and a Residentiary Canon of Chichester; and the names of David Curzon[5], Robert Lowth[6], Henry Drummond[7], Charles Sandby[8], *cum multis aliis*, have all, if I mistake not, been annex'd to good Church preferment.—With the above-mention'd Divines (omitting Doctor Phineas Pett) I was intimate;—they are all, I believe, alive, (and I hope well,) except Doctor Hall, and the much lamented Robert Louth:—I left them, when they were young, in the fostering bosom of *Alma Mater*, seldom or never to meet again! Though inhabiting the same island, and often,

P. 306.

---

[1] Charles Henry Hall; matr. June 3, 1779; Dean of Christ Church, 1809-24, of Durham, 1824 until his death in 1827.

[2] Phineas Pett; matr. June 1, 1779. aged 18; Principal of St. Mary Hall, 1801-15; Chancellor and Archdeacon of Oxford, 1797, until his death in 1830.

[3] Edward Christopher Dowdeswell; matr. Feb. 5, 1780, aged 15; Fellow of All Souls Coll.; Rector of Stanford Rivers, 1802 (of Langham, Essex, 1807-29), until his death in 1849.

[4] Charles Webber; matr. Oct. 17, 1778, aged 16; B.A. 1782; M.A. 1785; Vicar of Boxgrove, Sussex, 1786; Archdeacon of Chichester 1808, died 1848.

[5] David Francis Curzon; matr. Nov. 1, 1779, aged 17; B.A. 1783; M.A. 1787; Rector of Kedleston and Mugginton, died 1832.

[6] Robert Lowth; matr. July 6, 1779, aged 17; B.A. 1783; M.A. 1786; Prebendary of St. Paul's, 1789, and of Chichester, 1792.

[7] Henry Roger Drummond; matr. May 14, 1779, aged 18; B.A. 1783; M.A. 1788; Rector of Fawley, Hants; died 1806.

[8] Charles Sandby; matr. June 22, 1779, aged 18; B.A. 1783; M.A. 1786 (?); Vicar of Swell, county of Gloucester, 1795; of Belton, Leicester, 1807; and Rector of Honeychurch, Devon, 1816.

probably, sojourning in the same town together, our dissimilar avocations have placed us 'far as the poles asunder;'—*They* took the righteous road in life, and have prosper'd;—while I, like 'a reckless libertine,' preferr'd 'the primrose path' to wicked playhouses, and became, in every acceptance of the phrase, *a poor poet.*

Had my rage for scribbling, by the by, broken out before I quitted Oxford, I do not recollect any rival (the Professor of Poetry always excepted) whom I should have encounter'd in the whole University, but POET HARDING.—This man was a half crazy creature, (as Poets, indeed, generally are,) and was well known in most of the Colleges. He ran the Bell-Man hard in composition, but could not come up to him in rank, or in riches; living chiefly upon what he could get from the undergraduates, by engaging to find, instantaneously, a rhyme for any word in the english language;—and, when he could not find, he coin'd one; as in the case of *rimney* for chimney,—which he call'd a *wild* rhyme. To this *improvisare* talent, he added that of personification;—sometimes he walk'd about with a scythe in his hand as Time; sometimes with an anchor, as Hope.—One day, I met him with a huge broken brick, and some bits of thatch, upon the crown of his hat; on my asking him for a solution of this *prosopopœia*,—'Sir,' said he, 'to-day is the anniversary of the celebrated Doctor Goldsmith's death, and I am now in the character of his "*Deserted Village.*"'

While summing up my statement, I forgot to notice a declamatory practice of Lord Wellesley.—His Lordship occupied apartments in the Old Quadrangle, adjacent to mine; being on the same tier of building, although belonging to a separate staircase. Instead of a party-wall, there seem'd to be no intervening materials but canvass, lath, plaster, and the modern papering of our ancient rooms; so that

'thin partitions did our bounds divide.'

In consequence of so slender a barrier, I could not avoid

hearing his Lordship, at times, reciting, or reading aloud, what I conjectured to be the Orations of Demosthenes, and Tully; —these were, I presume, self-imposed exercises of a political Tiro, training himself for publick speaking, and ambitious of the eloquence which he has, since, so happily acquired :—But the medium, slight as it was, through which the tones were to penetrate, was sufficient to prevent me from distinguishing inflections of the voice, or, indeed, much of its articulation;— it was almost *vox et præterea nihil* ;—and, verily, under such obstructing circumstances, his Lordship's utterance did appear to me to be characterized by a most wearing and dismal P. 309. uniformity of sound !—calculated either to irritate the nerves of a next neighbour, or to lull him to sleep. . . .

As the Long Vacation approach'd, I was happy in the prospect of getting into London, although at a time when people of good taste are glad to get out of it. The Capital, even when its inhabitants are beginning to fry, still has charms for a young Oxonian ; and its fascinations for *me* lay in one of P. 310. the hottest parts of its heated atmosphere. . . .

II.

A little before Christmas, in 1780 . . . my father made a Vol. II. halt at Oxford, on his road to Wales, and took me with him P. 40. from Christchurch to Wynnstay,—that seat of festive opulence which so much delighted me. . . . It was late in January, P. 56. 1781, when I return'd from Wynnstay to Oxford ;—whence, in the ensuing Long Vacation, while the Dog Star raged, I revisited the Deserts of London, to enjoy another Summer's suffocation, in my father's theatrical hot-house. . . .

In the autumn of this year, an event occurr'd which pro- P. 61. duced a material revolution in my ' May of Life.'

The Hay-Market Theatre had closed, the Oxford Term was approaching,—when lo ! it pleased my father that I should keep Oxford Terms no more, nor enter London Theatres, for, at least, some seasons to come ;—in short, he banish'd me to Scotland; and sent me to King's College, in Old Aberdeen. . . .

P. 62. ¹ This was a just sentence,—or rather a well-intended parental measure, to remove me from scenes of idleness and dissipation, which not only London, but even Christ Church, presented, to those who sought after them, and into which I had been rushing *con gusto*.

XIX.

LETTERS FROM OXFORD, FROM 1790 TO 1794.

[Perhaps by John Skinner, of Trinity Coll.; *born* 1772; matr. Nov. 16, 1790, aged 18; B.A. 1794; Student of Lincoln's Inn, 1794; M.A. 1797; Rector of Camerton, Somerset; *died* Aug. 12, 1839. (From Bodleian MS. Top. Oxon. e. 41.)]

I.

Letter I.

To William ———, Esq.

For Chambers then I occupy,
Quite neat and roomy by the bye;
Twelve pounds a year must be bestow'd
For furniture:—it is the mode
To pay two thirds of all the sums
The former holder of the rooms
Has thereon spent:—my cost I found
Amounted just to thirty pound;
Twenty of which I may require
When I from College walls retire.
Warren[1] on equal terms has got
Some rooms adjoining to the spot
Which makes it pleasant, lodg'd so near,
To have the friend I most revere:

---

[1] Dawson Warren; matr. Nov. 16, 1790, aged 19; B.A. 1794; M.A. 1799.

P. 13.

Of President[1] we rent the same,
The buildings going by his name.
  Now for our garb—a trencher cap
Cas'd in black cloth, on pate we clap,
Fit emblem that the brains in head
For future trenchers must find bread.
Behind our gowns (black bombazeen)
Are seen two leading strings I ween,
To teach young students in their course
They still have need of Learning's nurse
To stay their steps, their progress guide
And o'er their devious steps preside.
So dress the Commoners:—The great
Proctors and Doctors march in state
With velvet sleeves and scarlet gown,
Some with white wigs so hugely grown
They seem to ape in some degree
The dome of Radcliff's Library.

. . . .

P. 15.

In silk, gay Lords the streets parade,
Gold tassels[2] nodding over head

. . . .

But weak my efforts to describe
The dress of all the motley tribe;
Such nice distinctions one perceives
In cut of gowns, and hoods, and sleeves,
Marking degrees, or style, or station
Of Members free, or on foundation,
That were old Cato here narrator
He must perforce have nomenclator[3].

---

[1] Joseph Chapman, President of Trinity Coll., 1776-1808; Vice-Chancellor, 1784-8. The buildings here alluded to were named Bathurst buildings, after a former President, Ralph Bathurst, and occupied the site on which the President's lodgings have since been built.

[2] The gold tassels of noblemen's caps were not abolished till about 1870.

[3] The slave who attended a Roman *patronus* to remind him of the names of his *clientes* or friends.

But the whole set, pray understand, P. 17.
Must walk full dress'd in cap and band,
For should grave Proctor chance to meet
A buck in boots along the street
He stops his course, and with permission
Asking his name, sets imposition,
Which to get done, if he's a ninny
He gives his barber[1] half a guinea.
This useful go-between will share it
With servitor in college garret,
Who counts these labours sweet as honey
Which brings to purse some pocket money.

. . . .

Enter we next the Public Schools P. 31.
Where now a death-like stillness rules:
Yet these still walls in days of yore
Back to the streets returned the roar
Of hundreds. . . . .
But since their champion Aristotle P. 33.
Has been deserted for the bottle
The benches stand like Prebends' stalls,
Lone and deserted 'gainst the walls,
And lads to wrangling who incline
Dispute at College over wine.

II.

LETTER III.

Description of a day spent in College, during the Winter of 1792.

To WM. P———, ESQ.

Why with such jangling notes and shrill, P. 47.
Like hateful harbinger of ill,
 Resounds that ceaseless bell;

---

[1] A book is still extant among the records of the Barbers' Company at Oxford, in which there is a list of the impositions written out, the price of each, and the undergraduates for whom they were done. The date of this curious paper is about 1810.

P. 49.
> [1] Say Scout, who thus uncall'd dost creep
> Like some foul fiend, to frighten sleep,
> Be quick—the reason tell?

SCOUT.

> Rouse, Master, rouse, and dress in haste,
> The quarter's chime is nearly past,
> Two minutes wants at most;
> I've put your breeches by your head
> And thick great coat have also laid,
> For bitter is the frost.

> There never sure was such a night,
> It froze two inches thick outright,
> On bedside stool I'll leave the light
> And run to Master Cooks;
> But how to reach him I don't know,
> So glib is now the trodden Snow,
> One slides as on the brooks.

P. 51.
> He vanishes:—at once I rise
> Rubbing my dim and misty eyes
> And leap upon the floor;
> But not the coldest marble hearth
> Nor plunge into Carshalton's bath
> Could chill my limbs much more.

> Bell stops:—unjustly blaming Scout
> For stockings turning inside out
> I hurry on my clothes,
> Stiff fingers, bungling much thro' haste
> But more so from the eastern blast
> Which thro' my casement blows.

> With little time to wash or comb
> Slipshod I quit my dressingroom
> And clatter down the stairs.

One instant finds my cap on pate,
My gown o'er coat ycleped great,
  My band beneath my ears.

Now shuffling to the Chapel door   P. 53.
Behind two sloven Students more
  I follow up the aisle;
Displeas'd, good-natur'd Chapman stares,
For nearly half done are the Prayers,
  And Lessons read meanwhile.

With chattering teeth and noses blue
We creep together to our pew
  Responses quavering out;
So cold is all devotion then
That by my faith the best of men
  Scarce know what they're about.

At length the benediction said
The President he takes the lead
  And Fellows follow fast;
Scholars and Commoners behind
Precedence, form, nor order, mind,
  The devil catch the last.

This sketch, dear Will, with flowing pen   P. 55.
I draw, to shew how College men
  Commence the morning here;
Doubtless their more restricted lot,
Yourself at ease, you envy not
  This season of the year.

But to proceed:—Your friend returns
To rooms to see if fire burns
  Or whether water boils;
For now again he must renew
By washing hands, and shaving too,
  Late interrupted toils.

Rolls smoking hot at half past eight
And George and butter on a plate
   The scarecrow Thomas brings;
Laying a napkin passing white
Tea equipage he puts in sight,
   Whilst loud the kettle sings.

P. 57.

Friend Warren takes accustom'd seat,
Pours tea on sugar very sweet
   And cream not over rich;
The rolls he cleverly does spread
Or from brown George[1] toasts slice of bread
   For Warren's always Bitch.

Perhaps, friend Will, you want to know
Why careful Warren's stiled so,
   I'll whisper in your ear:
Here then who 'stead of females take
The office tea and toast to make
   This honour'd title bear.

At half past nine—tea drinking o'er
And cups return'd thro' pantry door
   Our books we take instead;
By turns Virgilian murmurs please
Or thunders from Demosthenes
   Hurl'd 'gainst the Tyrant's head.

P. 59.

This author chiefest of the set
We lecture in to Tutor Kett[2],
   Must therefore come prepar'd:

---

[1] 'Brown George' was the name for a loaf. Samuel Wesley in his poem, 'A King turn'd Thresher,' mentions it:—

    'Here's an honest brown *George* which my Scrip does adorn;
    Here's a true *Houshold Loaf* of the hiew o' my Corn.'

[2] Henry Kett, Trinity Coll.; matr. March, 1777, aged 16; B.A. 1780; M.A. 1783; Fellow until 1824; Bampton Lecturer, 1790; died in 1825. He was author of a book on Logic and other works.

At one, exactly on the stroke,
The time expir'd for sporting Oak,
   My outer door's unbarr'd.

If day prove only passing fair
I walk for exercise and air
   Or for an hour skate,
For a large space of flooded ground
Which Christ Church gravel walks surround
   Has solid froze of late.

Here graceful gownsmen silent glide
Or noisy louts on hobnails slide
   Whilst lads the confines keep
Exacting pence from every one
As payment due for labour done
   As constantly they sweep.

A quarter wanting now of three   P. 61.
On ent'ring gates of Trinity
   For dressing will suffice
As Highland barber, far fam'd Duff,
Within that time will plenty puff
   Of lime in both my eyes.

Speaking of skating I declare
His motions far more rapid are
   Whilst up and down he runs;
At least he thirty has to dress,
Who all at the same instant press
   As clamorous as duns.

Now shrilly pealing kitchen bell
We find a diff'rent errand tell
   To that for morning Prayers;
It dinner, dinner, seems to call,
Enticing Students to the Hall
   By dozens down the stairs.

P. 63.
>Fellows then march in garments sable
>To upper seat yclep'd High Table
> And range them on each side,
>Where Commoners[1] of first degree
>In silk gowns clad, seem equally
> With them in state allied.

>The Batchelors upon the right
>And Scholars Table standing by't
> Are lower in the Hall
>Because some space it does require
>For the large grate and flaming fire
> Which blazes 'gainst the wall.

>Extending from the high rais'd floor
>In length—we count two tables more
> For me and my compeers;
>That is for youths with leading strings
>And sleeveless gowns, poor awkward things,
> Intitled Commoners.

P. 65.
>Our Hall arrangement being said
>We must add too the Griffin's head[2]
> In centre, made of brass.
>For what? you ask—why not to eat
>But for a kind of after treat
> Whilst grosser viands pass.

>Unlike that Griffin Chaucer told
>Who with good Pelican of old
> Convers'd in Ploughman's tale;

---

[1] I. e. Fellow Commoners.

[2] This 'griffin's head,' which is purely ornamental, is a large double-headed griffin—the College crest—on a brass pedestal, which used to stand in the Hall, but was removed, a few years ago, to the Antechapel; it was left to the College long ago by the butler of the period, and bears the following inscription on the pedestal:—

>'Ricardus . Beckford . Promus . D.D.
>Fidelis . in . Paucis.'

For this no Pride nor Popery speaks,
For Monks and Friars no credit seeks,
 Their tricks they now are stale.

For you must know when appetite
Is by repletion vanish'd quite
 And each has had enough,
(As by our seniors we are taught
Much as we can so much we ought
 Of luxuries to stuff.)

'Tis then before concluding grace   P. 67.
Some gownsman rising from his place,
 Whilst servants bustle out,
Towards the Griffin walking slow
To Fellows makes initial bow
 And then begins to spout.

Μηνιν αειδε θεα then
Or verses from the Mantuan pen
 Sound in melodious strains,
Or lines from Milton's Paradise
With emphasis deliver'd nice
 A just applause obtains.

Not that all equally excel
In speaking the narrare[1] well,
 For so the task we name,
As some the lines in cap will read
Drawling like peasant o'er his creed
 Before the village dame.

And here, en passant, I will state   P. 69.
A dialogue we heard of late
 Betwixt Vice Pres. and Chap,

---

[1] Christopher Wordsworth in his *Social Life at the Universities*, p. 119, writes:—
'So in 1792 there was a classical recitation from Homer, Virgil, etc., called a *narrare*, made at Trinity College, Oxon, by some undergraduate standing by the "Griffin's head," while the dons were finishing dinner.'

Who, not a friend to spouting, stood
At Griffin's head in surly mood,
  The verses in his cap.

But not being able to see well
To read them there, much less to spell,
  He silent kept his place.
Silent meanwhile were gownsmen all,
At least five minutes in the Hall,
  Full staring in his face.

He, bless'd with impudence enough
Now smil'd, now look'd grim and gruff,
  At verses now would peep;
Now with cap tassel would he play,
Now turn his body quite away
  From where the Fellows keep.

P. 71.

Moulding[1], Vice Pres., with visage round
As is a cheese of twenty pound
  Or moon in harvest week,
Than these not boasting more pretence
To features emanating sense,
  At length began to squeak:

Why, why, you stupid fellow, why
Are you thus silent, and not try
  Your tongue for to unloose?
Better behaviour, Sir, I beg,
You stand as foolish on one leg
  As any silly goose.

This sharp reproof when Freshman heard
A moment at fat Moulding star'd
  Not knowing what to do.

---

[1] John Bankes Moulding, Trinity Coll.; matr. May 30, 1774, aged 16; B.A. 1778; Fellow and Tutor; M.A. 1781; Proctor 1788.

But slow returning to his seat
He splutter'd out in rage and heat,
  I a'n't more goose than you.

Narrare finish'd—and grace said   P. 73.
Vice Pres. and Fellows take the lead
  And march away to wine.
We in our turn their steps pursue,
Sen. Coms., A.B.'s, and Scholars too,
  Where'er our steps incline.

For now some ten or dozen get
By fore appointment in a set
  To taste inviter's Port;
He glasses, plates, and spoons prepares,
Decanters, knives and forks and chairs,
  But each his own desert.

For with large baskets enters soon
A wily fruiterer styl'd Baloon,
  Who hands around his store,—
Apples and pears, and chesnuts too,
And oranges deck'd out to view,
  With many a bonne bouche more.

Should guest from other College come   P. 75.
Of course the master of the room
  Provides for his supply.
Our inmates carry to account
In fruiterer's book each day's amount
  Of what they taste or buy.

Meanwhile the jovial toasts go round,
The bottles jingle, glasses sound
  As each one drinks his fair;
The Chairman watches, bawls, and raps
Should any fill upon heel taps
  Or his good liquor spare.

At five, the Chapel bell again
Rings a loud peel—but rings in vain
   To move a single guest;
For while delighted they behold
Within all warm, without all cold
   Each loves fireside the best.

P. 77.

Time quickly passes, mirth and song
Do not the heavy hours prolong
   Like misery and woe;
Whilst wit, like fuel in the grate,
Enlivens all, dull care must wait
   Nor note how bumpers flow.

At six, dame Prudence well may see
It is high time to order tea
   If Prudence has her eyes;
But Bacchus, sly enchanter, draws
Her hoodwink'd captive to his laws,
   In short, now none are wise.

For lo! they tea and coffee spurn,
Whilst unsnuff'd candles dimly burn,
   Some hiccough, and some snore;
The Chairman vainly strives to speak
And mouths his English worse than Greek,
   In short, the game is o'er.

P. 79.

At nine, the blinking Scout appears
Whilst most are nodding in their chairs
   And bottles moves away;
For from the kitchen he has brought
What each one sober, might or ought
   T'have order'd in his tray.

Boil'd fowl, salt herrings, sausages,
Cold beef, and brawn, and bread and cheese,
   With tankards full of ale.

The sated guests he with delight
Counts o'er, for this his perquisite
  Is, when their functions fail.

Although in some respects he earns
The solace of these good returns
  For putting them to bed,
As many a curse, and many a kick
And many a pinch, and many a lick
  They give whilst being led.

Hush! hush! cries Tom, across quadrangle   P. 81.
In lanthorn stuck his two inch candle
  The President will hear.
Be quiet, Sir, and come along;
I wish you would not pull so strong
  Nor yet so loudly swear.

Yet my friend Will, you don't suppose
That thus alike all evenings close
  And gownsmen all are such?
No, no! believe me, now and then
They will exceed like other men,
  So did the grave phiz'd Dutch.

Warren and self in gloomy weather
Ofttimes a number get together
  Immediately we dine,
Who sit and chat till half-past five
With jest and song are all alive
  With quite sufficient wine.

Then Crotch[1] and two musicians more   P. 83.
And amateurs near half a score
  To play in concert meet.

---

[1] William Crotch, St. Mary's Hall; matr. 1791, aged 15; Organist of Christ Church and St. John's; Professor of Music, 1797; also Musical Composer and Writer; died 1847.

Our chairs to Warren's rooms we move
And those who strains melodious love
   Enjoy a real treat.

Crotch, as director of the band,
On harpsichord with rapid hand
   Sweeps the full chord:—this youth
Of late thro' Britain's realms was styl'd
The wondrous boy—Apollo's child—
   And such he was in truth.

For when five summers he had told
And scarce his hands a bow could hold
   He Handel's pieces knew;
The time and harmony would note
Not like a parrot, all by rote,
   But as a Master true.

P. 85.   Whilst years increas'd and science more
Augmented still his copious store,
   His genius brighter shone;
By pencil prov'd, and just design
Such knowledge in the graphic line
   As very few have done.

In such a lib'ral age as this
And such a place where merit is
   Or ought to be repaid,
May then his highly gifted mind
Some fost'ring friends, and Patron find
   And thrive in Oxford's shade.

The next performer, Mr. Jonge,
From high Dutch lineage lowly sprung,
   Loud on the fiddle scrapes;
Of ev'ry thing he has a smack
And like a real German quack
   Knows little what he apes.

After Parisian mode of speech P. 87.
French he professes us to teach,
   Italian, as at Rome;
Eke Spanish, Portuguese, and Dutch,
Of Latin too he knows as much
   As many here who come.

This lingo he at least can turn
To profit:—and from Barber earn
   What Servitors erewhile
Daily in College garrat did,
As he of task would soon get rid
   Not heeding sense nor style.

Once they pretend, by way of trick
A gownsman ask'd if Arabic
   Jonge could instruct him in.
Yes, looking big, th' imposter said,
'A fortnight hence, I'm not afraid
   My lectures to begin.

For books directly I'll procure P. 89.
And in that given space I'm sure
   I shall sufficient know;
All languages are much the same,
They differ chiefly but in name
   As I will shortly shew.'

So much for Jonge:—Inchbald the last
(Of those I thus now sketch in haste)
   With fingers large and fat
On his bass viol strums away
And little more can think or say
   Beyond a sharp or flat.

Whilst pause the flute's and viol's sound
The tea and toast are handed round
   Till each has had enough,

   And then brisk punch and lemonade
   May suit, when a full piece is play'd,
    Better than weaker stuff.

P. 91. At half past nine, the supper things
   In order Master Thomas brings
    And puts them on with care;
   For now the cunning rascal sees
   He has a diff'rent set to please
    Than those who tipsy are.

   The cloth removed, some negus sip
   And some regale on hot egg flip
    And some sing catch and glee;
   For each in turn must something do,
   Attempt old songs, or bawl out new
    By way of harmony.

   I wish friend Will that thou wert here
   To give thy favourite hunting cheer
    Or famous Tally-ho;
   Although perhaps the President
   Might start, and asking what it meant
    In haste send up to know.

P. 93. Eleven strikes :—and strangers strait
   Pass to their homes through College gate,
    The Porter lets them out:
   Meanwhile the rest to bed retire,
   Thus ends the day—and your desire
    To know what we're about.

III.

Letter VI.

To ——— Esq.

June 15, 1793.

At Folly Bridge we hoist the sail
And briskly scud before the gale
To Iffley—where our course awhile
Detain—its locks and Saxon pile
Affording pause:—to recommend
The Hobby-horse unto my friend
Our light-built galley: ours I say
Since Warren bears an equal sway
In her command:—as first, in cost
The half he shar'd: himself a host:
Whether he plies the limber oar
Or tows the vessel from the shore:
Or strains the main sheet tight astern
Close to the wind: of him I learn
Patient to wait the time exact
When jib and foresail should be back'd
To bring her round; or mark the strain
The boat on gunwale can sustain
Without aught danger of upsetting
Or giving both her mates a wetting.
We visit Sandford next, and there
Beckley provides accustom'd fare
Of eels, and perch, and brown beefsteak—
Dainties we taste oft twice a week,
Whilst Hebe-like, his daughter waits,
Froths our full bumpers, changes plates.
The pretty handmaid's anxious toils
Meanwhile our mutual praise beguiles:

> Whilst she, delighted, blushing sees
> The bill o'erpaid, and pockets fees
> Supplied for ribbon and for lace
> To deck her bonnet, or her face.
> A game of quoits will oft our stay
> Awhile at Sandford Inn delay;
> Or rustic nine-pins: then once more
> We hoist our sail, and tug the oar
> To Newnham bound: Can books bestow
> One half the joys we truants know
> Abroad?

P. 193.

IV

P. 205.

LETTER VII.

TO THE SAME.

October, 1793.

> Crossing the quadrangle we came
> Right to the river, where a dame
> Hooper yclept—at station waits
> For gownsmen, whom she aptly freights
> In various vessels, moored in view,
> Skiff, gig, and cutter, or canoe.
> Selection made, each in a trice
> Becomes transform'd, with trowsers nice,
> Jacket and catskin cap supplied
> (Black gowns and trenchers chuck'd aside):
> From students lo! see sailors rise
> Who glide like phantoms 'fore the eyes.
> Here to my friend, I point of course
> To our gay yacht the Hobbyhorse
> Moor'd in the stream: then on we wind
> Leaving aquatic sights behind
> And enter soon superb alcove

P. 217.

P. 219.

Curv'd like a vaulted arch above
By jutting boughs: and such 'tis said
First put th' idea in builder's head
Of forming roof to Gothic fane
With slender pillars to sustain
The concave ceiling: as one sees
Bent branches here diverge from trees.
At proper distances are made
Benches for strollers 'neath the shade,
Who may enjoy their noontide walk,
Their exercise, and social talk:
Charm'd with the vista op'ning strait
To fam'd Linnean Sibthorpe's[1] gate,
Whilst Merton's ancient towers between
Midway—improve the sombre scene.

Our circuit here complete, we tend
Our course to Carfax: here my friend
Smil'd at our learning, when he found
From Gallic origin the sound
Deriv'd—since clerks as well as boors
Pronounce it thus from Carrefours[2].

[1] That is, the Botanical (or more properly, Physic Garden. Dr. John Sibthorp was Professor of Botany from 1784 to 1796.

[2] It is now ascertained that Carfax is derived from *Quatuor furcas*, through the older English form carreforc's—furcs; see Dr. Murray's *New English Dictionary*.

XX.

JOSEPH BLANCO WHITE.

[*Born* at Seville, July 11, 1775; educated at the Dominican College, and the University of Seville for the Roman Catholic priesthood; after his ordination he escaped from Spain to England, 1810, where he ultimately entered the Established Church; finally adopted Unitarian views; *died* at Liverpool, May 20, 1841.]

Life of the Rev. Joseph Blanco White, Written by Himself. Edited by John Hamilton Thom. 3 vols. Lond. 1845.

Vol. I.
P. 216.

' I ESTABLISHED myself at Oxford solely for the purpose of perfecting my knowledge of Greek, and extending that which I had of Divinity.

I had made acquaintance with the Warden of New College (Dr. Shuttleworth[1]) at Holland House. Trusting in his good nature I requested him to look out for lodgings which I could make my permanent abode at Oxford. This he very kindly performed. I was soon settled with my small collection of books, very near New College. My removal took place I believe in October 1814. A Scotch gentleman whom I had met, at the house of my excellent friend Mr. James Christie, gave me a letter of introduction to the late Dr. Nicoll[2], who had just taken his Master's Degree. Nicoll, Shuttleworth and the brothers Duncan[3]

[1] Philip Nicholas Shuttleworth, Warden of New Coll., 1822-40; Bishop of Chichester, 1840, until his death, Jan. 7, 1842.

[2] Alexander Nicoll, Balliol Coll.; matr. Dec. 7, 1807, aged 14; B.A. 1811; M.A. 1814; Canon of Christ Church; Sub-Librarian, Bodleian Library; died 1828.

[3] John Shute Duncan, New Coll.; matr. May 5, 1787, aged 18; B.A. 1791; M.A. 1794; Keeper of the Ashmolean Museum, 1823-6; Barrister-at-law, Lincoln's Inn, 1798; died 1844.—Philip (Bury) Duncan, Scholar of New Coll.; matr. July 17, 1790, aged 18; B.A. 1794; M.A. 1798; Barrister-at-law, Lincoln's Inn, 1800; Keeper of the Ashmolean Museum, 1826-54; antiquary, naturalist, and philanthropist.

(those two models of everything that is most amiable and friendly) formed the whole circle of my acquaintance. I had not however been many days in my lodgings before Mr. (now Dr.) ¹ Charles Bishop¹, who had lately returned from Spain, P. 217. called upon me, bringing with him his two brothers, Mr. William ² and Mr. Henry Bishop³: the former already a clergyman, and Fellow of Oriel College; the other an undergraduate at that time, and subsequently a Clergyman. I cannot express the pleasure and advantage of which that visit was the source to me: from that moment to this moment, the friendship of William Bishop and his whole family has been to me a source of the highest gratification. If when proudest of my connection with England I was asked for a sample of the highest worth which the land can produce, I would point to the family of the Bishops, of Holywell, Oxford.

Mr. Parsons⁴, of Holywell, who was then employed in editing the Septuagint, did me also the favour of calling upon me, as a neighbour. . . .

¹ I had been in Oxford about a year when Lord Holland⁵, P. 218. returning from a foreign tour, unexpectedly made me the offer of being tutor to his son and heir, the Honourable Henry Fox⁶. This offer had certainly many attractions for me; but, at that time, I did not think my scholarship sufficient for that situation: I gave this as one of the principal reasons for declining an invitation so honourable and advantageous to me. But Lord Holland was kind enough to insist in a manner

---

[1] Charles Joseph Bishop, St. Mary Hall; matr. Dec. 5, 1816, aged 22; B.A. 1820; M.A. 1823; M.D. 1826.

[2] William Bishop, Wadham Coll.; matr. May 12, 1793, aged 17; B.A. 1797; Oriel Coll. M.A. 1801; Vicar of St. Mary's, Oxford.

[3] Henry Bishop, Oriel Coll.; matr. June 7, 1810, aged 17; B.A. 1814; M.A. 1816.

[4] James Parsons, Wadham Coll.; matr. Dec. 16, 1777, aged 15; B.A. 1781; M.A. 1786; B.D. from St. Alban Hall, 1815, and Vice-Principal; perpetual curate of Newnham and Little Dean, Gloucester, 1800, until his death in 1847.

[5] Henry Richard Vassall Fox, third Baron; born Nov. 1, 1773; died at Holland House, Oct. 22, 1840.

[6] Henry Edward Fox, of Christ Church; matr. Oct. 15, 1819, aged 17; fourth Baron Holland; M.P. for Horsham, 1816-7; died 1869.

which overcame my resistance. I yielded, and, having given up my little establishment, I settled myself at Holland House. . . .

P. 219.   'Restored to my liberty, but in a very bad state of health, I was in great doubt as to the choice of a residence. I might have returned to Oxford; but my not being a Member of the University had been a source of secret mortification while I lived there. I thought at one time of entering my name as an Undergraduate at Alban Hall, of which Mr. Parsons was then Vice-Principal: and in spite of the awkwardness of such a descent in literary rank, I believe I should have submitted to a second pupilage if I had not been called to Holland House. But time had of course increased the ground of my objections, and having no hopes of obtaining a degree, I gave up the idea of living at Oxford. . . .

P. 230.   'As I was now desirous of returning to Oxford, from a con-
P. 231.   viction that no residence was so favourable ' to the prosecution of my labours, I heard with great pleasure that it had been proposed¹ by the Hebdomadal Board to honour me with a degree of Master of Arts by Diploma. This was just what I could have wished, in order to remove the unpleasant feeling which I had formerly experienced at Oxford, arising from my recollection of the time when I belonged to a similar body, and my present exclusion from a body of graduates in the midst of which I was living. But the pleasure which the intentions of the Board had given me was soon mixed up with pain and anxiety. I learnt that an opposition to my degree

¹ 'In a Convocation to be holden on Thursday the 27 inst. at Two o'clock, it will be proposed to confer the Degree of Master of Arts by Diploma on the Rev. JOSEPH BLANCO WHITE, in consideration of his eminent talents and learning and of his exemplary conduct during his residence in Oxford, but more especially on account of those able and well timed publications by which he has powerfully exposed the errors and corruptions of the Church of Rome.

RICHARD JENKYNS,
Delegates' Room,   Vice-Chancellor.
April 24, 1826.'
University Notices, in the Bodleian.

The conferring of this degree was opposed, but was in the end carried by a majority.

was intended in Convocation. Two days elapsed between this notice and the arrival of my diploma—and certainly they were two days of bitterness. As I had not solicited the proposed honour I thought it very hard thus to be exposed to a public affront. Had the opposition succeeded I think I should have left the country. Thus the pleasure which at first filled me with joy was damped by the unfeelingness of party. Under the impulse of the passions which party-spirit sanctifies, even good men will employ the most cruel and unjust methods of forwarding their ends. I have every reason to think that the leader of the opposition had no personal objection against me. He has subsequently shown me all the kindness and hospitality to which he is naturally inclined; and I have accepted his civilities without a shadow of resentment. But this is exactly the evil of party violence: a generous and good-natured man will feel no scruple when he inflicts upon an innocent person severe loss and pain, only because it answers what he believes an important end. Had I been one who had raised himself to wealth and dignity by means of the party whom it was wished to mortify by affronting me—had I even shown an inclination to obtain anything in the Church during the many years which had elapsed since I subscribed the Articles, it might be said, that I must take the good together with the evil. But all that was proposed for me was an honour, which only restored me to a class to which I had belonged from my youth; an honour which I had sacrificed to my love of truth. I might have continued in this negative state and felt unhumbled; but what the opposition intended was a *positive affront* for which I had never received a compensation—if indeed there can be any compensation for dishonour—an affront which, by the confession of the opponents, I did not deserve. It was indeed necessary that time and the general kindness I experienced at Oxford should soften the painful impression which the opposition had made on my mind, before I could enjoy the gratification which I had expected from living there. At first indeed, I scarcely

P. 232.

met any one of whose friendship I had no previous proofs, without suspecting that he might be one of those who had objected to receive me as a fellow-graduate. But I must apologise for dwelling so long on this subject. My apology is one however which none but those who are thoroughly acquainted with ¹ the events of my life can either admit or understand. . . .

¹ In the year 1826, having received a diploma conferring upon me the degree of Master of Arts of the University of Oxford, I was confirmed in the resolution, which I had conceived a short time before, of taking my residence there. I cannot well describe the pleasure I felt upon finding myself again in that beautiful city, not, as before, a stranger to the University, but a graduate member of it, and enjoying all the rights and privileges of a Master. I felt young again, and in the full vigour of my early academical life. My health improved under these pleasurable impressions. Frank, sociable and unambitious of any thing but kindness, though I had been mortified by the opposition which my degree had met, there was now not one feeling of resentment in my breast against the person who prevented the unanimity of the Convocation in my favour. Nor had I any suspicion of the spirit which is not unfrequently found among the *fellows* of colleges, who constitute a kind of Aristocracy among the Masters. (It may be called *Hetairocracy*; a name which, if the state of the University should be thoroughly examined, would be frequently wanted to explain its internal life.) Oriel College, to which I requested admission, was, at that period, one of the most distinguished bodies of the University, and its *Common Room*—the *Fellows*' Common Room, as it is ¹ called, though Masters not on the Foundation may be admitted as members,—united a set of men who, for talents and manners, were most desirable as friends and daily companions. In the Oriel *Common Room* I met with great kindness. I now imagined I had found a home, but this was a delusion, which vanished as soon as I understood the constitution of the CLUB (for the

Common Room is nothing else) to which I had been admitted. I imagined that this admission had placed me upon an equality with the other Members; but it was not so. I found that even a probationary Fellow took precedence of me, whatever might be my seniority as a member of the Common Room. I was, in fact, only to be tolerated. The exceedingly good feeling of the Members who admitted me concealed my inferiority from me, for some time, till I first learnt it from the impertinence of a servant. Under these circumstances, I feared that notwithstanding the unresisting manner in which I submitted to my condition, the evil of it would increase in the course of two or three years, too much to be daily endured. As there is a perpetual change of Fellows, and their vacancies are recruited with very young Bachelors, it was evident that the time would soon arrive when I should find myself much too old indeed for my superiors of the Common Room. I must, however, thankfully acknowledge, that the various individuals who were elected Fellows during the five or six years that I spent as a resident Member of Oriel, treated me with the utmost kindness.[1] But I was in *a false position*: individual good nature could only relieve, but not remove my uneasiness.

I had brought to Oxford the *ideal* of a College—a place for the education of youth, for the improvement and completion of early learning during the vigour of life, and of external repose and internal activity for a few old votaries of knowledge, who, probably in consequence of that devotion, had continued an unmarried life till age had left them with only a few friends or distant connections. To this *ideal* the English Colleges did, in a great degree, answer, a century ago: but they are at variance with it in the present day. I conceive, nevertheless, that if my intellectual character had been in accordance with the *Genius Loci*, I might have found a resting-place at Oxford. But that result demanded a strict dependence on the most bigoted party, which will always govern the University. I began my residence in a state of the nearest approach which my mind could bear towards that party; from feelings which have been stated and explained elsewhere. I had silenced my understanding in favour of the Church of England, but this acquiescence was more an act of devotion than of conviction, least of all was it a voluntary surrender of my Reason: to that supreme faculty I [1] have preserved, during my whole life, its rights unviolated.

A natural consequence of the character and temper of my mind was the intimacy I soon contracted with Dr. Whately [1], a distinguished leader of whatever liberal spirit existed at Oxford. This connection did not prevent my being joined, by affection, with two individuals of a very different tone of mind— Mr. Ogilvie [2], of Baliol, and Mr. Cotton [3], now D.D., and Provost of Worcester College. Their tone of mind and my own were very different, if not opposite; but our *hearts* were in unison, and this was enough for me. We have been separated for some years by the impassable gulph of Orthodoxy; but I feel my heart yearn towards them, especially towards Dr. Cotton, than whom I never knew a more benevolent, upright, and sincere man.

So little sympathy with the governing party could not allow me to take root in the University. If my mind had been working in the direction of the Church, I might gradually have found favour and encouragement; but my thoughts pointed another way. I was truly at home with those who, though Orthodox enough to remain within the Church, were habitually struggling against the mental barriers by which she protects her power. It was therefore evident that I could not *serve* under the Church-and-King banners; and notwithstanding the politeness with which I was treated (two or three Heads of Houses made the only exception,) it was clear that

---

[1] Richard Whateley, Oriel Coll.; matr. April 6, 1805; Principal of St. Alban Hall, 1825-31; Archbishop of Dublin, 1831-63.

[2] Charles Atmore Ogilvie, Balliol Coll.; matr. Nov. 27, 1811, aged 18; Canon of Christ Church, 1849; Vicar of Ross, Hereford, 1839, until his death in 1873.

[3] Richard Lynch Cotton, Provost of Worcester, 1839-80.

I[1] could never hope to receive encouragement as a resident P. 130. Master.

I had solemnly engaged with myself not to accept preferment in the Church; and the publications which rounded my petty income into a comfortable sufficiency had been sacrificed to my theological and academical studies, so that I could not but feel the narrowness of my pecuniary means. Had I had supporters among the leading members of the University, it would have been easy to employ me in *editing* for the Clarendon Press, which is frequently the *secondary* employment of young men not particularly distinguished for their knowledge. But I was a foreigner, and not brought up at the University. These sources of jealousy (to which even Dr. Whately alludes in his friendly dedication to me of the *first* edition of his admirable work on Romanism[1]) could not be easily stopped: the leading Members might be well inclined towards me, but unless I had been totally *devoted* to their service, they would not have favoured me at the risk of exciting dissatisfaction.

I continued in this kind of neutrality, till the contest about Sir Robert Peel took place in 1829[2]. I was at that time in London, exerting myself in the difficult work of setting up a LONDON REVIEW, which totally failed of success. My first intention upon hearing of the approaching election, was not to vote at all. But a letter from Mr. (now Dr.) Pusey[3], at that time one of the most liberal members of the [1] University, P. 131. decided me to give my vote to Sir Robert Peel. The fury of the *No-Popery* party against me knew no bounds. I suffered greatly in my mind; but satisfied that I was acting properly,

[1] Essays, series 3.
[2] Early in Feb., 1829, Sir Robert Peel offered to resign his seat as Member for the University on the ground that he had felt it his duty as a Minister to recommend to the King some concessions of political status to Roman Catholics. His resignation was accepted, and a brief but perfervid period of excitement ensued, until on the 27th of the month, Sir Robert Inglis was elected Member by 755 votes to 609.
[3] Edward Bouverie Pusey, Fellow of Oriel, 1823–9; Canon of Christ Church and Regius Professor of Hebrew, 1828, until his death in 1882.

I endured all with fortitude. One of the secondary reasons which moved me to appear at the Election, was the wish to assert my right to vote as a *British subject*, though born abroad. I have always been very jealous of a privilege, which if I had remained neutral, most people would have doubted. My right of voting was examined by the two lawyers, who acted as assessors at the Poll, and was found incontestable. In company with my friend, Mr. Senior [1], I went to Oxford. I found the place in the utmost excitement, and, as it might be fully expected, had to endure the insolence of one or two, the killing looks of many, and the coldness of former friends, who were for the No-Popery Party. In this party I found, to my great surprise, my dear friend Mr. Newman [2], of Oriel. As he had been one of the annual Petitioners to Parliament for Catholic Emancipation, his sudden union with the most violent bigots was inexplicable to me. . . .

P. 132.   [1] Mr. Newman however continued on terms of intimacy with me after I had voted against his Candidate. That Mr. Cotton's friendship would not be diminished by my voting against his party, I was perfectly certain: indeed I know he said, when every one abused me, 'I am sure that only conscientious motives have decided Blanco White.' Valuing as I did Mr. Ogilvie, and knowing that he must have deeply reprobated my conduct at the election, I went to his rooms the day after I returned to reside at Oxford, having buried the still-born LONDON REVIEW. I told him I came to ascertain whether he was still my friend. He was cold at first, but

P. 133.   when I had explained to him my motives, his affection returned undiminished. But my separation from the Church put an end to our connection, more effectually than death itself.

I mention these particulars because they will suggest the

[1] See note, p. 227.
[2] John Henry Newman, Trinity Coll., matr. 14 Dec. 1816, aged 16; B.A. 1820; Fellow of Oriel Coll., 1822–45; M.A. 1823; Vice-Principal of St. Alban Hall, 1825; Vicar of St. Mary the Virgin, Oxford, 1828–43; seceded to Rome, 1845; Cardinal 1879; died 1890.

state of my feelings during the remainder of my residence at Oxford, more effectually than any description. I still had friends, but the mass of the senior members of the University preserved a scowl which I could not well endure. My health grew worse, and when Dr. Whately [1] left Oxford for his See of Dublin, I was so ill that I did not go out of my rooms for several months. But enough of external matters.

[1] In 1831.

XXI.

THOMAS FROGNALL DIBDIN.

[*Born* at Calcutta, 1776; matr. at St. John's Coll. 17 Jan. 1793, aged 16; B.A. 1801; M.A. 1825; of Lincoln's Inn, 1794; *died* 18 Nov. 1847.]

Reminiscences of a Literary Life. By Thomas Frognall Dibdin, D.D., 2 vols. Lond. 1836.

Vol. I.
P. 78.

> 'I NEVER hear the sound of thy glad bells,
> Oxford, and chime harmonious, but I say,
> (Sighing to think how time has worn away),
> Some spirit speaks in the sweet tone that swells,
> Heard, after years of absence, from the vale
> Where *Cherwell* winds.' BOWLES.

How sweetly and how truly do these 'speaking' verses describe the exact emotions of my heart! Forty-two years have passed away since I put on the freshman's gown—yet on every revisiting of ALMA MATER, there should seem to be some secretly-stirring spirit, which if it gently chide me for hours neglected, and studies shunned, still assures me that I have not lived altogether an unworthy or unprofitable Son. There is, and ever will be, an unspeakable pleasure, as well as a defensible pride, in this declaration. Peace to the spirits of such, who have revisited the ivied walls and grey battlements of EITHER university with emotions less honourable and consoling! I was matriculated an independent member and commoner of St. John's College during the vice-chancellorship of *Dr. Wills*[1]; a name that merits to be enrolled among those of the later 'WORTHIES of the University. Dr. Dennis[2] was the then president of the college. I had the slightest

P. 79.

---

[1] John Wills, Warden of Wadham Coll.; Vice-Chancellor, 1792–96.
[2] Samuel Dennis, President of St. John's Coll., 1772–1795.

possible knowledge of him; as, in those days, the distance between an independent freshman and the head of the college was great, unless an immediate approach was to be obtained through the medium of a letter of introduction. I had nothing of the sort; and why St. John's College was selected for me, neither my late master nor myself were ever able to ascertain. The introduction to the tutor, the Rev. Michael Marlowe[1], was one that afforded me the ' sincerest pleasure. P. 80. He was a gentleman and a scholar, uniting great diffidence with undoubted attainments. His conduct towards me, from first to last, was uniformly that of a sensible and kind-hearted man. In the third year of my residence, he succeeded to the presidentship, on the death of Dr. Dennis, by the unanimous votes of the Fellows. I regretted that, as a commoner, I had no vote to bestow, or he should have had a dozen from me, had I the means of giving them. On his election, the whole college (dependent and independent members) went *en trein*[2] to do homage to Christ Church. I thought this a very humbling piece of vassalage.

[1] Michael Marlow, Scholar and Fellow of St. John's Coll., afterwards President, 1795, until his death, Feb. 16, 1828. 'The first interview with Dr., then Mr. Marlowe, was short; but civil and decisive. One thing has ever since struck me. Dr. M. told Dr. Greenlaw that he thought I might maintain myself very respectably as a commoner for £120 per annum. To be sure, in those days port wine was to be had of Mr. Sims for £1 5s. per dozen. Claret was utterly unknown at any table.' [*Dibdin's note.*]

[2] 'We were received by the dean and chapter, as I supposed it to be, in full costume and formality. Dr. Cyril Jackson (than whom few men could dress themselves in the robes of authority with greater dignity and effect) was the Dean. What took place I know not; but we returned in rank and file, as we had issued out. In due course, the whole college was regaled with a sumptuous dinner by the newly-elected president, who came to our several common-rooms for drinking wine, to pledge us, and to receive in return the heartiest attestations of our esteem and respect for him—the masters by themselves, the bachelors by themselves, and scholars and commoners each in their particular banqueting room. I remember one forward freshman shouting aloud on this memorable occasion, as the new president retreated,

"Nunc est bibendum; nunc pede libero
Pulsanda tellus!" [Horace, Od. L xxxvii. 1-2.]

The stars of midnight twinkled upon our orgies: but this was a day *never to come again.* Dr. Marlowe sat thirty-three years in the president's chair of St. John's College.' [*Dibdin's note.*]

P. 81.   I had scarcely entered upon my studies, or joined my class, before I began to be conscious of my ¹ comparative backwardness; or rather of my premature entrance upon COLLEGE LIFE. Two years of stiff and steady discipline with a private tutor should have preceded it. The want, too, of an education at a *public school* was fancied to be felt; but my tutor, often seeing my misgivings and anxieties, spared me as much as possible. I always took pains before going up, and fancied I could master Herodotus and Xenophon with comparative ease; Demosthenes and Longinus required closer grappling with. Still all these lectures had only the air of schoolboy proceedings: nothing lofty, stirring, or instructive was propounded to us. There were no college prizes; and lecture and chapel were all that we seemed to be called upon to attend to. After lecture, the day was our own; and oh! what days were these.

Boating, hunting, shooting, fishing—these formed, in times of yore, the chief amusements of the OXFORD SCHOLAR. They form them now, and will ever form them; being good, and true, and lawful amusements in their several ways, when

P. 82.   partaken of in moderation. ¹ But who shall describe the inward glow of delight with which that same scholar first sees the furniture of his rooms as his own—and his rooms, a sort of castle, impervious, if he pleases, to the intruding foot! Everything about him begets a spirit of independence. He reads—he writes—he reposes—he carouses, as that spirit induces. All that he puts his hand upon, is his own. The fragrant bohea, the sparkling port; the friends, few or many, which encircle him; while the occupations of the past, and the schemes for the coming day, furnish themes which alternately soothe and animate the enthusiastic coterie. The anticipations of the morrow keep the forehead as smooth and the heart as warm as when the day of sport and of pastime has closed. There can be no let or hindrance. A lecture, which occupies a class only one hour, is as an intellectual plaything. It is over, and half the college is abroad; some few to wend their solitary steps 'where the harebells and violets blow,' and to return upon the bosom of Isis beneath the trembling radiance of the moon :—after having visited the ruins of Godstow, or entered the sacred antiquity of Iffley.

But I am dealing in generals, when, to be instructive, I ought perhaps to particularise. It was ¹ some time, and not till after keeping two or three terms, that I began to adopt what is called a systematic ¹ course of reading; the love of liberty, or rather of unrestrained recreation, having kept me previously very much out of college. Abingdon, Blenheim, Newnham,—in short, a new world, with a new set of ideas! But I had usually a pocket companion in the shape of a volume of English poetry or the drama. I had purchased Bishop Newton's Milton, Warburton's Pope, and Theobald's Shakspeare: but none took a stronger hold of me, in those days, than THOMPSON; and I loved his *Castle of Indolence* beyond measure. Of his Seasons, *Spring* was my ¹ favourite—and how natural the preference! How many 'summer suns' have 'rolled unperceived away' while, in the deepening glooms of Bagley Wood, or near the magnificent expanse of water at Blenheim, I have been seated with some one of the above authors in my lap! The *future* had nothing, then, so entirely rapturous as the *present*.

At length a sort of literary ambition began to be stirring within me. It was in the power of every one to row, sail, hunt, shoot, and fish; but to 'build the lofty rhyme,' to store the memory with deeds of other days, to think, speak, and write well, were objects which seemed to me to be of a more exalted and commanding cast of character. Still I was thrown upon myself and my own resources: there was no common link of sympathy. In my fellow-collegians, with some very few exceptions, I discovered no very obvious sparks or indications of a desire to strike out of the ordinary routine. But if I sought solitude, I found instruction in the society of those 'who speak without opening their mouths, and who chastise without the infliction of stripes.' Two works, at this ¹ crisis, con-

P. 83.
P. 84.
P. 85.
P. 86.
P. 87.

tributed, instantly and most effectually, to fasten me to my seat, and make me a constant inmate of college. These were Boswell's *Life of Johnson* and D'Israeli's *Curiosities of Literature*. Although composed of wholly opposite materials, they affected me in nearly the same degree. With Johnson and Boswell I used to sit hour after hour, and day after day, in our *groves* or *gardens*—a very paradise of their kind. I seemed to be one, however insignificant, of the circle described; and never knew how to admire sufficiently the masculine understanding, the vigorous reasoning, and colloquial eloquence, of the great sage of Litchfield. D'Israeli was the companion of my evening hours and lone musings beyond midnight. I once saw the gothic battlements outside my window streaked with the [1] dapple light of the morning, as I retired to rest closing 'the *Curiosities of Literature*.' I was always equally surprised and delighted to see from what sources the 'curious' intelligence contained in this work was derived. Never was truth attired in more attractive garments than in these volumes; and to *them* I owe my early passion for ENGLISH PHILOLOGY—a passion, which can only cease with my existence.

I loved history exceedingly; and, strange to say, took a violent affection for *Rushworth's Collections*, as a portion of that of our own country. Beyond measure was I pleased with that historian's account of the reign of James I., and the developement of [1] the intrigues of Gondomar and Buckingham, in negociating the marriage of Charles with the Infanta [1] of Spain. But Henry's[1] history was the sort of 'Hortus Adonidis' from which I strove to gather ripe and unperishing fruit. He was always on my *table*; and when I could, his authorities were by the side of him. Hume was my *sofa* companion; but his reign of Elizabeth (which I believe to have read through four times at the least) has always struck me as a piece of composition scarcely to be equalled. It is also very carefully got up on the score of authorities; while all the author's

---

[1] Dr. Robert Henry (d. 1790), author of the History of Great Britain.

Tudorian propensities and attachments are most adroitly interwoven in the narrative and reasonings of the text. Strange as may seem the juxta-position, yet *Burton* and *Gibbon* were frequently lying upon the same sofa or table. From causes utterly remote from each other, I loved these authors alike in respect to steadiness of attachment—although Gibbon always commanded a more consecutive attention and a more frequent reflection. The latter, in his 'Account of his Life and Writings,' was among the most winning of authors; and in his 'Decline and Fall' seemed to be the most dignified and instructive of historians. I read him, in the last mentioned work, with such authorities as I could muster together; but what was a lad of eighteen to do with the 'Body of the Byzantine Historians'? The shelves of the college library afforded, I believe, about one half of their number, but who could encounter such a phalanx as a matter of mere amusement?

Still there was something wanting, as I mellowed down towards the third year of my standing, to render a COLLEGE LIFE thoroughly congenial and satisfactory. College exercises were trite, dull, and uninstructive. The University partook of this distressing somnolency. There seemed to be no spur to emulation and to excellence. Whatever was done, was to be done only by means of private energy and enthusiasm. The STATUTES were at that time a sort of *caput mortuum*; and yet the members of the University were taught to view and to estimate them as the ancient Roman was taught to look upon the Rubicon, the sacred boundary of his confine—beyond which it was sacrilege to pass. The beadles paraded in rustling silks and glittering maces to St. Mary's, to the Divinity School, and to the Theatre. Sermons were preached, degrees conferred, commemorations celebrated; gaudies, or college anniversary festivals, went their joyous and spirit-stirring rounds; and dinners and deserts were at once plentiful and expensive. But, taking one day and one term with another, there was a sort of 'dull, aching void,' which, with young men of aspiring notions and ardent imaginations, nothing could thoroughly compensate or reconcile. The laws of the university were as the heavy sedge, or sea-weed, which only [1] encumbered exertion and darkened hope. Talents like those of Canning or of Copleston would doubtless have burst every 'searment'; but the aliment of an ordinary understanding required treatment of a more intelligible and invigorating nature. There was, as before intimated, plenty of private or individual energy, which only wanted sympathy or encouragement to break forth into public distinction; but the arms of *Alma Mater* dared not then embrace or cherish the hopes of her offspring. She might have commended the zeal, but she had neither the wisdom nor the spirit to 'move one finger' in giving it a right direction.

At length an experiment was made to break through all this miserable thraldom and melancholy state of things. Several members of several colleges (in the number of whom I was as proud as happy to be enlisted) met frequently at each other's rooms, to talk over and to concoct a code of laws, or of regulations, for the establishment of a society to be called a '*Society for Scientific and Literary Disquisition.*' It comprehended a debate and an essay, to be prepared by each member in succession, [1] studiously avoiding, in both, all topics of religious and political controversy. There was not the slightest attempt to beat down any one barrier of university law or regulation throughout our whole code. We were to meet in a hired room, at a private house, and were to indulge in our favourite themes in the most unrestrained manner, without giving ingress to a single stranger. Over, and over again, was each law revised, corrected, and endeavoured to be rendered as little objectionable as possible. At length, after the final touches, we demanded an interview with the vice-chancellors and proctors; and our founder, WILLIAM GEORGE MATON [1], of Queen's College, Messrs. STOD-

---

[1] William George Maton, Queen's Coll., matr. 1 July, 1790, aged 16; B.A. 1794; M.A. 1797; Physician extraordinary to the Queen; died 30 March, 1835.

DART[1], WHITELOCK[2], FALCONER[3], (of Christ Church, Queen's, and Corpus colleges) were deputed to meet the great men in office, and to report accordingly.

Dr. Wills was then vice-chancellor, of whom some slight mention has been already made. He received the deputation in the most courteous manner, and requested that our laws might be left with him, as much for his own particular and careful examination as for that of other heads of houses or officers whom he might choose to consult. His request was readily and as courteously complied with; and a day was appointed when the answer of the oracle might be obtained. In about a week, according to agreement, the same deputation was received within the library of the vice-chancellor, who, after solemnly returning the volume (containing the laws) into the hands of our worthy founder, addressed them pretty nearly in the following word[s]. '*Gentlemen, there does not appear to be anything in these laws subversive of academic discipline, or contrary to the statutes of the university—but* (ah, that ill-omened 'BUT!') *as it is impossible to predict how they may operate, and as innovations of this sort, and in these times, may have a tendency which may be as little anticipated as it may be distressing to the framers of such laws, I am compelled, in the exercise of my magisterial authority, as vice-chancellor, to interdict your meeting in the manner proposed.*' The deputation was not altogether unprepared for such a reply; as there had been previously frequent conferences between the Dean of Christ Church[4] and Dr. Wills, and the former was somewhat prone to consider *innovation* and *revolution* as synonymous.

There was, therefore, but one result to adopt—one choice

P. 96.

P. 97.

P. 98.

---

[1] John Stoddart, Christ Church, matr. 25 Oct. 1790, aged 17; B.A. 1794; knighted July, 1826; died Feb. 1856.

[2] William Whitelock, Queen's Coll., matr. 11 July, 1789, aged 20; B.A. 1793; M.A. 1797; Fellow until 1823; died 1836.

[3] Thomas Falconer, Scholar of Corpus, matr. 22 Jan. 1788, aged 16; B.A. 1791; M.A. 1795.

[4] Cyril Jackson, Dean of Christ Church, 1783–1809; died 1819.

left: and that was, to carry the object, so dear to our hearts, into effect within our private apartments, in rotation. There we might discuss, debate, and hear essays read *ad infinitum*; and, accordingly, our first meeting took place in Queen's College, at the rooms of our founder, afterwards so long and so well known in the medical world as Dr. MATON. Our society was quickly enlarged; and the present BISHOP OF LLANDAFF [1], then a student of Corpus College, and the Rev. JOHN HORSEMAN [2], afterwards a tutor in the same college, were enrolled members. The two MONCRIEFFS [3] of Baliol were [ ] also among our earlier acquisitions; and some gentleman-commoner of Trinity College (whose name I have forgotten) together with my oldest, and among my most valued friends, Mr. BARWIS [4] of Queen's, Mr. Gibson [5] (afterwards called Riddell) of Worcester, [ ] and George F [6] . . . of Lincoln—all united to give strength and respectability to our association. Our meetings were frequent and full. The essays, after having been read, were entered in a book; and I am not sure whether, at this very day, such book be not in existence. The subjects of debate usually were, as of old they ever have been, whether the merits or demerits of such a character (Cæsar or Queen Elizabeth, for instance) were the greater? Or whether the good or evil of such a measure, in legislation or in politics, be the more predominant? Of our speakers, the elder Moncrieff, and George F . . . of Lincoln were doubtless the most fluent and effective; especially the

[1] Edward Copleston, Scholar of Corpus; Provost of Oriel; Bishop of Llandaff, 1826; died 1849, aged 72.

[2] John Horseman, Corpus Christi, matr. 30 March, 1792, aged 16; B.A. 1795; M.A. 1799; Vicar of Little Chishall.

[3] William Moncreiff, son of Henry, of Cavil, Fife; Balliol Coll., matr. 20 March, 1793, aged 17; B.A. 1797; M.A. 1799; Barrister-at-law.—James Moncreiff, son of Henry, of Edinburgh; Balliol Coll., matr. 30 Nov. 1793, aged 17; B.C.L. 1800; Lord of Sessions and Justiciary until his death in 1851.

[4] John Barwis, Queen's Coll., matr. 16 May, 1793, aged 17; B.A. 1797; M.A. 1800.

[5] James Thomas Gibson, Worcester, matr. 5 July, 1792, aged 19; B.A. 1796; M.A. 1798.

[6] George Forster, matr. 6 June, 1791, aged 17; B.A. 1795; M.A. 1798.

latter, who had a fervency of utterance which was at times surprising. But the younger Moncrieff, in course of time, followed his brother, '*passibus æquis.*' Taking the art of speaking and the composition of an essay together, I think Mr. (now Sir John) STODDART of Christ Church beat us all. He was always upon his legs, a fearless opponent; and in the use of a pen, the most unpremeditating and successful. There were other members, of varying shades of merit, but I have forgotten their names. It is well to be able to particularise so much upon a subject brought to recollection after the lapse of upwards of forty years.

Meanwhile, the fame of our club, or society, began to be noised abroad; and those who felt no inclination to write essays, or to impose upon themselves the toil of reading and research for the purpose of making a speech, were pretty free in using sneering epithets, and in stigmatising by nick-names. There was, however, ONE nick-name which we instantly and courageously took to ourselves and adopted—and that was, the LUNATICS. Mad, indeed, we were, and desired so to be called—if an occasional deviation from dull and hard drinking, frivolous gossip, and Bœotian uproar, could justify that appellation. But let us hold the scales with an even hand, and ask what *weight* is NOW attachable to the names of our opponents and our deriders? A seed was sown—small, indeed, in itself, and perhaps slightly covered with earth—which has since grown up and expanded into a goodly tree, bearing perennial fruit; and when the fame of the ACADEMICS is known and admitted in London, let it not be forgotten that it is a *graft* upon this LUNATIC Society of Oxford. Nor must we conceal the truth, that, remotely and indirectly, the university *itself* was eventually benefited by the spirit engendered by such a society. I seem to trace the correction, and reconcoction, of those STATUTES, which were almost an insult to common sense, and a bar to progressive improvement—a very compound of monkish absurdity and puerile discipline — to the spirit awakened by the CONCLAVE OF LUNATICS. The same hand, 'which adorned everything that it touched,' both in that society and in either rostrum of the theatre[1], became busied, some dozen years afterwards, in the remodelling of the statutes in question; and, yet later, in throwing a seven-bull-hided shield over the University, against missile weapons of attack of no common manufactory. Oxford would be the most ungrateful of mothers if she did not bestow marks of peculiar favouritism upon this, her distinguished child. But may it be gently asked, and the question forgiven in asking,

'Why did he QUIT the studious cloister's pale?'

Two public events, of a very different but equally stirring nature, occurred during my undergraduateship at Oxford, which it may not be irrelevant to notice. The one was, the *Encænia* of the Duke of Portland[2] (on the death of Lord North or the Earl of Guildford) as Chancellor of the University; the other, the illumination of the whole town and the colleges, on the victory obtained by Earl Howe over the French, at sea, on the 1st of June, 1794. The first of these events, to a freshman, was likely to be of a most attractive description, and will never be wholly forgotten; although its splendor has well nigh faded away in the remembrance of the recent and more magnificent Encœnia of the Duke of Wellington[3]. London, in both instances, should seem to have emptied itself of its beauty and fashion. The brow of the tutor relaxed; the imposition no longer issued from head-quarters; logic and lectures were non-entities; Dun Scotus and Ockham were beaten with stripes, and Æschylus and Thucydides interdicted from opening their lips. It was all joy, all festivity, all delirium. The heart as well as the body seemed to be abroad. The graceful drapery of damsels was

---

[1] Edward Copleston (see p. 220) wrote the Latin prize poem in 1793, and in 1796 the English Essay. The rostra are the pulpits on either side of the Sheldonian Theatre, from which the prize poems and essays are delivered.

[2] See p. 151.

[3] In 1834.

seen to be gliding in those cloisters, or along those lawns, where, heretofore, the sable academic gown was trailing; while, through the gothic-arched windows, the radiant light of youth and beauty gleamed upon the gownsman and made him doubt the reality of the view. Meanwhile, the theatre is heavily besieged by the motley press of the young and the old—the countryman and the academic. Woe be to those with encumbered draperies! There is no deference—no distinction. The doors slowly open—the rush commences; screams, shrieks, laughter, shouts, intermingle their stunning sounds; and it is well if, on entrance, the visitor regain his recollection, and preserve his habiliments entire. Speeches, recitals, melodies, and choruses ensue. Degrees are conferred:—handkerchiefs wave, trencher-caps are beaten and split, and huzzas rend the roof!—as a popular candidate for these honours ascends to take his station among the '*Patres Conscripti*' of the assemblage.

The theatre ejects its suffocated occupants, but there is P. 111. no exhaustion; no diminution of excitation. In due course, a concert follows—and who would not be present to catch the spirit-stirring note of Braham, when he pours forth the sublime melody of *Scots wha hae wi' Wallace bled*? Evening approaches; and without knowing whether they have breakfasted and dined, or *not* breakfasted and dined, a sally is made for the ball-room—where anything but *room* rewards the aspirant's toil. Dense is the crowd. The thermometer rushes up to ninety: no matter, the mercury continues to advance, and the crowd to increase. Rents, fractures, loss of ornaments—mimic anger and determined struggle ensue. Everybody bewails the pressure, and everybody is determined to add to it. The chords of Weipart's harp are hardly heard to respond to their master's touch. An attempt is made to astonish by the *waltz* or the *gallopade*. Vain effort! As well strive to beat back the roaring sea ere the last surge is discharged upon the beach. Yet they are all joyous, all satisfied —deprecating the very pressure in which they seem to take delight. Encœnias are luckily not annual; or no physical stamina could encounter them.

P. 112.   ¹ Of a very different cast of character from the foregoing, was the *Illumination*, of which I have made mention, in consequence of the victory of Earl Howe, on the first of June. The country had been in breathless expectation and anxiety about the probable result of that great approaching conflict. Reports of the most idle as well as contradictory nature had gone abroad. At one time our gallant commander had been defeated; at another, he had twenty captured vessels in his wake. At length came *the truth*, and with it the most unbounded acclamation of a grateful country. The night of the illumination happened to be moonlight, but soft, calm, and unclouded; and the very paleness of 'Cynthia's brow,' in high summer, gave even additional picturesque effect to the grey battlements and minarets of the colleges. The candles were thickly placed outside, in fanciful groups, and unmolested by the slightest breeze; and those who remember the effect in the High-street, with its undulating sweep and gentle descent—of All Souls, University, and Queen's colleges—with the churches of All Saints and St. Mary's (which, after the Italian fashion, were also, I believe, illuminated on the outside) must admit that such a spectacle seemed to be altogether hardly terrestrial.

Meantime, a stir, of a very varying nature, soon began to betray itself. Many had sallied forth from foaming bowls
P. 113.   (the expression is Virgil's) and shouted ¹ aloud the names of HOWE and SPENCER! Others sung well-known national airs, as they passed along in hurrying groups. A rocket mounted here, a roman-candle blazed there. The roofs and parapet-walls were crowded by females of every description, who gazed with mixed wonder and delight upon the agitated scene below. The mails and the night coaches appeared at their usual hour. The 'roaring boys of Elysium,'—for they were anything but disciples of Heraclitus—insisted upon taking on the carriages another stage with their own hands.

Ribands (England's 'true blue') were brought forth in immeasurable quantities, wherewith to decorate the horses. Some genuine sons of Comus and Bacchus leapt within, and others upon the roofs of, the mails, determined upon taking *charge of the letters!* There was alternate scuffle, and laughter, and delay; and more than one, or one dozen, of patriotic academicians were not exactly aware of the *status in quo* till they reached the barriers of the metropolis.

But in the midst of this maddening uproar, there were hearts bleeding, and hearts cut in twain. A brother, a father, a friend, or ONE, combining all these endearing qualities, had fallen in the victory. Then it was that silence and sadness induced a different movement—and yet, SUCH was the VICTORY, and ' such the irrepressible exultation of all classes of society, that

'Sorrow, smiling through her tears,'

could not wholly turn away from *some* participation of so unprecedented a spectacle.

But it is time to bid adieu to 'the groves of Academus'; and to wish my beloved 'ALMA MATER' farewell. Yet a gentle word at parting. I have generalised rather than particularised. I have not even alluded to many acquaintances, rather friends, of whom death hath cut off the career when every bud of promise was about to be opened; or, acting a more friendly part, when the next step about to be taken would have involved the individual in misery and ruin. Others again, to one's utter amazement, ' have figured away in parts for which it was hardly possible to have conceived them to have been qualified; and now, that they bear themselves stiffly and proudly, will scarcely vouchsafe to recognise those to whom professions of indelible obligation were once profusely tendered. But this is LIFE; and its *drama* may be said to have begun when the unsuspecting confidence of undergraduateship has worn away. Farewell, *then*, to the plans, and schemes, and associations of early manhood!—

when every morning's dawn was bright, and the most lengthened day seemed to put on its wings of gold, and to fly too swiftly away! Of all the heads of colleges living, when I entered at Oxford, ONE only survives[1]. 'SERUS REDEAT IN CŒLUM.'

There is, however, or there *was*, a place, or street, in this university, 'hight' *Paradise;* and when I add that my future destinies were in some measure [1] regulated or fixed in this spot, the reader will be naturally prepared to *felicitate* me thereon. Sunshine and shade are alternately upon *all* the sons of men. I have felt the former with a grateful heart, but I have tarried longer in the latter: and yet, if I now trod a palace of marble I could scarcely feel such pure and bounding delight as when, in the time of life recorded, I saw those portals [2] open to which my approach was announced by raising the knocker annexed.

[1] Upon the whole, on a dispassionate and honest review of this tender, and, in many instances, trying period of human life, my conscience does not reproach me with the commission of the slightest act whereby, directly or indirectly, the character, comfort, or peace of mind, of any one individual acquaintance was injured or impaired. That I *quitted* college at a period of life when perhaps I ought to have *entered* it, may probably be admitted by many; but the die was cast, and the time is now gone by never to be recalled. Yet THAT TIME leaves no leaden weight upon the conscience for its abuse. With a limited income, and rather a large and miscellaneous acquaintance, I contrived not only to *buy* books, but to devote leisure to their *perusal*. I joined in the more manly and cheap exercises of the day, but studiously avoided those amusements which entailed a heavy expense, or tore up the constitution by the roots. If I could sometimes rise

---

[1] Martin Joseph Routh, President of Magdalen Coll., 1791-1855, is here alluded to.
[2] The 'portals' here alluded to, and of which Dibdin gives a sketch in his *Lit. Remains*, are still standing in Paradise Street, No. 22.

with the lark for a day's disporting upon the glassy surface of Isis, I could at others shut myself up in 'my den' for a week's consecutive hard reading, diversified by drawing, and an evening's ramble to Headington.

If, since I have taken my part upon this great THEATRE OF LIFE I have not been distinguished as filling a prominent character, I cannot yet allow myself to be classed amongst those who have had a merely mechanical part to perform, or who have exhibited the ingratitude and wrong-headednesses of such sons of 'Alma Mater' as are recorded in the quaint P. 118. verses of honest James Howell, the author of *Londinopolis*. As to the present scholastic discipline of the university, I P. 119. pretend not to say one word upon it; although, that it is capable of still greater extension and improvement, can scarcely be denied. The lectures of Dr. Buckland[1] form an æra in that discipline; and those of Mr. Senior[2] are not less entitled to notice and commendation. In the time of the 'Lunatics,' had such men sprung up to enlighten their brethren, the doors of all public buildings would have been shut upon their admission for so praiseworthy an object.

It remains only to say, although I had passed my examina- P. 120. tion (taking up Callimachus, Tacitus, and Juvenal) I left the university without taking my degree of B.A. till four years after I had quitted; and in 1825 took my present degree of D.D. per saltum.

---

[1] William Buckland, of Corpus and Christ Church; matr. 1801; Professor of Mineralogy, 1813-56, and of Geology, 1818-56; Dean of Westminster; died 1856.

[2] Nassau William Senior, of Magdalen; matr. 1807; Professor of Political Economy, 1825-30, and 1847-52; died 1864.

XXII.

HENRY FYNES CLINTON.

[*Born* January 14th, 1781; *died* October 24th, 1852; educated at Southwell and Westminster.]

Literary Remains of Henry Fynes Clinton, Esq., M.A. Lond. 1854. 8º.

ON April 6, 1799, my father accompanied me to Oxford; and in the evening we were introduced to Dr. Cyril Jackson, the Dean of Christ Church; with whom we found in his library Marsh[1], my future tutor, and Mr. Carey[2], afterwards successively Bishop of Exeter and St. Asaph, at that time Censor of the College, and subsequently the successor of Dr. Vincent[3], as Head Master of Westminster. The next day my father returned to London, and left me to myself. This commencement of my Oxford life was singularly pleasant: I found myself in possession of a new kind of liberty, being for the first time in my life considered and treated as a man. I was surrounded by my former companions and schoolfellows of Westminster, and with these I enjoyed the time at my disposal.

I remained at Christ Church, residing the whole of every term, for seven years and eight months, till December 1806, when a new scene opened upon me.

---

[1] Matthew Marsh, matr. 1788; Canon of Salisbury; died 1840.

[2] William Cary, Head Master of Westminster School, 1801; Bishop of Exeter, 1820; of St. Asaph, 1830; died 1846.

[3] William Vincent, Fellow of Trinity College, Cambridge; Head Master of Westminster, 1788-1801; Dean of Westminster, 1802-15, the year of his death. He was author and editor of several well-known works on classical subjects.

I carried with me to the University a more limited stock of classical reading than ought to have been possessed by a boy of eighteen, who had been ten years subjected to school discipline. But I had conceived a strong passion for literature, especially Greek. My curiosity to read through the Greek historians had been inflamed by the perusal of Mitford's History, and by the praise which he bestowed upon the original writers from whom he drew his materials. Fortunately Herodotus and Thucydides were the first authors that were put into my hands. I admired Demosthenes, though I had only read portions of him. Plato was my favourite. But the most solid literary advantage that I derived from Westminster was a taste for the Greek tragic poets, which was awakened in me by the study of the four plays of Sophocles, and the two of Euripides above mentioned, recommended and embellished by the able exposition of Dr. Vincent.

I was seized, at my first entrance upon Oxford, with the P. 9. desire of collecting books, especially Greek. My ambition was to have a legible text of each, without the encumbrance of Latin versions; for I had imbibed from my old master at Southwell[1] a dislike and contempt for versions, clavises, and all the pernicious helps by which the labour of learning is shortened to the student. He had taught us that the meaning of an author was to be sought by dilligent application to dictionaries and lexicons; that expedients for shortening the labour encouraged the negligent in their negligence; that what is easily learned is easily forgotten. My zeal in the adoption of these principles was such, that I mutilated my books to purify them from the accompanying Latin versions; and I at this time possess Brunck's Sophocles and Aristophanes, and the Euripides of Musgrave, from which I detached and destroyed the Latin versions.

In indulging my passion for collecting books, I often made great mistakes, from ignorance, and from the want of judicious

[1] Rev. Magnus Jackson. [*Clinton's Note.*]

advisers; sometimes purchasing a bad edition at a high price, sometimes parting with a valuable book in exchange for a worse.

My literary zeal was much increased by the conversation and example of two of my companions and contemporaries in particular—John Symmons[1] and John Conybeare[2]. Conybeare had no great depth of learning, for he had not the necessary diligence; but he had quick natural talents, a ready flow of eloquence, and a good taste. He delighted to talk on literary subjects, and had the talent of expressing himself plausibly, with a show of greater learning than he possessed. He had an excellent collection of books, of which he liberally permitted the use to his companions. In these conversations, questions of literature were started and discussed with ardour. I often found my literary inclination increased by his discourses, and by turning over the books which adorned his apartment. Symmons possessed in reality all that learning of which the other could only talk. Having had the advantage of good early instruction, he came to the University with a degree of erudition and critical knowledge of Greek, to which the usual course of academical reading could add but little. His extraordinary faculties, his wonderful memory, his strong relish for the beauties of literature, added to great application, qualified him to rise to the very first rank of critical scholars. The conversations and discussions of Symmons upon Greek literature inspired me with a zeal for those pursuits. We sometimes studied together; and, from the occasional information which fell from him (although information was not willingly given), but more especially from the enthusiasm of his discourses, inflaming me with a desire to emulate him and to acquire the same

---

[1] John Symmons, Christ Church; matr. April 11, 1799, aged 18; B.A. 1803; M.A. 1806.

[2] John Josias Conybeare, Christ Church; matr. June 19, 1797, aged 18; B.A. 1801; M.A. 1804; Student 1800-13; Rawlinsonian Professor of Anglo-Saxon, 1808-12; Professor of Poetry, 1812-21.

knowledge, I derived more advantage than from the instructions of the authorized teachers of the College.

These were my chief associates for almost the first two years of my College life. During this time, however, I was indolent: for the first time in my life I found myself at liberty, and master of my own time, and I abused that liberty. My reading was desultory, and an amusement rather than an occupation. I wandered from book to book in search of striking passages, till at the end of term my required portion of reading was still unprepared; and I was obliged to get it through by a hasty application of a few days or nights.

The first time that I began to study regularly was on the 17*th of January*, 1801, when I commenced the 'Prometheus' of Æschylus, which I read, with the commentary of the German editor, in three weeks. I employed another fortnight upon the 'Seven Chiefs,' which I studied in the same manner and with the same care. I then proceeded to the perusal of Livy for the first time, and finished the first Decade in about six weeks.

During the progress of these studies I removed to Fell's-buildings[1], a situation better adapted for study, in the month of *May* 1801; there I resided from that time till I quitted Oxford. From this period my studies became more systematic, my diligence was greater, and I no longer turned over books for amusement merely. From this period, *January* 1801, I date the beginning of a more useful habit of study and literary occupation. . . . .

1802.

In the spring of this year, I was diligently employed in preparing myself for examination, in the Public Causes of Demosthenes, and in Æschylus, and in the 'Rhetoric' of

---

[1] The range of rooms which used to look on the Broad Walk, on the site of part of the present Meadow Buildings.

Aristotle. My examination took place in the beginning of June. The persons examined were *Parry Jones*[1], *myself*, *Symmons*, *Gahagan*[2], *Heathcote*[3], and *Impey*[4]. The new system[5] had been just established, and we were, I think, the second set that were examined under the new regulations. We all acquitted ourselves pretty well. For myself, the Dean expressed himself satisfied, treated me with ' great kindness, and eventually made me a *student of Christ Church*.

In November, the two * * * were given to me as private pupils. They were exceedingly ignorant; never attempted Greek, and but little Latin. During the two years that they remained (till July 1804) they derived certainly no benefit from my instructions, nor was the office of their instructor desirable. It gave me however a footing in the College, and I became a student in December.

1803.

March 17, I took my Bachelor's degree. The long vacation was passed in Nottinghamshire. . . . Returning to Oxford *October* 15, I was appointed by the Dean private tutor to the Earl Gower[6] (the present Duke of Sutherland). I remained in this charge till June, 1806, three academical years. Lord Gower was a young nobleman of regular habits, disposed to

---

[1] Sir Love Parry Jones (who took the additional name of Parry in 1803); matr. May 8, 1799, aged 17; B.A. 1803; M.A. 1811; a Barrister, afterwards a distinguished officer and M.P.; died 1853.

[2] Henry Gahagan, matr. June 24, 1779, aged 18; B.A. 1803; M.A. 1806; a barrister.

[3] Richard Edensor Heathcote, Christ Church; matr. May 8, 1799, aged 18; B.A. 1803; M.A. 1805; died at Geneva in 1850.

[4] Elijah Barwell Impey, Christ Church; matr. May 22, 1799, aged 19; B.A. 1803; M.A. 1806; Student until his death, May 3, 1849.

[5] This of course refers to the new Examinations with Class Lists begun in 1802. By a statute of 1800, candidates could either offer themselves for an ordinary examination corresponding to our 'pass' in *any* term (as Clinton and his friends did) or in the *Easter* Term for an Honours' Examination.

[6] George Granville Gower, second Duke of Sutherland; born Aug. 1786; matr. at Christ Church, Oct. 21, 1803; B.A. 1805; M.A. 1810; created D.C.L., June 15, 1841; died Feb. 28, 1861.

application, desirous of acquiring knowledge, and was of
attainments very much superior to most young men of rank
who come to the University. As I trust our readings
together were of some service to him, so they certainly were
of advantage to myself in a literary point of view. . . . ¹ We P. 14.
read through the Odyssey, the whole of Thucydides, the
three orations of Æschines, the best orations (that is to say,
the longest) of Demosthenes, and the whole of Pindar.

1804.

In *June*, I experienced new marks of the Dean's kindness,
in being appointed to the *commemoration speech*[1], and in receiving the first Bachelor's prize: Moysey[2] had the second.

The long vacation was passed in Nottinghamshire. . . . In
October I returned at the usual time to Christ Church, and
to my office of assisting the studies of Lord Gower. The two
brothers, my former pupils, had quitted Oxford before the
vacation; but their place was now supplied by Sir James
————, to whom the Dean introduced me as private tutor.
. . . ¹ Between him and Lord Gower my morning hours were P. 15.
pretty well engaged and occupied. . . .

1805.

I had now begun the twenty-fifth year of my life, without
any other views for the future than those which were contained in the profession of a clergyman. I believed myself
destined for an academical life, which was to end in my taking
orders. In *March*, of this year, a new prospect was opened
to me. On the 17th of that month *Mr. Gardiner*[3] made

---

[1] These are allusions to Christ Church customs.

[2] Charles Abel Moysey, Christ Church; matr. June 6, 1798, aged 18; B.A. 1802; M.A. 1805; B.D. 1818; D.D. 1818; Bampton Lecturer, 1818; died 1859.

[3] It would seem that Isaac Gardiner, Esq. here mentioned (who died in 1811, probably at Wing in Buckinghamshire), was the son of a brother of the rich merchant of London, Henry Fynes, Esq., who died unmarried in 1758. Dr. Fynes
Clinton was then the grandson of another brother of Henry Fynes, and accordingly
the great nephew of Mr. Gardiner's mother.

himself known to ¹ my father. He told him, that his nephew being lately dead, he found himself, at eighty-one years of age, without an heir by the father's side, to whom he could bequeath his possessions; that he looked around him for the relations of his mother.... He therefore sought my father, who was the great nephew of his mother, and fixed upon his eldest son as his successor in his landed property....

Mr. Gardiner *particularly stipulated that I should not take orders*. His desire was that his heir should be a country gentleman, and capable of secular employments. My design of taking orders was consequently abandoned. I returned however to my usual literary occupations, and looked upon an academical life as my probable destiny for some time to come.

This year I was examined for the Master's degree, and as a preparation for it, I had employed the Christmas vacation in London in the careful perusal of Sophocles, with the Scholia; and the Easter vacation in reading over the whole of Livy. To these I added Thucydides, who had become familiar to me in the course of my readings with Lord Gower. After ¹ the examination, I passed the first six weeks of the long vacation in London, and at this time began the composition of the tragedy of 'Solyman ¹.' After the latter part of the long vacation at Cromwell, I returned to Oxford, October 14th, and took my Master of Arts degree.

1806.

.. I carried with me to London my brother Clinton ², then a boy of thirteen, and passed on to Oxford on the 21st of January, at the moment when the whole nation were in

---

[1] In 1807, the first year of his parliamentary life, Clinton writes :—'I printed the tragedy of "Solyman," which I brought with me from Oxford nearly finished. It had no sale ; scarcely fifty copies of it seem to have been called for by purchasers.' *Lit. Remains*, p. 26.

[2] Clinton James Fynes Clinton, Christ Church ; matr. May 28, 1811, aged 18 ; B.A. 1814; M.A. 1817 ; subsequently Barrister-at-law and M.P. for Aldborough, Yorkshire; died 1833.

anxious apprehension of the death of Mr. Pitt[1], whose recovery was then declared hopeless. I continued in the charge of my two pupils till the month of June, when Lord Gower quitted the University. The last books that we read together were Pindar, and the 'Rhetoric' of Aristotle. Our last literary interview was on the 20th of June; I took my leave of him with sentiments of regret and esteem.

' After the vacation had commenced I remained at Oxford till the 12th of July, engaged in the study of the Orators, in Reiske's edition. Among other parts of the collection I read Andocides, and a great part of Lysias. On the 12th of July I returned to Cromwell for the last long vacation. . . .

On the 17th of October I returned to Oxford. There I resumed my academical occupations with Sir James ———, now my sole pupil. I had already explained to the Dean my reasons for declining to engage any further in the tuition of the college, and he had taken my resolution in good part, and was satisfied with my reasons. But I still looked forward to literary occupations, although not official ' duties, in the University, and was applying my attention to objects of classical study, when about a week after my return I was surprised by a letter from my father, announcing the Duke of Newcastle's parliamentary intentions, and conveying an offer of bringing me in for Aldborough. My father mentioned this as a matter which required no hesitation, and to which there could hardly be imagined an objection; and that he had therefore accepted the proposal for me. Accordingly, on the 3rd of November, 1806, I saw myself declared one of the representatives for Aldborough. . . . ' I took my final leave of Oxford on the 15th December, 1806.

' The last two or three years of my Oxford life were passed very pleasantly. It happened at this time that an unusual number of my contemporaries remained resident, as Bachelors; so that I found myself, after taking my degree,

---

[1] William Pitt, second son of the Earl of Chatham; died Jan. 23, 1806, aged 47.

still surrounded by my former companions, without being driven to seek for new society among those who were below me, or those who were above me, in point of standing. It is sufficient for me to write the names of *Jones*[1], *Gaisford*[2], *Impey*, and *Mackensie*[3], in order to recall the memory of many hours pleasantly passed in the enjoyment of cheerful conversation, joint studies, literary discussions, and friendly meetings, in which some part of almost every day was spent. By the society of these four, I found my evil propensities corrected, my habits of regularity confirmed, my better affections improved. There were not a few of the hours which I passed with other companions (who, though very pleasant, were not sober-minded associates) which I remember with regret, and could wish to have been otherwise employed: but I have no cause to repent of any hours that were passed in the society of Jones, Gaisford, Impey, and Mackensie.

Though I had pursued classical learning with zeal, yet, at my leaving Oxford, my acquirements in Greek and Latin were not extensive. I was versed in the *language*, but unacquainted with the *writers* of ancient Greece. Not only the less obvious Greek authors were unknown to me, but many of those who ought to have been in the hands of one who had passed eight years in these studies. I had never heard, for instance, of Dion Cassius; I had never seen Isocrates, or Athenæus, or Pausanias, or Strabo, or Appian. I had not read any part of Plutarch in the original. Among the poets, neither Callimachus, nor Apollonius, nor Theocritus, nor Hesiod were known to me; and fourteen of the tragedies of Euripides were still unread. In Latin, my acquaintance with the chief authors was proportionably limited. Except the

---

[1] Probably Christopher Jones, Christ Church; matr. March 4, 1802, aged 18; B.A. 1805; M.A. 1808.

[2] Thomas Gaisford, Christ Church; matr. Oct. 26, 1797, aged 17; Student, 1800-16; B.A. 1801; M.A. 1804; Regius Professor of Greek, 1811-35; Dean of Christ Church, 1831, until his death June 2, 1855.

[3] Rev. Alexander Mackensie, Christ Church; matr. June 12, 1800, aged 18; B.A. 1804; M.A. 1807; died in college, July 21, 1809.

Orations, read at Southwell, I had not studied any part of the works of Cicero. I was ignorant of Quintilian, and Tacitus, and Pliny. I had twice perused Livy with attention; and this author formed the only addition to the stock of Latin which I brought with me from Southwell.

The amount of what I read in Greek in the seven years P 23 and eight months of my Oxford life, between April 6, 1799, and December 15, 1806, did not equal in quantity the *fifth part* of what I have since read in the same space of time,—between April 1810, and December 1817. I went through, at Oxford, about 69,322 verses of the Greek poets, and about 2913 pages of prose authors; making together an amount of about 5223 pages. The course of Greek reading which I had completed in the latter period, estimated, for the sake of a comparative view, by the same scale of pages, makes a sum of 28,887, being almost *six times* the amount of the former quantity.

The few authors, however, which I had read, I knew well; and they were the best. At the time of my leaving Oxford, I possessed the following writers.

Homer . . . verses	27,000	
Pindar	5,560	
Æschylus . . .	8,139	
Sophocles . . .	10,341	pp. 2,310
Aristophanes . .	15,282	
Of Euripides	3,000	
Thucydides . . . . pp.	786	
Demosthenes (harangues and Public Causes) . .	775	pp. 1,832
Æschines .	220	
Lycurgus . . .	51	
Andocides . . .	81	P. 24.
Lysias (half) . . .	100	
Of Plato	500	pp. 1,181
Of Aristotle (Rhetoric, Poetics, Ethics)	500	
	5,323	

(I forbear to add *Herodotus. Polybii* libb. i. ii., *Dionys.*

Halic. Critica Opera, because these were works which, though I often inspected, I did not accurately study.)

By the careful and repeated study of these few works, I had acquired, if not (in the language of Gibbon) 'a deep *and indelible knowledge of the first of languages,*' yet at least such a facility in it as to be able to read any writer that presented himself, without much help from a lexicon: a degree of proficiency which seems necessary in any language before it can be resorted to from choice, as a recreation;—before the study of it can become a *pleasant occupation,* instead of an *unwilling labour.*

I made, however, another acquisition of far greater importance, by applying myself, in the last two or three years of my residence at Christ Church, to the diligent study of the *Holy Scriptures.* I had never been a sceptic: my opinions, if the crude notions of a schoolboy may be called opinions, were those of a believer in Revelation. But I had no sound impressions [1] on religious matters: I easily joined in profane jests and light discourses, and with respect to these subjects was careless, childish, and ignorant. By degrees, time, reflection, more sober society, together with the necessity of making some preparation for the office of a tutor and the profession of a clergyman, brought me to better habits. I read through in order the whole of the Old Testament, devoting every Sunday to this study: I carefully noted down all the passages which prophetically applied to the Messiah. Proceeding then with the Greek Testament, I read St. Paul, with the Commentary of Locke. This course of study produced upon my mind the happiest effects.

P. 25.

1825.

. . . In the University of Oxford, at least, from the mode of conducting the Examinations, the Examiners discourage the young men from applying to a wide range of books. I have it upon the testimony of ―――― and ――――, both well

P. 229.

informed upon the subject (and I can speak from my own knowledge of what was the practice in my time, twenty years ago), that Isocrates, Isæus, Lysias, the Private Orations of Demosthenes, are never read at Oxford; that no part of the works of Plutarch, or of Plato, is studied; none of the philosophical works of Cicero; not Stobæus, not Athænæus, not Arrian; nor Dio Chrysostom, nor Dio Cassius, nor Dionysius of Halicarnassus. Young men, who obtain the honours of the first class, are not only not encouraged to bring any of these authors, but would find a prejudice excited against them, if they did. When this is the state of classical education at Oxford, can we expect in the cultivated classes of England the lofty speculations, or the depth and extent of research, for which the Germans are distinguished; or that we should maintain that rank in literature which we acquired in old times, in the days of Pearson, and Stillingfleet, and Bentley, and their contemporaries?

P. 230.

The Greek language appears certainly to be better studied now at Oxford than it was twenty years ago. When I first went thither, Greek learning was perhaps at the lowest point of degradation. During the seven years of my residence there (four of them as an Undergraduate) I never received a single syllable of instruction concerning Greek accents, or Greek metres, or the idiom of Greek sentences; in short, no information upon *any one point* of Grammar, or Syntax, or Metre. These subjects were never named to me. What I learned was struck out principally in my conversations with my companions Symmons and Gaisford. I lived much with Symmons during the first two years; and associated with Gaisford during the two or three last years of my academical life. These two eminent scholars guided me to the proper sources of information.

XXIII.

REGINALD HEBER.

[*Born* April 21, 1783, at Malpas, Chester; entered at Brasenose Coll., Nov., 1800; elected Fellow of All Souls Coll., 1804; Bishop of Calcutta, 1823; *died* at Trichinopoly, April 3, 1826.]

The Life of Reginald Heber, D.D. By his Widow. Lond. 1830. 2 Vols.

[To E. D. Davenport[1], Esq.]

Hodnet Rectory, Nov. 27, 1818.

'My Dear Davenport,

'. . . . I have myself been at home entirely, with the exception of a week's visit to Oxford, where I found sundry contemporaries grown bald and grave, and met sundry children of my friends in the country shot up into dashing young men. That same place always presents a curious gerometer to people who have long since ceased to be resident; but I do not know that I ever felt it so much before. In some respects, it is whimsically altered from what I remember it, though, of course, the whole outward show proceeds with less visible alteration than the library of Goëthe's grandfather, described in his Memoirs, where everything was so old, and in such good order, that it seemed as if time had stood still, or as if the watch of society had been put back for a century. But in Oxford, notwithstanding this outward monotony, there are certain changes which an observer less keen than yourself would not fail to discover.

[1] Edward Davies Davenport, of Capesthorne, Cheshire; matr. at Christ Church, 1797; M.P. for Shaftesbury, 1826-30; died 1847.

'First, when we remember Christ Church, it was an abso- P. 499. lute monarchy of the most ultra-oriental character; whereas the reigning dean[1] is as little attended to, to all appearance, as the peishwah of the Mahrattas; the whole government resting on an oligarchy of tutor[s], under whom, I think, the college flourishes, at least as much as under the cloud-compelling wig of the venerable Cyril[2]. My own old college is less altered in this respect; but the tutors there, as elsewhere in the university, are so different a race from the former stock, as to occasion a very ludicrous comparison. The old boys never stirred from home; these pass their whole vacations on the continent, are geologists, system-mongers, and I know not what. It is possible that, when we were lads, we rather underrated the generality of those set over us; but I cannot help thinking that this race of beings is, on the whole, considerably amended.

'Of the young men, I do not know that I can say much. The general story is, that they were never so diligent and so orderly as at present; all which is put down to the account of the system of examination. There is really, I think, much less lounging than formerly, which is produced, of course, by the greater frequency and regularity of lectures; but hunting seems practised to a degree considerably beyond our times; and so far as I can learn, in general they worship the same divinities who are enumerated in the Herodotean account of the university.'

Διονυσον και Αρτεμιδα και Αφροδιτην, ἐνιοι δε φασι ὁτι και τὸν Ἑρμην.

'If Bacchus is somewhat less honoured, (of which, from certain sounds which reached my ears during a nightly walk, I have some doubt,) the general change of manners, in this respect, has probably had as much efficacy as any strictness of discipline....'

[1] Charles Henry Hall, Dean of Christ Church, 1809-24; afterwards Dean of Durham till his death in 1827.
[2] Cyril Jackson, Dean of Christ Church.

NOTE A.

To John Thornton[1], Esq.

Oxford, Jan. 15, 1801.

'I AM very much obliged to you, my dear friend, for your kind invitation to Cambridge, and I could wish it were in my power to accept it. I have, however, been so completely engaged, and shall continue to be so, that an absence, however short, from college, will be attended with considerable difficulty and inconvenience. Our meeting must then be deferred till after this term, when I hope we shall both of us be in town.

'I write under the bondage of a very severe cold, which I caught by getting out of bed at four in the morning, to see the celebration of the famous All Souls' Mallard Feast[2]. All Souls is on the opposite side of Ratcliffe square to Brazen Nose, so that their battlements are in some degree commanded by my garret. I had thus a full view of the *Lord Mallard* and about forty fellows, in a kind of procession on the library roof, with immense lighted torches, which had a singular effect. I know not if their orgies were overlooked by any uninitiated eyes except my own; but I am sure that all who had the gift of hearing, within half a mile, must have been awakened by the manner in which they thundered their chorus, 'O by the blood of King Edward.' I know not whether you have any similar strange customs in Cambridge, so that, perhaps, such ceremonies as the All Souls' mallard, the Queen's boar's head[3], etc., will strike you as more absurd than they do an Oxford man; but I own I am of opinion that these remnants of Gothicism tend very much to keep us in a sound consistent track; and that one cause of the declension of the foreign universities, was their compliance, in such points as these, with the variation of manners.

'I have got into a habit of tolerably early rising, which I intend to

---

[1] Heber's schoolfellow during the three years he spent under the care of Mr. Bristow, at Neasdon.

[2] See '*Worthies of All Souls*,' by Professor Montagu Burrows, Appendix II, p. 429.

[3] This is a reference to a custom at Queen's College, where, on Christmas day, a boar's head is brought into the hall, to the accompaniment of an ancient carol.

adhere to; the plan is, that another man, who has been my companion in the course of mathematics which I have gone through, has agreed to read with me every morning from six till chapel, by which scheme we gain two hours of the best part of the whole day. This system must, however, be altered when chapel¹ begins at six, which it does in summer. I do not find "*Euclid de novo*" so irksome as your friend used to think. Though mathematics will never be the great rallying point of my studies, I should be very sorry to be ignorant of them, and that philosophy which depends on them. My class-fellow is agreeable and remarkably clever; though only sixteen, his acquirements and understanding are inferior to few in the college. He is at present a kind of tutor to a man at least five years his senior. Some traits in his manner and character have, I sometimes fancy, an imperfect resemblance to you; and, while they make me still fonder of him, serve to put me in mind of the only cause I have to regret that there are two separate universities in England.

'Term commences next Saturday, or at least the men come up then, as, strictly speaking, it began yesterday.'

The following account of the All Souls' Mallard Feast occurs in a volume of miscellaneous collections of the writings of one Hannibal Baskerville of Sunningwell (MS. Rawl. D. 810), having the following title prefixed: 'A transcript of some writings of Hanniball Baskervile, Esq., as they were found scattered here and there in his manuscripts and books of account.' (17th cent.)

'... Before I leave this Colledge and the good people in it, I must remember their mallard night. ffor the grave Judges have sometime their festivall days, and dance togeither at Sergeants Inn; The Country people will have their Lott-meads, and Parish ffeasts; And schollers must have some times of mirth to meliorate their great sobriety, for

> There is a time
> When wit and wine
> Will tickle the pate with pleasure
> And make one breath
> And vent with ease
> The debates o' the mind at leisure.

As touching the first institution of this Ceremony (which is very ancient saith Mr. Stodman) I cannot give any account of it; but when they have a mind to keep it, the time is always within a night or two of All Souls, then there are six Electors wch nominate ye Lord of the mallard, wch Lrd is to beare the expences of the Ceremony. When he is chosen he appoints six officers, who march before him with white staves in their hands, and meddalls hanging upon their breasts tied with a large blew ribbond, upon ye meddalls is cut on the one side the Lrd of the mallard with his officers, on the other ye mallard as he is carried upon a long Pole.

When ye Lrd is seated in his chair with his officers of state (as above s^d) before him, they carry him thrice about the Quadrangle and sing this song:

  Griffin Turkey Bustard Capon
  Let other hungry mortalls gape on
  And on their bones with stomacks fall hard
  But let All Souls men have the mallard
Hough the bloud of King Edward, by y^o bloud of King Edward
  It was a swapping swapping mallard.

  Stories strange were told I trow
  By Baker Holinshead and Stow
  Of Cocks & Bulls & other quere things
  That were done in the Reignes of their Kings
Hough the bloud, &c.

  Swapping he was from bill to eye
  Swapping he was from wing to thigh
  His swapping toole of generation
  Out swap'd all the winged nation
Ho the bloud, &c.

  The Romans once admir'd a gander
  More then they did their Chiefe Comander
  Because it sav'd if some don't foole us
  The P[lace] called from ye head of Tolus
Ho the bloud, &c.

  The poets fained Jove turned a swan
  But let them prove it if they can
  As for our profe tis not at all hard
  That twas a swapping swapping mallard
Ho the bloud, &c.

  Then let us sing and dance a galliard
  To the remembrance of the mallard
  And as the mallard does in Poole
  Let's dabble dive and duck in Bowle
Ho the bloud, &c.

[The following is a copy of the air to which the above song was sung, as given in the MS., and underneath it is a corrected version.]

The mallard song being sung by one man, all the rest y^t are present bearing the Chorus, when that is done they knock at all the middle-Chambers, where most of y^e Seniors lodge, of whome they demand Crowns a piece (I suppose a forfeiture for not assisting at the Ceremony) wch is readily given, then they go with 20 or 30 Torches (which are allways carried before them) upon the Leads of ye Colledge where they sing their song as before. This ended, they go into their common rooms where they make themselves merry with what wine every one has mind to, there being at that time great plenty of all sorts. When they have there sufficiently refresh'd themselves, to conclude all they go into the Buttery where every one has his Tumbler of Canary or other wine, Then he that bore the Mallard chops of his head dropping some of the bloud into every tumbler, which being drunk off every one disposeth of himselfe as he thinks fit, it being generally day-brake.'

XXIV.

JOHN TAYLOR COLERIDGE.

[*Born* at Tiverton, 1790; educated at Eton; Scholar of Corpus Christi; Fellow of Exeter; called to the Bar in 1819; in 1835 was appointed one of the Judges of the King's Bench; created D.C.L. in 1852; *died* at Heath's Court, Ottery St. Mary, Feb. 11, 1876.

Life of Dr. Arnold, by Arthur Penrhyn Stanley. 2 vols. Lond. 1881.

.... Arnold[1] and I, as you know, were under-graduates of Corpus Christi, a college very small in its numbers, and humble in its buildings, but to which we and our fellow-students formed an attachment never weakened in the after course of our lives. At the time I speak of, 1809, and thenceforward for some few years, it was under the ' presidency, mild and inert, rather than paternal, of Dr. Cooke[2]. His nephew, Dr. Williams[3], was the vice-president and medical fellow, the only lay fellow permitted by the statutes. Retired he was in his habits, and not forward to interfere with the pursuits or studies of the young men. But I am bound to record not only his learning and good taste, but the kindness of his heart, and his readiness to assist them by advice and criticism in their compositions. When I wrote for the Latin verse prize[4], in 1810, I was much indebted to him for advice

[1] Thomas Arnold, matr. Feb. 22, 1810, aged 15; Fellow of Oriel Coll.; Regius Professor of Modern History; Headmaster of Rugby School; died 1842.

[2] John Cooke, President of Corpus, 1783–1823.

[3] George Williams, matr. Nov. 6, 1777, aged 15; Sherardian Professor of Botany, 1796–1834; died Jan. 17, 1834.

[4] Coleridge gained the Latin Verse Prize in 1810, the subject being *Pyramides Ægyptiacæ*.

in matters of taste and Latinity, and for the pointing out many faults in my rough verses [1].

Our tutors were the present Sedleian Professor, the Rev. G. L. Cooke [2], and the lately deceased President, the Rev. T. Bridges [3]. Of the former, because he is alive, I will only say that I believe no one ever attended his lectures without learning to admire his unwearied industry, patience, and good temper, and that few, if any, quitted his pupil room without retaining a kindly feeling towards him. The recent death of Dr. Bridges would have affected Arnold as it has me; he was a most amiable man; the affectionate earnestness of his manner, and his high tone of feeling, fitted him especially to deal with young men; he made us always desirous of pleasing him; perhaps his fault was that he was too easily pleased; I am sure that he will be long and deeply regretted in the University.

It was not, however, so much by the authorities of the college that Arnold's character was affected, as by its constitution and system, and by the residents whom it was his fortune to associate with familiarly there. I shall hardly do justice to my subject, unless I state a few particulars as to the former, and what I am at liberty to mention as to the latter. Corpus is a very small establishment—twenty fellows, and twenty scholars, with four exhibitioners, form the foundation. No independent members were admitted except gentlemen commoners, and they were limited to six. Of the scholars several were bachelors, and the whole number of students actually under college tuition seldom exceeded twenty. But the scholarships, though not entirely open, were yet enough so to admit of much competition; their value, and still more, the creditable strictness and impartiality with which the examinations were conducted (qualities at that time more

---

[1] It is noticeable that it was considered fair that a College Tutor should correct verses intended for public competition as the work of an undergraduate.

[2] George Leigh Cooke, Sedleian Professor, 1810; Fellow of Corpus.

[3] Thomas Edward Bridges, President of Corpus, 1823-43.

rare in college elections than now) insured a number of good candidates for each vacancy, and we boasted a more than proportionate share of successful competitors for university honours. It had been generally understood (I know not whether the statutes[1] prescribe the practice) that in the examinations a large allowance was made for youth! certain it was that we had many very young candidates, and that of these, many remarkable for early proficiency succeeded. We were then a small society, the members rather under the usual age, and with more than the ordinary proportion of ability and scholarship; our mode of tuition was in harmony with these circumstances; not by private lectures, but in classes of such a size as excited emulation, and made us careful in the exact and neat rendering of the original, yet not so numerous as to prevent individual attention on the tutor's part, and familiar knowledge of each pupil's turn and talents. In addition to the books read in lecture, the tutor at the beginning of the term settled with each student upon some book to be read by himself in private, and prepared for the public examination at the end of the term in Hall; and with this book something on paper, either analysis of it, or remarks upon it, was expected to be produced, which insured that the book should have really been read. It has often struck me since, that this whole plan, which is now I believe in common use in the University, was well devised for the tuition of young men of our age. We were not entirely set free from the leading-strings of the school; accuracy was cared for; we were accustomed to *viva voce* rendering, and *viva voce* question and answer in our lecture-room, before an audience of fellow-students, whom we sufficiently respected; at the same time the additional reading, trusted to ourselves alone, prepared us for accurate private study, and for our final exhibition in the schools.

[1] The statutes do not seem to recommend any allowance for age, nor is it likely they should do so.

One result of all these circumstances was, that we lived on the most familiar terms with each other; we might be, indeed we were, somewhat boyish in manner, and in the liberties we took with each other; but our interest in literature, ancient and modern, and in all the stirring matters of that stirring time, was not boyish; we debated the classic and romantic question; we discussed poetry and history, logic and philosophy: or we fought over the Peninsular battles and the Continental campaigns with the energy of disputants personally concerned in them. Our habits were inexpensive and temperate: one break-up party was held in the junior common room at the end of each term, in which we indulged our genius more freely and our merriment, to say the truth, was somewhat exuberant and noisy; but the authorities wisely forbore too strict an inquiry into this.

It was one of the happy peculiarities of Corpus that the bachelor scholars were compelled to residence. This regulation, seemingly inconvenient, but most wholesome as I cannot but think for themselves, and now unwisely relaxed, operated very beneficially on the under-graduates; with the best and most advanced of these they associated very usefully: I speak here with grateful and affectionate remembrance of the privileges which I enjoyed in this way.

You will see that a society thus circumstanced was exactly one most likely to influence strongly the character of such a lad as Arnold was at his election. He came to us in Lent term, in 1811, from Winchester, winning his election against several respectable candidates. He was a mere boy in appearance as well as in age; but we saw in a very short time that he was quite equal to take his part in the arguments of the common room; and he was, I rather think, admitted by Mr. Cooke at once into his senior class. As he was equal, so was he ready to take part in our discussions; he was fond of conversation on serious matters, and vehement in argument; fearless too in advancing his opinions—which, to say the truth, often startled us a good deal; but he was ingenuous and candid, and though the fearlessness with which, so young as he was, he advanced his opinions might have seemed to betoken presumption, yet the good temper with which he bore retort or rebuke, relieved him from that imputation; he was bold and warm, because so far as his knowledge went he saw very clearly, and he was an ardent lover of truth, but I never saw in him even then a grain of vanity or conceit. I have said that some of his opinions startled us a good deal; we were for the most part Tories in Church and State, great respecters of things as they were, and not very tolerant of the disposition which he brought with him to question their wisdom. Many and long were the conflicts we had, and with unequal numbers. I think I have seen all the leaders of the common room engaged with him at once, with little order or consideration, as may be supposed, and not always with great scrupulosity as to the fairness of our arguments. This was attended by no loss of regard, and scarcely ever, or seldom, by even momentary loss of temper. We did not always convince him—perhaps we ought not always to have done so—yet in the end a considerable modification of his opinions was produced; in one of his letters to me,[1] written at a much later period, he mentions this change. In truth, there were those among us calculated to produce an impression on his affectionate heart and ardent ingenuous mind; and the rather because the more we saw of him, and the more we battled with him, the more manifestly did we respect and love him. The feeling with which we argued gave additional power to our arguments over a disposition such as his: and thus he became attached to young men of the most different tastes and intellects; his love for each taking a different colour, more or less blended with respect, fondness, or even humour, according to those differences; and in return they all uniting in love and respect for him.

There will be some few to whom these remembrances will speak with touching truth; they will remember his single-hearted and devout schoolfellow, who early gave up his

P. 12.

native land, and devoted himself to the missionary cause in India; the high-souled and imaginative, though somewhat indolent lad, who came to us from Westminster—one bachelor, whose father's connection with the House of Commons, and residence in Palace Yard, made him a great authority with us as to the world without, and the statesmen whose speeches he sometimes heard, but we discussed much as if they had been personages in history; and whose remarkable love for historical and geographical research, and his proficiency in it, with his clear judgment, quiet humour, and mildness in communicating information made him peculiarly attractive to Arnold—and above all, our senior among the undergraduates, though my junior in years, the author of the Christian Year, who came fresh from the single teaching of his venerable father, and achieved the highest honours of the University at an age when others frequently are but on her threshold. Arnold clung to all these with equal [1] fidelity, but regarded each with different feelings; each produced on him a salutary, but different effect[1]. . . .

P. 13.

P. 18.

[1] After I had ceased to reside, a small debating society called the Attic Society was formed in Oxford, which held its meetings in the rooms of the members by turns. Arnold was among the earliest members, and was, I believe, an embarrassed speaker. This I should have expected; for, however he might appear a confident advancer of his own opinions, he was in truth bashful, and at the same time had so acute a perception of what was ill-seasoned or irrelevant, that he would want that freedom from restraint which is essential at least to young speakers. This society was the germ[2] of the Union, but I believe he never belonged to it.

In our days the religious controversies had not begun, by which the minds of young men at Oxford are, I fear,

---

[1] It may be well to add the names of these friends: The Rev. John Tucker, the Rev. Geo. Cornish, the Rev. Francis Dyson, and the Rev. John Keble. [*Coleridge's Note.*]

[2] I can find no mention elsewhere of this fact or of the Society.

now prematurely and too much occupied; the routine theological studies of the University were, I admit, deplorably low, but the earnest ones amongst us were diligent readers of Barrow, Hooker, and Taylor. Arnold was among these, but I have no recollection of anything at that time distinctive in his religious opinions. .

XXV.

PERCY BYSSHE SHELLEY

[*Born*, 1792; educated at Eton, 1804–10; at University College, Oxford, April 1810–Mar. 1811; *died* July 8, 1822.]

AND T. J. HOGG.

T. J. Hogg's *Life of P. B. Shelley.* Lond. 1858; 2 vols.

I.

AFTER travelling for several days, we reached the last stage, and soon afterwards approached the point, whence, I was told, we might discern the first glimpse of the metropolis of learning. I strained my eyes to catch a view of that land of promise, for which I had so eagerly longed. The summits of towers, and spires, and domes appeared afar, and faintly; then the prospect was obstructed; by degrees it opened upon us again, and we saw the tall trees that shaded the colleges. At three o'clock on a fine autumnal afternoon we entered the streets of Oxford. Although the weather was cold, we had let down all the windows of our post-chaise, and I sat forward, devouring every object with greedy eyes. Members of the University, of different ages and ranks, were gliding through the quiet streets of the venerable city in academic costume. We devoted two or three days to the careful examination of the various objects of interest that Oxford contains. The eye was gratified; for the external appearance of the University even surpassed the bright picture which my youthful imagination had painted. The outside was always admirable: it was far otherwise with the inside. It is essential to the greatness of a disappointment, that the previous expectation should have been great: nothing could exceed my young anticipations,—nothing could be ¹ more complete than their overthrow. It P. 51. would be impossible to describe my feelings without speaking harshly and irreverently of the venerable University. On this subject, then. I will only confess my disappointment, and discreetly be silent as to its causes. Whatever those causes, I grew, at least, and I own it cheerfully, soon pleased with Oxford, on the whole; pleased with the beauty of the city, and its gentle river, and the pleasantness of the surrounding country.

Although no great facilities were afforded to the student, there were the same opportunities of *solitary* study as in other places. All the irksome restraints of school were removed, and those of the University are few and trifling. Our fare was good, although not so good. perhaps, as it ought to have been, in return for the enormous cost: and I liked the few companions with whom I most commonly mixed. I continued to lead a life of tranquil. studious. and somewhat melancholy contentment, until the long vacation, which I spent with my family, and, when it expired, I returned to the University.

At the commencement of Michaelmas term, that is, at the end of October, in the year 1810, I happened one day to sit next to a freshman at dinner; it was his first appearance in hall. His figure was slight, and his aspect remarkably youthful. even at our table, where all were very young. He ¹ seemed P. 52. thoughtful and absent. He ate little, and had no acquaintance with any one. I know not how it was that we fell into conversation, for such familiarity was unusual, and, strange to say, much reserve prevailed in a society where there could not possibly be occasion for any. We have often endeavoured in vain to recollect in what manner our discourse began, and especially by what transition it passed to a subject sufficiently remote from all the associations we were able to trace. The stranger had expressed an enthusiastic admiration for poetical and imaginative works of the German school. I dissented from his criticisms. He upheld the originality of the German writings. I asserted their want of nature.

'What modern literature,' said he, 'will you compare to theirs?'

I named the Italian. This roused all his impetuosity; and few, as I soon discovered, were more impetuous in argumentative conversation. So eager was our dispute, that when the servants came to clear the tables, we were not aware that we had been left alone. I remarked, that it was time to quit the hall, and I invited the stranger to finish the discussion at my rooms. He eagerly assented. He lost the thread of his discourse in the transit, and the whole of his enthusiasm in the cause of Germany; for as soon as he arrived at my rooms, and whilst I was lighting the candles, he said calmly, and to my great surprise, that he was not qualified to maintain such a discussion, for he was alike ignorant of Italian and German, and had only read the works of the Germans in translations, and but little of Italian poetry, even at second hand. For my part, I confessed, with an equal ingenuousness, that I knew nothing of German, and but little of Italian; that I had spoken only through others, and like him, had hitherto seen by the glimmering light of translations.

P. 53.

II.

P. 56.

I admired the enthusiasm of my new acquaintance, his ardour in the cause of science, and his thirst for knowledge. I seemed to have found in him all those intellectual qualities which I had vainly expected to meet with in an University. But there was one physical blemish that threatened to neutralise all his excellence. 'This is a fine, clever fellow!' I said to myself, 'but I can never bear his society; I shall never be able to endure his voice; it would kill me. What a pity it is!' I am very sensible of imperfections, and especially of painful sounds,—and the voice of the stranger was excruciating: it was intolerably shrill, harsh, and discordant; of the most cruel intension,—it was perpetual, and without any remission,—it excoriated the ears. He continued to discourse of chemistry, sometimes sitting, sometimes standing before the fire, and sometimes pacing about the room; and when one of the innumerable clocks that speak in various notes during the day and the ' night at Oxford, proclaimed a quarter to seven, P. 57. he said suddenly that he must go to a lecture on mineralogy, and declared enthusiastically that he expected to derive much pleasure and instruction from it. I am ashamed to own that the cruel voice made me hesitate a moment; but it was impossible to omit so indispensable a civility—I invited him to return to tea; he gladly assented, promised that he would not be absent long, snatched his cap, hurried out of the room, and I heard his footsteps as he ran through the silent quadrangle, and afterwards along High-street.

An hour soon elapsed, whilst the table was cleared, and the tea was made, and I again heard the footsteps of one running quickly. My guest suddenly burst into the room, threw down his cap, and as he stood shivering and chafing his hands over the fire, he declared how much he had been disappointed in the lecture. Few persons attended; it was dull and languid, and he was resolved never to go to another.

'I went away, indeed,' he added, with an arch look, and in a shrill whisper, coming close to me as he spoke,—' I went away, indeed, before the lecture was finished. I stole away; for it was so stupid, and I was so cold, that my teeth chattered. The Professor saw me, and appeared to be displeased. I thought I could have got out without being ' ob- P. 58. served; but I struck my knee against a bench, and made a noise, and he looked at me. I am determined that he shall never see me again.'

'What did the man talk about?'

'About stones! about stones!' he answered, with a downcast look and in a melancholy tone, as if about to say something excessively profound. 'About stones!—stones, stones,

stones!—nothing but stones!—and so drily. It was wonderfully tiresome—and stones are not interesting things in themselves!'

We took tea, and soon afterwards had supper, as was usual. He discoursed after supper with as much warmth as before of the wonders of chemistry; of the encouragement that Napoleon afforded to that most important science; of the French chemists and their glorious discoveries; and of the happiness of visiting Paris, and sharing in their fame and their experiments. The voice, however, seemed to me more cruel than ever. He spoke likewise of his own labours and of his apparatus, and starting up suddenly after supper, he proposed that I should go instantly with him to see the galvanic trough. I looked at my watch, and observed that it was too late; that the fire would be out, and the night was cold. He resumed his seat, saying that I might come on the morrow, early, to breakfast, immediately after chapel. He continued to declaim in his rapturous strain, asserting that chemistry was, in truth, the only science that deserved to be studied. I suggested doubts. I ventured to question the pre-eminence of the science, and even to hesitate in admitting its utility. He described in glowing language some discoveries that had lately been made; but the enthusiastic chemist candidly allowed that they were rather brilliant than useful, asserting, however, that they would soon be applied to purposes of solid advantage.

'Is not the time of by far the larger proportion of the human species,' he inquired, with his fervid manner and in his piercing tones, 'wholly consumed in severe labour? And is not this devotion of our race—of the whole of our race, I may say (for those who, like ourselves, are indulged with an exemption from the hard lot are so few, in comparison with the rest, that they scarcely deserve to be taken into the account)—absolutely necessary to procure subsistence; so that men have no leisure for recreation or the high improvement of the mind? Yet this incessant toil is still inadequate to procure an abundant supply of the common necessaries of life : some are doomed actually to want them, and many are compelled to be content with an insufficient provision.'

III.

.... He suddenly remarked that the fire was nearly out, P. 65. and the candles were glimmering in their sockets, when he hastily apologised for remaining so long. I promised to visit the chemist in his laboratory, the alchemist in his study, the wizard in his cave, not at breakfast on that day, for it was already one, but in twelve hours—one hour after noon—and to hear some of the secrets of nature; and for that purpose, he told me his name, and described the situation of his rooms. I lighted him down-stairs as well as I could with the stump of a candle which had dissolved itself into a lamp, and I soon heard him running through the quiet quadrangle in the still night. That sound became afterwards so familiar to my ear, that I still seem to hear Shelley's hasty steps.

I trust, or I should perhaps rather say, I hope, that I was as much struck by the conversation, the aspect, and the deportment of my new acquaintance, as entirely convinced of the value of the acquisition I had just made, and as deeply impressed with ¹ surprise and admiration, as became a young P. 66. student not insensible of excellence, to whom a character so extraordinary, and indeed almost preternatural, had been suddenly unfolded. During his animated and eloquent discourses I felt a due reverence for his zeal and talent, but the human mind is capable of a certain amount of attention only. I had listened and discussed for seven or eight hours, and my spirits were totally exhausted; I went to bed as soon as Shelley had quitted my rooms, and fell instantly into a profound sleep; and I shook off with a painful effort, at the accustomed signal, the complete oblivion which then appeared to have been but momentary. Many of the wholesome usages of antiquity had ceased at Oxford; that of early rising, however, still lingered.

As soon as I got up, I applied myself sedulously to my academical duties and my accustomed studies. The power of habitual occupation is great and engrossing, and it is possible that my mind had not yet fully recovered from the agreeable fatigue of the preceding evening, for I had entirely forgotten my engagement, nor did the thought of my young guest once cross my fancy. It was strange that a person so remarkable and attractive should have thus disappeared for several hours from my memory; but such in truth was the fact, although I am unable to account for it in a satisfactory manner.

At one o'clock I put away my books and papers, and prepared myself for my daily walk; the weather was frosty, with fog, and whilst I lingered over the fire with that reluctance to venture forth into the cold air, common to those who have chilled themselves by protracted sedentary pursuits, the recollection of the scenes of yesterday flashed suddenly and vividly across my mind, and I quickly repaired to a spot that I may perhaps venture to predict many of our posterity will hereafter reverently visit, to the rooms in the corner next the hall of the principal quadrangle of University College; they are on the first floor, and on the right of the entrance, but by reason of the turn in the stairs, when you reach them, they will be upon your left hand. I remember the direction given at parting, and I soon found the door: it stood ajar. I tapped gently, and the discordant voice cried shrilly,—

'Come in!'

It was now nearly two. I began to apologise for my delay, but I was interrupted by a loud exclamation of surprise—

'What! is it one? I had no notion it was so late; I thought it was about ten or eleven.'

'It is on the stroke of two, sir,' said the scout, who was engaged in the vain attempt of setting the apartment in order.

'Of two!' Shelley cried, with increased wonder, and presently the clock struck, and the servant noticed it, retired, and shut the door.

I perceived at once that the young chemist took no note of time. He measured duration, not by minutes and hours, like watchmakers and their customers, but by the successive trains of ideas and sensations; consequently, if there was a virtue of which he was utterly incapable, it was that homely, but pleasing and useful one, punctuality. He could not tear himself from his incessant abstractions to observe at intervals the growth and decline of the day; nor was he ever able to set apart even a small portion of his mental powers for a duty so simple as that of watching the course of the pointers on the dial.

I found him cowering over the fire, his chair planted in the middle of the rug, and his feet resting upon the fender: his whole appearance was dejected. His astonishment at the unexpected lapse of time roused him: as soon as the hour of the day was ascertained, he welcomed me, and seizing one of my arms with both his hands, he shook it with some force, and very cordially expressed his satisfaction at my visit. Then resuming his seat and his former posture, he gazed fixedly at the fire, and his limbs trembled and his teeth chattered with cold. I cleared the fire-place with the poker and stirred the fire, and when it blazed up, he drew back, and looking askance towards the door, he exclaimed with a deep sigh,—

'Thank God, that fellow is gone at last!'

The assiduity of the scout had annoyed him, and he presently added—

'If you had not come, he would have stayed until he had put everything in my rooms into some place where I should never have found it again!'

He then complained of his health, and said that he was very unwell; but he did not appear to be affected by any disorder more serious than a slight aguish cold. I remarked

the same contradiction in his rooms which I had already
observed in his person and dress; they had just been papered
and painted; the carpet, curtains, and furniture were quite
new, and had not passed through several academical generations, after the established custom of transferring the whole
of the movables to the successor on payment of thirds, that is
of two-thirds of the price last given. The general air of
freshness was greatly obscured, however, by the indescribable
confusion in which the various objects were mixed; notwithstanding the unwelcome exertions of the officious scout,
scarcely a single article was in its proper position.

Books, boots, papers, shoes, philosophical instruments,
clothes, pistols, linen, crockery, ammunition, and phials innumerable, with money, stockings, prints, crucibles, bags, and
boxes, were scattered on the floor and in every place; as if
the young chemist, in order to analyse the mystery of
creation, had endeavoured first to re-construct the primeval
chaos The tables, and especially the carpet, were already
stained with large spots of various hues, which frequently
proclaimed the agency of fire. An electrical machine, an
air-pump, the galvanic trough, a solar microscope, and large
glass jars and receivers, were conspicuous amidst the mass of
matter. Upon the table by his side were some books lying
open, several letters, a bundle of new pens, and a bottle of
japan ink, that served as an inkstand; a piece of deal,
lately part of the lid of a box, with many chips, and a
handsome razor that had been used as a knife. There
were bottles of soda water, sugar, pieces of lemon, and the
traces of an effervescent beverage. Two piles of books
supported the tongs, and these upheld a small glass retort
above an argand lamp. I had not been seated many minutes
before the liquor in the vessel boiled over, adding fresh stains
to the table, and rising in fumes with a most disagreeable
odour. Shelley snatched the glass quickly, and dashing it
in pieces among the ashes under the grate, incrcased the
unpleasant and penetrating effluvium.

He then proceeded, with much eagerness and enthusiasm, to show me the various instruments ¹ especially the electrical P. 71. apparatus; turning round the handle very rapidly, so that the fierce, crackling sparks flew forth; and presently standing upon the stool with glass feet, he begged me to work the machine until he was filled with the fluid, so that his long, wild locks bristled and stood on end. Afterwards he charged a powerful battery of several large jars; labouring with vast energy, and discoursing with increasing vehemence of the marvellous powers of electricity, of thunder and lightning; describing an electrical kite that he had made at home, and projecting another and an enormous one, or rather a combination of many kites, that would draw down from the sky an immense volume of electricity, the whole ammunition of a mighty thunderstorm; and this being directed to some point would there produce the most stupendous results.

In these exhibitions and in such conversation the time passed away rapidly, and the hour of dinner approached. Having pricked *æger* that day, or, in other words, having caused his name to be entered as an invalid, he was not required, or permitted, to dine in hall, or to appear in public within the college, or without the walls, until a night's rest should have restored the sick man to health.

He requested me to spend the evening at his ¹ rooms; I P. 72. consented, nor did I fail to attend immediately after dinner. We conversed until a late hour on miscellaneous topics. I remember that he spoke frequently of poetry, and that there was the same animation, the same glowing zeal, which had characterised his former discourses, and was so opposite to the listless languor, the monstrous indifference, if not the absolute antipathy, to learning, that so strangely darkened the collegiate atmosphere. It would seem, indeed, to one who rightly considered the final cause of the institution of an University, that all the rewards, all the honours, the most opulent foundation could accumulate, would be inadequate to remunerate an individual whose thirst for knowledge was so intense, and his activity in the pursuit of it so wonderful and so unwearied. I participated in his enthusiasm, and soon forgot the shrill and unmusical voice that had at first seemed intolerable to my ear.

He was, indeed, a whole University in himself to me, in respect of the stimulus and incitement which his example afforded to my love of study, and he amply atoned for the disappointment I had felt on my arrival at Oxford. In one respect alone could I pretend to resemble him, in an ardent desire to gain knowledge; and as our tastes were the same in many particulars, we immediately became, through sympathy, most intimate and altogether inseparable companions. We almost invariably passed the afternoon and evening together; at first alternately at our respective rooms, through a certain punctiliousness, but afterwards, when we became more familiar, most frequently by far at his; sometimes one or two good and harmless men of our acquaintance were present, but we were usually alone. His rooms were preferred to mine, because there his philosophical apparatus was at hand; and at that period he was not perfectly satisfied with the condition and circumstances of his existence, unless he was able to start from his seat at any moment, and seizing the air-pump, some magnets, the electrical machine, or the bottles containing those noxious and nauseous fluids, wherewith he incessantly besmeared and disfigured himself and his goods, to ascertain by actual experiment the value of some new idea that rushed into his brain. He spent much time in working by fits and starts and in an irregular manner with his instruments, and especially consumed his hours and his money in the assiduous cultivation of chemistry.

IV.

Notwithstanding our difference of opinion as to the importance of chemistry, and on some other questions, our intimacy rapidly increased, and we soon formed the habit of passing the greater part of our time together; nor did this constant intercourse interfere with my usual studies. I never visited his rooms until one o'clock, by which hour, as I rose very early, I had not only attended the college lectures, but had read in private for several hours. I was enabled, moreover, to continue my studies afterwards in the evening, in consequence of a very remarkable peculiarity. My young and energetic friend was then overcome by extreme drowsiness, which speedily and completely vanquished him; he would sleep from two to four hours, often so soundly that his slumbers resembled a deep lethargy; he lay occasionally upon the sofa, but more commonly stretched upon the rug before a large fire, like a cat; and his little round head was exposed to such a fierce heat, that I used to wonder how he was able to bear it. Sometimes I have interposed some shelter, but rarely with any permanent effect; for the sleeper usually contrived to turn himself, and to roll again into the spot where the fire glowed the brightest. His torpor was generally profound, but he would sometimes discourse incoherently for a long while in his sleep. At six he would suddenly compose himself, even in the midst of a most animated narrative or of earnest discussion; and he would lie buried in entire forgetfulness, in a sweet and mighty oblivion, until ten, when he would suddenly start up, and rubbing his eyes with great violence, and passing his fingers swiftly through his long hair, would enter at once into a vehement argument, or begin to recite verses, either of his own composition or from the works of others, with a rapidity and an energy that were often quite painful. During the period of his occultation I took tea, and read or wrote without interruption. He would sometimes sleep for a shorter time, for about two hours; postponing for the like period the commencement of his retreat to the rug, and rising with tolerable punctuality at ten; and sometimes, although rarely, he was able entirely to forego the accustomed refreshment.

We did not consume the whole of our time, when he was

awake, in conversation; we often read apart, and more frequently together: our joint studies were occasionally interrupted by long discussions—nevertheless I could enumerate many works, and several of them are extensive and important, which we perused completely and very carefully in this manner. At ten, when he awoke, he was always ready for his supper, which he took with a peculiar relish: after that social meal his mind was clear and penetrating, and his discourse eminently brilliant. He was unwilling to separate; but when the college clock struck two, I used to rise and retire to my room. Our conversations were sometimes considerably prolonged, but they seldom terminated before that chilly hour of the early morning; nor did I feel any inconvenience from thus reducing the period of rest to scarcely five hours.

A disquisition on some difficult question in the open air was not less agreeable to him than by the fire-side; if the weather was fine, or rather not altogether intolerable, we used to sally forth, when we met at one.

P. 79.
I have already pointed out several contradictions [1] in his appearance and character; his ordinary preparation for a rural walk formed a very remarkable contrast with his mild aspect and pacific habits. He furnished himself with a pair of duelling pistols, and a good store of powder and ball; and when he came to a solitary spot, he pinned a card, or fixed some other mark upon a tree or a bank, and amused himself by firing at it: he was a pretty good shot, and was much delighted at his success. He often urged me to try my hand and eye, assuring me that I was not aware of the pleasure of a good hit. One day when he was peculiarly pressing, I took up a pistol and asked him what I should aim at? And observing a slab of wood, about as big as a hearth-rug, standing against a wall, I named it as being a proper object. He said that it was much too far off, it was better to wait until we came nearer; but I answered—'I may as well fire here as anywhere,' and instantly dis-

charged my pistol. To my infinite surprise, the ball struck the elm target most accurately in the very centre. Shelley was delighted; he ran to the board, placed his chin close to it—gazed at the hole where the bullet was lodged—examined it attentively on all sides many times, and more than once measured the distance to the spot where I had stood.

I never knew any one so prone to admire as he was, in whom the principle of veneration was so ¹ strong; he extolled my skill, urged me repeatedly to display it again, and begged that I would give him instructions in an art in which I so much excelled. I suffered him to enjoy his wonder for a few days, and then I told him, and with difficulty persuaded him, that my success was purely accidental; for I had seldom fired a pistol before, and never with ball, but with shot only, as a schoolboy, in clandestine and bloodless expeditions against blackbirds and yellowhammers. P. 80.

The duelling pistols were a most discordant interruption of the repose of a quiet country walk, besides, he handled them with such inconceivable carelessness, that I had perpetually reason to apprehend that, as a trifling episode in the grand and heroic work of drilling a hole through the back of a card, or in front of one of his father's franks, he would shoot himself, or me, or both of us. How often have I lamented that Nature, which so rarely bestows upon the world a creature endowed with such marvellous talents, ungraciously rendered the gift less precious by implanting a fatal taste for perilous recreations, and a thoughtlessness in the pursuit of them, that often caused his existence from one day to another to seem in itself miraculous. I opposed the practice of walking armed, and I at last succeeded in inducing him to leave the pistols at home, and to forbear the use of them. ¹ I prevailed I believe, not so much by argument or persuasion, as by secretly abstracting, when he equipped himself for the field, and it was not difficult with him, the powder-flask, the flints, or some other indispensable article. One day, I remember, he was grievously discom- P. 81.

posed, and seriously offended, to find, on producing his pistols, after descending rapidly into a quarry, where he proposed to take a few shots, that not only had the flints been removed, but the screws and the bits of steel at the tops of the cocks, which hold the flints, were also wanting. He determined to return to College for them,—I accompanied him. I tempted him, however, by the way, to try to define anger, and to discuss the nature of that affection of the mind, to which, as the discussion waxed warm, he grew exceedingly hostile in theory, and could not be brought to admit that it could possibly be excusable in any case. In the course of conversation, moreover, he suffered himself to be insensibly turned away from his original path and purpose. I have heard, that some years after he left Oxford he resumed the practice of pistol-shooting, and attained to a very unusual degree of skill in an accomplishment so entirely incongruous with his nature.

Of rural excursions he was at all times fond; he loved to walk in the woods, to stroll on the banks of the Thames, but especially to wander about Shotover Hill. There was a pond at the foot of the hill, before ascending it, and on the left of the road: it was formed by the water, which had filled an old quarry; whenever he was permitted to shape his course as he would, he proceeded to the edge of this pool, although the scene had no other attractions than a certain wildness and barrenness. Here he would linger until dusk, gazing in silence on the water, repeating verses aloud, or earnestly discussing themes that had no connexion with surrounding objects. Sometimes he would raise a stone as large as he could lift, deliberately throw it into the water as far as his strength enabled him; then he would loudly exult at the splash, and would quietly watch the decreasing agitation, until the last faint ring and almost imperceptible ripple disappeared on the still surface. 'Such are the effects of an impulse on the air,' he would say; and he complained of our ignorance of the theory of sound,—that the subject was obscure and mysterious, and many of the phenomena were contradictory and inexplicable. He asserted that the science of acoustics ought to be cultivated, and that by well-devised experiments valuable discoveries would undoubtedly be made; and he related many remarkable stories, connected with the subject, that he had heard or read. Sometimes, he would busy himself in splitting the slaty stones, in selecting thin and flat pieces, and in [1] giving them a round form; and when he had collected a sufficient number, he would gravely make ducks and drakes with them, counting, with the utmost glee, the number of bounds, as they flew along skimming the surface of the pond. He was a devoted worshipper of the water-nymphs; for whenever he found a pool, or even a small puddle, he would loiter near it, and it was no easy task to get him to quit it. He had not yet learned that art, from which he afterwards derived so much pleasure—the construction of paper boats. He twisted a morsel of paper into a form that a lively fancy might consider a likeness of a boat, and committing it to the water, he anxiously watched the fortunes of the frail bark, which, if it was not soon swamped by the faint winds and miniature waves, gradually imbibed water through its porous sides, and sank. Sometimes, however, the fairy vessel performed its little voyage, and reached the opposite shore of the puny ocean in safety. It is astonishing with what keen delight he engaged in this singular pursuit. It was not easy for an uninitiated spectator to bear with tolerable patience the vast delay, on the brink of a wretched pond upon a bleak common, and in the face of a cutting north-east wind, on returning to dinner from a long walk at sunset on a cold winter's day; nor was it easy to be so harsh as to interfere with a harmless gratification, that was [1] evidently exquisite. It was not easy, at least, to induce the ship-builder to desist from launching his tiny fleets, so long as any timber remained in the dockyard. I prevailed once, and once only; it was one of those bitter Sundays that commonly receive the new year; the sun had set, and it had almost begun to snow. I had exhorted

P. 83.

P. 84.

him long in vain, with the eloquence of a frozen and famished man, to proceed; at last, I said in despair—alluding to his never-ending creations, for a paper-navy that was to be set afloat simultaneously lay at his feet, and he was busily constructing more, with blue and swollen hands,—' Shelley, there is no use in talking to you; you are the Demiurgus of Plato!' He instantly caught up the whole flotilla, and bounding homeward with mighty strides, laughed aloud—laughed like a giant, as he used to say. So long as his paper lasted, he remained riveted to the spot, fascinated by this peculiar amusement; all waste paper was rapidly consumed, then the covers of letters, next letters of little value: the most precious contributions of the most esteemed correspondent, although eyed wistfully many times, and often returned to the pocket, were sure to be sent at last in pursuit of the former squadrons. Of the portable volumes which were the companions of his rambles, and he seldom went out without a book, the flyleaves were commonly wanting,—he had applied them as our ancestor Noah applied Gopher wood; but learning was so sacred in his eyes, that he never trespassed farther upon the integrity of the copy; the work itself was always respected. . . . .

V.

But to return to Oxford. Shelley disliked exceedingly all college-meetings, and especially one which was the most popular with others—the public dinner in the hall; he used often to absent himself, and he was greatly delighted whenever I agreed to partake with him in a slight luncheon at one, to take a long walk into the country, and to return after dark to tea and supper in his rooms. On one of these expeditions we wandered farther than usual, without regarding the distance or the lapse of time; but we had no difficulty in finding our way home, for the night was clear and frosty, and the moon at the full; and most glorious was the spectacle as we approached the City of Colleges, and passed through the silent streets. It was near ten when we entered our college ; not only was it too late for tea, but supper was ready, the cloth laid, and the table spread. A large dish of scalloped oysters had been set within the fender, to be kept hot for the famished wanderers.

Among the innumerable contradictions in the character and deportment of the youthful poet was a strange mixture of a singular grace, which manifested itself in his actions and gestures, with an occasional awkwardness almost as remarkable. As soon as we entered the room, he placed his chair as usual directly in front of the fire, and eagerly pressed forward to warm himself, for the frost was severe, and he was very sensible of cold. Whilst cowering over the fire and rubbing his hands, he abruptly set both his feet at once upon the edge of the fender; it immediately flew up, threw under the grate the dish, which was broken into two pieces, and the whole of the delicious mess was mingled with the cinders and ashes, that had accumulated for several hours. It was impossible that a hungry and frozen pedestrian should restrain a strong expression of indignation, or that he should forbear, notwithstanding the exasperation of cold and hunger, from smiling and forgiving the accident at seeing the whimsical air and aspect of the offender, as he held up with the shovel the long-anticipated food, deformed by ashes, coals, and cinders, with a ludicrous expression of exaggerated surprise, disappointment, and contrition. It would be easy to fill many volumes with reminiscences characteristic of my young friend, and of these the most trifling would perhaps best illustrate his innumerable peculiarities. With the discerning, trifles, although they are accounted such, have their value. A familiarity with the daily habits of Shelley, and the knowledge of his demeanour in private, will greatly facilitate, and they are perhaps even essential to, the full comprehension of his views and opinions. Traits that unfold an infantine simplicity, the genuine simplicity of true genius, will be slighted by those only who are ignorant of the qualities that

P. 87.

constitute greatness of soul: the philosophical observer knows well, that to have shown a mind to be original and perfectly natural,¹ is no inconsiderable step in demonstrating that it is also great.

Our supper had disappeared under the grate, but we were able to silence the importunity of hunger. As the supply of cheese was scanty, Shelley pretended, in order to atone for his carelessness, that he never eat it; but I refused to take more than my share, and notwithstanding his reiterated declarations, that it was offensive to his palate and hurtful to his stomach, as I was inexorable, he devoured the remainder, greedily swallowing not merely the cheese, but the rind also, after scraping it cursorily, and with a curious tenderness. A tankard of the stout brown ale of our college aided us greatly in removing the sense of cold, and in supplying the deficiency of food, so that we turned our chairs towards the fire, and began to brew our negus as cheerfully as if the bounty of the hospitable gods had not been intercepted.

We reposed ourselves after the fatigue of an unusually long walk, and silence was broken by short remarks only, and at considerable intervals, respecting the beauty of moonlight scenes, and especially of that we had just enjoyed; the serenity and clearness of the night exceeded any we had before witnessed; the light was so strong it would have been easy to read or write. 'How strange was it, that light proceeding from the sun, which¹ was at such a prodigious distance, and at that time entirely out of sight, should be reflected from the moon, and that was no trifling journey, and sent back to the earth in such abundance, and with so great force!'

Languid expressions of admiration dropped from our lips, as we stretched our stiff and wearied limbs towards the genial warmth of a blazing fire. On a sudden, Shelley started from his seat, seized one of the candles, and began to walk about the room on tiptoe in profound silence, often stooping low, and evidently engaged in some mysterious search. I asked him what he wanted, but he returned no answer, and continued his whimsical and secret inquisition, which he prosecuted in the same extraordinary manner in the bed-room and the little study. It had occurred to him that a dessert had possibly been sent to his rooms whilst we were absent, and had been put away. He found the object of his pursuit at last, and produced some small dishes from the study; apples, oranges, almonds and raisins, and a little cake. These he set close together at my side of the table, without speaking, but with a triumphant look, yet with the air of a penitent making restitution and reparation, and then resumed his seat. The unexpected succour was very seasonable; this light fare, a few glasses of negus, warmth, and especially rest, restored our lost vigour, and our spirits. We spoke[1] of our happy life, of Universities, P. 90. of what they might be; of what they were. How powerfully they might stimulate the student, how much valuable instruction they might impart! We agreed that, although the least possible benefit was conferred upon us in this respect at Oxford, we were deeply indebted, nevertheless, to the great and good men of former days, who founded those glorious institutions, for devising a scheme of life, which, however deflected from its original direction, still tended to study, and especially for creating establishments that called young men together from all parts of the empire, and for endowing them with a celebrity that was able to induce so many to congregate. Without such an opportunity of meeting we should never have been acquainted with each other; in so large a body there must doubtless be many at that time, who were equally thankful for the occasion of the like intimacy; and in former generations how many friendships that had endured through all the various trials of a long and eventful life, had arisen here from accidental communion, as in our own case.

If there was little positive encouragement, there were various negative inducements to acquire learning; there were no interruptions, no secular cares; our wants were well supplied without the slightest exertion on our part, and the exact regularity

T

of academical existence cut off that dissipation of the hours and the thoughts, which so often prevails where the daily course is not pre-arranged. The necessity of early rising was beneficial; like the Pythagoreans of old, we began with the Gods; the salutary attendance in chapel every morning not only compelled us to quit our beds betimes, but imposed additional duties conducive to habits of industry; it was requisite, not merely to rise, but to leave our rooms, to appear in public, and to remain long enough to destroy the disposition to indolence, which might still linger if we were permitted to remain by the fire-side. To pass some minutes in society, yet in solemn silence, is like the Pythagorean initiation, and we auspicate the day happily by commencing with sacred things. I scarcely ever visited Shelley before one o'clock; when I met him in the morning at chapel, he used studiously to avoid all communication, and, as soon as the doors were opened, to effect a ludicrously precipitate retreat to his rooms.

'The country near Oxford,' he continued, as we reposed after our meagre supper, 'has no pretensions to peculiar beauty, but it is quiet, and pleasant, and rural, and purely agricultural after the good old fashion; it is not only unpolluted by manufactures and commerce, but it is exempt from the desecration of the modern husbandry, of a system which accounts the farmer a manufacturer of hay and corn: I delight to wander over it.' He enlarged upon the pleasure of our pedestrian excursions, and added—' I can imagine few things that would annoy me more severely than to be disturbed in our tranquil course; it would be a cruel calamity to be interrupted by some untoward accident, to be compelled to quit our calm and agreeable retreat. Not only would it be a sad mortification, but a real misfortune, for if I remain here I shall study more closely and with greater advantage than I could in any other situation that I can conceive. Are you not of the same opinion?'

'Entirely.'

'I regret only that the period of our residence is limited to four years; I wish they would revive, for our sake, the old term of six or seven years. If we consider how much there is for us to learn,'—here he paused and sighed deeply through that despondency which sometimes comes over the unwearied and zealous student,—'we shall allow that the longer period would still be far too short!'

I assented, and we discoursed concerning the abridgement of the ancient term of residence, and the diminution of the academical year by frequent, protracted, and most inconvenient vacations.

'To quit Oxford,' he said, 'would be still more unpleasant to you than to myself, for you aim at objects that I do not seek to compass, and you ¹ cannot fail, since you are resolved to place your success beyond the reach of chance.'

He enumerated with extreme rapidity, and in his enthusiastic strain, some of the benefits and comforts of a college life.

'Then the *oak* is such a blessing,' he exclaimed with peculiar fervour, clasping his hands, and repeating often—'the oak is such a blessing!' slowly and in a solemn tone. 'The oak alone goes far towards making this place a paradise. In what other spot in the world, surely in none that I have hitherto visited, can you say confidently, it is perfectly impossible, physically impossible, that I should be disturbed? Whether a man desire solitary study, or to enjoy the society of a friend or two, he is secure against interruption. It is not so in a house, not by any means; there is not the same protection in a house, even in the best-contrived house. The servant is bound to answer the door; he must appear and give some excuse: he may betray by hesitation and confusion that he utters a falsehood; he must expose himself to be questioned; he must open the door and violate your privacy in some degree; besides there are other doors, there are windows at least, through which a prying eye can detect some indication that betrays the mystery. How different is it here! The bore arrives; the outer door is shut; it is black and solid, and perfectly impenetrable, as is your secret; the doors are all alike; he can distinguish mine from yours by the geographical position only. He may knock; he may call; he may kick, if he will; he may inquire of a neighbour, but he can inform him of nothing; he can only say, the door is shut, and this he knows already. He may leave his card, that you may rejoice over it, and at your escape; he may write upon it the hour when he proposes to call again, to put you upon your guard, and that he may be quite sure of seeing the back of your door once more. When the bore meets you and says, I called at your house at such a time, you are required to explain your absence, to prove an *alibi* in short, and perhaps to undergo a rigid cross-examination; but if he tells you, " I called at your rooms yesterday at three, and the door was shut," you have only to say, "Did you? was it?" and there the matter ends.'

' Were you not charmed with your oak? did it not instantly captivate you?'

' My introduction to it was somewhat unpleasant and unpropitious. The morning after my arrival I was sitting at breakfast; my scout, the Arimaspian, apprehending that the singleness of his eye may impeach his character for officiousness, in order to escape the reproach of seeing half as much only as other men, is always striving to prove that he sees at least twice as far as the most sharpsighted: after many demonstrations of superabundant activity, he inquired if I wanted anything more; I answered in the negative. He had already opened the door: " Shall I sport, sir?" he asked briskly as he stood upon the threshold. He seemed so unlike a sporting character, that I was curious to learn in what sport he proposed to indulge. I answered—"Yes, by all means," and anxiously watched him, but to my surprise and disappointment he instantly vanished. As soon as I had finished my breakfast, I sallied forth to survey Oxford; I opened one door quickly, and not suspecting that there was a second, I struck my head against it with some violence. The blow taught me to observe that every set of rooms has two doors, and I soon learned that the outer door, which is thick and solid, is called the oak, and to shut it is termed, to sport. I derived so much benefit from my oak, that I soon pardoned this slight inconvenience: it is surely the tree of knowledge.'

'Who invented the oak?'

'The inventors of the science of living in rooms, or chambers —the Monks.'

'Ah! they were sly fellows; none but men who were reputed to devote themselves for many hours to prayers, to religious meditations, and holy abstractions, would ever have been permitted quietly to place at pleasure such a barrier between themselves and the world. We now reap the advantage of their reputation for sanctity; I shall revere my oak more than ever, since its origin is so sacred.'

The sympathies of Shelley were instantaneous and powerful with those, who evinced in any degree the qualities, for which he was himself so remarkable—simplicity of character, unaffected manners, genuine modesty, and an honest willingness to acquire knowledge, and he sprang to meet their advances with an ingenuous eagerness which was peculiar to him; but he was suddenly and violently repelled, like the needle from the negative pole of the magnet, by any indication of pedantry, presumption, or affectation. So much was he disposed to take offence at such defects, and so acutely was he sensible of them, that he was sometimes unjust, through an excessive sensitiveness, in his estimate of those, who had shocked him by sins, of which he was himself utterly incapable. Whatever might be the attainments, and however solid the merits of the persons filling at that time the important office of instructors in the University, they were entirely destitute of the attractions of manner; their address was sometimes repulsive, and the formal, priggish tutor was too often intent upon the ordinary academical course alone to the entire exclusion of every other department of knowledge: his thoughts were wholly engrossed by it, and so narrow were his views, that he overlooked the claims of all merit, however exalted, except success in the public examinations.

'They are very dull people here,' Shelley said to me one evening soon after his arrival, with a long-drawn sigh, after musing awhile; 'a little man sent for me this morning, and told me in an almost inaudible whisper that I must read: "you must read," he said many times in his small voice. I answered that I had no objection. He persisted; so, to satisfy him, for he did not appear to believe me, I told him I had some books in my pocket, and I began to take them out. He stared at me, and said that was not exactly what he meant: "you must read *Prometheus Vinctus*, and Demosthenes *de Coronâ*, and Euclid?" Must I read Euclid? I asked sorrowfully. "Yes, certainly; and when you have read the Greek works I have mentioned, you must begin Aristotle's Ethics, and then you may go on to his other treatises. It is of the utmost importance to be well acquainted with Aristotle." This he repeated so often that I was quite tired, and at last I said, Must I care about Aristotle? what if I do not mind Aristotle? I then left him, for he seemed to be in great perplexity.'

Notwithstanding the slight he had thus cast upon the great master of the science, that has so long been the staple of Oxford, he was not blind to the value of the science itself. He took the scholastic ¹ logic very kindly, seized its distinctions with his accustomed quickness, felt a keen interest in the study, and patiently endured the exposition of those minute discriminations, which the tyro is apt to contemn as vain and trifling.

It should seem that the ancient method of communicating the art of syllogising has been preserved, in part at least, by tradition in this university. I have sometimes met with learned foreigners, who understood the end and object of the scholastic logic, having received the traditional instruction in some of the old universities on the Continent; but I never found even one of my countrymen, except Oxonians, who rightly comprehended the nature of the science: I may, perhaps, add, that in proportion as the self-taught logicians had laboured in the pursuit, they had gone far astray. It is possible, nevertheless, that those who have drunk at the fountain-head, and have read the 'Organon' of Aristotle in the original, may have attained to a just comprehension by their unassisted energies; but in this age, and in this country, I apprehend the number of such adventurous readers is very inconsiderable.

Shelley frequently exercised his ingenuity in long discussions respecting various questions in logic, and more frequently indulged in metaphysical inquiries. We read several metaphysical works [1] together, in whole, or in part, for the first time, or after a previous perusal, by one, or by both of us.

The examination of a chapter of Locke's 'Essay concerning Human Understanding' would induce him, at any moment, to quit every other pursuit. We read together Hume's 'Essays,' and some productions of Scotch metaphysicians, of inferior ability—all with assiduous and friendly altercations, and the latter writers, at least, with small profit, unless some sparks of knowledge were struck out in the collision of debate. We read also certain popular French works, that treat of man, for the most part in a mixed method, metaphysically, morally, and politically. Hume's 'Essays' were a favourite book with Shelley, and he was always ready to put forward in argument, the doctrines they uphold.

VI.

The long vacation is an admirable and blessed institution, worthy of all honour and of perpetual observance; but the short vacations at Christmas and at Easter deserve utter execration, and exist only to be abolished. They are a pernicious interruption of the course of study, which is broken off almost as soon as it is fully begun, and an unseasonable disruption of studious friendships and agreeable society. If they were tolerable to young men, whose families reside at a moderate distance from the University, they were insupportable to those unfortunates who must travel by coaches, perhaps two whole days, and certainly two nights, to reach their household gods, and for the like space of time to return to college. All lectures, all instruction ceased, public libraries and every other place of amusement or resort were closed during these ferial days, even the entertainment of attending chapel was denied. The tutors departed, as well as all the undergraduates; the porter and the master shut themselves up close in their respective lodges; and the College servants could seldom be found. A dinner was provided certainly, but not in the Hall; the inhospitable table was spread in some mysterious apartment, which I never entered at any other time, and which seemed to have vanished as soon as term recommenced, so that I have sometimes wondered what became of it. At the dinner I commonly found myself alone. It consisted of a joint of meat, potatoes, and bread; all very good of their kind, no doubt; but it was impossible to obtain anything else—any of those little extras for which one might *battel* in term-time; the very cheese suffered dim eclipse, not a slice was to be procured. The College cook, in truth, would have felt that he was unworthy of his important office if he had approved himself less lazy than the masters and tutors.

Many and great reforms were needed at our famous University in those days, which were far more pressing and urgent than the discouragement of metaphysical speculations in the active minds of a few studious youths.

It was manifest that my presence in the vacant seat of learning was unwelcome. To travel to the north of England, to rest myself for a few days there after my journey, and then to come back in the dark, as it were, in an ungenial season and the shortest days, was too severe a sacrifice to be made even to the grossest abuse of educational trusts; so I determined to go to London.

VII.

Twenty years ago, the young men at our Universities were satisfied with upholding the political doctrines of which they approved by private discussions : they did not venture to form clubs of brothers, and to move resolutions, except a small number of enthusiasts, of doubtful sanity, who alone sought to usurp, by ¹ crude and permature efforts, the offices of a matured understanding and of manly experience.

Although our fellow-collegians were willing to learn before they took upon themselves the heavy and thankless charge of instructing others, there was no lack of beardless politicians amongst us: of these, some were more strenuous supporters of the popular cause in our little circles than others ; but all were abundantly liberal. A Brutus, or a Gracchus, would have found many to surpass him, and few, indeed, to fall short, in theoretical devotion to the interests of equal freedom. I can scarcely recollect a single exception amongst my numerous acquaintances: all, I think, were worthy of the best ages of Greece, or of Rome ; all were true, loyal citizens, brave and free.

VIII.

The rare assiduity of the young poet in the acquisition of general knowledge has been already described ; he had, moreover, diligently studied the mechanism of his art before he came to Oxford. He composed Latin verses with singular facility. On visiting him soon after his arrival at the accustomed hour of one, he was writing the usual exercise which we presented, I believe, once a week—a Latin translation of a paper in the Spectator. He soon finished it, and as he held it before the fire to dry, I offered to take it from him ; he said it was not worth looking at ; but as I persisted, through a certain scholastic curiosity to examine the Latinity of my new acquaintance, he gave it to me. The Latin was sufficiently correct, but the version was paraphrastic, which I observed; he assented, and said that it would pass muster, and he felt no interest in such efforts, and no desire to excel in them. I also noticed many portions of heroic verses, and even several entire verses, and these I pointed out as defects in a prose composition. He smiled archly, and asked, in his piercing whisper—'Do you think they will observe them? I inserted them intentionally to try their ears! I once showed up a theme at Eaton to old Keate, in which there were a great many verses; but he observed them, scanned them, and asked why had I introduced them? I answered, that I did not know they were there: this was partly true and partly false; but he believed me, and immediately applied to me the line, in which Ovid says of himself—

"*Et quod tentabam dicere, versus erat.*"'

Shelley then spoke of the facility with which he could compose Latin verses; and, taking the paper out of my hand, he began to put the entire translation into verse. He would sometimes open at hazard a prose writer, as Livy, or Sallust, and by changing the position of the words, and occasionally substituting others, he would transmute several sentences from prose to verse—to heroic, or more commonly elegiac, verse, for he was peculiarly charmed with the graceful and easy flow of the latter—with surprising rapidity and readiness. He was fond of displaying this accomplishment during his residence at Oxford, but he forgot to bring it away with him when he quitted the University; or perhaps he left it behind him designedly, as being suitable to academic groves only and to the banks of the Isis.

IX.

During the whole period of our residence there, the University was cruelly disfigured by bitter feuds, arising out of the late election of its Chancellor[1]: in an especial manner

[1] See Cox's *Recollections of Oxford*, 2nd ed. (1870), p. 65.

was our own most venerable college deformed by them, and by angry and senseless disappointment.

Lord Grenville had just been chosen. There could be no more comparison between his scholarship and his various qualifications for the honourable and useless office, and the claims of his unsuccessful opponent, than between the attainments of the best man of the year and those of the huge porter who, with a stern and solemn civility, kept the gates of University College,—the arts of mulled-wine, and egg-hot being, in the latter case, alone excepted.

The vanquished competitor, however, most unfortunately [P. 255.] for its honour and character, was a member of our college; and in proportion as the intrinsic merits of our rulers were small, had the vehemence and violence of electioneering been great, that, through the abuse of the patronage of the church, they might attain to those dignities, as the rewards of the activity of partisans, which they could never hope to reach through the legitimate road of superior learning and talents.

Their vexation at failing was the more sharp and abiding, because the only objection that vulgar bigotry could urge against the victor was his disposition to make concessions to the Roman Catholics; and every dull lampoon about popes, and cardinals, and the scarlet lady, had accordingly been worn threadbare in vain. Since the learned and the liberal had conquered, learning and liberality were peculiarly odious with us at that epoch. The studious scholar, particularly if he were of an inquiring disposition, and of a bold and free temper, was suspected and disliked: he was one of the enemy's troops. The inert and the subservient were the loyal soldiers of the legitimate army of the faith. The despised and scattered nation of scholars is commonly unfortunate; but a more severe calamity has seldom befallen the remnant of true Israelites than to be led captive by such a generation! Youth is happy, because it is blithe and healthful, and [P. 256.] exempt from care; but it is doubly and trebly happy since it is honest and fearless—honourable and disinterested.

In the whole body of undergraduates, scarcely one was friendly to the holder of the loaves and the promiser of the fishes, Lord Eldon. All were eager—all, one and all—in behalf of the scholar and the liberal statesman; and plain and loud was the avowal of their sentiments. A sullen demeanour towards the young rebels displayed the annoyance arising from the want of success, and from our lack of sympathy; and it would have demonstrated to the least observant, that, where the Muses dwell, the quarrels and intrigues of political parties ought not to come.

By his family and his connexions, as well as by disposition, Shelley was attached to the successful side; and although it was manifest that he was a youth of an admirable temper, of rare talents and unwearied industry, and likely, therefore, to shed a lustre upon his college and the University itself; yet, as he was eminently delighted at that wherewith his superiors were offended, he was regarded from the beginning with a jealous eye.

A young man of spirit will despise the mean spite of sordid minds; nevertheless, the persecution which a generous soul can contemn, through frequent repetition, too often becomes a severe annoyance in ' the long course of life; and Shelley frequently and most pathetically lamented the political divisions which then harassed the University, and were a more fertile source of manifold ills in the wider field of active life. For this reason did he appear to cling more closely to our sweet studious seclusion; and from this cause, perhaps, principally arose his disinclination,—I may say, indeed, his intense antipathy, for the political career that had been proposed to him. A lurking suspicion would sometimes betray itself that he was to be forced into that path, and impressed into the civil service of the state,—to become, as it were, a conscript legislator.

X.

The ordinary lectures in our college were of much shorter duration, and decidedly less difficult and less instructive, than the lessons we had received in the higher classes of a public school; nor were our written exercises more stimulating than the oral. Certain compositions were required at stated periods; but, however excellent they might be, they were never commended,—however deficient, they were never censured; and, being altogether unnoticed, there was no reason to suppose that they were ever read.

The University at large was not less remiss than each college in particular: the only incitement proposed was an examination at the end of four years. The young collegian might study in private as diligently as he would at Oxford, as in every other place; and if he chose to submit his pretensions to the examiners, his name was set down in the first, the second, or the third class,—if I mistake not, there were three divisions,—according to his advancement. This list was printed precisely at the moment when he quitted the University for ever;—a new generation of strangers might read the names of the unknown proficients, if they would.

It was notorious, moreover, that, merely to obtain the academical degrees, every new comer, who had passed through a tolerable grammar-school, brought with him a stock of learning, of which the residuum that had not evaporated during four years of dissipation and idleness, would be more than sufficient. The languid course of chartered laziness was ill-suited to the ardent activity and glowing zeal of Shelley.

Since those persons, who were hired at an enormous charge by his own family and by the state to find due and beneficial employment for him, thought fit to neglect this, their most sacred duty, he began forthwith to set himself to work. He read diligently,—I should rather say he devoured greedily, with the voracious appetite of a famished man,—the authors that roused his curiosity: he discoursed and discussed with energy; he wrote—he began to print—and he designed soon to publish various works.

XI.

Although Shelley was of a grave disposition, he had a certain sly relish for a practical joke, so that it were ingenious and abstruse, and of a literary nature; he would often exult in the successful forgeries of Chatterton and Ireland; and he was especially delighted with a trick that had lately been played at Oxford, by a certain noble viceroy, at that time an undergraduate, respecting the fairness of which the University was divided in opinion, all the undergraduates accounting it most just, and all the graduates, and especially the bachelors, extremely iniquitous, and indeed popish and jesuitical. A reward is offered annually for the best English essay on a subject proposed: the competitors send their anonymous essays, each being distinguished by a motto; when the grave arbitrators have selected the most worthy, they burn the vanquished essays, and open the sealed paper endorsed with a corresponding motto, and containing the name of the victor.

On the late famous contention, all the ceremonies had been duly performed, but the sealed paper presented the name of an undergraduate[1], who is not qualified to be a candidate, and all the less meritorious discourses of the bachelors had been burnt, together with their sealed papers—so there was to be no bachelor's prize that year.

XII.

We had read together attentively several of the metaphysical works that were most in vogue at that time, as 'Locke concerning Human Understanding,' and 'Hume's

---

[1] The case mentioned appears to be that of W. Attfield, 1811, but though an undergraduate he had exceeded four years from his matriculation on 5 May, 1811, and so would seem to have been duly elected. The part played by the 'noble viceroy' is not clear, nor are the dates quite consistent.

Essays,' particularly the latter, of which we had made a very careful analysis, as was customary with those who read the Ethics and the other treatises of Aristotle for their degrees. Shelley had the custody of these papers, which were chiefly in his handwriting, although they were the joint production of both in our common daily studies. From these, and from a small part of them only, he made up a little book, and had it printed, I believe, in the country, certainly not at Oxford.

XIII.

His little pamphlet[1] was never offered for sale; it was not P. 274. addressed to an ordinary reader, but to the metaphysician alone; and it was so short, that it was only designed to point out the line of argument. It was in truth a general issue; a compendious denial of every allegation, in order to put the whole case in proof; it was a formal mode of saying, you affirm so and so, then prove it; and thus was it understood by his more candid and intelligent correspondents. As it was shorter, so was it plainer, and perhaps, in order to provoke discussion, a little bolder, than Hume's Essays,—a book which occupies a conspicuous place in the library of every student. The doctrine, if it deserves the name, was precisely similar; the necessary and inevitable consequence of Locke's philosophy, and of the theory that all knowledge is from without. I will not admit your conclusions, his opponent might answer; then you must deny those of Hume: I deny them; but you must deny those of Locke also; and we will go back together to Plato. Such was the usual course of argument; sometimes, however, he rested on mere denial, holding his adversary to strict proof, and deriving strength from his weakness.

The young Platonist argued thus negatively through the P. 275. love of argument, and because he found a noble joy in the fierce shocks of contending minds; he loved truth, and sought it everywhere, and at all hazards, frankly and boldly, like a man who deserved to find it; but he also loved dearly victory

[1] Entitled *A Defence of Atheism.*

in debate, and warm debate for its own sake. Never was there a more unexceptionable disputant; he was eager beyond the most ardent, but never angry and never personal; he was the only arguer I ever knew who drew every argument from the nature of the thing, and who could never be provoked to descend to personal contentions. He was fully inspired, indeed, with the whole spirit of the true logician; the more obvious and indisputable the proposition which his opponent undertook to maintain, the more complete was the triumph of his art if he could refute and prevent him.

To one who was acquainted with the history of our University, with its ancient reputation as the most famous school of logic. it seemed that the genius of the place, after an absence of several generations, had deigned to return at last; the visit, however, as it soon appeared, was ill-timed.

XIV.

P. 277.   Wiser and better men displayed anciently, together with a more profound erudition, a superior and touching solemnity; the meek seriousness of Shelley was redolent of those good old times before mankind had been despoiled of a main ingredient in the composition of happiness, a well-directed veneration.

Whether such disputations were decorous or profitable may be perhaps doubtful; there can be no doubt, however, since the sweet gentleness of Shelley was easily and instantly swayed by the mild influences of friendly admonition, that, had even the least dignified of his elders suggested the propriety of pursuing his metaphysical inquiries with less ardour, his obedience would have been prompt and perfect.

Not only had all salutary studies been long neglected in Oxford at that time, and all wholesome discipline was decayed, but the splendid endowments of the University were grossly abused; the resident authorities of the college were too often men of the lowest origin, of mean and sordid souls, destitute

of every literary attainment, except that brief and narrow
course of reading by which the first degree was attained; the
vulgar sons of vulgar fathers, without liberality, and wanting
the manners and the sympathies of gentlemen.

A total neglect of all learning, an unseemly turbulence, the
most monstrous irregularities, open and habitual drunkenness,
vice, and violence, were tolerated or encouraged, with the
basest sycophancy, that the prospect of perpetual licentiousness might fill the colleges with young men of fortune;
whenever the rarely exercised power of coercion was exerted,
it demonstrated the utter incapacity of our unworthy rulers by
coarseness, ignorance, and injustice.

If a few gentlemen were admitted to fellowships, they were
always absent; they were not persons of literary pretensions,
or distinguished by scholarship; and they had no more share
in the government of the college than the overgrown guardsmen, who, in long white gaiters, bravely protect the precious
life of the sovereign against such assailants as the tenth Muse,
our good friend, Mrs. Nicholson[1].

As the term was drawing to a close, and a great part of
the books we were reading together still remained unfinished,
we had agreed to increase our exertions and to meet at an
early hour.

It was a fine spring morning on Lady-day, in the year
1811, when I went to Shelley's rooms: he was absent; but
before I had collected our books he rushed in. He was
terribly agitated. I anxiously inquired what had happened.

'I am expelled,' he said, as soon as he had recovered himself a little, 'I am expelled! I was sent for suddenly a few
minutes ago; I went to the common room, where I found
our master[2], and two or three of the fellows. The master
produced a copy of the little syllabus, and asked me if I were
the author of it. He spoke in a rude, abrupt, and insolent
tone. I begged to be informed for what purpose he put the

---

[1] This refers to Shelley's *Posthumous Poems of my Aunt Margaret Nicholson*.
[2] James Griffith, Master of Univ. Coll. 1808-21.

question. No answer was given; but the master loudly and angrily repeated, "Are you the author of this book?" If I can judge from your manner, I said, you are resolved to punish me, if I should acknowledge that it is my work. If you can prove that it is, produce your evidence; it is neither just nor lawful to interrogate me in such a case and for such a purpose. Such proceedings would become a court of inquisitors, but not free men in a free country. "Do you choose to deny that this is your composition?" the master reiterated in the same rude and angry voice.' Shelley complained much of his violent and ungentlemanlike deportment, saying, 'I have experienced tyranny and injustice before, and I well know what vulgar violence is; but I never met with such unworthy treatment. I told him calmly, but firmly, that I was determined not to answer any questions respecting the publication on the table. He immediately repeated his demand; I persisted in my refusal; and he said furiously, "Then you are expelled; and I desire you will quit the college early to-morrow morning at the latest." One of the fellows took up two papers, and handed one of them to me; here it is.' He produced a regular sentence of expulsion, drawn up in due form, under the seal of the college.

Shelley was full of spirit and courage, frank and fearless; but he was likewise shy, unpresuming, and eminently sensitive. I have been with him in many trying situations of his after-life, but I never saw him so deeply shocked and so cruelly agitated as on this occasion. A nice sense of honour shrinks from the most distant touch of disgrace—even from the insults of those men whose contumely can bring no shame. He sat on the sofa, repeating, with convulsive vehemence, the words, 'Expelled, expelled!' his head shaking with emotion, and his whole frame quivering. The atrocious injustice and its cruel consequences roused the indignation, and moved the compassion, of a friend, who then stood by Shelley. He has given the following account of his interference:

'So monstrous and so illegal did the outrage seem, that

I held it to be impossible that any man, or any body of men, would dare to adhere to it; but, whatever the issue might be, it was a duty to endeavour to the utmost to assist him. I at once stepped forward, therefore, as the advocate of Shelley; such an advocate, perhaps, with respect to judgment, as might be expected at the age of eighteen, but certainly not inferior to the most practised defenders in good will and devotion. I wrote a short note to the master and fellows, in which, as far as I can remember a very hasty composition after a long interval, I briefly expressed my sorrow at the treatment my friend had experienced, and my hope that they would re-consider their sentence; since, by the same course of proceeding, myself, or any other person, might be subjected to the same penalty, and to the imputation of equal guilt. The note was despatched; the conclave was still sitting; and in an instant the porter came to summon me to attend, bearing in his countenance a promise of the reception which I was about to find. The angry and troubled air of men, assembled to commit injustice according to established forms, was then new to me; but a native instinct told me, as soon as I entered the room, that it was an affair of party; that whatever could conciliate the favour of patrons was to be done without scruple; and whatever could tend to impede preferment was to be brushed away without remorse. The glowing master produced my poor note. I acknowledged it; and he forthwith put into my hand, not less abruptly, the little syllabus. "Did you write this"? he asked, as fiercely as if I alone stood between him and the rich see of Durham. I attempted, submissively, to point out to him the extreme unfairness of the question; the injustice of punishing Shelley for refusing to answer it; that if it were urged upon me I must offer the like refusal, as I had no doubt every man in college would—every gentleman, indeed, in the University; which, if such a course were adopted with all,—and there could not be any reason why it should be used with one and not with the rest,—would thus be stripped of every member. I soon perceived that arguments were thrown away upon a man possessing no more intellect or erudition, and far less renown, than that famous ram, since translated to the stars, through grasping whose tail less firmly than was expedient, the sister of Phryxus formerly found a watery grave, and gave her name to the broad Hellespont.

'The other persons present took no part in the conversation: they presumed not to speak, scarcely to breathe, but looked mute subserviency. The few resident fellows, indeed, were but so many incarnations of the spirit of the master, whatever that spirit might be. When I was silent, the master told me to retire, and to consider whether I was resolved to persist in my refusal. The proposal was fair enough. ' The next day, or the next week, I might have given my final answer—a deliberate answer; having in the mean time consulted with older and more experienced persons, as to what course was best for myself and for others. I had scarcely passed the door, however, when I was recalled. The master again showed me the book, and hastily demanded whether I admitted, or denied, that I was the author of it. I answered that I was fully sensible of the many and great inconveniences of being dismissed with disgrace from the University, and I specified some of them, and expressed an humble hope that they would not impose such a mark of discredit upon me without any cause. I lamented that it was impossible either to admit, or to deny, the publication,—no man of spirit could submit to do so ;—and that a sense of duty compelled me respectfully to refuse to answer the question which had been proposed. "Then you are expelled," said the master angrily, in a loud, great voice. A formal sentence, duly signed and sealed, was instantly put into my hand : in what interval the instrument had been drawn up I cannot imagine. The alleged offence was a contumacious refusal to disavow the imputed publication. My eye glanced over it, and observing the word *contumaciously*, I said calmly that I did not think that term was justified by my behaviour. Before I had

concluded the remark, the master, lifting up the little syl- P. 284.
labus, and then dashing it on the table, and looking sternly
at me, said, "Am I to understand, sir, that you adopt the
principles contained in this work?" or some such words; for,
like one red with the suffusion of college port and college ale,
the intense heat of anger seemed to deprive him of the power
of articulation; by reason of a rude provincial dialect, and
thickness of utterance, his speech being at all times indistinct.
"The last question is still more improper than the former,"
I replied,—for I felt that the imputation was an insult; "and
since, by your own act, you have renounced all authority over
me, our communication is at an end." "I command you to
quit my college to-morrow at an early hour." I bowed and
withdrew. I thank God I have never seen that man since:
he is gone to his bed, and there let him sleep. Whilst he
lived, he ate freely of the scholar's bread, and drank from his
cup; and he was sustained, throughout the whole term of his
existence, wholly and most nobly, by those sacred funds that
were consecrated by our pious forefathers to the advancement
of learning. If the vengeance of the all-patient and long-
contemned gods can ever be roused, it will surely be by some
such sacrilege! The favour which he showed to scholars, and
his gratitude, have been made manifest. If he were still alive,
he would doubtless be as little desirous that his zeal should
now be remembered as those bigots who had been most P. 285.
active in burning Archbishop Cranmer could have been to
publish their officiousness, during the reign of Elizabeth.'

Busy rumour has ascribed, on what foundation I know not,
since an active and searching inquiry has not hitherto been
made, the infamy of having denounced Shelley to the pert,
meddling tutor of a college of inferior note, a man of an in-
salubrious and inauspicious aspect. Any paltry fellow can
whisper a secret accusation; but a certain courage, as well as
malignity, is required by him who undertakes to give evidence
openly against another; to provoke thereby the displeasure
of the accused, of his family and friends; and to submit his

own veracity and his motives to public scrutiny. Hence the illegal and inquisitorial mode of proceding by interrogation, instead of the lawful and recognised course by the production of witnesses. The disposal of ecclesiastical preferment has long been so reprehensible,—the practice of desecrating institutions that every good man desires to esteem most holy is so inveterate,—that it is needless to add that the secret accuser was rapidly enriched with the most splendid benefices, and finally became a dignitary of the church. The modest prelate did not seek publicity in the charitable and dignified act of deserving; it is not probable, therefore, that he is anxious at present to invite an examination of the precise nature of his deserts.

P. 286.

The next morning, at eight o'clock, Shelley and his friend set out together for London on the top of a coach; and with his final departure from the University the reminiscences of his life at Oxford terminate.

XV.

P. 287.

Thus not only were we driven rudely and lawlessly from a common table, spread for us by the provident bounty of our pious and prudent forefathers, where we had an undoubted right to be fed and nurtured; but my incomparable friend and myself were hunted hastily out of Oxford. The precipitate violence and indecent outrage was the act of our college, not of the University; the evildoers seemed to fear that, if we remained among them but a little while, the wrong might be redressed. It is true that I was told, but as it were at the moment of departure, that if it was inconvenient to us to quit the place so suddenly, we might remain for a time; and that, if Shelley would ask permission of the master to stay for a short period, it would most probably be granted. I immediately informed him of this proposal, but he was far too indignant at the insult which he had received, and at the brutal indignity with which he had been treated, to apply for any favour whatever, even if his life had depended on the P. 288. concession. The delicacy of a young high-bred gentleman makes him ever most unwilling to intrude, and more especially to remain in any society, where his presence is not acceptable. Nevertheless, I have sometimes regretted, and more particularly for the sake of my gifted friend, to whom the residence at Oxford was exceedingly delightful, and, on all accounts, most beneficial, that we yielded so readily to these modest, retiring feelings. For if license to remain for some days would have been formally given upon a specific application, no doubt it would have been tacitly allowed; although no request had been made, permission would have been implied. At any rate it is perfectly certain that force—brute force—would not have been resorted to; that the police of the University would never have been directed to turn us out of our rooms, and to drive us beyond the gates of our college, roughly casting the poor students' books into the street. The young martyr had never been told—he never received any admonition, not even the slightest hint, that his speculations were improper, or unpleasing to any one; those persons alone had taken notice of, or a part in, them to whom they were agreeable; persons, who, like himself, relished them, and had a taste for abstruse and, perhaps, unprofitable discussions.

XVI.

If he had disregarded repeated admonition (I am confident P. 289. that he would have yielded to the first monitor) the milder punishment of rustication should have been first tried. To have been banished from Oxford, for a term or two, would have been a less immoderate chastisement, and it would have been deeply felt by an ingenuous youth to whom a college-life was in all respects suitable, and indeed charming; who seemed to be one of those modest, studious, recluse persons for whose special behalf universities and colleges were founded and are maintained.

P. 290.   Our college was denominated University College, but Liberty Hall would have been a more correct and significant name. Universal laziness was the order of the day, except so far as half-a-dozen scholars were concerned, who subsisted, in some measure, on eleemosynary foundations, and were no acquisition to the society; such people being usually the vulgar relatives or friends of the vulgar authorities of the place. In the evening unceasing drunkenness and continual uproar prevailed.

The observation, therefore, was not less just than happy, that our college must have been founded, not by King Alfred, as was asserted, but by his foes, the Danes; by barbarians, who quaffed mead to furious intoxication out of the skulls of their enemies; all men being accounted such who would read and write, or who had an inclination for such pursuits. The disorder was, in truth, intolerable. The perpetual intoxication doubtless was profitable, if not to the interests of learning and education, to the Oxford vintners; to vintagers, that from the fruit of the white blossomed sloe,

'Crushed the black poison of misused wine.'

To ascribe a college to a particular county or district, is to devote it at once to vulgarity and barbarism; and fellowships, and other foundations, confined to some particular county or school, are invariably ill-bestowed, wasted, and thrown away.

P. 291.   This was our unfortunate position, and to a striking degree—in an excess—the milk of bounty had turned sour, our aliment was corrupted, our natural nutriment most unnaturally had become poison! In such a state of things nothing seemed to be forbidden; the notion that every one might follow his own devices, and do whatever he pleased, was perhaps a mistake; but it was a natural and surely a pardonable one. It ought to have been corrected by salutary precept and admonition, not blindly and fiercely chastised and overwhelmed by injustice, indignity, and insult. But it was necessary that the divine poet should fulfil his destinies ; his high vocation was to be before and above his age. It was inevitable, and he could not but pursue it !

One thing, at least, is certain, that I bear them no ill-will ; on the contrary, I earnestly desire to return good for evil—and indeed the greatest of all good—viz., to reform their famous and admirable university; to reform it effectually and thoroughly, so that it may be a credit to themselves, and a blessing to the country and to posterity: and I feel strongly that it is my vocation to do this.

I heard an anecdote which may be repeated now, for it can never be out of place, respecting the University of Oxford, from a venerable friend who had resided many years in Italy ; at Venice and Padua. The greater part of his time he had spent [1] at the latter remarkable and interesting city, and he had long been intimate with the professors of its celebrated university. Some of them he had found to be truly learned and liberal-minded men ; of one professor in particular—I regret that I have forgotten his name—he often spoke with admiration, and related many things concerning him highly to his credit.

This gentleman had long been animated by an honourable curiosity to inform himself touching the condition of the other universities of Europe, and for several years had employed his leisure and vacations in visiting the most renowned of these institutions. He obtained introductions to the principal authorities at each seat of learning, and had been passed, duly furnished with letters of recommendation, from one university to another.

The Paduan professor had remained some weeks at Oxford, and had conversed with the principal persons. He said that he had been forcibly struck there with two very remarkable peculiarities, neither of which he had ever met with in any other university. The first was this: wherever he went it had been his practice to inquire, Whom do you consider as the

P. 292.

first man among you in learning and talent? Who is the second? And who is your third? In every other university he had received a prompt and decided answer to these questions; here and there he had met with some difference of opinion as to the name which ought to rank as the third,—but as to the first and second, they had been everywhere unanimous; and certainly his three questions had everywhere received an immediate and unhesitating answer. But at Oxford and at Oxford only, as if they were all in a conspiracy together,—the phrase is the professor's—to keep it a profound secret, nobody would ever tell him who stood first. In what way, in what walk of science, in what department, in what branch of knowledge? Pray, tell me who is the first among you in any way? There was no answer; they all stood mute. Why was this?

The second remarkable peculiarity was this,—and, the Professor added, it made the first peculiarity still more striking and peculiar. At every other mart of learning he had often heard the answer 'I do not know'; but at Oxford, never. Elsewhere I have asked a professor of astronomy some question regarding anatomy, or botany, and he had the courage and honesty at once frankly to answer, 'I do not know.' But at Oxford it really seemed as if everybody considered himself equally bound to be universal, to know everything, and to be able to give some sort of affirmative answer to every question, however foreign it might be to his ordinary and proper pursuits. There is so much wisdom in answering seasonably, 'I do not know,' that in an university which has been celebrated, and accounted most wise for nine or ten centuries, I thought, for the credit of the place, I ought to get it once, at least, before I went away; so I tried hard, but I could never obtain it. Why was this?

I had called Oxford 'a seat of learning.' 'Why do you call it so?' Shelley asked, warmly; 'you have no right to call it so; such a place cannot be a seat of learning?' 'Yes, it is a seat of learning, and I have a right to call it so. It is a seat in which learning sits very comfortably, well thrown back, as in an easy chair, and sleeps so soundly, that neither you, nor I, nor anybody else, can wake her.'

It has been affirmed by ardent spirits,—and not, perhaps, altogether without some show of reason,—that if any of the scholars be suffered to quit Eton without a moderate, but lively feeling of religion, the authorities of that famous seminary ought to be scourged to death. And, moreover, that if a single student be permitted to depart from the Universities of Oxford or Cambridge, unimbued with genuine piety, the appliances of both universities, and especially of the former, being duly estimated, the heads of houses, the professors and tutors, deserve to be impaled alive, with their cold Bampton Lectures, tame unedifying discourses, evidences, probabilities, credibilities, and the whole farrago of frigid rationalism, suspended round their necks. The Oxford Tracts, however, have, of late years somewhat redeemed the character of this ancient and renowned school of orthodox theology; had it been the fate of my incomparable friend to have met with these, or rather with some of them, with how much delight and instruction would he not have perused and profited by them.

Some slight advances have unquestionably been recently made towards removing the stigma of utter uselessness with which the University of Oxford has been branded; until lately it seemed to exist only for the discouragement of learning. For many years I desired, I trust, with no illiberal curiosity, and for a long time I desired it eagerly, to consult certain Greek and other MSS., deposited in the Bodleian and other libraries. I ventured sometimes to hint my wish to persons who were in a position to have granted it very easily; but I found no encouragement. At the best I was told, that if I went to Oxford, and procured the recommendation of some Master of Arts, I might enter those well-closed depositories, as others might, and could do as they did; what this was, I could never discover; probably to return as wise as they came. The

P. 295.

P. 296. scanty information, costively imparted, tempted [1] me only to postpone indefinitely the gratification of my wishes.

We had determined to quit Oxford immediately (this probably was a mistake), being under the ban of an absurd and illegal sentence. Having breakfasted together, the next morning, March 26, 1811, we took our places on the outside of a coach, and proceeded to London.

XXVI.

FREDERICK OAKELEY.

[Sixth son of Sir Charles Oakeley, first Baronet; *born* Sept. 5, 1802; Prebendary of Lichfield, 1832; afterwards of St. George's, Westminster; a Canon in Holy Orders of the Church of Rome; *died* Jan. 29, 1880.]

The Month. Vols. 3-4. Lond. 1865-66.

I.

CHRIST CHURCH UNDER DEAN HALL[1].

DEAR MR. EDITOR,—You are so kind as to think that the public may be interested in my personal recollections of Oxford, going back, as they do, nearly half a century, and ranging over some twenty years of an important period; and you wish accordingly that I should put them on paper. I will do as you desire, upon one condition; and that is, that you will allow me to throw my narrative into the form of one or more letters to yourself. It is thus only that I can shield myself in the view of the public from the appearance of an absurd piece of egotism. Moreover, I suppose that most people can write on popular subjects more easily when addressing an individual than when discharging the contents of their memory, or their imagination, as it were, into the air.

I do not possess any written memoranda of the times to which you recall me, but the scenes of my youth are still vividly before my mind; and although, in trying to reproduce them on paper, I shall no doubt omit many things necessary to the completeness of my picture, yet I think I can pro-

Vol. III. P. 508.

---

[1] Charles Henry Hall, Dean of Christ Church, 1809-24; Dean of Durham, 1824; died March 16, 1827.

mise tolerable accuracy in the description of what I do remember.

I happen to have just been reading for the first time Dean Stanley's beautiful Life of Dr. Arnold, in the earlier part of which you will remember that there occurs a very long letter from one of Arnold's most distinguished and most valued friends[1], containing a graphic delineation of undergraduate life at Oxford, when he and several eminent men yet living were companions together. In reading that interesting letter I could not help feeling, with a sense of deep personal humiliation, what a different idea it gives of Oxford undergraduate society from that which I obtained as the result of my own experience,—different not only as respects the general character of the life which it represents, but as respects also the moral tone of the individuals who gave to that life the character which is impressed on it. We are accustomed to suppose that the moral tone of Oxford has been in a progressive course of improvement since the beginning of the present century; yet the picture to which I refer belongs to a period more remote by several years than that which is present to my mind. However, as I have said, the contrast suggests feelings of personal humiliation in arrest of any precipitate judgment as to ¹ the historical differences between Oxford in 1810 or 1812 and Oxford in 1820 or 1822.

I cannot tell how much of the gloom which hangs over my impression of undergraduate life at Oxford in my time is attributable to my own misuse of its actual opportunities; yet that the darkness of these recollections is not merely self-reflected, I am thoroughly convinced, though it still may be that my lot as an undergraduate was cast in a sphere peculiarly unfavourable for the exhibition of what Oxford even in those days was actually capable of effecting. I do really think that Christ Church, the college at which I entered, as it was the highest in repute for the advantages of this world, was also, in my time, the most degraded in respect

[1] Sir John Taylor Coleridge. See above, p. 247.

of all that relates to the true end of our existence. The letter to which I have just alluded conveys the idea of a small knot of men, belonging to one or more of the lesser colleges, living constantly with one another, and finding their chief interest in literary pursuits, rational converse, and harmless recreation. I will say confidently that such a picture as this had no kind of counterpart at Christ Church during the earlier years of my undergraduate life. I cannot recollect any set of men, however regular in ordinary college duties. and however given to reading, of whom I do not feel sure that, with whatever possible exceptions in the case of individuals, they were. as a set, addicted to vice and loose conversation. I remained long enough at Oxford to witness a vast improvement; but the favourable testimony I shall hereafter give would be of no value if I attempted in any way to disguise the fact which I have just placed on record.

On the other hand, I am well aware that my own personal antecedents were in many respects unfavourable to my gaining from Oxford all the advantages of which it might have been productive in the case of another. Hence it is that I am led to mistrust the almost total absence in myself of those feelings of enthusiastic attachment to the place which are common to men of such diametrically opposite views and temperaments as the late Dr. Arnold on the one side, and Dr. Newman, Mr. Keble, and Sir John Coleridge on the other. As time went on, I got to like Oxford far better than I did during the greater portion of my life as an undergraduate; but my early impressions of it were so exceedingly the reverse of pleasant, that I could never wholly conquer them; and I left with but little regret a place which I entered with the most glowing anticipations of happiness.

I have always traced my want of congeniality with Oxford in a great measure to the fact of its having been the first place of my public education. I do not mean merely that I was never at a public school ' but that I was never at any school at all which could deserve the name. Hence I had to

P. 510.

encounter at the age of eighteen those trials which most boys get through and leave behind them at the age of eight,—the trial of feeling oneself suddenly in an entirely new world, and that a world of the most inconsiderate and unsympathising portion of the rational creation. I went up to Oxford in 1820 from a private tutor, whose house was but a prolongation of home, and that under the most delightful aspect; that is to say, it was a home in which there was discipline to give vigour to work and zest to recreation,—not such a discipline as ever galled or fretted its subjects. In my tutor I had one who united the authority of a father with the tenderness of a mother; and whatever he wanted to the full development of the maternal relation was supplied by a simple and kind-hearted wife, whose tastes were remarkably congenial to my own, and who took in me more than ordinary interest, as in one who was transplanted under her roof from an eye which had watched over him during eleven years of sickness and infirmity. Fancy what it was to be abruptly drafted from a home like this into a great college, teeming with bustle and excitement of the most boisterous and heartless character; to become the butt of badgering tutors and the sport of overbearing undergraduates; and to feel that the manifestations of discomfort and shyness which were inevitable in so new an atmosphere could only contribute to increase the evil of which they were the result. But I am getting off the line of my narrative.

My available knowledge of Oxford dates from the summer of 1820, when I went up from my private tutor's to be matriculated at Christ Church. It happened to be the time of the Commemoration, and I was taken by my graduate friend to witness the imposing spectacle in the Theatre, with the view of firing my young ambition by a sight of the triumphs accorded by the University to the conquerors in one department of the academical arena. To a youth educated mainly in the country, and never at any school, no sight could be more impressively brilliant than that which this annual gathering presents. It is a spectacle which is said to have struck the imperial and royal visitors of 1814[1] almost more than any of the festive scenes which were got up for their entertainment. There is the sweeping semicircle of Doctors of Divinity and Law in their robes of scarlet and pink, backed by the rising tiers of particoloured ladies, beaming with bright and jubilant countenances; the whole surmounted by a crown of undergraduates, with their lively summer costume, contrasting so curiously with that ugliest of professional badges—the undergraduate gown. The area below is filled with Masters of Arts, and their gaping lions. On the occasion to which I refer there were one or two notable circumstances. The first of these was the extraordinary unpopularity of the Senior Proctor of that year,—my kind friend and sometime tutor, Mr. (afterwards Doctor) Bull[2], of Christ Church. By a certain absurd donnishness and unevenness of manner, which laid him open to the charge of adapting himself too much to his company, this really kind-hearted man had contrived to earn for himself the unpopular characters of a tyrant and a tuft-hunter; and the undergraduate world poured forth upon him, at the annual saturnalia, the pent up fury of the preceding two terms. The rosy-faced official bore his trial with unruffled placidity; but to a youth—inexperienced alike in the misdeeds of the proctor and in the system which allows so great a license to public opinion in the subjects of a great educational institution—this display of excited feeling was, as may well be imagined, a complete enigma. They hissed, they yelled, they roared like a bull, with a manifest allusion to the proctor's ill-starred name; and they did their best to give force to the contrast which they wished to make between the object of

P. 511.

---

[1] The Prince Regent, the Emperor of Russia and the King of Prussia, who visited the University, June, 1814.

[2] John Bull, Christ Church, matr. May 27, 1808, aged 18; B.A. 1812; M.A. 1814; Proctor, 1820; D.D. 1825.

their fury and his colleague, whom they invested for the occasion with an exaggerated popularity.

The other incident of the year was of a more pleasing character,—it was the unusual interest attracted by the Latin prize-poem, the reputation of which had preceded its delivery. The fortunate competitor was Mr. William Ralph Churton [1], of Queen's College, who some years later became domestic chaplain to Dr. Howley [2], and died—as is recorded in a very elegant Latin epitaph at St. Mary's, Oxford—in the prime of youth and promise. The subject of the prize which he gained in 1820 was 'Newtoni Systema'; and he handled the Newtonian theory of gravitation altogether in the spirit of Lucretius. I remember too his felicitous description of the characteristics of the different planets; and his elegant allusion, at the mention of the Georgium Sidus, to the death of the sovereign who gave his name to that planet, which had occurred in the course of the preceding year:—

> . . . .   dum tua lucet
> Stella polo, semper grato sub corde fovemus
> Ingenium, moresque aureos, memorande, colentes.'

Churton was run hard for the prize by Ewart [3] of Christ Church, and Dr. Copleston [4] was called in as umpire. That eminent Latin scholar gave his judgment in favour of the successful candidate; and the somewhat inordinate expectations of Ewart's friends were but poorly satisfied by his victory in the Newdigate of the same year.

The opening of my residence at Christ Church in the following October presented a painful contrast to this bril-

---

[1] William Ralph Churton, Lincoln Coll., matr. Jan. 14, 1819, aged 17; Queen's Coll. B.A. 1822; Fellow of Oriel, 1823-8; M.A. 1825; died 1828.
[2] William Howley, Canon of Christ Church; Bishop of London, 1813-28; Archbishop of Canterbury, 1828, until his death in 1848.
[3] William Ewart, Christ Church, matr. Oct. 22, 1817, aged 17; B.A. 1821; M.A. 1865; of Broadleas, Wilts; Barrister-at-law, Middle Temple, 1826; M.P. for Bletchingley, 1828-30; Liverpool, 1830-1, 1831-7; Wigan, 1839-44; Dumfries in six Parliaments, 1841, until his death in 1869.
[4] See notes, pp. 220, 222.

liant inauguration. For the whole of the first term I was bandied about from one set of rooms to another; and at length, to my great joy, sent home for want of a place where to lay my head. During those few weeks I conceived a disgust of college-life, which I never wholly conquered till after I took my degree. I found myself quite out of harmony with the society of the place. I would not go through for a trifle what I used to suffer in having to pass through a knot of buoyant undergraduates in Peckwater or at Canterbury Gate. My tutor, the aforesaid Bull, kindly introduced me to two reading-men, who however, I suppose, were reading so hard that they did not want to be troubled with a new acquaintance, for both of them cut me the day after the introduction. I used to find relief in a good cry when I came to my unutterably dismal rooms in Fell's Buildings[1], after morning chapel or after hall, when I had seen clusters of my happier companions go off in high spirits to their several breakfast or wine-parties.

And now about wine-parties. They were divided into two kinds: parties consisting of ten or twelve members of the same 'set'; or, on the other hand, what were called 'spreads'; that is to say, entertainments for an indefinite number, at which successions of men entered for several hours,—some remaining a longer and some a shorter time, and some merely sitting down for a few minutes, drinking two or three glasses of wine, eating a few almonds and raisins or some preserved ginger, and then walking off. To a shy and solitary freshman like myself, to appear at one of the former kind of wine-parties was a penance most excruciating, but happily not frequent. He was not usually invited to small parties, unless once in a way by some person whom he happened to know at 'home,' and who had been requested by his mother or maiden-aunt to show some attention to George ——, who had just gone up to Oxford. A freshman was usually invited to the more indiscriminate entertainments, where he was not

[1] See note, p. 231.

so uncomfortably situated, because the party was too large for general conversation, and he was always introduced by his host to his next neighbour, who must have been a brute indeed if he did not at least address to him a few words of civility. Those with which a freshman was usually accosted were as formal and stereotyped as the phrases in a traveller's conversation book, and invariably consisted of such characteristic commonplaces as these: 'When did you come up?' 'Where are your rooms?' 'Who is your tutor?' The answer to which latter query was in my time followed by a rapid survey of that tutor's physical, moral, and intellectual qualities: e.g. 'A good fellow ——.' '—— is an ass,' '—— is a humbug,' etc. Indeed these 'spreads' often gave our hapless freshman the best chance he was likely to get of forming an agreeable or valuable acquaintance, since they were occasions on which both he and those with whom he was thrown were apt to appear to the best advantage. The parties were too large for overbearing or exclusive or unpleasant conversation, or indeed for any uniform conversation at all; and every one knows that a shy man feels himself most at home in such a society. The hosts also at these parties, to do them justice, were often gentlemanly fellows, who had imbibed true ideas of hospitality from their 'governors,' as they called them; perhaps, in some cases, might have been accustomed to take the bottom of the table at home. Among these ideas, one was that it was the host's duty, on the one hand, to disparage the good things at his table; and, on the other, to press them benevolently on his guests. I once heard of a ludicrous instance of the way in which these somewhat conflicting duties were occasionally brought into an awkward juxtaposition. 'This ice,' said the host, 'is atrocious, perfectly beastly.' Then, after a short pause, 'My dear fellow, do take some of it.'

Still, putting things at their best, it was a dreary state of existence for one like myself. Often would I throw up my window and gaze—as best I could through the bars by which it was secured against the exit of some disorderly tenant, or the entrance of some undesirable visitor—at the moon, on which I had been accustomed to look under circumstances so different: nor was it without a feeling of inexpressible relief that I hailed the 'gown-and-town' rows consequent upon the acquittal of Queen Caroline, which brought the term of college-residence to an earlier end than usual in the winter of 1820.

The undergraduate body of Christ Church in my time contained more than one of our existing notabilities. Dr. Pusey[1] was drawing toward his examination in the Schools. I did not know him, and have no definite recollection about him, except that he was a hard reader. We had also several members of the aristocracy, who have since created a reputation for themselves, though under names which have since been merged in hereditary or acquired titles. Lord Derby[2], as Mr. Stanley, was of a former generation, though his fame was still vigorous. There were, however, the present Lord Stanley of Alderley[3], then Mr. Stanley; Mr. Robert Grosvenor[4], now Lord Ebury; and Lord Ashley[5], now Lord Shaftesbury. But by far the most distinguished of the aristocratic coterie was George Howard[6], who as Lord Carlisle has lately passed away from this earthly scene. In the

---

[1] See note, p. 209.

[2] Edward Geoffrey Smith Stanley, fourteenth Earl of Derby, Christ Church, matr. Oct. 17, 1817, aged 18; gained the Chancellor's Prize for Latin verse by his poem 'Syracuse,' 1819; D.C.L. by diploma, 1852; Chancellor of the University, 1852–69; First Lord of the Treasury, 1852, 1858, and 1866; died 1869.

[3] Edward John Stanley, second Lord Stanley of Alderley, Cheshire, Christ Church, matr. Jan. 18, 1822, aged 19; B.A. 1825; created Lord Eddisbury, 1848; Postmaster-General, 1860; died 1869.

[4] Robert Grosvenor, Christ Church, matr. Dec. 9, 1818, aged 18; B.A. 1821, of Lincoln's Inn; created Baron Ebury, 1857.

[5] Anthony Ashley Cooper, Baron Ashley, Christ Church, matr. Oct. 27, 1819, aged 18; B.A. 1823; M.A. 1832; created D.C.L. 1841; seventh Earl of Shaftesbury; died 1885.

[6] George William Frederick Howard, seventh Earl of Carlisle, Christ Church, matr. Oct. 15, 1819, aged 17; B.A. 1823; M.A. 1827; Lord Lieutenant of Ireland, 1855–8 and 1859, until his death, 1864.

P. 514.

year 1821 he became the *monstratus digito* ¹ *prætereuntium*, as the successful competitor for both the undergraduate prizes. The subjects were 'Eleusis' and 'Pæstum'; and the latter was a really beautiful poem on the far-famed temples of Southern Italy, which made so great an impression on me that I could even now recite it off by heart. I have a kindly remembrance of Howard, for he was always very civil to me. He bore an irreproachable character as an undergraduate, and united, to an extent remarkable in a young man, a dignified bearing with affable and amiable manners. I wrote for both the prizes which he gained, and each succeeding year for the Newdigate, which I never was so fortunate as to get; and I think that one reason of my failure, among others, was that I always aimed at the sublime, while my judges properly preferred the simple. One year (1822) when the subject was 'Palmyra[1],' I got rightly served for my tendencies towards the bombastic. I spent some three months in concocting a poem (only, be it remembered, fifty lines) on the merits of the ancient Tadmor of the Desert, in which I threw off what I regarded as a stunning line, and it ran as follows:—

'High o'er the waste of Nature and of Time.'

A wicked wag of my acquaintance came into my room when I was absent, and finding my manuscript, which I had incautiously left on the table, erased the word 'Nature' from the above line, and substituted for it the word 'paper'; so that my pet line reappeared on my return in the following shape:—

'High o'er the waste of *paper* and of time;'

and was thus converted into a very apt description of the progress and result of my literary labours in this instance.

How strangely things come about in the course of years! The author of this amusing joke, who was as eccentric as he

---

[1] Gained by Ambrose Barber, Wadham.

was clever, afterwards became a Catholic and a priest, and was murdered some twenty years ago while bathing in the Adriatic, by a party of ruffians, who took that method of plundering him of valuables which he had left with his clothes on the beach.

I must say a few words of the college-authorities who presided over the education at Christ Church in my time. At the head of them when I first went and for two or three ,years later, was Dean Hall—a very handsome and gentlemanlike old man, who was said to have got himself into great difficulties by profuse expenditure and who at length exchanged his deanery of Christ Church for the more valuable one of Durham. He was, like other contemporaries of Dr. Cyril Jackson, a great imitator of the manners and ways of [1] that singular and popular man. I can see him now P. 515. marching up and down Christ Church hall at Collections, with the senior censor by his side, his hand planted in the belt of his cassock, and his cap almost perched upon the bridge of his nose. His manner, at least to me, was always haughty and overbearing, and I have no pleasant recollections about him. Next to him in dignity among the college-authorities was Dr. Barnes[1], the Sub-dean, a good-hearted old man; for he was old, or at least looked so to us youngsters even then, though he died a comparatively short time ago. He always took a prominent part at Collections, and there were all kinds of stories about his examinations. He was very regular and punctual at morning chapel, which was more than could be said of the Dean, who generally sailed in just before the 'Prayer of St. Chrysostom,' to the great relief of a host of undergraduates, who took advantage of his known habits, and waited in the nave till they gained admittance in the sweep of his tail.

The tutorial staff consisted of Bull, already mentioned;

---

[1] Frederick Barnes, of Christ Church, matr. June 9, 1790, aged 19; B.A. 1794; M.A. 1797; D.D. 1811.

Short[1], now Bishop of St. Asaph; Cramer[2], who died some years ago as Dean of Carlisle; and Longley[3], the present Archbishop of Canterbury. Bull, who was my tutor, did himself, as I have already said, injustice by his manner. Like his principal the Dean, he was of the school of Cyril Jackson, and reflected the peculiarities of his model, but in a far more amusing and attractive form. He adopted a certain phraseology, which had often an irreverent sound, though not, I hope, profanely meant. His strong Christ-Church feeling, inherited from old Cyril,' broke out in the most ridiculous prejudice against what were called ' ex-college men,' that is, the members of all other colleges; and this prejudice elicited, as was natural, a corresponding sentiment of antipathy in the other colleges to what they in their turn sometimes called ' *house*-men,' in reference to the pedantry by which Christ Church disdained the name of a college. When Bull was proctor, and had to take down the names for the public examinations, his room was of course besieged by a troop of these 'ex-college men'; and when his own class came in afterwards to lecture, he would ostentatiously throw open his window, in order, as he said, 'to purify the atmosphere.' But full half of all this was fun, though I do not deny that there was reality in it also. I cannot think of Bull without finding a smile arise on my lips; but it is far from being an unkindly smile,—rather it expresses the sort of half-playful melancholy which Shakespeare has so touchingly thrown into Hamlet's souvenir of his friend Yorick. Bull was an excellent scholar, and had the liveliest perception of the beauties of classical literature, as well as a great power of communicating it to

---

[1] Thomas Vowler Short, Christ Church, Bishop of Sodor and Man, 1841–6; of St. Asaph, 1846–70; died 1872.

[2] John Anthony Cramer, Principal of New Inn Hall (which he rebuilt), 1831–47; Regius Professor of Modern History, 1842–8; Dean of Carlisle, until his death, 1848.

[3] Charles Thomas Longley, Headmaster of Harrow, 1829–36; Bishop of Ripon, 1836–57; of Durham, 1856–60; Archbishop of York, 1860–2; of Canterbury, 1862, until his death in 1868.

others. ¹ His instincts of taste and scholarship were so acute, P. 516. that if a man in lecture made a false quantity, or was guilty of any literary vulgarism, he would jump about the room like a parched pea. I remember a good little man of the name of Wingfield¹ who once shortened the penultima of 'Eriphyle.' Bull screamed out as if he had been wounded the termination of Virgil's line, 'mœstamque Eriphȳlen.' Such incidents, trifling as they are, may serve to give reality to the scenes described in the eyes of some before whom these pages may chance to fall. Bull would recite whole passages of Virgil or Milton with evidences of the keenest relish. He used to say that the melody of euphonious versification was never exemplified more perfectly than in the lines :—

> 'Qualis populea mœrens Philomela sub umbra
> Amissos queritur fœtus, quos durus arator
> Observans nido implumes detraxit; at illa
> Flet noctem, ramoque sedens miserabile carmen
> Integrat, et mœstis late loca questibus implet.'
>
> [*Virgil.*]

He was also peculiarly fond of these touching lines of Horace :—

> 'Linquenda tellus, et domus, et placens
> Uxor; neque harum quas colis arborum
> Te præter invisum cypressum
> Ulla brevem dominum sequetur.'

I think his favourite Greek poet was Pindar. He wrote Latin verse with ease; and in 1821 dressed up a composition of mine after it had the good luck, rather than the merit, to gain the college-prize. It was full of disgraceful blunders; but Bull told me that the judges thought it more poetical than its more accurate competitors. He was pleased with descriptions which it contained of the boa-constrictor and of an elephant hunt. The subject was 'Taprobane' (the Island of Ceylon), a word the prosody of which I do not know to this day, and so am glad that I have to write it instead of

---

¹ Probably the Rev. Edward John Wingfield, Christ Church; matr. Oct. 19, 1820, aged 18; B.A. 1825; M.A. 1827; died Feb. 4, 1830.

pronouncing it. In my poem I made the first three syllables a dactyl; but Gaisford[1] (no mean authority on such a subject) declared that the penultima was long, in spite of the authorities I gave him. Of Gaisford I will speak presently; in the meantime I must complete my description of the tutors of Christ Church in my undergraduate days.

Next to Bull in order of seniority was a man as unlike him as one man could be unlike another. Those who are acquainted with the present respected Bishop of St. Asaph, and who know that a character so simple, so truthful, and so upright is not the creation of a day, will not be surprised to hear that the well-known Thomas Vowler Short, of forty-five years ago, was the precise counterpart of the honest Welsh prelate, minus the wrinkles, gray hair, apron, and lawn sleeves. Among the many sorrowful recollections connected with my undergraduate days, not one of the least is that I did not fall more directly under the practical influence of that truly good man. As it was, I knew only enough of him to be cowed and repelled by his blunt and somewhat uncouth manner, especially after a withering examination which he once gave me at Collections in the fifth book of Ethics. It was told of Short —I think upon good authority, but whether the story represented a fact or merely an antecedent probability I cannot say—that the first thing he did, upon hearing that his name was in the double first class, was to sit down and enter upon the study of St. Paul's Epistle to the Romans. A man who could do this was worthy of being a Jesuit.

Next to Short was John Anthony Cramer, an elegant-minded man, afterwards Dean of Carlisle; and next to him was Charles Thomas Longley, the present amiable and accomplished Primate of the Established Church,— the scholar and the gentleman everywhere. He was, as may well be imagined, a very popular tutor, and a welcome guest at the principal houses in Oxford. He was also, in my time, an

---

[1] Thomas Gaisford, of Christ Church; Regius Professor of Greek, 1811-35; Dean of Christ Church, 1831, until his death, 1855.

active steward of the music-room, and the πρόξενος of a series of *prima donnas*. Longley completed the tutorial staff in my early days; though, before I left Christ Church, it had received some less distinguished additions.

Of course I did not know Cyril Jackson, who had retired from Christ Church some years before, and was then spending his latter days at his living of Felpham, near Bognor. It had been commonly supposed that he would die, as the saying is, in harness; for he was often heard to declare that he did not think he could exist out of the sound of Great Tom. He was generally understood to have refused the archbishopric of York, as well as many inferior dignities, and it used to be said that he was much more than a bishop, for that he was a bishop-maker. He was consulted by Lord Liverpool[1] upon all the Church-appointments, though I cannot say whether his advice was invariably followed. No man who has left so few tangible records of greatness ever contrived to impress his character and manner more powerfully on those who surrounded him. I have already mentioned that Dr. Hall copied him to the extent of poising his cap on the bridge of his nose, and that Bull used to echo his phraseology in ordinary conversation. In fact, he was the founder of a school of copyists, and the author of a family of traditions. But we have lived long enough to see the last of his great imitators die off, and the most cherished of his traditions become obsolete. Poor Bull had vainly hoped that this school of opinions might have endured; and he had fixed upon a man singularly devoid of its faults, the late Robert Hussey[2] of Christ Church, some time Professor of Ecclesiastical History, as the agent by whom the old traditions were to be propelled into futurity. But Hussey was cut off by death in the prime of manhood, and the heathen entered into the sanctuary. Bull broke down under the pressure of the disappointment, and died in 1857.

[1] Charles Jenkinson, Earl of Liverpool; died 1808.
[2] Robert Hussey, Christ Church, matr. June 2, 1821, aged 19; B.A. 1825; M.A. 1827; Regius Professor of Ecclesiastical History, 1842, until his death in 1856.

One of the most pleasing recollections of my undergraduate life is that of the kind hospitality shown me by eminent men of considerable standing and great name in Oxford, who either belonged to other colleges or were *emeriti* in my own. I had the advantage of bringing introductions to this class from a brother[1] who had distinguished himself in the University some years before, and from other friends. I was thus brought into agreeable personal intercourse with two men of most opposite characters, but each of them famous in his generation. One of these was Gaisford, the celebrated Grecian, who, when I went up to Christ Church, occupied a small house in Holywell with an amiable wife and young family. There I received much kindness. I was invited to dinner once a term, and had the *entrée* when I liked ; nor did the great scholar, whom I always found up to his ears in folios, manifest the least annoyance at the interruption to his literary labours occasioned by the visits of a somewhat lazy undergraduate. I never felt the least afraid of him, and derived advantage as well as pleasure from his conversation. I have still a note of his, characteristically laconic, among other interesting autographs, dated June 21st, 1821. Gaisford was an amiable, kind-hearted man, much misunderstood, especially when, some years later, he became Dean of Christ Church, and was thus placed in a false position. He was not a man of the world, and had no notion of dealing with young men as a class, nor of supporting the dignity of the head of a college like Christ Church, and, as Dean, he always seemed out of his element.

A contrast to Gaisford in every respect was my other patron as an undergraduate, Philip Nicholas Shuttleworth, then Fellow, afterwards Warden of New College, and at last Bishop of Chichester. He had passed his youth at Holland

---

[1] Sir Herbert Oakeley, third Baronet, Christ Church, matr. April 25, 1807, aged 16; B.A. 1811; M.A. 1813; Dean and Rector of Boking, 1834-45; Archdeacon of Colchester, 1841; Vicar of Ealing, Middlesex; died 1845.

House[1], in the society of the men who frequented that celebrated haunt of polished infidelity, and was perfectly familiar with the objections to Christianity current in the class of his former associates. He was an eloquent and practical preacher, and a man of elegant taste and ready conversation. His connection with Holland House made him acquainted with all the young scions of the literary aristocracy of England; and when they came up to Oxford he was their patron and friend. His dinner-parties [1] were very agreeable, and his fund of anecdote P. 519. inexhaustible. He showed me many real kindnesses. As time went on he became a bitter enemy of the Tractarian movement; and one of his latest acts as Bishop of Chichester was to write me a long letter to warn me against it. On the other hand, it redounds to his credit that he was the first person who brought Dr. Manning forward into public life, little thinking that he was taking under his wing a future Archbishop of Westminster.

This kind of society created a pleasant diversion in my miserable undergraduate existence. But the miseries of its early stage were somewhat abated as time went on, though only to give place to worse. A freshman who does not at once drop into a respectable set is in imminent danger of finding himself in a bad one. This was soon my case. I was so thoroughly lonely that I caught at the first hand of fellowship held out to me; and, though I had little in common with most of my companions, their good-nature afforded me a relief from the intolerable dullness of my rooms, of which some idea may be formed when I say that they now consisted of two dreary attics in the Regius Professor of Divinity's vacant house, abutting on the cathedral, and within the immediate sound of bells which carried with them no enlivening ideas. I lived in this set for a twelvemonth, and very soon found that I was beginning to suffer, partly in moral sensitiveness, and still more in character and estimation, from my connection with it. I got into the habit of card-playing and attending late suppers;

[1] The seat of Lord Holland, at Kensington.

not adverting to the fact that my name went up every morning to the senior censor with those which were in no good odour. I also grew irregular at morning chapel, and was constantly visited by a scout bearing in his hand a folded slip of paper, in which were inscribed the words, 'One hundred lines of Virgil, Wednesday, M.C.' (morning chapel). It may well be imagined that Herodotus and Euclid did not flourish in such an atmosphere. Now, considering that I was a youth who had his way to make in the world, and who went up to the University with a certain promise, I began to see that all this would not do, and that I must make an abrupt turn out of the broad road along which I was proceeding. This resolution was furthered by some very kind admonitions from my tutor and friends at home, and I lost no time in carrying it into effect. But I soon found how much harder it is to get out of a bad set than to get into it, and the effort cost me much sacrifice of feeling. Some of my companions had really a liking for me; but I saw at once that I must have no more to do with them. The painfulness of the effort to emancipate myself from their society can easily be imagined, and I do not like to think of it. However, in a short time I succeeded; but it was then too late to get into another set, and accordingly I hovered over the society of Christ Church for the remainder of my undergraduate life without ever again penetrating into it. It was not till I had taken my degree and resided at Oxford for three years as a Bachelor of Arts that I fully tasted the sweets of an academical life, and enjoyed some of the experiences which enable me in a measure to understand the enthusiasm with which its advantages are described by those who have made a better use of them than I did in my undergraduate days. The pleasure I used to find in the life of a reading-man, when at length I took to it, is still in my memory: the freshness of the spring morning air in going to and from chapel; the opening lights of Aristotle or Thucydides gradually breaking upon a diligence of research, without which the same authors had appeared inexpressibly difficult and dull; the solitary walk round Christ Church Meadow, going through a brilliant mental examination in which the respondent enjoyed the advantage of being himself the proponent of his questions; or the no less charming stroll through St. John's gardens, bursting into the luxuriance of their vernal beauty, with a miniature Pindar or Sophocles in hand, and a pencil to note down the most successful rendering of some sententious or glowing passage in an ode or chorus, suggested by the indescribable tranquillity of the scene.

But nothing of all this was sufficient to repair the damage of an undergraduate career passed in comparative idleness till within a few months of the final examination. I lost my first class as I deserved, and was nearly plucked for my divinity to boot; but I passed sufficiently well in other things to encourage even to the last, in myself and my friends, the hope that I should gain the highest honours; and it was a great disappointment to them and to me when I found that my name came out in the second class; and the disappointment was all the greater because the standard of the time was not particularly high. My next paper will introduce a somewhat different idea of academical history.

II.

Christ Church under Dean Smith[1].

Before I had ended my undergraduate course at Christ Church, Dr. Hall was promoted to the golden deanery of Durham, and replaced in the headship of the College by Dr. Smith, one of the canons; a man who, I suppose, owed that important piece of preferment to private influence, as he was remarkable for nothing but his good nature. The removal of Dean Hall satisfied a growing public opinion, that in his bestowal of studentships, servitorships, and chorister-

---
[1] Samuel Smith, Dean of Christ Church, 1824–31.

ships, he had looked rather to other considerations than to the merits of the candidates, or to the advantage of the society over which he presided; a society, be it remembered, partaking at once of an academical and ecclesiastical character. With regard indeed to choristerships, even his celebrated predecessor, Dean Jackson, seems to have shared somewhat of this indifference to personal claims, if credit may be attached to a story once told me by old Cyril's pupil, Bishop Lloyd[1]. Lloyd said that once upon a time a boy appeared before the Dean as a candidate for a vacancy in the choir. 'Well, boy,' said the Dean, 'what do you know of music?' 'Please, sir,' said the boy, 'I has no more ear nor a stone, and no more voice nor an ass.' 'Never mind,' said the Dean, 'go your ways, boy; you'll make a very good chorister.' Those who remember the musical portion of the service in Christ Church Cathedral at the time of which I am speaking will not be disposed to acquit the successive deans of this indifference to the professional qualifications of those who took part in them. But Cyril certainly had one great advantage over his successor. In the disposal of studentships, at all events, he was often guided by a regard to merit; whereas in the days of his successor, more than one young man who would have done credit to the college was lost to it for want of being placed on the foundation. Bull used to lament this circumstance with all the energy of his characteristic *esprit de corps*. He had failed to secure a place on the foundation for his distinguished pupil Ewart, of whom I had occasion to speak in the last paper. But the loss to the college which he most deplored was that of John Carr[2], a very elegant and accomplished scholar, who gained a brilliant first-class, and afterwards became a Fellow of Balliol. In fact, merit-studentships were never given in my time, except to such cases of literary excel-

---

[1] Charles Lloyd, Christ Church, matr. Feb. 4, 1803, aged 18; B.A. 1806; M.A. 1809; Bishop of Oxford, 1827, until his death in 1829.

[2] John Carr, Christ Church, matr. March 15, 1815, aged 18; B.A. 1819, Balliol Coll.; M.A. 1823; Rector of Brattleby, Lincoln, 1835. until his death, 1861.

lence as could hardly have been overlooked without creating public scandal. It was thus that James Shergold Boone[1] was made an exception to the general rule in consequence of his gaining both the Chancellor's undergraduate prizes and the Craven Scholarship in his first year; and that Augustus Page Saunders[2], the present amiable Dean of Peterborough, received an act of tardy justice in being placed on the foundation of his college as a reward for his success in the two first classes. The other distinguished men of my time had either come to Christ Church as Westminster students, or were not in circumstances to be placed on the foundation. This limitation of the most substantial college-rewards to cases of unusual merit left a considerable margin of private patronage to the Dean and Canons. It is needless to add that, in this matter of academical patronage, vast improvements have been made since the days to which I refer. While speaking of distinguished Westminster students, I must not forget to pay a tribute of honour to two men whom Bull once described in his annual censor's speech as ' pari apud juniores modestia, pari erga seniores reverentia.' These were my friend Robert Hussey, afterwards Professor of Ecclesiastical History, and Edgerton Vernon Harcourt[3]. Both of them were excellent scholars and hard readers, besides bearing a high character for their moral qualities.

After I had passed my public examination in the schools, I formed a resolution for which I have every reason to be grateful, since, in its remoter effects, it has been the origin of many valuable friendships, as well as a determining cause of

---

[1] James Shergold Boone, Christ Church, matr. May 30, 1816, aged 17; B.A. 1820; M.A. 1823, of Lincoln's Inn; a Master at Charterhouse; Incumbent of St. John's, Paddington, 1832, until his death, 1859.

[2] Augustus Page Saunders, Christ Church, matr. May 14, 1819, aged 18; B.A. 1824; M.A. 1825; Headmaster of Charterhouse School; Dean of Peterborough, 1853; died 1878.

[3] Edgerton Venables Vernon Harcourt, Christ Church, matr. June 2, 1821, aged 18; B.A. 1825; M.A. 1828, of Whitwell Hall, Yorks; Barrister-at-law, Inner Temple; died 1883.

those events in my after-life in which I have the most reason to rejoice. Instead of leaving Oxford for good, after my examination in the schools, I resolved upon remaining there to read for a fellowship, and thus to do all which was left to me towards repairing the neglect of my undergraduate life, and justifying the outlay which a generous parent had made towards the charges of my education. This resolution was kindly and warmly seconded by my tutor and other college authorities, who, to do them justice, were always desirous of encouraging residence in the case of bachelors of arts whom they considered likely to avail themselves of its advantages. I had now been long enough at Christ Church as an undergraduate to obliterate the remembrance of my earlier breaches of college discipline, which my tutor, with characteristic kindness, was always disposed to attribute rather to weakness than wilfulness. I accordingly returned to Oxford in the Michaelmas term of the year in which I passed my examination, and never again left it, except for a short period, for¹ the next fifteen years. I entered upon my new course of residence under those advantages the want of which had been so serious an obstacle to my comfort at the beginning of my academical life. Before I took my degree of B.A., I had formed some pleasant acquaintances, with whom I was now able to associate much more habitually than when I was reading for the schools. I became a member of a social coterie, and we used to meet for wine in each other's rooms every evening. Among those who took part in these agreeable re-unions was the present Lord Stanhope[1] and Lord Devon[2]. I was likewise often invited to the Senior Common Room, the society of which was extremely agreeable. I read regularly, though not hard; and Oxford soon began to smile

[1] Philip Henry, fifth Earl of Stanhope, Christ Church, matr. April 19, 1823, aged 18; B.A. 1827; created D.C.L. 1834; M.A. 1854; Historian and Biographer; died 1875.
[2] William Reginald Courtenay, twelfth Earl of Devon, Christ Church, matr. March 30, 1824, aged 18; B.A. 1828; Fellow of All Souls' Coll. 1828-31; created D.C.L. 1837; died 1888.

upon me. In the following year I gained the Chancellor's [1] prize for the Latin Essay, and later on, the other also. These are honours of greater *éclat* than real worth; and though they have the name of University prizes, and are actually open to competition to all bachelors of art, they really represent little more than the competition of the resident bachelors. Yet such successes were of solid use to me, by giving me somewhat more of confidence in myself, and by qualifying me to become a candidate, without appearance of undue presumption, for the more substantial advantages of a fellowship on one of the open foundations. I had not long to wait for this opportunity, since in 1826 two vacancies at Oriel enlisted every bachelor of the slightest pretensions in the contest to supply them. The names of the twelve candidates who entered the lists were thus commemorated in Homeric verse by one of the fellows of Oriel; and I leave them to the interpretation of ingenious commentators [2]:—

> Ἄνερες οἴδε δυώδεκ' ἐς Ὀριελ ἦλθον ἀγῶνα·
> Φροῦδος, Τοξοφόρος, καὶ Ἀλέκτορες Ἰχθύος ὦα,
> Κρίθος ἀμῶν, Κορύφαια πέτρη, Δρυοείκελος, Ἄγρος,
> Καλὸν ὄρος, Βιότου δ' ὅγ' ἐπώνυμος ἡμετέροιο [3]
> Ὤρας δ'οὔνομ' ἔχων, καὶ Ἕκων ἀέκοντί γε θυμῷ.

The well-known name of Mr. Froude [4] will speak for itself in its Greek representative; and the very happy rendering of that of Mr. Wilberforce [5], with which the above list concludes, will suggest the remembrance of Mr. Froude's companion in success, the late lamented Archdeacon of Yorkshire, so early

---

[1] In 1825 Oakeley gained the Latin Essay Prize, the subject being *De Tribunitia apud Romanos Potestate*; and in 1827 that for the English Essay, the subject of which was *The Influence of the Crusades upon the Arts and Literature of Europe*.

[2] The suggested solution of this riddle will be found on p. 345. The words and accents are left in their original state.

[3] 'Cobham,' the name of the poet's 'living.' [*Oakeley's Note.*]

[4] Rev. Richard Hurrell Froude, Oriel Coll., matr. April 13, 1821, aged 18; B.A. 1824; M.A. 1827; Fellow 1826, until his death in 1836.

[5] Robert Isaac Wilberforce, Oriel Coll., matr. Feb. 14, 1820, aged 17, B.A. 1824; M.A. 1827; Fellow, 1826-33; Vicar of Burton Agnes, Yorks., 1840-56; Archdeacon and Canon of York, 1841, until he seceded to Rome in 1856; died 1857.

cut off from the promise of a useful and distinguished career as a convert to the Catholic Church. An examination for an open fellowship—at least the *viva-voce* portion of it—is a far more nervous affair than an examination in the schools, and that at Oriel was especially so. You were taken up into a sort of tower, from which you looked down upon your examiners, who [1] made their presence visible to your eyes by expressions of countenance too readily interpreted in an unfavourable sense; and audible to your ears in scratchings of the pen or pencil, which were multiplied in proportion as you felt yourself getting into a hobble with a crabbed passage of an unfamiliar author, left in your hands to manage as best you could. These disadvantages were of course common to you with all your fellow-competitors; but this was a conclusion of the reason which was not adequate as a relief to the pressure of such facts upon the imagination. I remember when I afterwards stood for a fellowship at another college, and was suffering under the real torture of this ordeal, how great an alleviation of my embarrassment it was to see the head of the college regaling himself over a basin of soup. I suppose that I had expected to see him feasting on nectar and ambrosia. As I did not succeed at Oriel, my residence at Christ Church continued without interruption during nearly the whole of my bachelor's career, and I continued to receive marks of kindness and favour from the college authorities, which I remember with sincere gratitude. The pecuniary advantages of a studentship were almost made up to me by the proceeds of an exhibition and constant advances of money, about which I am to this day ignorant how they arose, except that I know I was told to apply to the treasurer from time to time, and that I never came away empty-handed. This period of my Oxford life is that upon which I look back with the greatest human pleasure, though very possibly it was not that which was the most useful to me.

It was at this time principally that I attended Lloyd's celebrated private Divinity Lectures. Thither repaired all the *élite* of graduate Oxford,—Pusey, Newman, Edward Denison[1], Froude, Robert Wilberforce, William Churton, Moberly, and about twenty or thirty more. Lloyd was the very prince of college-lecturers—a master in the art in which I have known so many failures. Two qualifications are above all necessary in a college-lecturer, as will be better understood when we remember what college lectures are. They are not like professorial lectures, in which the lecturer talks away to a body of silent hearers arranged in ranks before him ; but partake far more of a free and colloquial character, where the lecturer rather converses than dogmatises, and the pupils feel themselves at liberty to propose to him as many difficulties as he is benevolent enough to receive. Hence it is in the first place necessary that the lecturer should have a sufficient command of his subject, since he is generally devoid of those resources which enable a man who is making a speech—and especially a speech he has often made before—to disguise his ignorance under a showy display of knowledge. In fact, tutorial lectures [1] bear just the same relation to professorial which paper examination does to *viva-voce*, the comparative advantages of which are so well described by Dr. Arnold in one of his letters[2] on the London University. The next, and no less important requisite in a lecturer, is that he should not be afraid of his class, or of any one in it ; and a part of this qualification is that he should not be ashamed of confessing his ignorance, or rather that he should know enough of what he is expected to know to allow of the confession of his ignorance of what is merely supplemental to the subject which he undertakes. He has to deal with the most critical, and even captious, of all possible audiences, by which his shortcomings and unavoidable defects are sure to be noticed and canvassed,—perhaps even drawn out by what is regarded

P. 610.

---

[1] Edward Denison, Oriel Coll., matr. June 23, 1818, aged 17 ; B.A. 1822 ; Fellow of Merton, 1826-37 ; M.A. 1826 ; Vicar of St. Peter's in the East, Oxford, 1826-37 ; Bishop of Salisbury, 1837, until his death, 1854.

[2] Stanley's *Life of Dr. Arnold*, vol. ii. p. 101.

as justifiable malice. There was once a tutor at one of the principal colleges at Oxford, who was a good scholar and a clever man, but he wanted the tact to manage a class of aristocratic and intelligent pupils. He had the misfortune not to be able to pronounce the letter *r*, to which he always gave the sound of *w*. Two of his pupils, in whose names the proscribed letter happened to be prominent, entered into an agreement with one another that whatever question he might ask as to the meaning of a proper name, they would answer in one of two ways—and always in the wrong way—by saying alternately that it meant 'a noble Roman,' or 'a river in Thessaly.' These replies produced the desired effect, in a burst of indignation from the tutor, giving opportunity for a reiterated employment of the letter which he was in the habit of mispronouncing. This only shows what might be the results of the system where the lecturer was no match for his class in point of tact and presence of mind. Yet its immense use was in point of fact independent of any possible abuse. Not merely did it give the opportunity of acquiring that deep and practical knowledge of the subject in hand which is peculiarly the gift of an Oxford education, but it encouraged those relations of mutual confidence between the teacher and the taught which constitute one especial advantage of the tutorial as compared with the professorial method.

Lloyd's peculiar excellence with his private Divinity class was, no doubt, the result in part of his former experience as a college-tutor; indeed, some of his pupils in that class had also been his pupils when he was tutor. As far as my recollection serves me, the tact and presence of mind which he showed with his class were characteristic of the Christ Church lecturers in general; certainly of those which I attended as an undergraduate, as well as of his own. Never were there two men of more opposite characters than Bull and Short; yet all that I knew of Bull's lectures from personal experience, and all that I have often heard of Short's from his own pupils, convinces me that, however different might be the character of their several teaching, they had alike the same command of their subjects and of their classes. One of their merits was that they were perfectly self-possessed, and adequate to all those possible emergencies which no man in a public situation can foresee or control, but which may easily damage the influence of one who does not know how to deal with them in a befitting way. I have known college-tutors who met this difficulty by desiring that no message of any kind might be brought to them during the hour when they were occupied with their class. I do not wish to say a word against this mode of escaping awkward conjunctures; but I conceive that which was preferred by Bull and Short to have been the more heroic, and, upon the whole, the more successful. They used to run their chance of such interruptions, under a conviction that they were fully equal to the encounter. Thus it would sometimes happen that, while Short was engaged in illustrating the Fifth Book of Ethics by the laws of political economy, or while Bull was in a *furore* of classical enthusiasm over an ode of Pindar or a chorus of Sophocles, there would enter the manciple,—a pale, placid official connected with the culinary department,—who came to Bull as the senior censor, or, in his absence, to Short as the junior, to take their pleasure as to the dinner at the Master's table for the day; and the answer of each college authority used to be given with a courageous indifference to the criticisms and comparisons to which it might have been expected to lead, and actually did lead, among their respective pupils. To the manciple's interrogative Short would reply, with a slight manifestation of impatience at the interruption, ' Oh, anything you've got,—a boiled leg of mutton and a pudding.' Bull, however, always seemed to have his reply at hand in some such form as the following : 'A fricandeau, a pheasant, and an omelette *au sucre*.' The respective classes of the two tutors used to agree that when they became masters of arts they would never dine when Bull dined out.

I hope the reader will pardon this little episode upon college-lecturers, which really bears more than he may be aware upon the subject in hand. And now to return to Lloyd. Some of his divinity-lectures were given before he became Bishop of Oxford and some afterwards; but his elevation to the dignity did not produce the slightest difference in his demeanour, or even in his dress; the only symbol of it being his wig, which used to hang upon a peg in the door. He always wore a long loose coat, little removed from a dressing-gown, and carried in his hand a coloured pocket-handkerchief, as a necessary accompaniment of his habits as a professed snuff-taker. Those of his class under whose eyes these papers may chance to fall will remember that he never sat down, but always instructed peripatetically, making the circuit of his large class once and again, and accosting its several members, or those at least whom he might choose to select, with a question which in its turn formed the handle of a reply of his own, full of information conveyed in a most attractive form. His treatment of his pupils, particularly of those with whom he was well acquainted, or who had established a claim to his favour, was familiar and free to an extent upon which few men but himself could have ventured. He generally accosted them by a kick on the shin, or by pulling their ears or noses to a degree which made them tingle; but these methods of address, far from being resented as a liberty, were received as the greatest of all possible compliments, inasmuch as they were rightly understood to be proofs of his especial confidence and regard. He had some peculiar phrases which will recall him to mind after many long years. When any one answered a question from his own imagination, or produced some strange piece of information on it, Lloyd would ask whether he had received a letter on the subject. The word 'special' was a favourite with him, and he always pronounced it with peculiar emphasis; and he generally drew attention to what he was saying by a copious use of the interrogative 'D'ye see?' Thus, for example, he would go up to some man to whom he considered he might suitably address himself on such a subject, and, after the friendly kick, would go on as follows: 'I suppose, Mr. Woods, you have been taught from your cradle upwards that it is the special duty of a Christian to abuse the Roman Catholics'; then, with another kick, 'that. d'ye see? I hold to be a mistake.' Then he would proceed to say, 'When I was a youngster, I happened to know some of the French emigrant clergy, and a better set of men never existed; I got a great deal out of them about their religion, and came to very different conclusions about it from those in which I was brought up.' Lloyd's method of lecturing exhibited with the happiest effect the peculiarly ethical character of the Oxford system, which has been often remarked by those best acquainted with it as one of its greatest advantages. There was not one of his pupils who did not feel that he was a friend to whom he might have recourse at any period, or in any case of difficulty, with an assurance that he would always be kindly received. Lloyd's death in 1829 was a great blow to the University; for although the precedent of private divinity-lectures set by him has been followed, I believe, by all his successors, he could not transmit to posterity those peculiar qualifications of personal character and influence which con- P. 613. stituted their chief attraction, and imparted to them their extraordinary value.

As a bachelor of arts living chiefly among those of my own standing, or with the very oldest of the undergraduates, I had no opportunity of forming any judgment of the moral and religious state of Christ Church during the period at which I have arrived; but I have every reason to believe it was in a state of progressive improvement. Some young men of what was called the Evangelical party had now come into residence there; and as they were amiable as well as religious, and as there was sufficient good-feeling among their contemporaries to secure them against molestation, even if not to obtain for them a certain respect, they had an influence for good beyond the sphere of the small circle in which they lived. With this exception, I do not remember that the idea of religion as a practical rule of life was ever suggested to me while I was at Christ Church, although dissuasions from immorality in one shape or another were occasionally put before me by those who had authority over me. More than this was certainly done at other colleges; for I remember that a friend of mine who was at Oriel used to tell me how great an impression had been made upon him by his excellent tutor Hawkins[1], the present Provost, in the course of walks which he had been asked to take with him. At Christ Church the only way in which religion, as such, was put before us was in the public prayers at the college, than which nothing could well have been more adverse to its proper influence. The services were so managed that it would have been hardly possible for any one to make a good use of them, even had he wished it, and I do not think that such a wish was largely shared. Little or no care was taken to secure even the decent behaviour of those who attended chapel as a general rule; and it was only when that behaviour broke out, as was sometimes the case in the evening, into the most disgraceful irreverence, that authorities interposed to control it. The names of those present used, when I was at Christ Church, to be noted by the registering student during the time of the service itself; and the period chosen was especially during the Creed, when every one turned round towards the Communion-table. During the greater part of my undergraduate time the most irregular and unpunctual attendant at the chapel was the Dean himself. But an improvement in these respects was set on foot before I left Christ Church, and has, I believe, continued to proceed. One practice which existed in other colleges was unknown at Christ Church—I mean that of forcing the men to go to Communion once a term. This, as far as it went, was an advantage; though the alternative was, after all, one between profaneness and irreligion.

P. 614. About this time the Union Debating Society, which was first established somewhere about the year 1823, had begun to as-

[1] Edward Hawkins, Provost of Oriel, 1828-82.

sume much of the importance which afterwards belonged to it. I have no doubt that it has been in two ways of great use to Oxford; as a means of moral improvement, to say nothing of its advantages as a school of oratory and parliamentary practice to those of whom so many are likely to be called into positions where such a preparation must prove of signal use to them. The Union Society, by placing men of all the various colleges upon a footing of perfect equality, has operated more than any other single agency towards the removal of those invidious distinctions and college rivalries to which I adverted in my last paper. There can be no doubt also that it has been of great service in furnishing useful and innocent subjects of conversation and pursuit to many, who before it existed were led to seek pleasure in topics and interests of a less praiseworthy character. For a long time the authorities of the University discouraged the Union, and even after they ceased to discourage it, were unwilling to give it anything like an avowed protection; but I believe they have learned by experience that its tendency to draw undergraduates from the characteristic studies of the University is far more than counter-balanced by its advantage in another direction; and that, even in the light of an academical institution, its benefit has been far from inconsiderable in widening the range of useful knowledge, and bringing the light of modern political experience to bear upon the history of ancient times. Need I add, that the great living representative of the benefits—both intellectual and moral—of the Oxford Union Society is to be seen in the person of Mr. Gladstone, who, as an undergraduate of Christ Church, was alike the foremost orator of the Union and an example to his companions of the possibility of combining youthful virtue with that deportment of humility and social kindliness which is best calculated to win others to the imitation of it.

I now bid adieu to Christ Church, not without regret; and must reappear, if at all, in another neighbourhood.

III.

BALLIOL UNDER DR. JENKYNS[1].

Vol. IV.
P. 50.

Balliol is now by general consent one of the first, if not the very first, college in Oxford. When I was an undergraduate it had the character of a good reading college, but nothing more. The credit it has since attained was then in its infancy; and even before I left Oxford, in 1839, Balliol had made rapid advances towards its present height. Dr. Jenkyns was elected to the headship, I think, in 1819, and soon proved himself desirous of carrying on, to the best of his ability, the work of improvement which had been begun by Dr. Parsons[2]. He had one advantage at least over his predecessor during the greater part of his headship—that he was able to devote his undivided energies to the interests of his college. Dr. Parsons was a bishop as well as Master of Balliol; thus uniting in his own person offices either of which was, or ought to have been, sufficiently laborious to engage the sole attention of one man. I believe that the college received the chief part of Dr. Parsons' attention, and that even before his death it had begun to lift its head among its compeers. It must have been in his time that two men, to whom it afterwards owed a great deal, were qualifying themselves to be placed on its foundation—Charles Atmore Ogilvie[3] and James Thomas Round[4]; nor could the literary advantages of a college be small which contributed to form two such valuable men. When Jenkyns was elected Master, or soon afterwards, Ogilvie and Round were both fellows; and about the same time the college received the advantage of admitting upon its foundation Mr. John Carr of Christ

---

[1] Richard Jenkyns, Master of Balliol, 1819-1854.
[2] John Parsons, Master of Balliol, 1798-1819; Bishop of Peterborough, 1813.
[3] See note, p. 208.
[4] James Thomas Round, Scholar of Balliol, matr. Dec. 13, 1816, aged 18; B.A. 1820; Fellow 1820-35; M.A. 1823; Prebendary of St. Paul's, 1843; died 1860.

Church, of whom I spoke in my last paper as one of the most distinguished men of his time.

Dr. Jenkyns was a remarkable instance of what a man of ordinary talents can do towards effecting an important work by dint of industry and devotion to a single object. He was literally wedded to his college; it engaged all his thoughts and enlisted all his sympathies. Its failures or successes were the subjects of his keenest disappointments and most exciting pleasures. In his zealous labours for its advancement he was powerfully supported by Mr. Ogilvie, a man of intellectual ability, accurate scholarship, and keen insight into human nature; an elegant English writer, a discreet preacher,[1] and possesed of unwearied vigilance as tutor and dean of his college. He was literally Jenkyns's right-hand man, and often threw the broad shield of his ability and influence over the defective powers of his principal. Round was one of the most admirable men I ever knew; zealous, painstaking, and conscientious, even to the verge of scrupulosity.

The effect of Dr. Jenkyns's administration soon came to be felt. He brought about an improvement in two important particulars—in the character of his fellows and in that of his undergraduates. He looked about him for the most distinguished men of the University who were not on the foundation of other colleges, or to whom, at all events, the temptation of a Balliol fellowship was sufficient to draw them away, and encouraged them to present themselves as candidates for admission to his Society. He also increased the strictness of the examination for entrance, and was thus enabled to make his selection from among the number of those who sought to obtain admission to his college. The more the college rose in reputation, the more of course did this selection become practicable. He was also extremely diligent in advancing the studies of the junior members of his Society, always making a point of looking over and criticising their exercises, and taking a personal and active part in the ex-

P. 51.

aminations at the end of the term. Meanwhile the discipline of the college, as well as its literary distinction, were greatly promoted by Mr. Ogilvie.

One of the most important reforms effected by Dr. Jenkyns was that of throwing open to competition the scholarships on the foundation. By a clause in the statutes, the holder of a scholarship enjoyed a preference, *ceteris paribus*, in the examination for a fellowship. In former times these scholars were merely the nominees of the different fellows; and it was therefore a creditable and disinterested act on the part of the Society to throw the scholarships open to public competition. Two of the fellowships, however, still remained under the disadvantage of being closed against all candidates except those who had been educated at one particular school; and this was a flaw in the Society which the Master deeply regretted, but which the conditions of the benefaction rendered unavoidable. There was also another and a similar drawback upon the literary excellence of the college, which was also a subject of grievance to him. This consisted in the misapplication, as he used to consider it, of a valuable piece of patronage[1] in connection with the college enjoyed by Glasgow University—the appointment, namely, to certain valuable exhibitions, held for several years. It is, however, a remarkable fact that Dr. Jenkyns should have lived to see two of the most distinguished members of his Society created out of these sorry materials. One of them was Dr. Temple[2], the present Master of Rugby, who, although the holder of a close fellowship, possessed abilities and attainments which would probably have secured his election to an open one against almost any competition; the other was a Scotch exhibitioner, whose history is still more remarkable, and shall be recounted.

---

[1] The Snell Exhibitions.
[2] Frederick Temple, Balliol Coll., matr. Oct. 12, 1838, aged 16; B.A. 1842; Fellow 1842-8; M.A. 1847; Hon. Fellow of Exeter Coll.; Headmaster of Rugby School, 1858-69; Bishop of Exeter, 1869; of London, 1885.

In the year 1830, among the crowd of candidates who came up in the summer term to pass their examinations for entrance, was a fair-haired young Scotchman, who pleased his examiners by the intelligence and good sense with which he mastered the difficulties of the Greek and Latin passages upon which his scholarship was tried. In the following year he presented himself as a candidate for an open scholarship; but an objection was understood to have been made to his election on the ground that he held one of the valuable exhibitions already mentioned, and should therefore be considered under a disqualification, in comparison with poorer candidates. Some of his examiners are said to have been of opinion, however, that this objection, although sufficient to prejudice him in a case of equality of merit, ought not to outweigh the claim of superiority in the examination, however slight, over his fellow-candidates; and, in the judgment of the majority of electors, the young Scotchman had evidently vindicated his claim to a preference. Two years later he obtained a first class in *literis humanioribus*, and soon afterwards presented himself as a candidate for a fellowship at his own college. His exhibition having still some time to run, the objection made to his election as a scholar was probably renewed at his examination for the fellowship, and with still greater force in proportion as the prize to be gained was far more lucrative. However, the good fortune of the young Scotchman did not desert him on this occasion also, and he was elected to a fellowship. The young Scotchman in question was no less a person than Archibald Campbell Tait[1], present Bishop of London. A few words more on the college career of one who has attained so high a position in this country may not be uninteresting to the reader. From a fellow Mr. Tait soon became a tutor; and his lectures were distinguished by that

---

[1] Archibald Campbell Tait, Scholar of Balliol, matr. Jan. 29, 1830, aged 18; B.A. 1833; Fellow 1834-42; M.A. 1836; Headmaster of Rugby, 1842-50; Bishop of London, 1856-69; Archbishop of Canterbury, 1868, until his death, 1882.

ability and power of lucid explanation which had contributed to his earlier successes. It is well known that he was one of the four tutors who took part against the celebrated Tract 90. On the lamented death of Dr. Arnold, he was elected to the head-mastership of Rugby school; and his subsequent career is sufficiently well known. Both as an undergraduate and as a tutor Mr. Tait was popular among his companions and pupils, who saw in his practical talent and great prudence an omen of his future success in life. In fact, those who pretended to the character of prophets used to say, 'Depend upon it, old Tait will be Archbishop of Canterbury.' His successful colleague, in the election of a fellowship, was Mr. William George Ward, afterwards so well known in connection with the Tractarian movement.

In 1826 two remarkable men had been added to the list of fellows—Francis William Newman[1], brother of his illustrious namesake, and George Moberly[2], the present head-master of Winchester school. The Society rang for years with the praises of Mr. Newman's examination for the fellowship. The writer of these pages desires to commemorate him in a different way, as one of the first persons who impressed him with the seriousness of religion. Mr. Newman's career at Balliol was brief and eccentric. His religious opinions did not square with those of the college, and he had conscientious difficulties about subscribing the Articles. He soon resigned his fellowship, and went as a missionary to the East; since which time the present writer has never, to his knowledge, seen him, but retains a deep respect for the strict conscientiousness and noble spirit of devotion, with which the remembrance of his keen eye, placid countenance, and ascetical habits is still

---

[1] Francis William Newman, Worcester Coll., matr. Nov. 29, 1822, aged 17; B.A. 1826; Hon. Fellow, 1883; Fellow of Balliol, 1826-30; Professor of Latin at University Coll., London, 1846-69.

[2] George Moberly, Balliol Coll., matr. March 13, 1822, aged 18; B.A. 1825; Fellow, 1826-34; M.A. 1828; Headmaster of Winchester Coll. 1835-66; Rector of Brightstone, Isle of Wight, 1866-9; Bishop of Salisbury, 1869-85.

associated. Mr. Moberly fully justified his election by his great ability as tutor, examiner, and select preacher. He was a man of keen and penetrating intellect, accurate and elegant erudition, and rare accomplishments. His sermons were much and justly admired, and, what was far better than force of logic or elegance of composition, they were evidently directed, and, I believe, were greatly instrumental, to the moral and spiritual advancement of his hearers. Mr. Oakeley, who had been an unsuccessful competitor for a fellowship when Mr. Newman and Mr. Moberly were elected, was placed on the foundation in the following spring, as one of the fellows to whose charge the duties of college chaplain are attached.

The rise of Tractarianism, which was by far the most important incident in the epoch to which I refer, had a great effect in disturbing the harmony and dislocating the internal arrangements of Balliol. To the Master it was a constant source of fret and worry; and it altered the position, both social and professional, of more than one of the fellows. Mr. Ogilvie, though a High Churchman, was strongly opposed to this manifestation of an orthodoxy which he regarded as visionary and dangerous. With the rise of Tractarianism his influence with a large section of the University seemed to decrease. Mr. Keble, Mr. Froude, and others with whom he had been intimately associated both in State and University politics, had stolen a march upon him in their religious and ecclesiastical predilections. The separation of feeling between him and his former friends, which had begun to manifest itself before Mr. Froude's death, was brought out into something like active hostility by the publication of the celebrated *Remains*. Mr. Ogilvie, who, about the time of Sir Robert Inglis's[1] election in 1829, was the leader of the High Church party in Oxford, now felt himself unable to act with some of his former friends, and left the University, to become domestic chaplain to Archbishop Howley. He had been

P. 54.

[1] See p. 209, note 2.

generally designated in public opinion as the future Master of Balliol; but Tractarianism changed the aspect of affairs with the force of a volcanic eruption, and nowhere was the effect more powerfully felt than in the little Society of Balliol. Mr. Round sided with Mr. Ogilvie in his fear and dislike of the new opinions. Mr. Moberly, on the contrary, was inclined to them. Mr. Oakeley soon found the atmosphere of the college somewhat oppressive, and retreated to Margaret Chapel. Mr. Ward [1] remained at his post, and took up the new opinions with characteristic energy and intensity. The Master began to deal blows against the obnoxious doctrines on the right hand and on the left—some of them effectual, but more of them impotent. The undergraduates were more vulnerable than the fellows, and more frequently wounded. The criticism of the weekly themes gave the Master many opportunities of dealing his anathemas against the new school; but his most powerful weapon was the terminal examination at collections. He had certain trial passages of the New Testament which he employed as the criteria of the religious tenets of an undegraduate suspected of 'Puseyism.' One of those most frequently produced was that in which the errors of the Pharisees are exposed. When a man had completed his translation of some such passage, the Master would proceed as follows: 'Now, tell me, Mr. ———, of all the various religious sects and parties which exist among us, which would you say corresponds the most with the Pharisees of the Gospel?' If the examinee was not fully up to the import of the question, he would perhaps answer, 'The Puritans, sir.' This was a safe reply, and in quieter times would have been the best for the purpose; but just then a more powerful antipathy even than the dread of Puritanism was uppermost in the academical mind; and he who wished to receive the

---

[1] Rev. William George Ward, Christ Church, matr. Nov. 26, 1830, aged 18; B.A. from Lincoln Coll. 1834; Fellow of Balliol, 1834-45; M.A. 1837; author of *Ideal of a Christian Church*, 1844, which was condemned in Convocation, 1845, and its author deprived of his M.A. degree; he seceded to Rome shortly after, was many years editor of the *Dublin Review*; died 1882.

Master's highest commendation would always answer, 'The Roman Catholics, sir.' This reply was so satisfactory, that, under the influence of the pleasure which it excited, an examiner would sometimes go on to say, 'And is there any sect among ourselves which tends to introduce the errors of the Roman Catholics into our Protestant Church?' To this question of course there could be but one answer.

The social body at Balliol was strengthened between the years 1830 and 1840 by three important additions. There had been elected ¹ into it Mr. Edward Cardwell[1], the present Colonial Secretary; Mr. Robert Scott[2], the present Master of the College; and Mr. Jowett[3], the present Regius Professor of Greek. Mr. Cardwell has done honour to his college chiefly by the credit which his political career has reflected upon himself and his electors. He remained but a short time in residence, and soon vacated his fellowship by marriage.

P. 55.

Mr. Scott, however, has conferred on the college of his adoption not merely lustre, but the solid advantage of able and laborious service. He was elected into the Society from a studentship of Christ Church; the reward as well as the forerunner of a brilliant academical reputation. He neared the Ireland scholarship for two or three years, and at length bore it off. It is needless to add that he obtained the highest classical honours of the schools. After fulfilling with exemplary diligence the duties of college tutor for several years, and making time out of their interstices to edit, in conjunction with the present Dean of Christ Church, the most valuable Greek and English lexicon which has been produced in modern times, he retired to a col-

[1] Edward Cardwell, Balliol Coll., matr. March 25, 1831, aged 17; B.A. 1835; M.A. 1838; created D.C.L. 1863; Barrister at-law, Inner Temple; Secretary at War, 1864-74; created Viscount Cardwell, 1874.

[2] Robert Scott, Christ Church, matr. Oct. 21, 1829, aged 18; B.A. 1833; Fellow of Balliol, 1835-40; M.A. 1836; Master, 1854-70; Dean of Rochester, 1870, until his death in 1887.

[3] Benjamin Jowett, Balliol Coll., matr. Nov. 30, 1835, aged 18; B.A. 1839; M.A. 1842; Fellow 1838-70; Master since 1870.

lege living; whence, upon the death of Dr. Jenkyns, he was recalled to occupy the important post of Master. It cannot be said that he found the college of brick, and will leave it of marble; but it may truly be said that he has contributed to mould into more perfect form, and to polish into a fairer beauty, the materials which he received into his hands. The third of the important acquisitions which Balliol received during the ten years aforesaid, was that of Professor Jowett, whose name has been too often before the world to make it necessary that we should refer to his very marked opinions upon questions of the day, or to those indefatigable labours in his profession and those amiable and popular manners which have won him the respect and affection even of those who most strongly object to his views on religious subjects.

The rapid progress of Tractarian opinions which took place during the interval in question was the occasion of many collisions between the Master and those of the fellows who were either connected or thought to be connected with the new school of opinions. The fellows, of course, were less tractable subjects of the anti-Tractarian head of the college than the undergraduates. They had their status in the Society, and their rights. which justified them in making a stand against any vexatious or unconstitutional opposition wherever such was seriously contemplated ; but matters did not, as a fact, ever proceed to extremities, and stopped short in 'brushes' or 'scenes,' which partook rather of the ludicrous than the serious. This circumstance was mainly owing to the remarkable forbearance and indomitable good temper of the most prominent representative of Tractarianism [1] in the college, Mr. Ward. Had he been as touchy and pugnacious as he was ardent and determined in the cause of the opinions which he held so sincerely and advocated so ably, it would have been difficult to foresee the extent to which the conflict might have proceeded. But as it was, his patience and amiable deportment completely took the sting out of the good little Master's intense animosity to his religious views. It was likewise a point in his favour that the college stood in great need of a mathematical tutor, and could ill dispense with the services of one who discharged the duties of that office with singular ability. On the other hand, it could not escape so vigilant and ubiquitous an eye as that of Dr. Jenkyns, that the same attractive qualities of personal character, which disarmed his opposition in spite of himself, were also gaining for Mr. Ward a powerful influence over the minds of his pupils, as well as of the junior fellows. He therefore came to the resolution of removing Mr. Ward from the mathematical lectureship; not because there was any very obvious relationship between mathematics and theology, but because he suspected that the mathematics might be made a medium for communications of a less dry and abstract character than themselves. The crisis of the movement is related to have taken a form eminently characteristic of the two high contending parties. The mathematical lecturer, of suspected orthodoxy, is summoned into the presence of the Master, who is discovered in the plenitude of his dignity and academics, and intrenched behind an impregnable fortification of ancient statutes. The culprit enters the apartment with an air of imperturbable serenity, which slightly discomposes his judge; but the statutes are at hand to nerve his failing powers, and quicken his faltering eloquence. The silent accused is confronted with chapter this, and section that; and his accuser awaits, not without anxiety, a reply to his charges at once subtle, elaborate, eloquent, and conclusive. What, then, is his surprise and relief when he finds that the culprit has come with the intention of placing an unqualified resignation in his hands! The reaction from a state of official severity, dignified condescension, and nervous alarm, into one of peaceful triumph and assured success, is too much for the equanimity of this really kind-hearted and amiable man. At once the whole pomp of an academical tribunal is put to flight. The Master throws himself back in his chair, and with a passionate burst of gratitude towards his deliverer, exclaims in a tone singularly different from that of the moment before,

'My dear Ward, this is just like your generosity. I have been reading your book; I had no idea you went such lengths.'

P. 57.   The moral tone of Balliol was remarkably high, both among the fellows¹ and undergraduates. In the latter class there were, of course, those exceptions which must be looked for in any large collection of young men between the ages of eighteen and twenty-one. There were occasional noisy parties, and nightly irruptions into the college garden, with college meetings in the morning as their consequence. But there were, on the other hand, excellent men, who set the fashion of the college in a right direction. To this honourable distinction of Balliol several causes contributed. One was, that the rules of the college did not admit of the reception of noblemen and gentlemen-commoners as a privileged class; so that there was no recognition of a lower standard of regularity than that to which the undergraduates, as a body, were bound to conform. There were no cases of men who had large incomes at their disposal, with the accompanying temptations to vicious extravagance. The good-natured affability of the Master contributed to the same result. His little peculiarities of manner and deportment were the subjects rather of amusement than of severe criticism; and he had the good sense not to mind being laughed at where he knew that the laughter was quite innocent, and really consisted with a great deal of sincere regard. It was one of his misfortunes that he was not a good rider, and yet used to ride a great deal. He was a little man, and he had a little pony; and everyone knows that a little man with a little pony is not likely to escape a great deal of playful criticism on the part of tall men who ride tall horses. Thus, it would sometimes happen that the Master and his pony would fall in with a party of riders returning from the hunt. The riders would trot at a quick pace behind the Master and his pony; and the latter, fretted by the noise behind it, would start off at a gallop, and thus place the Master in the awkward position of seeming to head a party of his own undergraduates on their return from the hunting field. On one occasion the excitement was too much for the pony, which kicked up, and deposited the Master in a ditch. One of the hunters, an undergraduate of his own, foresaw that the incident might be of serious moment to himself and his companions, and determined upon a politic expedient. He went up to his unhorsed principal, and benevolently tendered his good offices in catching the pony and restoring its rider to his seat. The Master could not but accept this offer under the circumstances; and, of course, the undergraduate who made it thus secured for himself and his companions an indemnity against the consequences of so awkward an encounter.

Another and very principal cause of the high moral tone which prevailed at Balliol, was the absence of a donnish exclusiveness on the part of the tutors. They associated freely with their pupils, yet in such a way as to conciliate goodwill without compromising influence. Where tutors mix with undergraduates without proposing to themselves the moral and religious improvement of their companions as a definite object, such associations tend only to lower the one party without elevating the other. On the other hand, where they show themselves too solicitous about gaining influence, and obtrude their advice in a dictatorial spirit, or at unseasonable times, their excellent intentions are most likely to be met by little else than expressions of forced and complimentary agreement on the part of the junior, indicating no very substantial promise of a good result. The sort of intercourse which used to exist between tutor and pupil at Balliol struck the balance very successfully between these extremes, and is, I believe, remembered with gratitude by those on both sides who were the parties to it.

Nor must we forget among the causes which contributed to the high moral tone of Balliol the valuable influence of Dr. Arnold's pupils, who began to flow into it in rapid succession after he had been at Rugby a sufficient time to form the characters of his boys by means of an intercourse not unlike that which I have just described. It is difficult to estimate, for

P. 58.

instance, the moral advantage which must have resulted to any society from the example of such a member as Arthur Penrhyn Stanley[1]; uniting, as he did, the rarest abilities and attainments with a deportment characterised by unaffected humility and universal kindness.

But a main cause of the same result is no doubt to be found in the general character of the governing body, which, as a body, was distinguished by high principle and irreproachable conduct. The influence of Mr. Ogilvie and Mr. Round had been materially instrumental towards this effect; and it was an influence which outlived the immediate presence of those who had created it. It is not too much to say that any conversation by which religion or morality might have been compromised would have been instantly hushed, or rather effectually anticipated by the known feelings and sentiments of the Balliol common-room. Nor could anyone be present at the ordinary social meetings of the fellows and their friends without carrying away, if he pleased, some profitable impression. Those of the Society who have since become Catholics will feel, at once admiringly and regretfully, how much of the valuable influence which was there stored up, as it were, in bond, was debarred from its legitimate effect for want of a grander field of operation, and a still higher elevation of object. They will mourn over the number of 'vocations' missed, and the strength of energies wasted, in a comparatively contracted sphere, where there was so little in the opportunities to correspond with the promise. In the very images of certain individuals, still, after many years, impressed upon their mind's eye, they will be apt to see counterparts of those whom they have since known as priests and religious, and in whose telling power upon the world, or high spiritual attainments, they will discern a contrast, as

---

[1] Arthur Penrhyn Stanley, Scholar Balliol Coll., matr. Nov. 30, 1833, aged 17; B.A. 1838; Fellow of University Coll. 1838–51; M.A. 1840; Regius Professor of Ecclesiastical History, and Canon of Christ Church, 1856–64; Dean of Westminster, 1864, until his death, 1881.

painful as it is beautiful, to the subsequent careers or premature ends of some of the admirable men whose entrance on public life they remember. They will find reason to lament that those who had in them the making of saints should have been dwarfed for want of room in which to expand. Why was not —— a son of St. Ignatius, or —— of St. Dominic? or that simple-minded and generous heart which was so apt to be touched by the recital of misfortune, and moved to the most self-denying sacrifices for its relief—why does it beat in the breast of a Protestant Rector, instead of that of a Catholic Missionary or Brother of Charity? Why have those valuable men been distanced in the pursuit of truth by some who were once their inferiors in spiritual advancement, and who might have learned so many lessons of true wisdom at their feet? Often did they set an example of Catholic virtues at the very moment when they were defaming Catholic truth. Let us humbly hope and fervently pray that, in the merciful judgment of our Heavenly Father, the unconscious testimony of their lives may outweigh the unknowing prevarications of their lips. *Fiat, fiat!*

[CANDIDATES FOR THE ORIEL FELLOWSHIP IN 1826.

(See p. 323.)

Φροῦδος .	. Richard Hurrell Froude, of Oriel.
Τοξοφόρος .	F. Bowman, of Exeter.
Ἀλέκτορες .	William H. Cox, of Pembroke.
Ἰχθύος ᾠά .	William C. Rowe, of Balliol.
Κρῖθος ἀμῶν	. G. Moberly, of Balliol.
Κορυφαία πέτρη	. W. J. Copleston, of C.C.C.
Δρυοείκελος .	. The Writer of these Reminiscences.
Ἀγρός . .	. C. G. Du Pre, of St. Mary Hall.
Καλὸν ὄρος .	. . A. J. Beaumont, of Queen's.
Ἐπώνυμος κτλ .	. J. B. Cobham, of Oriel.
Ὥρας	. T. Vores, of Wadham.
Ἑκὼν ἀέκοντί γε θυμῷ	Samuel Wilberforce, of Oriel.]

XXVII.

ST. ALBAN HALL, OXFORD.

By HENRY ROBINSON, D.D.

[Matr. Oct. 25, 1838, aged 19; B.A. 1842; M.A. 1854; D.D. 1871; a Member of Merton, 1882; Rector of Kilkhampton, Cornwall, 1857-9; *died* in 1887].

London Society, Feb. 1887.

As an old alumnus of St. Alban Hall, which now exists no longer, having been merged into Merton College, I have written down some few recollections of the old place . . .

My connection with St. Alban Hall commenced in 1838. Dr. Cardwell, professor of ancient history, was principal, and the Rev. Henry Wall, vice-principal. Mr. Wall afterwards became fellow of Balliol and professor of logic. There were only seven undergraduates in my first term; they afterwards became more numerous, but there were never more than a dozen in residence in my time. One reason of the small number was that Dr. Cardwell would not, like his predecessors, receive men from other colleges. In one term, soon after Dr. Cardwell's appointment, there was ' only one undergraduate in residence. His name, strange to say, was Tenant; he was called the 'solitary tenant of Alban Hall.'

I will now give a few recollections of my undergraduate days from 1838 to 1842. The vice-chancellor who matriculated me was Dr. Gilbert, principal of Brasenose. He was a very handsome man, and he afterwards became Bishop of Chichester. He had a very large family, all of whom but two were daughters; one of his daughters was blind. The two first proctors I remember were the Rev. W. Ricketts, fellow of Merton, and the Rev. T. T. Bazeley, fellow of Brasenose. The vicar of St. Mary's, the university church, was the celebrated John Henry Newman; the vicar of St. Peter's-in-the-East was the Rev. W. K. Hamilton, who afterwards became Bishop of Salisbury. My rooms were on the ground floor facing Merton Street and next to Merton College. The staff of servants were the cook, the manciple, the porter, and a boy. The cook and manciple were husband and wife. Having no chapel, we had prayers in the hall once on a week day and twice on the Sunday. On one Sunday in each term we went to St. Peter's-in-the-East to Holy Communion. Our sole tutor was the vice-principal; the principal, however, lectured on divinity. In Lent term, 1840, I passed responsions; the two examiners before whom I appeared were Mr. Jelf, of Christ Church, and Mr. Henry, of Pembroke. In Michaelmas term, 1841, I passed the final examination. My three examiners were Dayne, Tait, and Donkin. Tait became at last Archbishop of Canterbury. The number of undergraduates in 1838 was much fewer than they are now. At New College there are now more than 200 undergraduates. I doubt much if there was one-tenth of that number in 1838. At New College, Magdalen, and Corpus there were no commoners, and at Merton there were not above ten; twenty-six, including scholars, formed the whole number under instruction.

There was a cricket ground on Cowley Marsh, and another on Bullingdon Green, but there was no football, no tram-cars and no omnibuses. If we wanted to go home by coach at the end of the term, it was necessary to book our places at least a week beforehand. The coaches were well horsed and very fast. One used to go by the Henley Road, 58 miles to London, in five and a quarter hours. Boating was a favourite amusement then as it is now, but the pace has much increased.

The chief inn at Oxford was the 'Angel.' It is now pulled down and the new schools are built on its site. The 'Mitre' still exists, as does also the 'Star,' but this last has changed its name; it is now called the 'Clarendon.' At St. Mary Hall, Dr. Hampden was the principal. He did not, however, take much part in its management as he lived at Christ Church, where he was a canon and regius professor of divinity. He left it all to the Rev. W. H. Cox, the vice-principal, who was also Rector of Carfax.

At St. Edmund Hall, Dr. Grays[1], the principal, left all to the Rev. John Hill, the vice-principal, a well-known Evangelical clergyman, who, like Mr. Simeon, of Cambridge, did much to promote religion among the undergraduates. Mr. Hill, whose residence was 65, High Street, had been a long time vice-principal, and was the immediate successor of Daniel Wilson, who was afterwards Bishop of Calcutta.

At Magdalen Hall, Dr. Macbride, the principal, like Dr. Cardwell, attended to the religious instruction of his pupils. He was a layman, as well also as Dr. Marsham, the warden of Merton. The vice-principal of Magdalen Hall was Mr. Jacobson, who afterwards became regius professor of divinity and at last Bishop of Chester; Dr. Hampden, of St. Mary Hall, became Bishop of Hereford.

The principal of New Inn Hall was Dr. Cramer, who died Dean of Carlisle. He had no vice-principal when I was an undergraduate. Having been a student of Christ Church was one reason why men sent away from Christ Church generally entered at New Inn Hall.

I believe that the members of St. Alban Hall were quite as well done for as at any of the others. It was rather an expensive place, the number being so few, and there was no endowment. There is one member and alumnus of Alban Hall whom I should not forget, the late Stephen Reay, B.D., professor of Arabic and senior assistant librarian at the Bodleian.

---

[1] Anthony Grayson must be here meant, Prin. St. Edmund Hall, 1824-43; as there was no Principal named Gray at that time.

So Alban Hall has this century had the honour of educating the two Professors, Reay and Wall. The other principals and vice-principals received their education at other colleges. There was a blind man a few years before my time who got second-class. This was a Mr. Seymer, whose sister used to read to him. She came up to Oxford for the purpose. There is an Alban Hall alumnus, a Mr. Kitto, whom the Bishop of London (after he had done a great work in the East End of London for many years) has just presented to the important living of St. Martin's-in-the Fields. He matriculated in 1856. Many of my contemporaries have naturally passed away, perhaps the greater part of them. It has been calculated that on an average an Oxford man lives for 33 years after taking his B.A.

Magdalen Hall is still in existence as Hertford College. Mr. T. C. Baring, M.P., I was told by one of the fellows, has given as much as £200,000 for the endowment of fellowships and scholarships. When we think of this place and of Keble College, we see a good prospect that the work of education will be carried on efficiently as in the days of Wykeham and Wainflete.

St. Edmund Hall will be carried on in connection with Queen's College, who always have appointed the principal, and who will continue to do so.

St. Alban Hall is destroyed because it has no friends. No one was interested in it except the principal, and he has been pensioned [1] off. A new chapel, which was built a few years ago by subscription, is now secularised.

P. 194.

In days gone by, the scholars of Merton, called Postmasters, lived in a tenement called Bean Hall, and had for their principal one of the fellows. Even to this day one of the fellows is styled Principal of the Postmasters. Alban Hall, having both a chapel and a hall would have been a much more suitable place for the Postmasters to lodge in than Bean Hall. It would then have an existence as St. Edmund Hall has now.

The undergraduates of St. Alban Hall in my days were a very friendly body. We all knew one another intimately, as was only likely in such a small community. Breakfasting together so frequently, as well as spending our evenings together, caused us to waste more time than we should have done, but yet it was very pleasant. Our vice-principal used to boast that there had never been a pluck since he had held his appointment. Having never more than twelve pupils to attend to, he could and did for them almost as much service as if he had been a private tutor. I must say that the recollection of our intercourse with each other is very pleasant, and every one of our alumni whom I have come across has always expressed the same opinion. There was none of that party spirit which is so common in undergraduate society. We were there, and were all disposed to make the best of it. The principal was too great a man to interfere in any way, and the vice-principal lived away with his mother and sister. In my time, any one who wished to go in for honours had to take a private tutor. The most popular coach then was Bob Lowe, of Magdalen—the present Lord Sherbrooke. Bob might often be met with on the water, pulling a lusty stroke oar while his wife steered. As an examiner he was not so popular; for he was too hasty in his decisions. He afterwards went out to Australia, practised at the Bar there, and when he returned to England, took to politics. This coaching does very well for a few years, but it does not do for a man to make it the business of his life. There was a man named Robertson[1], of Lincoln, who had, at one time, a great reputation; but his pupils gradually falling off, and having a wife and family, he had, I fear, much to do to make both ends meet before his death at 70 years of age. Another celebrated coach was the well-known Mr. Hughes, of Trinity. He held a great many offices; he was rector of St. Clement's, chaplain of All Souls, clerk of the market, etc., etc. He was usually called by undergraduates 'the fast man's friend,' and he was by no means ashamed of the title. He lived and died in Oxford, and lies buried in Holywell Church-

---

[1] Probably George Thomas Roberson, exhibitioner of Linc. Coll., 1820; there is no *Robertson* of Linc. Coll. to whom this could apply.

yard. He came up from Rugby as captain of the school, got a scholarship at Trinity, then a high honour, but did not obtain a fellowship, as he married, when quite young, a daughter of Mr. Vicary, the organist of Magdalen. He was always applying for various places. In addition to those I have mentioned P. 195. he was proctor of the Vice-Chancellor's court, besides holding such places as pro-proctor, master of the schools, select preacher, etc. But for all this, I am sure he would have left his family better off had he got a fellowship at Trinity, and succeeded in time to one of the college livings.

Cardinal Manning was a select preacher before the university in my undergraduate days, and was very much thought of. He was then Archdeacon Manning. He and Samuel Wilberforce, successively Bishop of Oxford and Winchester, married two sisters. Manning, before his marriage, had been fellow of Merton College. Manning's father was head of the firm of Manning and Anderdon, West India merchants, and had been governor of the Bank of England. In my undergraduate days I have heard two men preach before the university who are now cardinals of the Church of Rome. Manning might be thought more of by the junior members, but Newman would be decidedly the favourite with those of longer standing. Pusey was remarkable for very long sermons, he has preached for two hours.

During my undergraduate career I believe there was only one college tutor who was not in holy orders; this was Travers Twiss, of University. At Merton, William Adams, author of *The Shadow of the Cross*, was a tutor; at Magdalen, William Palmer, brother of Sir Roundell Palmer. now Lord Selborne. As a public examiner he was thought much of by the undergraduates; he died a member of the Church of Rome. The two censors of Christ Church were Robert Hussey and Jacob Lee; the present Dean Liddell was then one of the junior tutors. But by far the most distinguished college tutor at that date was William Sewell, of Exeter; he had originally been of Merton College; he had one brother a fellow of Magdalen and another, fellow of New College. This last is now warden, and has been vice-chancellor. William Sewell was a great promoter of education. He was a High Churchman, but not altogether in agreement with Pusey and Newman. Sidney Smith said of Sewell, 'Thou art *suillus*,' i.e. a little pig, because he would not, as the saying is, 'go the whole hog.' The most remarkable of the heads was Gaisford, Dean of Christ Church. He was regius professor of Greek. The canons at that time were Barnes, Dowdeswell, Woodcock, Buckland, Pusey, Bull, Jelf, and Hampden. Jelf and Dowdeswell were non-resident. Jelf was in Hanover as tutor to the Crown Prince; Dowdeswell had never resided, I was told. Christ Church was then, as it is now, the chief college; there would, perhaps, be five or six noblemen in residence and perhaps thirty gentlemen-commoners. One of these gentlemen-commoners was John Ruskin, who gained the Newdigate prize poem, which I heard him recite at Commemoration. He was nearly always to be seen with some female relation, which was rather remarkable at that day, but would not be thought so much of now.

P. 196. Another remarkable event in my time was the condemnation of Newman's celebrated Tract 90 by the Hebdomadal Board, that is the heads of houses and proctors. This condemnation was procured by the remonstrance of four college tutors— Churton, of Brasenose; Tait, of Balliol; Wilson, of St. John's, and Griffith, of Wadham. Churton, though a good man, was not remarkable; Tait was remarkable for his extraordinary success in life, for he rose to be Archbishop of Canterbury; Wilson took a country living, and would not have been remembered except he had written one of the seven Essays and Reviews, which were so much condemned for their want of orthodoxy; Griffith became Warden of Wadham, and died rich and respected a year or two ago. The vice-chancellor who succeeded Dr. Gilbert was Dr. Wynter, of St. John's. It was Dr. Wynter who suspended for two years Dr. Pusey, on account of a sermon; this was thought rather a high-handed proceeding. The vice-chancellor has no authority beyond the precincts of the university; Dr. Pusey, during those two years. lectured as usual and preached away from Oxford. It was, I think, after I took my degree, I believe in 1844 . . .

Another celebrated canon of Christ Church is Dr. Buckland, professor of geology, who afterwards became Dean of Westminster. Dean Buckland, like Dean Swift, failed in mind before he failed in body. Their minds were worn out first. This is a sad ending for a great man. Dr. Routh, the president of Magdalen, was another Oxford celebrity, but except at chapel he was rarely seen during the last twenty years of his life. He was president from 1791 to 1854, and died in his 100th year. He is buried at the entrance of his college chapel. Dr. Jenkyns, the master of Balliol, had raised his college to be one of the foremost in the university, though it was not then a very large college. The senior tutor was Frederick Oakeley, who afterwards joined the Catholic Church, and was thought much of as an eloquent preacher in Islington. The first time I attended a university sermon, which was on Easter Day, 1838, he was the preacher. I do not think he was much thought of as a preacher while he was at Oxford, but certainly he was a good tutor and examiner. The university sermons were much better attended in those days than they are now.

Another man of mark was Richard Greswell, tutor of Worcester College. He was not then a fellow because he had married. The head of Worcester [1] was an amiable man, and Dr. Pusey's brother-in-law. Strange to say, for nobody who knew him in after life would have thought it, he had been when a young man a skilful four-in-hand whip. One coachman in my day had certainly been an undergraduate. He was employed by Coster. A four-in-hand coachman would be as different from a cabdriver as a canon of St. Paul's from a Welsh curate. St. Ebbe's Church had a non-resident rector. There were three curates who did the duty, who had

[1] Dr. Cotton.

each taken a double first, Charles Baring, of Christ Church, Samuel Waldegrave of All Souls, and Edward A. Litton of Oriel. Baring became Bishop of Durham, and Waldegrave Bishop of Carlisle. I do not suppose there was another parish in England which could say it had three curates who had each taken a double first-class. It was the Bishop of Durham's eldest son who behaved so munificently to Hertford College We have had one visit from royalty, which I remember; the Queen and Prince Albert came, but I think they stayed at the Archbishop of York's, at Nuneham Courtenay. This was perhaps the occasion when the Duke of Wellington came as Chancellor of the University, for I remember him once at Commemoration. He looked a fine old man, though it must have been more than twelve years before his death. I noticed that he wore his cap the hinder part foremost.

Dr. Ingram, the president of Trinity, was a great antiquarian. He published the *Memorials of Oxford*. It was at Trinity College where John Henry Newman was a scholar before he became a fellow of Oriel. Newman was the son of a Lombard Street banker. Dr. Symons, warden of Wadham, resigned his headship when he was eighty years of age, but he lived to be ninety-five. He had been both proctor and vice-chancellor, as also were the present Rector of Exeter College and the present Dean of Christ Church.

When I first came to Oxford, Dr. Shuttleworth was warden of New College. He became Bishop of Chichester, but he did not live long afterwards. His successor at New College was Dr. Williams, who had been head master of Winchester School. He was genial and popular. New College choir in those days had a great reputation. The warden himself could intone the service well.

Magdalen Choir was also thought much of; the cathedral then was very poor, but it has greatly improved since.

The warden of All Souls was the Rev. Lewis Sneyd, M.A. From some cause or other he would not take his D.D. as was usual. When I first knew him he was quite bald, but after the long vacation he appeared with what seemed a fine head of hair. But alas! he, like Major Pendennis, wore an exceedingly well-made wig. He was not married. It was All Souls where Bishop Heber was a fellow. He was an undergraduate of Brasenose, and while there gained the Newdigate prize for English verse.[1] He recited it at the following Commemoration. The subject was Palestine. Another youth, a B.A. of Edmund Hall, gained the English prose essay. He was Daniel Wilson. The subject was 'Common Sense.' Both these two became in their time Bishops of Calcutta.

P. 198.

It was a standing joke in the university that the fellows of All Souls were required to be *bene nati, bene vestiti, et moderate docti*. This is true no longer; a candidate for a fellowship is required to have taken a first-class in one school at least, or to have gained a university prize. I have now brought my remarks to a conclusion, but I must express my regret that this little society, which has maintained a respectable existence since 1239, should exist no longer. It is more for the authorities of the university than for a private individual to take the matter in hand. I should rejoice if Alban Hall was resuscitated and revived. I am sure its extinction was not called for, but there was no one to speak up for it. The Chancellor of the University is the visitor of all the halls, and he holds his place in trust for his successor.

XXVIII.

TOURNAMENTS HOLDEN AT OXFORD, 1863.

By AN OLD OXONIAN.

The Boys' Own Volume, 1863.

DURING the long summer evenings, it was a custom among our undergraduates to bring out their chairs and sit in the 'quad.,' i. e. the quadrangle, where they could take their modest after-dinner sherry, and enjoy the coolness of the evening breeze. Now, it so happened that, on one of these evenings, a restless gownsman, who was sitting in a large, low, easy chair, began to push himself along by pressing his feet against the ground. After a few moments his speed increased, and he drove his chair round the quad., challenging any one to race with him. Of course, such a challenge was not likely to pass unheeded, and in a moment another arm-chair was drawn up alongside that of the challenger, and a race was organised, the umpires, referee, and judge being appointed with as much care as if the Derby or Cup were being run for, and the locality were Epsom or Ascot. Three times round the quad. was the distance ; the competitors tossed up for choice of place, and at a given signal off they started on this novel course.

They dashed round the quad., going at a wonderful pace, and steered by the advice of anxious partisans, he who had won the best place trying to keep it, and his competitor endeavouring to wrest the advantage from him. Each time they encircled the quad. (which seems, by the way, to be a mode of squaring the circle) they had to cross four sunken stone gutters, causing no slight bumping to the chairs, and seriously endangering their castors. Just as they began the third round, one of the competitors began visibly to flag in his exertions, while the other dashed forward still more rapidly, got well in front of his antagonist, cut him out of his advantageous ground, and won easily.

The fact was, that the winner was one of the 'eight' of the college crew, and, in consequence, was in good condition, while his opponent was incapable of sustaining severe exertion for any lengthened period in consequence of his want of training. The task was much more difficult than it would seem to be to an uninitiated observer. To propel a heavy chair by an unusual mode of action, over a rough and gravelly surface, which soon gets torn up and lets the castors cut deeply into its substance, requires no light exertion, and no one who was not in thoroughly good condition could hope to keep it up for any length of time.

Of course, races became quite fashionable and the custom extended to other colleges, much to the benefit of the upholsterers, who had continually to supply fresh castors, and even fresh legs, to the much-enduring chairs.

This sport endured for some weeks, being the regular evening's amusement, and causing as much excitement as if the chairs were racehorses, and their owners jockeys. The quads. of the various colleges were classed according to the facilities which they offered for chair-racing, and many were the laments over a well-proportioned and smoothly-paved quad. which was infested with fellows, tutors, and other objectionable beings. Our own quad. being far removed from the domains apportioned to the tutors, being tolerably spacious, and having no grass in the middle, was considered as the very type of a quad., and many a race was decided within its precincts by men of other colleges.

Thus affairs proceeded for some time, when a sudden change took place in the amusement. Two of the chairs happened to come into collision; one was overturned, and both jockeys were thrown from their wooden steeds. Winged words flew swiftly about, each fallen antagonist laying the fault on the other, and at last it was decided that they should settle the matter by single combat.

Accordingly, the two chairs were taken to opposite sides of the quad., their riders placed in them, with their feet against the wall, so as to insure a good start, and, at a given signal, off they went, intending to meet in the middle of the quad. As the combatants were sitting back to back, neither could see the other. Bad steering frustrated their intentions, and they shot harmlessly past each other. Again and again the combatants were brought into action with the same result, until a bright thought struck one of the bystanders.

Taking a walking-stick in his hand, he drew a line across the quad. by scraping a furrow into the gravel with the ferrule of the stick, set the chairs upon the line, and directed the combatants to keep their feet upon the groove, so as to insure their meeting in the middle of the quad. Off they went with a mighty creaking of wheels and scraping of feet, and great was the crash of [1] their meeting, the breath being quite driven out of the combatants by the sudden shock. Loud shouts of applause greeted the successful passage-at-arms, the panting opponents were removed from their steeds by their supporters, and their chairs taken to the starting-points in readiness for the next assault. A second time they met with equal success; the third shock nearly sent one of the combatants out of his chair; and, on the fourth assault, one of the chairs swerved slightly from the line, was struck at a disadvantage, and went over on its side, leaving the victorious opponent to career triumphantly over the course.

Races were now voted slow, and tilting became the order of the day. The upholsterers were still better pleased with this, for, the existing chairs being soon smashed, the men took to ordering new ones, made very strongly, for the express purpose of tilting, with solid oak backs, well-braced arms, and large broad wheels instead of castors.

Course after course was run, chair after chair was smashed, and the gravel of the quad. assumed the aspect of a well-ploughed field. Just as the tilting mania began to decline, it was suddenly raised again to its former height by a proposal from the same inventive genius that had suggested the plan by which the tilters might insure the meeting of their steeds. Calling to his assistance a couple of friends, he disappeared into one of the ground-floor rooms, and presently returned bearing a sofa (N.B.—it was not his own), which he placed on the ground, manned it with four of his own party, and began to propel it about by their united action. Out came the sofas, on went the men, and in a few minutes a couple of sofas were driving full tilt against each other. Crash came the sofas together, smash went a leg, over went both sofas, and on the spot was seen a mixed heap of furniture and human beings, reminding one of a railway collision in everything but its consequences.

I have witnessed many a pervading mania, but never saw one that spread so rapidly or was so absorbing while it lasted . . .

This tilting mania was, in my opinion, the swiftest and most absorbing mental epidemic that has ever overrun a city. Men really seemed to think and talk of nothing but their tournaments, and every object was referred to one single standard. We all know how a sporting man (not a sportsman) looks upon every event as a vehicle for betting, how a naval man measures everything by nautical rule, and how a mathematician wants to turn every idea into a proposition. Thus did the unfortunates who were bitten by this tarantula learn to look upon chairs and sofas merely according to their capabilities in a tilting match; any smooth and hard patch of road was immediately pounced upon as *such* a sweet spot for

[1] P. 154.

a tournament, and the merits and demerits of mutual acquaintance were all weighed in the same balance.

One man would ask another, 'What do you think of Smith, of Ch. Ch.?' to whom he had just been introduced, and would probably get for answer, 'Oh! he's not much good; Jones on my staircase would knock him over like ninepins.' Or perhaps the opinion might be more favourable—'Smith of Ch. Ch.? First-rate! Saw him cut over half-a-dozen of our men without giving them a chance.' Or perhaps the opinion might run thus:—'What do I think of Smith? Why, I think he has the best chair in the 'Varsity.'

All such mental fevers, like those of the body, *must* run their course. The authorities of the University, popularly called the 'dons,' were perfectly aware of this truth, and, instead of opposing the mania, were judiciously blind, knowing that opposition would only strengthen the influence which they desired to destroy. The climax of absurdity seemed to be reached in the '*mêlées*,' where the combatants divided themselves into two parties, arranged themselves on opposite sides of the quad., and, at a given signal, sofas, chairs, and all wheeled furniture came crashing together in general confusion.

It was a remarkable and significant fact that the movement received its death-blow in the college in which it originated.

One evening, after a 'joyous and gentle passage at arms' had been held, resulting in the smashing of much furniture and the infliction of many bruises, all the combatants adjourned to a wine party and drank each other's healths with such hearty good-will that they forgot the swift passage of time, and midnight found them still engaged upon their revelries.

Now, there is a very useful institution called a 'gate-bill,' which is worked in various ways at the different colleges. In my own college the gate was closed at nine o'clock P.M., and any one who entered after that hour paid a penny, and had his name put down in the porter's book. A penny is not much to pay; but if the authorities find that you are frequently out of college after the gates are shut, they naturally infer that you are not likely to do the college much credit in the schools, and that you prefer wine parties to study. So the tutor sends for you, and offers a friendly remonstrance, which, if not heeded, changes its tone, and becomes rather stern on the next occasion.

Entering college after the gate is shut is technically called 'knocking in,' because you have to knock at the gate in order to call the porter. Practically, 'kicking in' would be the better term, as no one runs the risk of hurting his knuckles by striking them against a heavy door knobbed and plated with iron. The belated individual discharges a hearty kick, which, when rightly directed, communicates a mighty shake to the door, and makes its antique bolts and chains rattle loud enough to wake the porter from the soundest sleep.

If you knock in after eleven P.M. you pay sixpence, and if after twelve you are mulcted in a shilling, and are sure, after morning chapel, to receive a visit from the porter, who gives a quiet single knock at your door, opens it about six inches, and inserts his head, with, 'Beg pardon, sir, for interruptin' of you at your breakfast, sir, but the dean wishes to see you immediately, sir.' Now, in college there is a peculiar phraseology. The dean is by no means the chief of [1] a cathedral, but is the officer who looks after the conduct and morals of the undergraduates. Off you go to the dean, who holds the gate-bill in his hand, and very blandly requests your reasons for remaining out of college to so late an hour; and if you cannot satisfactorily account for your time—why, I would rather that you, and not I, were the delinquent.

If you visit a friend belonging to another college, and leave his rooms after midnight, the porter always asks you, 'Whose rooms, sir?' and enters the name on his gate-bill. You have to pay as much for each friend who gives the porter the trouble of letting him out as if you gave him the trouble of letting you in, and his gate-bill has the advantage of being a countercheck, which at times is useful both to dean and undergraduate. For example, if you say to the dean, 'I was wining with Smith of Ch. Ch., sir, and quite forgot the time,' he will probably dismiss you with a gentle warning not to offend again under certain penalties made and provided. But it *may* be that your conduct has not been very satisfactory, or perhaps the dean may be unpleasantly suspicious. In either case, he quietly calls at Ch. Ch. in the course of the day, and ascertains whether Mr. Smith's gate-bill corresponds with your assertion.

The reader will now understand that, when the midnight hour struck, all the jousters were taken by surprise, and the out-college men made a rush for their gowns. (N.B. There is no particular property in a gown, and very little in caps. Any one takes any gown that happens to be handiest ; and, provided a cap happens to fit, its ownership is a matter of small consequence.)

On this occasion one of the party suggested that, as twelve o'clock *had* struck, they might as well be hung for a sheep as a lamb, and that a few jovial jousts would make an agreeable finish to the evening. So they had their tilting, and were enjoying their game immensely, when one of the combatants pretended to turn recreant, backed out of the *mêlée*, and fled from the battle-scene, closely pursued by his antagonist. Instantly the tilt was changed to a hunt, and, with loud shouts of 'Tally-ho!' the entire party set off in chase of the recreant knight. They were rapidly gaining upon him, when he wheeled his chair suddenly round, darted through the archway that led to the quadrangle sacred to fellows and tutors, and boldly invaded those decorous precincts.

All the hunt followed him, and the quiet and respectable quad. resounded with shouts and the rush of chairs and sofas careering over the smooth gravel. Suddenly up went the dean's window, out popped the dean's head, decorated with a white and tasselled cap, and the dean's voice was heard demanding the names of the rioters. A shout of laughter drowned his appeal; there was a sound of wheels scurrying over gravel, and, before the dean could get into his clothes, the revellers had disappeared, and the college was quiet and deserted.

Next morning all the undergraduates were summoned to the hall, at the end of which stood the dean, a lighted candle on the table by his side, his hand full of ominous-looking papers, and a settled purpose written on his brow. When we were all arranged before him, the innocent and guilty alike, the dean addressed us as follows:—

'Gentlemen,' said he, 'you cannot but be aware of the reason for which I have called you together this morning. The proceeding is unusual, and so is the occasion. You must feel that, however indulgently the college may look upon the natural outbursts of youth, it is wholly impossible that the disgraceful riot of last night can be overlooked. In this college we have always entertained a great objection towards the infliction of minor punishments, because we desire to treat you like gentlemen, and not like schoolboys. But we expect that, when you are considered as gentlemen, you will behave like gentlemen; and if you persist in acting after this schoolboy manner you will force us to change our system, and will have yourselves only to thank for the more stringent rules which we shall be obliged to enforce. In the present case you have laid yourselves open to severe penalties. Were I to take official notice of your conduct, there would be no other course open to us but to send you home for the remainder of the term, if not for a still longer period. It is true that, owing to the darkness[1] of the night, I could not recognise your faces, but I could not mistake your voices, and I only need look round me to discover those who have wasted their evening in dissipation. We have held a consultation as to the best method of dealing with the present matter, and I have ventured to take upon myself the responsibility. I leave the case in your own hands. I am willing to suppose that you erred from thoughtlessness, and did not deliberately plan the discourtesy of which you were guilty. If, therefore, you will apologise for your conduct, and give me your promise, as gentlemen, that it shall never be repeated, I will, on my own responsibility, assure you that this disagreeable affair shall be forgotten, and burn these papers in your presence.'

I have seldom seen men look so heartily ashamed of themselves as the guilty parties. There was first a dead silence, so completely had every one been taken by surprise; then there was a general shout of 'On my honour, sir!' 'Much obliged to you, sir!'

The dean held up his hand to command silence.

'I thought that I could depend upon you,' said he, at the same time holding the papers to the candle. 'But be pleased to remember that I have acted in opposition to several of my colleagues, and that, if you should again forget yourselves, you will not only draw on yourselves a very severe punishment, but you will also compromise me. Now, gentlemen, I wish you all a good morning.'

And so saying, he dropped the flaming fragments on the ground, placed his foot upon them, and left the hall.

Out rushed all the men. 'Three cheers for the dean!' cried six or seven voices simultaneously; and I am very much mistaken if ten times that number of lusty shouts were not given for the man who had acted so kindly and yet so judiciously. Ever after that day his influence was supreme, and a kindly reverence has always been felt for him by those whom he ruled so mildly and yet so firmly.

All my readers would know his name, were I but to mention it; and, for my own part, I hope to see him wearing an archbishop's mitre, for I am sure that such talents would find a fit scope in that elevated and difficult position.

Thus came the tournaments to an end. They never flourished kindly in any other college, though they were fashionable enough for a time; and, after that memorable morning, chairs and sofas were permitted to stand peacefully in the rooms of their owners. I ought to say that every one of the delinquents waited privately on the dean, thanked him for his kindness, and exonerated all those who had taken no part in the disturbance.

XXIX.

OLD AND NEW OXFORD.
By T. E. KEBBEL.

[Thomas Edward Kebbel, Exeter Coll., matr. May 10, 1845, aged 18; Exhibitioner of Lincoln, 1847–51; B.A. 1849; M.A. 1865; Barrister-at-law, Inner Temple.]

To a Tory and High Churchman of the old school, Oxford represented almost everything which he held dear. Anglicanism, hereditary monarchy, the scholar and the gentleman: the whole circle of traditions in fact, in which his moral nature lived and moved and had its being. As the busy world of London and great cities told him more and more of irresistible change, and of the passing away of all his landmarks the more would he love to find in the society of these ancient towers and these stately elms, the sympathy denied himself elsewhere. Not, however, that the *genius loci* spoke to him out of the past; or that all its spell lay in its historic associations. The mere natural beauty of Oxford, and its character as the hereditary seat of learning, where literature has lived so long as to have acquired all the grace and the sweetness and the dignity which are the prerogatives of ancient lineage are sufficient by themselves to make it holy ground for every mind not absolutely void of imagination. *Cornhill,* Sept. 1879, p. 336.

———

The National Review, June, 1887 (revised by the author).

P. 452. NOTHING, of course, can deprive Oxford of its romantic and literary associations, and nothing, that is likely to happen, of its natural and material glories; only the extinction of civilization can obliterate the former, and only brute violence destroy the latter. Oxford is still the Oxford of Campion, and Holt, and Arden, the young Elizabethan revivalists, of Cavaliers and Jacobites, of Addison and Johnson, of Wellesley and Canning, of Keble and Newman. The hand of improvement has not yet touched Magdalene Tower, or New College Gardens, or St. Mary's Church, or the noble sweep of the High Street. These are all there as they were a hundred years ago, and will be, let us hope, a hundred years hence. Even here, however, some of those useful deformities have crept in which bagmen call progress and men of taste vandalism. Tramcars run down 'The High,' and Magdalene Bridge has been widened to make room for them. But what will make the deepest impression on the gaze of the long absent visitor, is the change which has taken place in the environs of Oxford. Formerly, whether we approached Oxford from the east or from the west, from the north or from the south, there was nothing to mar the effect of the *coup d'œil*, which was in store for us. We came straight from the woods and the meadows into the heart of the University, and found ourselves at once surrounded by its colleges and churches, without having passed through any intermediate zone of modern brick and mortar. St. Clement's, indeed, might call itself a suburb, but it was very short, and there was no other. Now, on the contrary, the visitor approaches Oxford through a fringe of genteel villas such as you may see at Highbury, or Camberwell, bespeaking the growth of a new world outside the old one, and little in harmony with the ideas of Oxford which he carried away with him a generation ago. It is true that many of these houses are inhabited by tutors and professors. But one likes to think of a tutor or a professor living either actually in his college or at least under the shadow of its walls, and within the sacred area of the solemn and stately structures which made Oxford what she is. But alongside the academic race which peoples the outskirts of the University, there is also a great influx of immigrants from other quarters, who have settled near Oxford for the sake of getting a cheaper University education for their sons, and hoping to turn Oxford into a big day-school, like the institution in Gower Street. Formerly all round and about Oxford it was difficult to find anything that was commonplace. ¹ Now she is surrounded with it; and though doubtless P. 453. it is one mark of prosperity, it spoils the effect of that semimonastic repose which was one of the chief characteristics of the place in the olden time . . .

What the pilgrim may still do with little to alloy his satisfaction is to revisit all his old familiar haunts in the neighbourhood of Oxford: Bagly Wood, and Witham, and Cumnor, and Bablock Hythe, where the scholar gipsy was seen returning with his wild flowers from 'distant Wychwood'—now, alas, no more—and Iffley and Sandford and Shotover and Stow Wood and Beckly, and tumble-down old Islip, and Water Eaton and Elsfield. The bean-fields, I dare say, smell as sweet as ever by the side of the unfrequented footpath which leads from Headington to Stow Wood ; but where is the very pretty girl who brought you eggs and bacon at the Royal Oak, as modest and good as she was pretty? Alas! it is the change in the human element, both in and around the University, which reminds us that we did not quit it yesterday. I wonder what has become of the very remarkable waiter at the Inn at Ensham, and whether men still go there to shoot, as they used to do in my time, coming home perhaps with a rabbit and a water-hen, and thinking they had done well. I remember once going there in a more ambitious spirit to shoot through two or three woods, the terms being a sovereign for the day, and take what you killed, and my bag that day really did boast of a pheasant, a hare, and two rabbits. But are there such men in Oxford now as the 'cad' who rode with us on the dog-cart, and officiated as beater during the day, in company with another gentleman of essentially the same species, whom he picked up by the way? Has 'Windy Davis' left any successor to his name and his reputation, and his garments, to say nothing of his hunger and his thirst? I remember, after dinner, that when we objected to the enormous sum that was charged for our two ragged attendants, the waiter aforesaid assured us, in an injured tone, that they had had quite a plain dinner—'Just a loin of pork, Sir, and a plain ¹ pudding, with two quarts of ale apiece.' Are these things still done, I ask?

But to return to the University itself, from which we have been too long absent. The first thing that strikes one after a long absence from Oxford, in strolling along the principal streets, is the scarcity of 'men,' by which, of course, every old University man will understand me to mean the favoured class to whom that term was applied *par excellence.* 'Men,' of course, do not now wear their caps and gowns out of college so generally as they used to do, if at all. But in my time it was easy enough to distinguish a member of the University without his academicals. When last at Oxford I remember passing lots of young fellows in the streets whom I could not, for the life of me, assign to any class of society. They did not look like townsmen; they did not look like gownsmen; they did not look like public school men come up to try for scholarships. I could not tell what they were . . .

The change in the style of dress, and what I may call college etiquette, is a fact. The appearance of Charles Reade at Magdalen as Dean of Arts, in a green coat and brass buttons, was such a shock to the college traditions that it created a panic even among the junior members. Thirty years ago no man was ever seen in the streets of Oxford after lunch without being dressed as he would have been in Pall Mall. Tail coats were sometimes worn in those days in the morning, and the fast men still wore cutaways. But the correct thing for the quiet gentlemanly undergraduate was a black frock-coat, and tall hat, with the neatest of gloves and boots, and in this costume he went out for his country walk, the ' admired of all beholders, as he passed through Hinksey or Headington. In the same dress he usually went into hall, and appeared at wine parties; though, now, I believe, shooting-jackets of all patterns, in which it is not given to every man to look like a gentleman, have taken the place of this decorous garb in which every one looked well. This change alone is one that makes a considerable difference in the outward aspect of under-graduate life at Oxford to one who remembers what it was.

P. 455.

The life of undergraduates has changed as well as their attire. The introduction into the University of quite a new class of men, belonging to a lower rank of life has led to the formation of new social habits among men of the old stamp, which are, however, but an inadequate compensation for what has passed away. In the pre-Reform days, the whole body of Oxford men were, in many respects like one gigantic common room : all members of a highly-exclusive society; all members of the Church, and, with some very few exceptions, which did not in the slightest degree affect the tone or manners of the place, all gentlemen. To belong to the class to which, in those days, a University education was practically limited was a social distinction. It was considered a good deal to be able to say of one that he was a University man; and though certain faults might be fostered in such an atmosphere which may have caused many people to rejoice over its dispersion, yet I do not know whether it did not tend to make Oxford a more pleasant place of residence for undergraduates than it has been since. . . . Every individual felt himself the member of a little aristocracy, and was conscious of the dignity of privilege. Now, however, with the abolition of Tests, the introduction of unattached students, and the foundation of a Non-conformist college, all is changed. The change was probably unavoidable. As soon as the whole nation woke up to the advantages of a University education it was obliged to be brought within their reach. While classical culture, even in a very moderate form was the luxury of a few, and learning of still fewer, the half-monastic, half-patrician, and wholly exclusive system of Oxford might continue to flourish. But when the Laity began to clamour for the wine of knowledge as well as for the bread, there was no withstanding the demand.

P. 458. ¹ Whatever changes have taken place in the undergraduate world at Oxford have had their parallels among the fellows of colleges; and I fancy that in these changes, also, one well acquainted with the old and the new *régime* would see the same mixture of things to be regretted and things to be desired which is to be found in all human vicissitudes. I remember that in the days of old Oxford it used frequently to be lamented, by persons, perhaps, who had never considered very carefully the difficulties in the way of such a change, that there was so little familiar intercourse between the younger tutors and the undergraduates. Unquestionably mistakes were made for want of it. But with the system of collegiate discipline which ruled at Oxford thirty years ago, it would have been almost impossible.

At the same time I must readily admit that for want of that better knowledge of the undergraduate population which might in that way be obtained, tutors used to make egregious errors in their judgment of individual men. Mr. Pycroft[1] tells us that men's characters were discussed by the Dons over their wine in the common room. But they could judge only from the outside: by regularity at chapel and at lecture, quiet habits in college, and deferential civility to themselves. Such were the virtues which the Dons used to delight to honour, though all might be combined with indolence, dulness, and even vice: while other men of more lively temperament, high animal spirits, and literary tastes, who only wanted taking by the hand, and a little encouragement and advice, to display steady application, were frowned upon as idle and dissipated. Mr. Pycroft thinks the Dons learned all that it was necessary to know from the scouts. But, without objecting to a system of espionage, which the peculiar circumstances of the case might render necessary, I have no hesitation in saying that no scout in the world could tell a tutor what he ought to want to know of the men under his charge, if he is to do them real justice. What does the scout know about the mortification, disappointment, and anger experienced by the man who finds himself thoroughly misunderstood; of the shyness and nervousness which often prevent him from explaining himself; of the recklessness which takes possession of him when he finds that he can do nothing right, that his best efforts

[1] Rev. James Pycroft, B.A., in his *Oxford Memories*.

fail to win him a single smile or nod of friendly recognition from those whom he is solicitous to please, while performances much inferior to his own are selected for public commendation? The scouts cannot help the Common Room to save itself from errors such as these; but junior fellows mixing freely with the undergraduates could; and, other considerations apart, would certainly form a very useful link in the chain between the older Dons and the men still *in statu pupillari*. It must be remembered, however, that then, as now, the number of young resident fellows who were not tutors, was comparatively small. After the year of probation was passed, those who did not intend to devote themselves to college work usually went elsewhere; some to curacies, some to the Inns of Court, some to the public schools, some into the Civil Service; and at the present day, I imagine it would be more true to say that there are no resident fellows at all who are not engaged in academic work of some description.

I recollect more than one example in my own time of men whose careers were in great danger of being wrecked through the blindness or prejudices of particular Dons, who, however, were really able to plead the excuse that they knew no better. One man I remember, of considerable humour and a brilliant scholar, who, after carrying off one of the great University prizes, was warned by the tutors of his college to beware of the pride of intellect. This was all the honour he got in his own country; all the thanks he received for a distinction conferred upon his college such as it had not won for many years. This quaint return for months of hard work spent on what everybody supposed to be a legitimate object of ambition, had a two-fold effect upon the man. It made the authorities ridiculous in his eyes; and, secondly, brought him to believe that he should never be able to gain their good opinion. ' What was the result? He became wild, mutinous, and dissolute; and though he continued to read, and distinguish himself still more highly, he ruined his chance of a fellowship, and lived and died in obscurity.

I knew another, whose misfortunes were rather comic than serious, yet they illustrate the want of closer communication between fellows and undergraduates even still more closely. This man came up to college with a great love of scholarship and literature, which might easily have been nurtured into habits of assiduous study. But he was fond of pleasure, irregular at chapel, and not always prepared for lecture. In some men at Oxford, if the Dons took a fancy to them, these were venial errors. But my friend was shy, even a little awkward, and certainly possessed none of the arts of a courtier. What made me say that his misadventures were comic, was a circumstance that arose directly out of this deficiency in his character. One morning, five minutes before lecture, he found he had no shoes ready to wear. He roared for his scout, but in vain. The time passed, and he was obliged to stay away, for to have attended lecture in a pair of red and green slippers would in those days have been regarded as a deliberate insult to the tutor. Now, mark—when sent for to explain his absence, this man was too shy to give the real reason; he fancied he should make himself ridiculous by saying he had no shoes, so what he did say was simply this: 'If you please, Sir, I couldn't come.' The tutor dismissed him with the remark that this was a very insufficient answer, as indeed it was, and thenceforth gave out in all companies that S—— was the idlest man in college. The character clung to him. He heard of it, and very naturally resented it. But what we are said to be at school and college we often end by being, and S—— became more irregular than ever, and though in reality a strong conservative, with the highest reverence for authority, and a keen interest in Oxford studies, he became in the eyes of 'the Dons' a radical, a rebel, and a prodigal, who never opened a book! He was not any one of the three. He took good honours, and did well afterwards, but his career at Oxford was a failure. He missed the fellowship which was necessary to him, and just escaped going to the dogs. I mention these two instances because they show how invaluable would be the assistance and information which the college authorities might derive from men of their own order who mixed freely with the undergraduates, and understood the public opinion of the college. From such a medium of communication they would have learned at once that neither S. nor R. was the man they took him for. Much mortification would have been spared to both of them, much injustice would have been avoided, and a mistake which at one time seemed to threaten both of them with ruin would never have been made . . .

Lastly, there is the alteration in the status of the fellows themselves. A Don in my day was only partially associated in the undergraduate mind with the ideas of education and learning. Each college was then a close, powerful, and wealthy corporation, doing what it liked with its own, repelling interference from without, and, perhaps it is hardly too much to say, a little University in itself. The members of this corporation, as long as they remained unmarried, and unbeneficed, held their fellowships for life, and were practically irremovable. A fellowship was a freehold; and the tenant of it was simply in the position of a small landed proprietor, rich in the possession of an income sufficient for all his wants, able to do exactly as he pleased, and much more independent than a Duke with fifty thousand a year. Now between such a position as this and that of a salaried teacher, there is all the difference in the world. As work is more honourable than idleness, and learning than the want of it, so in some respect, of course, the rank of a lecturer or professor in a great University like Oxford, is more honourable than that of a simple college fellow who only amuses himself. But the position of a drone—I mean an independent drone—whose cell is his castle, is not without a certain dignity; and if not honourable, is, to judge from the efforts which men make to attain it, decidedly enviable. And a man of this kind, representing the traditions and history of the college, and embodying in his own person all that made it powerful and independent, appealed much more strongly to the imagination than one who is obliged to work for his living. This a man could do anywhere. In Oxford and Cambridge alone were found these ancient immemorial nests of life-long leisure, the occupants of which succeeded each other like rooks in a rookery, where the tall elms tell of centuries of undisturbed repose and inviolate prescription. Individual birds were very often laughed at, it is true; but collectively they shared in the respect which was paid to the system as a whole; and helped to invest the idea of 'Donship' in general with attributes very different from the admiration and sympathy which we feel for a very clever set of schoolmasters, lecturers, and professors . . .

Another great difference between Old Oxford and New, is in the character of the Long Vacation. Charles Reade, we are told, always retained his five rooms at Magdalen 'facing, on the south, the cloisters and towers of ancient Magdalen, and on the north overlooking the grove, with its browsing deer and the romantic water walk': and here he came in the depth of the Long Vacation to have Oxford to himself, and to shoot over the college property at Tubney. I can conceive no kind of life more nearly resembling Paradise than this. In those old Long Vacations $\pi\rho\grave{\iota}\nu$ $\grave{\epsilon}\lambda\theta\epsilon\hat{\iota}\nu$ $\hat{\upsilon}\hat{\iota}as$ Ἀχαιῶν, Oxford was delightful. For a Don, with his own rooms in a beautiful college like Magdalen, and enjoying at the same time, country life and field sports, it must have been perfectly delicious. With all the dignity of a college fellow in the olden days, with all the ease and freedom of an inn, breathing an atmosphere of literature and romance, surrounded by libraries, and within easy reach of a little sung partridge-shooting, such a man must have wished, forty years ago, that August and September might endure for ever. The Undergraduates had all vanished. The Educational Machine was still. Only here and there a stray coach, with a stray pupil, was to be seen. A great calm had settled down upon the queenly city. Her gardens and her spires, her hoary quadrangles and her melancholy cloisters, acquired fresh charms and spoke to one in deeper tones. Then and then only did one know what real repose meant. But nowadays, as I understand, there is no real Vacation, or only a short one, at Oxford. Men and Dons remain in residence. The work of the University goes briskly on, and the September Sabbath is no more.

XXX.

THE O. D. A.

By the Rev. WILLIAM KIRKPATRICK RILAND BEDFORD.

[Matr. at Brasenose, June 5, 1844, aged 17; B.A. 1848; M.A. 1852; Rector of Sutton Coldfield, Warwick, 1850.]

Time, April, 1880 (revised by the author).

WE were an enterprising college at Brasenose five-and-thirty years ago. B. N. C. might not be much to the fore in the class-list; but we had as good oars, as skilful cross-country riders, and as prominent humorists as any community in Oxford, and we were reckoned excellent hands at inventing new kinds of diversion. Legends of the exploits of Theodore Hook, Thomas Ingoldsby, and of Surtees (the author of the immortal *Jorrocks*) still lingered in the college, and it had recently sent into the reading world two admirable Oxford jest books—*The Art of Pluck* and *Hints to Freshmen*, the latter the composition of that most genial of writers, Canon Reynolds Hole[1], whose towering form had just been invested with the sleeves which marked the 'new-made Baccaulere.' Our latest performance in the way of relieving the tedium of the Lent term had been the institution of a fancy-dress ball in college, all the guests being of the sterner sex, but sundry ludicrous

[1] Samuel Reynolds Hole, Brasenose Coll., matr. March 26, 1840, aged 20; B.A. 1844; M.A. 1878, of Caunton Manor, Notts; Prebendary of Lincoln Cathedral, 1875; Vicar of Caunton since 1850; Dean of Rochester, 1887.

assumptions of female attire furnishing a semblance of the other element in ordinary reunions. The best mimic among the undergraduates had appeared in lawn sleeves, and made a speech at supper in exact imitation of the tone and manner of the late principal, Dr. Gilbert[1], newly promoted to the see of Chichester; the stroke oar of our boat, a hirsute giant, had assumed the garb of a Red Indian, and made himself so intolerable, as the violence of his exertions in the war-dance caused the paint with which he was plentifully besmeared to dissolve, that he had been forcibly requested to retire to his wigwam. In fact, to the somewhat feeble standard of university fun, the whole thing had been a great success and an exquisite joke, and the more enterprising spirits in the college longed for a new field of amusement.

It was just at this juncture that my turn came 'to sit in the Schools,' a custom now happily abolished, which was performed in this wise: A certain number of undergraduates took their places as audience in the room where the examination for 'Greats' was held; and, with a brief interval for luncheon, had to retain them until the end of the sitting, when they became entitled to a certificate, without which they were not permitted in their turn to present themselves for examination; the reason assigned for this proceeding being that they should not be able to assert that they were unaware of the mode of procedure in the examination schools. Although strict silence was the rule, and an offender incurred the risk of being turned out (of course losing his certificate) by a vigilant or ill-natured examiner, yet the tedium was so intolerable, that written or whispered conversations were constantly carried on; and thus I glided into a chat with my neighbour, a Christ Church man named Chilton[2], about our ball, and into the suggestion that theatricals would be better

---

[1] Ashurst Turner Gilbert, Principal of Brasenose Coll., 1822-42; Bishop of Chichester, 1842.

[2] George Robert Comyn Chilton, Christ Church, matr. May 31, 1844, aged 18; B.A. 1848; M.A. 1852; Vicar of Wanborough, Surrey, 1861; Barrister-at-law, Inner Temple, 1850 ?).

fun, and not quite impracticable, in spite of the ban under which in those days they were known to labour. 'Do you know Talfourd[1] of the "House?"' that being the term by which Christ Church men (*Ædis Christi Alumni*) designated their college. On my replying that I did not, an invitation to meet him, and hear a burlesque he was writing, followed in due course; and I made the acquaintance of that most enthusiastic dramatist, Frank Talfourd, and heard the first draft of his now well-known *Macbeth Travestie*.

It was soon arranged that we should get it up for performance at the forthcoming Henley Regatta, and a consultation upon a company to perform it ensued. The author admitted that he had written Lady Macbeth for himself, and meant to act the part; but was anxious to have a good Macbeth, who could sing well, to support his dramatic, and supplement his somewhat questionable vocal, exertions. I fortunately remembered a house in Gower-street, where a boy-friend of mine used to perform the *Midsummer Night's Dream* with little dressed dolls on a toy-stage with the assistance of his sisters, and at once volunteered to write to Sam Brandram[2] of Trinity, who had just passed his Schools, to come up and act with us. The other *dramatis personæ* were sustained by an extremely scratch company, hardly one of whom had ever made an essay at acting—selected therefore for all manner of reasons, as, for instance, one excellent country gentleman (who has come forward more than once of late years as a parliamentary candidate in the Liberal interest), who was promoted to the *rôle* of First Witch in consideration of his rooms in Brasenose being, from their size and remoteness, eminently suitable for rehearsals. The most amusing and conspicuous figure of all was the representative

---

[1] Francis Talfourd, Christ Church, matr. May 5, 1845, aged 17; Barrister-at-law, Middle Temple, 1852; author of burlesques and plays; died at Mentone, 1862.

[2] Samuel Brandram, Trinity Coll., matr. May 23, 1842, aged 17; B.A. 1846; M.A. 1847; Barrister-at-law, Lincoln's Inn, 1850; Public Reader and Elocutionist.

of the principal of Banquo's assassins, 'Paddy' Nicholson [1]—afterwards a banker, and author of sundry grave works on the currency question—then the hugest and rowdiest of Irish undergraduates. He could never rehearse, he declared, except in his stocking-feet. No one who was present will easily forget the dismay of our prompter, a little man from Drury Lane, recommended by W. H. Payne, when Paddy proceeded to deliver an entirely new version of his principal speech. He had armed himself with a huge blunderbuss or *trabuco*, with several barrels; and upon the prompter venturing to interfere, [P. 84.] he turned and took deliberate aim at him with the firearm, and continued, in a more stentorian voice than usual,

> 'The young bhoy, beneath the moon's pale light,
> The turf I lit my poipe with sees,
> And says, I scent tabaccky in the breeze.
> Come on, says Banquo, I don't care a curse!
> The son replies, Go, father, and fare worse [2].'

I need hardly add that he was permitted to use the Hibernian version. But the eccentricities of some of our recruits were much more embarrassing on the night of representation; for instance—I was Rosse, and shared the stage management with Talfourd—a despairing voice suddenly burst on my ear: 'That wretch W—— has got screwed, and vows he won't go on without a sword '—as the Gentlewoman forsooth—and a dirk had to be assigned to the fair creature before the sleep-walking scene could be presented. In spite of all this—and of the most amazingly shabby scenery, dug out of a broken shed in Clare Market, and such an orchestra!—the performance was a great success. Brandram and Talfourd of course were excellent; and

---

[1] Nathaniel Alexander Nicholson, Trinity Coll., matr. Oct. 26, 1843, aged 16; B.A. 1849; M.A. 1858; died 1874.

[2] 'When the young boy, beneath the moon's faint light
  The glimmering of my stiletto sees,
  And cries, "Pa, I scent treason in the trees!"
  "Come on," says Banquo, "I don't care a curse;"
  The son replies—"Go *Father*, and fare worse!"'
  Macbeth Travestie, Act ii. Scene 2.

so was Winter[1] of B. N. C., a man whose admirable sketches of Eton and Oxford are the ornament of many an English squire's or parson's study to this day. He was rowing in the 'Varsity boat, and shouts of delight greeted his appearance in the combat scene as Macduff, his helmet having been mislaid, in the well-known hard straw and broad blue ribbon of the Oxford eight. He was a good fencer, too, and his combat with Macbeth went off with immense spirit. *Bombastes Furioso* was the after-piece, with Talfourd as Bombastes; Johnson[2], the King; Brandram, Fusbos; and the writer, Distaffina. One more incident deserves record in connection with this 17th June, 1847. We closed the first act, after the appearance of the whole *corps dramatique* in their night-gear with chamber-candlesticks, and the chorus and dance which ensued, by a tableau modelled on the then famous print of the *pas de quatre*, in which Taglioni and other stars of the ballet were represented—Macbeth and his consort, Macduff and Rosse, being the four central figures. I was desirous of having a reminiscence of the play, and I took a very crude sketch to 'Sugary' Thompson, the printseller of Oxford, for him to get a drawing made for me. In due course I received a very spirited coloured sketch, and in the corner was the name of the artist: ('A promising young man,' observed Thompson) G. A. Sala[3]. I gave the drawing to Talfourd when I left Oxford, and would give a trifle to recover it now.

During the winter of 1847 Brandram and the two Talfourds, with several of their friends, with whom I was numbered, gave several performances at the judge's house in Russell-square, the pieces being Talfourd[4] *père's* tragedy of *Ion* and his son's *Macbeth* ' *Travestie*. On more than one of these occasions a p. 85.

---

[1] George Robert Winter, Brasenose Coll., matr. Feb. 27, 1845, aged 18; B.A. 1848; M.A. 1851; Rector of East Bradenham, Norfolk, 1851-72; Vicar of Swaffham, 1872; Hon. Canon, Norwich, 1886.

[2] Frederick Pigot Johnson, Ch. Ch., 1845, Rector of Oakey, Wilts.

[3] George Augustus Sala, critic and journalist.

[4] Sir Thomas Noon Talfourd, Barrister; created Serjeant-at-Law, 1835; M.P. for Reading in 1835; succeeded Mr. Justice Colman as Judge of the Court of

most brilliant audience approved our efforts; chief justices and chief barons and other legal friends of the host mingled with literary men like Dickens and Albert Smith, and artists like Leech and the Keeleys. I was not there on the night when Serjeant Talfourd—as he was then—essayed to act Adrastus, and signally failed to realise his own conception; but I was one of the performers on a night recorded by Crabb Robinson, when the diarist with prescient judgment picks out 'one Brandon, an Oxford man,' for high approval and promise of distinction in the histrionic field.

In consequence we all returned to Oxford in the summer full of great ideas for the 'Oxford Dramatic Amateurs,' as we began to call ourselves. Of course, the programme for Henley was the same as our winter one; but the character of Ianthe in the tragedy, which had been sustained by Miss Ely in Russell-square, had to be transferred to a male representative, whom we found in a Westminster schoolfellow of mine, R. M. Preston, whose make-up and elocution were equally commendable. But we had several unlucky accidents. The Archdeacon of Buckingham (Cust[1] of B. N. C. in those days) will forgive me for reminding him that he deserted us for a Queen's ball, leaving his part of Medon to be read by G. W. Latham[2], who was not, under the circumstances, quite a satisfactory representative of the part. Then our wardrobe was very shady indeed: Austin[3] and I, who played Ion's two fellow-conspirators, had but one pair of sandals between us,

---

Common Pleas in 1849; created Knight in 1850. In his early years he had been on the staff of several periodicals, and was the author of several plays, *Ion* being the chief; Hon. D.C.L. Oxford, 1844; died 1854.

[1] Arthur Perceval Purey Cust, Brasenose Coll., matr. June 9, 1846, aged 18; B.A. 1850; Fellow of All Souls', 1850–4; M.A. 1854; Hon. Canon of Christ Church, 1874; Dean of York, 1880.

[2] George William Latham, Brasenose Coll., matr. May 22, 1845, aged 18; B.A. 1849; M.A. 1852; Barrister-at-law, Inner Temple, 1852; M.P. Cheshire; died 1886.

[3] Wiltshire Stanton Austin, Exeter Coll., matr. April 17, 1845, aged 19; B.A. 1849; of Lincoln's Inn, 1850 (?), author (with J. Ralph of Queen's Coll.) of the *Lives of the Laureates*, 1853, died 1875.

about which we squabbled all the while we were off the stage. But the second night the most ludicrous finale took place. The play ends by Ion, who has slain himself to appease the anger of the gods, hearing the messenger announce that the plague is stayed, raising himself for a moment and exclaiming, 'The offering is accepted; all is well!' Our messenger was no actor, though a most popular fellow, and generally required to be pushed on after his cue had been delivered. On this night he totally lost his presence of mind, and regardless of the frantic whispers of the prompter, blurted out, 'The people have got well of the disease!' The corpse of Ion quivered with irrepressible laughter, and down went the curtain.

But the accident which was most to be lamented arose in a measure through my fault, in this wise. I had a servant, Adam by name, a vast favourite with my undergraduate friends, a bit of a character, and, alas, a bit of a tippler also. He was set to act as checktaker at the top of the stairs which led to the loft or long workshop, which served as our theatre, as well as a place of worship for some heterodox denomination on Sundays. Just as I was dressed for the first piece I heard a horrible din of voices and scuffling, and in a moment one of our managers appeared in mingled amusement and P. 86. wrath. The Mayor of Henley had obtained from me a free admission for self and party; but on presenting my order had been promptly denied admission by Adam, doubly vigilant and consequential in consequence of many friendly drinks round, which had been going on in honour of some Oxford victory; and after a brisk altercation the affair had culminated by Adam knocking his worship down-stairs, an act hardly to be condoned even by the abject apology immediately proffered. It might be the result of the fracas that we never played at Henley again, a fact much to be regretted, as the drive from Oxford was delightful, especially on a drag, or behind a tandem, with a load of choice spirits. If any of us wanted to go down on theatrical business we seldom lacked a volunteer coachman. I remember Charles Hanbury [1] (Hanbury Lennox), Paddy Dungarvan (Lord Cork [2]), John Severne [3] (now member for Shropshire), poor Mark Southwell [4] (who died in Canada), and 'Cherry' Angell [5], all acting at one time or other in that capacity. But though Henley was abandoned, we did not feel disposed to break our alliance; in fact, we soared a little higher at first, by taking 'Miss Kelly's' (the Royalty) Theatre for the night of the University Boat-race of 1849, where we did the everlasting *Macbeth Travestie* again, preceded by a drama the very name of which I have forgotten [6], the characters being sustained by Brandram, another friend of Talfourd's, and Mrs. Stirling; *Box and Cox*—Brandram and Talfourd again, with the writer as Bouncer; and a scene from *Othello* for the two Talfourds. The burlesque was really good; Morgan John O'Connell as the sleepy porter of Macbeth's castle was inimitable, and 'Joe' Colquhoun [7] an excellent Duncan. But it was the last combined performance of the old stagers. An attempt to get up a company for Henley that year failed, though, I see, a rehearsal was held of the *Thumping Legacy*, with a gentleman not unknown to the Editor of *Time* as Jerry [8] (he was paying a visit in Oxford), Charles Kegan Paul [9] as Rosetta, and South-

---

[1] Hon. Charles Spencer Bateman Hanbury Kincaid Lennox, of Lennox Castle, Stirlingshire, Brasenose Coll., matr. July 5, 1845, aged 17; B.A. 1848; Fellow of All Souls', 1848-62; M.A. 1853; assumed the surnames of Kincaid Lennox by royal licence in 1862; M.P. for Herefordshire and Leominster; some time Captain in the Life Guards.

[2] Richard Edmund St. Lawrence Boyle, present Earl of Cork and Orrery, Christ Church, matr. May 27, 1847, aged 18; M.P. for Frome, 1854-6.

[3] John Edmund Severne, Brasenose Coll., matr. June 6, 1844, aged 18; B.A. 1848; M.A. 1854, of Thenford, North Hants; High Sheriff, 1861; some time Captain 16th Lancers.

[4] Marcus Richard Southwell, Exeter Coll., matr. June, 1846, aged 18; B.A. 1850; M.A. 1856; assistant Chaplain to the Forces; died 1860 circ.

[5] Benedict John Angell, Magdalen Coll., matr. June 22, 1848, aged 18.

[6] I am informed by Mrs. Stirling that the title of the play was *Patronage*.

[7] James Charles Henry de Colquhoun, Trinity Hall, Camb., resided at Cannes; died 1890.   [8] Edmund Yates.

[9] Charles Kegan Paul, Exeter Coll., matr. Jan. 29, 1846, aged 17; B.A. 1849; M.A. 1868; Vicar of Sturminster Marshall, Dorset, 1862-75; of London, publisher.

well as the smuggler. However, better success attended a proposal to perform at Maidenhead, where we did a farce of Talfourd's called, I think, *Number 1 A*; *Box and Cox*, the two Talfourds being the hatter and the printer (for Brandram could not act, and only sang 'Caller Herrin'' between the pieces); and as a finale, Reynolds Hole's *Hamlet Travestie*, which was literally murdered for want of rehearsals. The first act went fairly, Murray [1], an admirable singer, doing justice to the Ghost; and the first scene of the second act, between Polonius (Cust) and Ophelia (the writer), was smooth enough; but the remainder of the piece was a scramble with the prompter and the property-man, and a disgraceful hash altogether. And this was our last exhibition. No doubt many of us carried our tastes into our respective spheres of action; some of us have trasmitted them to our children; but the O. D. A. were numbered among the shadowy traditions of the past, and a good many years elapsed before amateur theatricals established themselves at either University . . .

[1] George William Murray, Queen's Coll., B.A., 1850; M.A., 1853; Vicar of Shrivenham, Berks, 1859-89.

XXXI.

MY OXFORD DAYS.

By the Right Hon. EDWARD HUGESSEN KNATCHBULL-HUGESSEN, M.P.

[Educated at Eton and Magdalen; B.A. 1851; M A. 1854; M.P. for Sandwich, 1857, until created Baron Brabourne, 1880; a Lord of the Treasury, 1859-66; Under-Secretary for the Home Department, 1866; for the Colonies, 1871-4.]

Time, No. 6, Sept. 1879.

I DULY matriculated at Oxford upon the 9th July, in the year 1847, and swore with befitting alacrity to my belief in the Thirty-nine Articles, of which I probably knew as much—or as little—as the majority of youths who had to undergo the same performance for the same reason. The Oxford of those days was very different from the Oxford of to-day, and the standard of examination for entrance into most of the colleges was by no means high. I am not sure that there was any standard at all for 'gentlemen commoners,' in which capacity I was duly entered at Magdalen College. Dear old Magdalen! I could break out into a rhapsody about the place with the greatest ease; but although I avoid this, for reasons connected with the feelings of such as may chance to become my readers, none the less I will take this opportunity of saying that I always cherish a warm affection for the college in which were spent three of the happiest years of my life. That I ever entered it at all was owing to a singular chain of circumstances. My father had cherished the old-fashioned belief that 'influence' could (as perhaps it might have done in former days) obtain for a boy to whom it was accessible admission into any college which his father selected for him. Accordingly he neglected to put my name down for any college at all, and was much surprised and annoyed, on applying to his old friend, Dr. Marsham[1], the Warden of Merton, to take me into that respectable establishment, to find that there was such a thing as 'a list' kept by the Heads of Colleges, that the Warden's list was full, and that for some time to come there would be no chance of my admission. That a Marsham should refuse a favour to a Knatchbull appeared to him incomprehensible; but so it was, and my father then required me to try for a Postmastership at Merton, which would have been an excellent way of obtaining an entrance to the college, but that it entailed success in a competitive examination. As boys could be idle at Eton in those days (whatever it may be now), and I had taken full advantage of that possibility, it is not surprising that I was beaten in the contest, and again failed in my attempt to become a member of Merton. Thus repulsed, and destined to be neither a 'commoner' nor a 'scholar' of that ancient college, a choice was given me between two positions, that of 'commoner' at Christ Church or 'gentleman commoner' at Magdalen. It was a curious choice to offer to a boy; but the explanation was that my cousin, the Rev. J. M. Rice[2], for whom my father had a great regard, had just become a 'Fellow' of Magdalen; and as there were at that time, and for some time afterwards, no 'commoners' there, I must have entered as a 'gentleman commoner,' or not at all. I elected to do so, which was perhaps natural enough under the circumstances.

Much as I enjoyed my Magdalen days, I am bound to say, in the interests of truth, that there never was a greater

[1] Robert Bullock-Marsham, Warden of Merton, 1826-81.
[2] John Morland Rice, Postmaster, Merton Coll., matr. July 9, 1842, aged 19; Demy Magdalen Coll. 1846-7; B.A. 1847; Fellow, 1847-64; M.A. 1849; Bursar, 1853; Rector of Boyton, Wilts, 1860-1, and Bramber, Sussex, 1864.

academical error committed in a University than the institution of 'gentlemen commoners.' I will not waste time in proving this proposition, because I hardly think that any one will deny it; but it is incomprehensible to me how the 'order' could have been allowed to exist as long as it did. In Magdalen it was certainly an unmitigated evil. There were three other gentlemen commoners there when I entered the college, and a fourth shortly afterwards joined us. As our relations were from first to last of the most friendly character, it must not be supposed for a moment that I am attacking individuals whilst exposing the evils of a system. They were all 'good fellows,' but none of them came to Oxford with any intention of securing that degree which is supposed to be the legitimate end and object of an academical career. They came to enjoy themselves for three or four years, according to their ideas of enjoyment—to hunt, give supper-parties, play billiards, shirk lectures, and spend money in various kinds of ways not entirely conducive to any satisfactory results. These three or four men were thrown down into the college, of which some twenty 'Demies' (scholars) were the only other undergraduate members, very much, I imagine, to the detriment of the latter in every way. It was hard for a scholar, probably the son of a poor man, with a restricted allowance, to be exposed to the temptations afforded by the society of men to whom expense was apparently 'no object,' and whose talent for 'making a row' was by no means favourable to the quiet pursuit of classical knowledge. We were a 'rackety' set when I first entered the college; for I freely confess that I yielded to the spirit of the place, which was a step absolutely essential for my own comfort as a new-comer. I could tell tales of our doings which would be more amusing than edifying, but they are perhaps better buried in the past, especially as the college has long since undergone a complete change; the race of 'gentlemen commoners' has been swept away, and a number of 'commoners' exist, as in other colleges, who may safely boast that for comfort, good management, and good tutors, their college is second to none in the University. It was not a wise, though a natural, choice I made in accepting the 'gentleman commoner' alternative, so far at least as concerned my scholastic career. It settled the question of my taking 'a class,' for the temptations to be idle were too great, and, as a matter of fact, I was the only one of the five of my 'order' whom I have mentioned who took a degree at all. Within a year of my last examination, my tutor, the present respected and in every way excellent President of Magdalen [1], sent for me to entreat me to 'go in for a class,' telling me fairly that I had wasted too much time to make it probable that I could now get 'a first,' but that he could almost guarantee me 'a second' if I would but try. My ambition, however, did not lie that way, and I had not yet learned the pleasures as well as the advantages of work. So I neglected his advice, and it is no use being sorry now. The mention of the word 'President' reminds me of the venerable Dr. Routh [2], who occupied that position when I first entered the college, and in fact did not die until I had left it several years. He was elected in 1791, and was at that time supposed to be in delicate health, for which reason I have always heard he was elected by those who thought their own chance was only temporarily postponed. But he disappointed all such calculations, if indeed they were really made—expectant Presidents arose, lived, and passed away, and Dr. Routh was in his hundredth year when he died in 1855, although we had a legend in Magdalen that he was a hundred years old some time before. He was a very extraordinary man, and wrote a book which was read in the Schools not many years before his death. This, at least, I have often been told, and I hope no one will contradict it and spoil the illusion, if it be one. I am prouder of two autograph letters of his than of almost any others I possess (Canning's and the Duke of Wellington's are those I have in

---

[1] Frederic Bulley, President of Magdalen, 1855-85.
[2] Martin Joseph Routh, President of Magdalen, 1791-1855.

my mind's eye when I say 'almost'), and I value them highly. One of these affords a curious commentary upon the manner in which encouragement was given to young men who wished to read at Oxford in my day. Having become somewhat anxious about my degree (the natural result of habitual idleness) I wrote to the President to ask if I might return to Oxford two or three weeks before the term began, in order to read, adding that I was going to 'coach' with one of the Fellows of the college. Dr. Routh wrote back *a refusal*, though couched in very gracious terms. He explained that for an undergraduate to come up and read out of term-time was an innovation which could not be recognised or permitted; but, taking his analogy from that cock-fighting which I suppose had been among the favourite sports of his youth, he added, 'allow me to say, sir, you require *no feeder to make you fight.*'

His other letter to me was one of congratulation upon my marriage in 1852—a spontaneous and very kind effusion. The President, at his advanced age, was naturally somewhat deaf; but he was more or less so according to his desire to hear or not to hear what was said. It was genuine deafness, I imagine, which caused him to fall into a mistake at the beginning of one summer [1] term, when a senior undergraduate went on behalf of the rest of us to ask if we might, as usual, practise archery in the park behind the 'new buildings' at Magdalen. It should be explained that there is a small herd of deer there, which add greatly to the beauty of the park. So, when the ambassador had made his request that 'the butts' might be put up there to be shot at by the college archers, the old President, after listening attentively, burst forth with an astonished exclamation: 'Shoot at the *bucks*, sir—shoot at the *bucks*! I should think not, sir, indeed. I never heard of such a thing!' Fortunately for our archery, however, a speedy explanation satisfactorily settled the question. Another instance of his deafness, real or feigned, is somewhat more amusing. Between the Sunday services some of the little choristers had occasionally amused themselves with playing bowls upon the smooth lawn between the old and new buildings. Some zealous man among the Fellows, whose righteousness was too much for him on Sundays, felt bound to wait upon the President one day to represent to him the enormity of this proceeding, and how that these unhappy boys were perilling their own souls, and affording to others a pernicious example of juvenile depravity in thus breaking the Sabbath. But the President would not hear the good man. Somehow or other he was deafer than ever that morning, and misinterpreted everything which the other tried to say to him. At last, when the advocate of repression had bawled himself hoarse, and, almost in despair, made one more tremendous effort to be heard, the good old President turned and looked him in the face for a moment, whilst with great energy he enunciated this sentiment: 'I'm no Sabbatarian, sir—I'm no Sabbatarian'; and not another word could his persecutor extract from him. If it was not that I fear to be wearisome, I could relate sundry other anecdotes of Dr. Routh. He was always most civil to me when I saw him, although that was, as a rule, not more than once or twice a term. Sometimes, however, I had the honour of dining with him— an honour only vouchsafed to a very few of the undergraduate members of the college, and one with which, to say the truth, we would most of us readily have dispensed. For the good old man preserved the ancient custom of dining in academical costume, and 'dons' and undergraduates alike had to appear duly clad in cap and gown—the latter of which was an uncomfortably warm addition to one's evening clothes in rooms which, as those of the President, had a terrible paucity of ventilation . . .

Besides the President, there were several notable Fellows P. 687. at Magdalen in my day. Amongst these was J. B. Mozley [1], the well-known writer of the articles in the *Christian Remem-*

[1] James Bowling Mozley, Oriel Coll., matr. July 1, 1830, aged 16; B.A. 1834; M.A. 1838; Fellow of Magdalen Coll. 1840-56; Vice-President, 1849; Regius Professor of Divinity and Canon of Christ Church, 1871-8; Vicar of Old Shoreham, Sussex, 1856, until his death, 1878.

brancer; and also the Rev. William Palmer[1], elder brother of Lord Selborne, who occupied rooms immediately over mine, and was intent upon reconciling the Greek and Anglican Churches, to which I should have had no objection if it had not caused him to indulge in long nocturnal perambulations, which constantly disturbed my rest, and were all the more trying because he was lame, and consequently walked about overhead with a stick. Then there was Dr. Ellerton[2], who delivered a lecture at early chapel once a term, the subject being the Pope, against whom he dealt out anathemas which might possibly have demolished the Pontiff of Rome if he had ever heard them. Fortunately for him, however, he was not compelled to do so, as were the Magdalen undergraduates, much to their disgust. As an instance of the sort of discipline exercised over 'gentlemen commoners' at this time, it is a fact that we deliberately claimed exemption from attendance at Dr. Ellerton's lecture, not, I am bound to say, that we loved the Pope, but that we hated early chapel and services of any description. I was deputed to conduct the appeal to the Dean upon the subject, which I did in the most formal and solemn manner. The college authorities took time to consider; but it is right to say that, after full deliberation, they came to the conclusion that the statutes of the college nowhere gave any such right to any one as that which we claimed, and I was duly informed of this decision by a letter from the Dean, which I still possess as a curious memento of those days. Apart, however, from this enforcement of discipline (at which we were rather surprised) great latitude was allowed to our 'order.' Our lectures were few, we had as many friends as we liked to dine at our special table, and we

---

[1] William Palmer, Magdalen Coll., matr. July 27, 1826, aged 15; Demy, 1826-32; B.A. 1831; M.A. 1833; Fellow, 1832-55, when he joined the Church of Rome; died 1879.

[2] Edward Ellerton, University Coll., matr. Nov. 19, 1789, aged 16; B.A. 1792; M.A. 1795; Fellow of Magdalen Coll. 1803-31; D.D. 1815; Rector of Theale, Berks, 1831; and perpetual curate of Sevenhampton, Gloucs. 1825, until his death in 1851.

'knocked in' after twelve o'clock at night, again and again, without anything being said to us. One of our 'privileges' was to have a 'common room' of our own; but against this I made war from the first, thinking it far preferable to breakfast, lunch, and 'wine' in one's own room, and to choose one's own company; and to this view the others came round in my second term.

I said I would not chronicle the undergraduate doings of my time; but after all they were probably an improvement on those of past generations, and the tone of things has since those days been so greatly raised and improved, that the relation of a few strange proceedings will probably only cause to any young Oxonians who may chance to read these pages a laudable feeling of self-congratulation that they live in a more sober and respectable epoch. We were great at supper-parties, as I have already said. Every man who took his degree, or passed his 'Smalls' successfully, gave a supper-party, and other excuses were not wanting to justify similar entertainments. Indeed, one of my brother 'gentlemen commoners' had supper spread in his room almost every night in the week when nothing on a larger scale was going on, and was quite offended if one did not pretty frequently drop in. At the larger parties no inconsiderable quantity of fiery port, strong sherry, and full-bodied claret went down throats which would have been far better without either; and mulled claret, 'Bishop,' and other stomach-destroying compounds were always to be had in abundance. The youthful brain was not only inflamed by these potations, but was further stimulated by a baneful practice of drinking toasts to a chorus. This game consisted of the whole party singing three times over to a certain tune the words, 'A pie sat on a pear-tree'; at the conclusion of the third time of repeating the line, the verse ended with, 'Sing hi, sing ho, sing he'; then followed, 'Once so merrily hopped she—twice so merrily hopped she—thrice so merrily hopped she—sing hi, sing ho, sing he.' At each 'hopped she' everybody took a sip at his glass, and all glasses had to be emptied in time for the whole party to join in the final, 'Sing hi,' &c.; of course the older hands at the game, by singing fast and drinking quickly, were able to fluster and confuse the younger ones not a little, and anyhow the result was that most of the party usually imbibed somewhat more than was good for them. There was one excellent young man who would not join in these festivities,— there may have been more, but this is the only one I recollect,—and he had, moreover, some ecclesiastical notions of which we foolish undergraduates did not approve, probably because we did not understand them. I suppose he would have been called a Ritualist now, but the name had not been invented then. Anyhow, on two occasions we behaved very badly to this non-convivial gentleman. After one more excited supper than usual we seized him, laid him on a shutter (I am not sure whether it was not his own door), carried him into the inner 'quad.,' tossed him in a blanket, and held over him an animated debate whether or no we should throw him into the Cherwell from the bridge close by. I decline to say which way I gave my vote, but I know it was a near thing, and it was only the arrival of two or three less excited individuals upon the scene of action which decided the matter in favour of restoring him unducked to his room. Had it been otherwise, the consequences would probably have been serious. On another occasion we had planned to put this unfortunate individual into a stone pulpit[1], which formed an excrescence

---

[1] Ingram, in his *Memorials of Oxford*, writes: 'The curious and extraordinary little pulpit of stone, at the north-west angle of the ancient oratory, was erected, probably by Waynflete, for the delivery of public sermons on the festival of John the Baptist, and other solemn occasions. On the former occasion, being Midsummer-day, and the day on which the hospital was dedicated, of which this pulpit once formed an appropriate termination westward, there was usually assembled in ancient times a large concourse of people, with the authorities of the University, who had seats placed for them; whilst the ground was covered with green rushes and grass, as well as the surrounding buildings with the verdant boughs of trees and flowers, to imitate the preaching of St. John in the wilderness. This custom was continued till about the middle of the last century. But the sermon on this day, as well as that on St. Mark's day, from Simon Parret's benefaction, had been before transferred to a pulpit in the ante-chapel.' Vol. ii. p. 14.

from the wall between the porter's lodge and the chapel, and to which there was no approach from inside, so that a ladder (as well as ropes to secure him) had to be provided for the purpose. It so happened, however, that the Dean of that year was rather popular; and as he gave leave for the supper that evening, with a stipulation (very necessary, had he known of the project) that there should be 'no row afterwards,' we felt bound in honour to refrain from a proceeding which could hardly have taken place without something of the kind. I beg leave to observe here that these occurrences all took place in the earlier part of my career, and that the college gradually became much quieter and more orderly. I remember a tremendous race one night at this time, a race with armchairs in the new cloisters, one man pushing another along in a chair, and racing against another in a similar position. I saw Charlie Ridding[1] (brother of the present Head Master of Winchester) come the most terrible 'cropper' imaginable whilst engaged in this laudable pastime. The armchair which he was pushing stuck, or broke down, or did some thing unexpected of the sort, and over he went on his head, with a force which I should have thought would have broken any skull in Europe. But I do not believe he was a bit the worse. Talking of races, I remember I was matched to run a hundred yards for a small sum of money with one of the Demies, who came to me a day or two before the race, and said that he was shortly going to take holy orders, and did not think it right to run for money. With sad irreverence I promptly offered to run him for a Bible, but the match never came off. It was an honest and conscientious scruple on his part, and I always respected him for it.

One very sad event sobered our youthful spirits during these old college-days, though it occurred later on than the events of which I have been writing. This was the death of

---

[1] Charles Henry Ridding, Trinity Coll., matr. Nov. 14, 1844, aged 18; Demy Magdalen Coll. 1847–56; B.A. 1848; M.A. 1851; Fellow, 1856–66; Vice-President, 1863; Rector of Slimbridge, Glouces. 1865.

one of our Demies, little Daubeny[1], who was a general favourite with the college. He had been up with the college-boat, and the crew had left the boat and were walking home, when in crossing an unfinished bridge he fell off upon his head, and received injuries from which he died in two or three days, on the 5th March, 1850. The funeral was on the 9th March, when all the members of the college met 'in Hall' at a quarter before nine, and followed the body round the cloisters to the outer gate of the college, whence it was taken to his home in the country, three of the Demies going with the members of his family to see the last of the poor little fellow. This event cast, as might have been expected, a gloom over the whole college. I shall never forget the impression made upon me by that solemn procession round the cloisters. I remember, as well as if it were yesterday, how Blyth[2] the organist played the 'Dead March in Saul' on the day the boy died, and how the anthem was 'In the midst of life we are in death,' and how sad and sober we all felt.

Talking of Blyth reminds me of quite a different matter, to which I immediately turn in order to get rid of the sorrowful memories awakened by the last recital. Blyth stood for some small University office, the precise nature of which I cannot recollect, but which was contested by some one else, who, I think, beat him. 'Dick Berens[3],' the jovial Bursar of All Souls, an old friend of my father's, and always civil to me, asked me to dinner about this time, and had promised to vote for Blyth. At dinner he was much pressed by some friends to vote for the other man, whom they stated to have far superior claims, and to be eminently qualified for the office. I can see before me as I write the merry face and twinkling eyes of the dear old Bursar as, to every good qualification

---

[1] Giles Edwin Daubeny, Wadham Coll., matr. 21 April, 1847; Demy of Magdalen Coll. 1847, until his death, Feb. 25, 1850.

[2] Benjamin Blyth, Magdalen Hall, matr. July 6, 1824, aged 31; Mus. Doctor, 1833.

[3] Richard Berens, Christ Church, matr. Feb. 10, 1800, aged 18; B.A. 1804; All Souls', B.C.L. 1807; D.C.L. 1813.

attributed to the other candidate, he merely replied, with a peculiarly jolly chuckle of his own, ' So's Blyth—so's Blyth,' until at last they gave up the attempt in despair. All Souls was a charming place to dine at in those days—not only on account of its undeniable port and some brown sherry of special virtue, but because the company was agreeable and select. So it ought to have been, for at that time social qualifications (to the entire disregard of academical distinction and scholarship) were the best recommendations of a candidate who stood for an All Souls fellowship. Dr. Sneyd[1] was then ' the Head,' a polished gentleman, of whom were written those two lines which most old Oxonians will recollect as epitomising the particular merits and demerits of the respective ' Heads' of All Souls and Christ Church :—

> ' Gaisford and Sneyd each other's lectures seek ;
> The *one learns manners, and the other Greek.*'

I have slipped away naturally from Magdalen to All Souls; but in truth, when I begin to chronicle the recollections of my old Oxford days, the difficulty I find is not a want, but a superfluity, of material. I lived a great deal with Eton men, and this took me to Christ Church, Merton, University, and, most of all, to Balliol, where my brother[2] came into residence after I had been at Oxford about a ¹ year. The great drawback of Magdalen was its distance from most of the other colleges, so that my old Eton friends could not lounge into my room just before or after chapel or lecture, but had to undertake a real journey to pay me a visit. This was atoned for, however, in some degree, by the facility which the easy discipline of the college afforded for entertaining one's friends at various meals. I take up a somewhat irregularly-kept diary which I seem to have had in 1848, and find in the first

---

[1] Lewis Sneyd, Christ Church, matr. Oct. 24, 1805, aged 17 ; B.A. 1809; Fellow of All Souls', 1809–27; M.A. 1813; Warden 1827 ; Rector of East Lockinge, Berks, 1827, until his death, 1858.

[2] Reginald Bridges Knatchbull, Balliol Coll., matr. Dec. 8, 1848, aged 17 ; B.A. 1852 ; Rector of Cheriton, Kent, 1866–76 ; of Mersham, Kent, 1876–84.

week of the spring term the following entries: 'Jan. 31. Austen Leigh[1] dined with me. Feb. 1. Lord Robert Cecil[2] dined *tête-à-tête* with me in my rooms. Feb. 2. Hall began. Hutton[3] (Balliol) came to go to chapel with me, and dined with me in Hall; Regy (my brother) dropping in in eve. Feb. 4. Dined with Snowden of University. 6th. Hanbury[4] and Colquhoun[5] dined with me.' And so on throughout the term. I got my out-college society and preserved my Eton friendships by a series of dinners, for the goodness of which our Magdalen cook was somewhat famous. His name was Whiting. I recollect, and he had a singular manner of replying to questions of an ordinary nature by scriptural texts whenever (as was generally the case) he could find one appropriate to the subject. For instance, I well remember speaking to him once when there was a storm going on, and remarking upon its violence, when he promptly replied, 'Yes, sir, yes—the blast of the terrible ones is as a storm against the wall'; and upon another occasion some one asked him if he had any family, to which he forthwith responded, 'Write ye this man childless.' He was a good cook, however, and the under-cook, Davis, who used to go the rounds of the college to discover the intentions of its members with regard to each day's dinners, was a suggestive and remarkably polite person, who never spoke to you without bowing repeatedly, in a manner at once respectful and ludicrous. I should like to be able to recall the conversations of some of those *tête-à-tête* dinners to which I have alluded. 'Lord Robert Cecil' is now

[1] Cholmeley Austen Leigh, Balliol Coll., matr. March 17, 1847, aged 17; Scholar Trinity Coll. 1848–52; B.A. 1851; Fellow, 1852–64; M.A. 1856; Barrister-at-law, Lincoln's Inn, 1856.

[2] Robert Arthur Talbot Gascoigne, Christ Church, matr. Dec. 1, 1847, aged 17; B.A. 1850; M.A. 1853; Fellow of All Souls', 1853; D.C.L. by diploma, 1869, third Marquis of Salisbury; Chancellor of the University since 1869.

[3] Henry Edward Hutton, Balliol Coll., matr. June 17, 1847, aged 18; B.A. 1852; M.A. 1859.

[4] Probably? Arthur Allen Bateman Hanbury, Christ Church, matr. June 16, 1848, aged 17; B.A. 1852; M.A. 1863; Rector of Shobdon, Hereford, 1853.

[5] Archibald Campbell Colquhoun, Christ Church, matr. May 27, 1847, aged 18; B.A. 1852, of Killermont and Garscadden, N.B., died 1872.

Marquis of Salisbury; but in those days no Schouvaloff Memorandum, Berlin Treaty, or similar State anxiety troubled his brain. We probably discussed the affairs of the Oxford Union, in which we both took an active part, each of us being (let the truth be confessed) a Tory of Tories as regarded our political creed. Happy Cecil, who could remain in the same creed down to this time, or at least be called by the same political name, for the creed of a Tory is hardly the same in 1879 as it was in 1848. Still, I suppose a man who has called himself a Tory in both years may claim to have been consistent throughout; and there is a feeling of respectability even in a nominal consistency which is highly appreciated by Englishmen. I would have been consistent too, but I could not have been honest at the same time. Cecil could; and therefore again I say, 'Happy Cecil!' If we were ¹ to have a *tête-à-tête* dinner now I daresay we should fall to talking of the old subjects again—at least I think I should try to do so, and forget all the political events which have occurred since.

But the political reflections have nothing to do with Magdalen dinners, my notice of which I conclude by stating that, with a curious love for statistics (long since discarded), I seem to have kept a record of my entertainments in tabular form during the years 1848 and 1849, from which I perceive that in the Michaelmas term of the former year (which will be sufficient for a sample) I entertained eighty people at dinner and twenty-seven at lunch, being meanwhile entertained at dinner by twenty-one and at lunch by ten. Such was the exchange of hospitality by which I managed to keep up a great many old friendships and make not a few new ones. Some of these originated or were cemented in the Union; but this is a subject which must be dealt with, if at all, in a separate article, as a description of its doings would spin this paper out to an unreasonable length. I 'took my Smalls,' or, in other words, 'passed my Little-go' or 'Responsions,' on the 15th February, 1849, and my Degree examination—vulgarly, 'Greats'—on 11th November, 1850; taking my departure from the University upon the 20th of the same month.

As I look back upon this period of my life, and contrast it with the last twenty years, I can scarcely believe that I can have been such a fool as to waste my Oxford time as I certainly did; and feel that if I had worked one-half or one-third as hard during the former as I have during the latter period, I should have been a far more useful and satisfactory member of society. I suppose this is not an uncommon reflection for a man in his fifty-first year to make; but although I certainly *do* make it, and with a most sincerely regretful feeling, I cannot deny that I was supremely happy at Oxford, and have most pleasant memories of my University career. An Eton man who is 'worth his salt' must be happy at either University, because he has friendships to carry on with less restrictions than were imposed upon them by the discipline of school-life, and a wide field of new acquaintance opened before him, which cannot fail to be attractive to any one who loves the society of his fellow-men. This I confess I have always done. There is a great charm in it to me. There is information or amusement to be derived from almost every man that you meet through life; and if you only try to look at the bright side of every one, and ignore faults which you are not obliged to discover, your pleasure and benefit are likely to be all the greater. In the society of young men, especially, fresh from public schools, and not yet tossed about and hardened in the storms of life, there is a peculiar charm, which I own I hardly feel the less now that I have ceased to be a young man myself. I felt it very much when I was one of them, and thoroughly enjoyed the society of the Oxford of my day. I began by saying that it was a very different Oxford from what it is now. That is true enough; but in one sense it is the same—the same constant supply of high-spirited manly English boys still comes up from our great public schools to the University, and in the three years passed there the boyish character receives an impression for good or evil which is likely to endure through life. To those who are happy enough to come to her, Oxford still gives a training which, if rightly taken advantage of, is invaluable; and now, as in my day, I believe a man to be worth very little indeed who, on leaving the University, does not carry away with him feelings of veneration and love for her which only end with his existence.

APPENDIX.

[The following is a hitherto unpublished letter written by Robert Southey, from Miss Tyler's house, College Green, Bristol, to Thomas Davis Lamb, of Rye, Sussex, Nov. 23, 1792. Southey was admitted commoner of Balliol, 3 Nov. 1792, matriculated same day, aged 18; was created D.C.L. 1820; and died 1843. Lamb matriculated at Ch. Ch., about a year later. This letter is inserted not on account of its poetical worth, but simply as an unstudied description of Southey's first experience of Oxford. The original is in the Bodleian.]

DEAR TOM—again
I take my pen
Resolv'd to write to you,
Resolv'd to send
To you, my friend,
A story long and true.

To say as how,
If time allow,
To Oxford I went down;
And eke to tell
What me befell
Within that gallant town.

Ordine rect.,
Without neglect,
Confusion too without,
We will approach
Towards the coach
And thence we will set out.

But by the by,
To tell no lie,
I ought to say the mail,
For this I rhyme;
At no one time
Shall falsehood cloud my tale.

A veil of clouds
The welkin shrouds,
Full dismal look'd the sky;
Inside no room!
Unlucky doom;
Upon the roof get I.

And by my side
Did one more ride,
A lawyer's clerk was he;
His horn guard blows—
I blew my nose—
And merrily on went we.

Scarce ten miles got
(Unhappy lot!)
When down descends the rain—
'No hope, I fear,'
Said I, 'is near,
'I wish I was home again.'

'Faint heart,' then said he,
'Ne'er won fair Lady,
Perhaps the weather 'll mend—
And should it not,
'Twill be forgot
When your journey's at an end.'

Now if you will,
Dear Tom, stand still
And listen to my dress,
You then shall hear
What much, I fear,
You'd never be able to guess.

For next my breast
Poor I was drest,
With my father's warm fir cap;
As in inside
I could not ride
It serv'd me thus by hap.

My own old bear
Was over there,
To speak of more were vain;
Half the guard's coat set
To keep out wet,
For bitterly came the rain.

To Faringdon
Suppose we're gone,
The lawyer's clerk got down;
The whole coat mine,
Miles nine and nine,
No more from Oxford town.

But there a man
His journey began,
Of whom we'll more anon;
His name indeed
I can't areed,
Whether Dick, Jemmy, Martin, or John.

At Oxford town,
As I got down,
I saw them all intent
Upon the ground
In searching round,
However, in I went.

There as awhile
I sat in stile
My negus was prepar'd,—
My trunk upstairs
The coachman bears,
And with him comes the guard.

Into my hose
My hand then goes
Some money them to give,—
God help us all!
No purse at all
I found as sure as you live.

''Tis gone I swear,—
No purse is there.'
No purse can there be found!—
'Why to be sure
That purse wer'nt yours
We found upon the ground?'

'I will soon say,
Perhaps it may,
Of leather it was made;
I do declare
Two pockets there
Wherein guineas four were laid.'

'God help us all,'
They both outcall,—
'The man that was with you
Did that purse own.
None could disown
What all believ'd was true.

Perhaps we can
Find out this man.'
'Perhaps,' I said, 'we may.
Where he is gone,
We ask anon,
And find he went away.

Coachman and guard
Both now prepar'd
Along with me to pack;
  Two waiters wait
  On us in state,
And follow'd them boot-jack.

Hap-hazard we go,
Not very slow,
Towards the inn next door:—
  A waiter out came,
  Who was call'd to by name
Before we proceed any more.

'Stop, stop,' they cry,
'Here come to I,
To speak a bit we want ye:
  Say has there been
  Unto your Inn
A man with a hare and portmanteau,

Who just came down
Into this town
On outside of the mail?'
  The guard thus said,
  And scratch'd his head,
And listen'd for the tale.

But here, my friend,
I must make an end
Tho' only for a time:
  In a post or so
  I'll let you know
The rest of the story in rhyme.

Why I proceed after this you will soon see, but though I go on, that is no reason why you should—if you are one half as tired with reading as I am with writing, you will fling the letter behind the fire.

As you may read,
I thought indeed
Before to make an end:
  But I will say
  Without delay
Why I go on, my friend.

I thought it better,
Stead of one letter
To send my tale in two;
  Until I gues't
  You'd think it best
To make one postage do.

Call'd by his name,
The waiter came
To us along the way;
  He scratch'd his head,
  And then he said
What I am going to say.

'Just now, there came
One just the same
As you describe I grant ye;
  I do declare
  He had a hare,
And likewise a portmanteau.'

We cry 'O-ho!
And is it so?
Where is he?' waiter said—
  And so says John,
  'Why he is gone
This minute up to bed.'

All in a row
Up stairs we go;—
Our anger you may guess.
  But here we stay,
  Tom, whilst I say
What was this honest man's dress.

His shirt did hide
His meagre side,
The jordan in his hand,
  A nightcap red
  Upon his head,
As barefooted he did stand.

'Where is the purse?'—
With a hearty curse,—
Says he,'Was that purse thine?'
  'No, no,' says I,
  As I stood by,
'But that same purse is mine.'

'O-ho,' says he,
'That, Sir, may be,
I only took the same
  With me to keep
  Whilst I did sleep,
Lest any rogue should claim.'

And then to me
The purse gave he.
'Tis well it is no worse.—
  ''Twas hard,' (I say),
  'To walk away
To take care of my purse.'

Full many a name
Of evil fame
This fellow then they gave;
  As 'cheating rogue,'
  And 'gallows dog,'
'Thief,' 'villain,' 'rascal,'
    'knave.'

Whether he slept or no,
I do not know.
One guinea still remain'd;
  This guinea too,
  With much ado,
We from the gutter gain'd.

With many a thank,
This last was drank
By those who got my purse;
  And going to bed
  We all of us said,
''Tis well it is no worse.'

Next morn I rise
And ope my eyes,
My little trunk I make fast;
  A letter write,
  And send to invite
The king of men to breakfast.

How you would stare
To see his hair,
It looks so royal well,
  Which when at school
  He made a rule
To grease as we can tell.

Why should I express
What you can guess,
His rooms how neat and fine;
  So cleanly too,
  (Tom, without you),
Without your help or mine?

Why say how fine
The royal wine,
How ruby red his nose?
  Of all such stuff
  Enough, enough,
The morning past suppose.

I go, God save me,
To Dr. Davey[1],
Of Baliol College head,—
  And when he came,
  My own sweet name
In modest manner said.

[1] John Davy, Master of Balliol, 1785–98.

Dear Tom, his wig
Is not so big
As many Doctor's more;
And so I may
Presume to say
His wisdom is the more.

So instantly,
To look at me,
For fellows two did he send;
And luckily,
Whom should I spy,
In one but a very good friend.

Oh my dear Thomas,
Indeed I promise
That I was very glad,
Without examination,
Or any vexation,
To swear away like mad.

As they provide them
To dare my fidem
And go to the Vice-Chancellor;
And, nothing loth,
To buy an oath
Of which he was the seller.

He then a book,
Very shabby to look,
Gave me—wasn't that kind?
For which nice gift
Indeed I left
But one-pound-four behind.

Now I'm on clover.
When all is over,
When without being examined,
I'm capp'd, gown'd, and
swore,
And what is more,
To conclude, matriculated.

My rooms to see
Away went we;
Rooms which my good friend
found;
One room to keep in,
Another to sleep in,
The floor upon the ground.

But every chair,
Dear Thomas, there,
Is like the roaring sea:—
There's a simily good
As Homer could,
For no bottom we could see.

Tho' mine be small,
Yet none at all
You know would never do;
So I must have,
As you perceive,
Some chairs, Dear Thomas,
new.

To church next day
I went my way
A sermon grand to hear;
But to say next
What was the text,
Would be as tiresome as the
sermon, I fear.

As, Thomas Davis,
Your friend not grave is,
Enough such sight to stand;—
The great wigs all,
Each in his stall
With a trencher in his hand.

Like so many old women
A very odd trim in;
Black gown with stripes of red.
So dull the sermon by hap,
That they all took a nap,
And nodded each one his great
head.

So here's an end,
My very dear friend,
Without any more adoe.
I need not tell
That I got home well,
Else I should not be writing
to you.

Some compliment,
Pray Tom, present
To all my friends at Rye.
Pray write and tell
If, (as I hope), you're well:
And so, dear Thomas, good-
bye.

All this whole sheet I have written without intermission—my hand really aches—pray write and let me know what is become of you?

INDEX.

(The index heading of OXFORD is spread over the whole index: see especially COLLEGES; UNIVERSITY.)

Abbot, Charles. See COLCHESTER.
Aberdeen, George Colman sent to, 182.
Abingdon, mentioned, 47, 215.
Academical disputations, 74, 91, 161.
Academical dress, 113, 162, 184–5; Oakeley's description of, at the Commemoration, 305; 362; not worn out of college generally, as in former days, 369; dining in, 391; at church, 407.
'Academics,' the, 221.
Act, The, at St. Mary's, 21, 26; at the Sheldonian Theatre, 29–31; mentioned, 33, 50.
Act of Grace, pleading, 71, 75, 85.
Adams, William, author of *The Shadow of the Cross*, 351.
Addison, Joseph, mentioned, 366.
Admission and matriculation, account of, 68–70, 130. See MATRICULATION.
Age of competitor taken into account by electors to a scholarship, 53.
Aldborough, Clinton, M.P. for, 235.
Allestree, Dr., mentioned, 31, 32.
Allowance, of an undergraduate. See UNIVERSITY—Expenses.
All Saints Church, illuminated on the occasion of the victory of Earl Howe, 224.
ALL SOULS' college. See under COLLEGES.
Alma Mater, 179; revisiting of, 212, 218, 225; sons of, 227.
Alumni Oxonienses, vii.
AMHURST, Nicholas See under TERRÆ FILIUS.
Amusements. See under UNIVERSITY.
Anatomy School, 23.
'Angel' Inn, the, chief at Oxford, 348.

Angell, Benedict John, Magd., as a volunteer coachman, 384.
Answering under bachelor, 162.
Apsley, Henry, Lord. See BATHURST.
Arden, the young Elizabethan revivalist, 366.
Arguments necessary for *doing generals*, 162.
Arm-chair races, 356–65; in Magdalen cloisters, 395.
ARNOLD, Thomas, undergraduate at Corpus Christi, 247; mentioned, 248; comes from Winchester, winning scholarship, 250; vehement in argument, 250–1; his friends, 252; member of the Attic Society, 252; mentioned, 303, 336; his pupils from Rugby, 343.
'Art of chopping logic,' 72.
Arundel marbles, 26, 31.
Assizes, attendance of R. L. Edgeworth at, 155; statute concerning the attendance of gownsmen, 155 note.
Attfield, W., competition for English Essay Prize, 286, note.
Attic Society, 252.
Auckland, William Eden, Lord, mentioned, 158.
Austin, Wiltshire Stanton, a member of the O.D.A., 382.
Austins. See under *Doing Austins*.

Bablock Hythe, mentioned, 368.
Bachelors, *answering under*, 162; place of, in Hall, 190; vacant fellowships filled with very young, 207, 213, note; several scholars at Corpus are, 248; —scholars compelled to reside, 250.
Bagley Wood, mentioned, 215, 368.
BALLIOL College. See under COLLEGES.

[16th cent. pp. 1–3; 17th, pp. 4–56; 18th, pp. 57–201; 212–27; 403–8; 19th, pp. 202–11; 228–402.]

'Baloon,' the fruiterer, 193.
Bampton Lectures, 148 note ; 299.
Barber, Ambrose, gains the Newdigate, 310.
Barbers, employed by undergraduates to write impositions, 185 note, 197.
Baring, Charles, Ch. Ch., curate of St. Ebbe's, 354.
Baring, T. C., M.P., benefactor of Hertford Coll., 349.
Barlow, Thomas, Provost of Queen's, Bodley's Librarian, 22, 25, 27, 29.
Barnes, Frederick, Canon of Ch. Ch., 311, 352.
Barwis, John, Queen's Coll., member of the *Society for Scientific and Literary Disquisition*, 220.
Baskerville, Hannibal, his account of the All Souls' Mallard Feast, 243.
Bathurst Buildings. See under COLLEGES—Trinity.
Bathurst, Henry, Lord Apsley, third Earl of, 178.
Bathurst, Ralph, Pres. of Trin. Coll., 27, 33.
Battels, college, 64–5.
Baylie, Richard, Pres. of St. John's Coll., Dean of Salisbury, mentioned, 5 ; account of, 18.
Bazeley, Rev. T. T., Fellow of Brasenose, 347.
Beam Hall, inhabited by Postmasters of Merton Coll., 349.
Bearblocke, John, Exeter Coll., elected proctor, 2.
'Beardless politicians,' 281.
Beaumont, A. J., Queen's Coll., candidate for Oriel Fellowship, 345.
Beckley, 368.
Beda, MS. lent from St. John's Coll., 11.
Bedell of Arts, 64, note.
BEDFORD, Rev. William Kirkpatrick Riland, author of 'The O.D.A.,' 377; sits in the Schools, 378 ; is invited to meet Talfourd, 379 ; assists in the performance of *Macbeth Travestie*, 379–81 ; joins in some private performances in London, 381 ; is a member of the Oxford Dramatic Amateurs, 382 ; acts at Henley, 382–3 ; at Maidenhead, 385. See TABLE OF CONTENTS; PREF. viii. note.
Bedmaker, mentioned, 69, 163, 175.
Benson, Martin, Bp. of Gloucester, 110.
Bentham, mentioned, 127.
Bentinck, William Henry Cavendish. See PORTLAND.
Bentley, Dr. Richard, 239.

Berens, Richard, 'the jovial bursar of All Souls,' 396.
Bishop, Charles Joseph, calls on Blanco White, 203.
Bishop, Henry, Oriel Coll., friend of Blanco White, 203.
Bishop, William, Fellow of Oriel, friend of Blanco White, 203.
Black book of the Proctors, the, 71, 75, 79 ; charge against Mr. Meadowcourt in the, 80, 89.
Blackstone, Sir William, 129, 150.
Blenheim, mentioned, 215.
Blyth, Benjamin, organist at Magdalen, 396.
Boar's head at Queen's Coll. See COLLEGE CUSTOMS.
Boating. See UNIVERSITY—Amusements.
Bobart, Jacob, first keeper of the Physic Garden, 26.
Bodleian Library, the, Bodley 'sets up his staff at the door of,' 2–3 ; rarities of, 22 ; Evelyn visits, 34, 165 ; difficulty in gaining admission, 299.
BODLEY, Sir Thomas, account of, 1 ; sent to Oxford, 1 ; elected proctor, 2 ; University Orator, 2 ; leaves England, 2 ; returns to Oxford, 2 ; his library, 3. See TABLE OF CONTENTS.
Bombastes Furioso, acted by the O.D.A., 381.
Book of Strings, 74.
Boone, James Shergold, student at Ch. Ch., 321.
Boswell's *Life of Johnson*, Dibdin's admiration of, 216.
Botanic Garden. See PHYSIC GARDEN.
Bowling-green, mentioned, 46 ; Penton's visit to the, 50.
Bowman, F., Exeter Coll., candidate for Oriel Fellowship, 345.
Boyle, Hamilton. See CORK AND ORRERY.
Boyle, Richard Edmund St. Lawrence. See CORK AND ORRERY.
Boyle, Hon. Robert, mentioned, 25.
Braboutne, John, New Inn Hall, 87.
BRABOURNE, LORD, Edward K. Hugessen, matriculates at Oxford, 386 ; enters as gentleman-commoner at Magdalen, 387–9 ; undergraduate doings, 393 ; intercourse with Eton men, 397 ; entertains friends, 398, 399 ; takes his degree, 400. See TABLE OF CONTENTS ; PREF. viii. note.
Bradley, Edw., *Verdant Green*, PREF. vii.
Bradshaw, George, Master of Ball. Coll., mentioned, 18.

INDEX. 411

Braham, the 'spirit-stirring note' of, at the *Encænia*, 223.
Brandram, Samuel, Trin. Coll., 379-85.
BRASENOSE college. See under COLLEGES.
Bridges, Thomas Edward, Pres. of Corpus Christi Coll., mentioned, 248.
'Brown George,' 188, see note.
Buckland, William, Dean of Westminster, his lectures, 227, 352, 353.
Bull, John, unpopularity of, as Senior Proctor, 305; as Oakeley's tutor, 307, 311-14, 315; laments the carelessness at Ch. Ch. in the disposal of studentships, 320; his censor's speech, 321; his lectures, 326-7; Canon of Ch. Ch., 352.
Bulley, Frederick, Pres. of Magd. Coll., 389.
Bullingdon Green, cricket ground on, 347.
Burton, mentioned by Gibbon, 127; Dibdin's love of, 217.
Butler, James. See under ORMOND.
Byzantine Historians, the, 217.

Calvin's Institutions, read at New Coll., 5.
Campion, mentioned, 366.
Candidates for the Oriel fellowship, 323, 345.
Canning, talents of, 218, 366; autograph letter of, 389.
Canterbury Gate. See COLLEGES—Ch. Ch.
Canterbury Quadrangle. See COLLEGES—Ch. Ch.
Cap, ring, and kiss, 21 note; 31.
Cardwell, Edward, Viscount, account of, 339.
Cardwell, Dr., Prin. of St. Alban Hall, 346.
Carey, William, Bp. of St. Asaph, mentioned, 228.
Carfax, 201, note.
Carlisle, George William Frederick Howard, Earl of, at Ch. Ch., gains the undergraduate prizes, 310.
Carr, John, Fellow of Balliol, 320, 332.
Carty, Basil, University Coll., kept from his degree, 80.
Castle, the, Whitefield receives Sacrament at, 105.
Cathedral choir, 320, 354.
Catholic Emancipation, Mr. Newman an annual petitioner to Parliament for, 210.

Cavendish, Thomas, circumnavigator, mentioned, 16, note.
Cecil, Robert Arthur Talbot Gascoigne, Lord. See under SALISBURY.
Ceremonies, of cap, ring, and kiss, 21, 31; at St. John's, 213 note. See COLLEGE CUSTOMS; UNIVERSITY—Ceremonies.
Chapman, Joseph, Pres. of Trin. Coll., 184; at morning Chapel, 187.
Charles II, the question as to the successor of, 51; enforces the expulsion of John Locke from Ch. Ch., 146.
Chedworths, the, invite Richard Graves to their party, 98.
Chemists, French, Shelley praises the discoveries of, 258.
Cherwell, a row on the, 200-1, 212, 394.
Chesterfield, Earl of, mentioned, 32.
Chesterfield, Philip Dormer, Lord, fourth Earl, 149.
Chillingworth, mentioned, 115, 139.
Chilton, George Robert Comyn, of Ch. Ch., 378.
CHRIST CHURCH. See under COLLEGES.
Christie, Mr. James, gives Blanco White a letter of introduction to Dr. Nicoll, 203.
Christmas day sermon and communion in college chapels, 6.
Church, Thomas, referred to by Gibbon, 125.
Churton, William Ralph, gains the Latin poem prize, 306; attends Lloyd's divinity lectures, 225; remonstrates against Newman's *Tract No. 90*, 352.
'Clarendon' Hotel, formerly the 'Star,' 348.
Clarendon, Lord, bequest, 128, and note.
Clarendon Press, editing for the, 209.
Claret drinking, 158; utterly unknown, 213 note, 393.
Class list, new examinations with, 232, 285; Oakeley gains a second in the, 319, 389.
Cleaver, Dr., Bp. of Chester, 128, note.
CLINTON, Henry Fynes, account of, 228; taken to Oxford by his father and introduced to Dr. Cyril Jackson, 228; love of literature, 229; collects books, 229; his friends John Symmons and John Conybeare, 230; his studies, 231-2; examined under the new system of examinations with Class lists, 232; made student of Ch. Ch., 232; private tutor to Earl Gower,

[16th cent. pp. 1-3; 17th, pp. 4-56; 18th, pp. 57-201; 212-27; 403-8; 19th, pp. 202-11; 228-402.]

232; takes his B.A. degree, 232; appointed to the commemoration speech, and receives the first Bachelor's prize, 233; becomes the heir of Isaac Gardiner, Esq., 233-4; begins the composition of the tragedy 'Solyman,' 234; takes his M.A. degree, 234; M.P. for Aldborough, 235; leaves Oxford finally, 235; declares his classical learning to be most limited, 236-7; list of Greek writers possessed by him on leaving Oxford, 237; studies the Holy Scriptures, 238; study of the Greek language at Oxford, 238-9. See TABLE OF CONTENTS.

Clinton, James Fynes Clinton, mentioned, 234.

'Coach,' Bob Lowe the most popular, 350; 390.

Coach drive, to London, 347; Southey's, to Oxford, 403-4.

Cobham, J. B., Oriel Coll., candidate for Oriel Fellowship, 323, 345.

Coffee houses, first in England, 19, note; mentioned, 51; prohibited from taking in 'Terræ Filius,' 72; mentioned, 119.

Colchester, Charles Abbot, Lord, mentioned, 178.

COLERIDGE, John Taylor, account of, 247; writes for Latin verse prize, 247; description of Corpus, 248-50; of Arnold, 250-1; the Attic Society, 252; Oxford's freedom from religious controversies, 252; Oakeley mentions Coleridge's letter concerning Thomas Arnold, 302, 303. See TABLE OF CONTENTS.

Collections, Cyril Jackson at, 311; Thomas Vowler Short at, 314.

Collectors, 95, 96.

Colleges and Halls :—

ALL SOULS, Evelyn visits, 22; picture in the chapel, 26; illuminated in honour of the victory of Earl Howe, 224; Mallard Feast, 242-6; fellows of, 355; 'charming place to dine at,' 397.

BALLIOL, Evelyn a fellow-commoner of, 18; he sups in hall, 21; Joseph Somaster invited to, 60, 62-3; Somaster's scholarship at, 66-7; under Dr. Jenkyns, 332-45, 397.

BRASENOSE, 127; Heber's garret at, 242; Heber an undergraduate of, 355, 377.

CHRIST CHURCH, library of, 23; cathedral and hall, 24; coursing against, 36; Great Tom, 84, 315; Whitefield receives Sacrament at, 106; he prays in the Walk at, 108; improved discipline at, 127, note; 133; expulsion of John Locke from, 145-6; Westminsters the ruling party at, 149; Colman at, 168; Peckwater Quadrangle, 172; Colman's chief companion at, 172; early grievances at, 173-7 distinguished men at, 177-9; Old Quadrangle, 180; skating on the floods at, 189; on the election of their President, all the members of St. John's Coll. go to do homage to, 213 note; Clinton goes to, 228; Fell's Buildings, 231, 307; Clinton student of, 232; he obtains prizes at, 233; Heber's recollections of, 241; under Dean Hall, 301-19; Peckwater Quadrangle, 307; under Dean Smith, 319-31; men sent from, generally entered at New Inn Hall, 348; censors of, 351; chief college, 352; choir at, very poor, 354; 'The House,' the term by which their college is designated by members of, 379; mentioned, 170, 182, 238, 397.

CORPUS CHRISTI, Potenger gains a scholarship at, 53; Edgeworth is gentleman-commoner at, 152; description of, 247-50; no commoners at, 347.

EXETER, their comedy, 20; Lord Shaftesbury at, 35; altering beer at, 37; tucking freshmen at, 37-8; opposition to the incorporation of Hart Hall by, 57, 66; the Rector of, 354.

HART HALL, incorporation of, 57 note; disturbance among the students, 57; an attempt to obtain the evacuation of, 58; Joseph Somaster's behaviour at, 59; tutors at, 60-2; expenses at, 62-6.

HERTFORD, Hart Hall converted into, 57, note; fellowships and scholarships, 349.

JESUS, Richard Meadowcourt denied, when he stood for his grace, by an M.A. of, 89.

KEBLE, mentioned, 349.

MAGDALEN, library and chapel, 24; painting in the chapel, 26; Gibbon matriculated at, 113; 'new buildings' and walks of, 114; period of Gibbon's residence, 116; description of, 119-21; its gates for ever shut against Gibbon, 126; vindication of, 130-48; custom of declaiming at, 135; terminal exercises at, 136-9; no commoners

INDEX. 413

at, 347; choir, 354; tower, 366; Charles Reade at, 369, 375; Knatchbull-Hugessen a gentleman-commoner at, 386, 387; Dr. Routh, President of, 389-91; archery at, 390; notable fellows at, 391-2; lax discipline at, 392-3; undergraduate doings at, 393-5; stone pulpit, 394; its distance from other colleges, 397; cook, 398; dinners, 399. See DEMIES.

MAGDALEN HALL, Thomas Hobbes at, 14; Evelyn visits Dr. Hide at, 25; account of, 57 note; 348; now Hertford Coll., 349.

MERTON, Bodley a probationer of, 1; reads a public lecture at, 1; the case of Richard Meadowcourt, of, 71, 75-90; Earl of Malmesbury at, 157-8; ancient towers of, 201; St. Alban Hall merged into, 346; 347; scholars of, live at Beam Hall, 349; mentioned, 387, 397.

NEW, Laud's objection to the studies at, 4; Lord Say and Sele at, 7; Evelyn visits, 23, 26; Blanco White settles near, 202; undergraduates at, 347; choir at, 354; gardens, 366.

NEW INN HALL, men sent from Ch. Ch., generally entered at, 348.

ORIEL, the rebels besiege, 70; Blanco White's description of, 206-7; candidates for a fellowship at, 323, 345; mentioned, 127 note; 330, 354.

PEMBROKE, Shenstone at, 97; Whitefield becomes a servitor at, 104.

QUEEN'S, first meeting of the *Society for Scientific and Literary Disquisition* takes place at, 220; illumination of, in honour of Earl Howe's victory, 224; St. Edmund Hall to be carried on in connection with, 349.

ST. ALBAN HALL, Blanco White thinks of entering as an undergraduate of, 204; an account of, 346-55.

ST. EDMUND HALL, 348; to be carried on in connection with Queen's Coll., 349.

ST. JOHN'S, Laud President of, 8; lending a volume of Beda from, 11; Sir William Paddy a benefactor of, 11; Evelyn's visit to, 23; doing homage to Ch. Ch., 213 note; groves, 216; gardens, 319; mentioned, 212.

TRINITY, John Skinner at, 183; Bathurst Buildings, 184, note; description of a day spent in, 185-98; Newman at, 354.

UNIVERSITY, illuminated in honour of Earl Howe's victory, 224; Shelley's rooms at, 260, 262; porter at, 283; Master and Fellows of, 289-93; account of, 296; mentioned, 397.

WADHAM, Evelyn sups at, 22; Dr. Wilkins's gardens at, 24; letter to *Terræ Filius* from, 71.

College, Blanco White's ideal of a, 207; Balliol, the first, 332; Ch. Ch., the chief, 352, 374. See under COLLEGES, *supra* and *infra*; FELLOWS; HALL; SCHOLARS; TUTORS, &c

College chapel, Christmas Day sermon and communion at, 6; stated hours of, 113; Edgeworth's non-attendance at, 154; 176; a new surplice in, 177; description of, at Trinity, 187; 194; 214; at Brasenose, 243; beneficial effect of morning attendance at, 274; Dr. Barnes very punctual at, 311; Oakeley grows irregular at, 318; irreverence at Ch. Ch., 330; — of St. Alban Hall secularised, 349; Dr. Routh buried at the entrance of his, 353; 392.

College customs, reading *Calvin's Institutions* at New Coll., 5; Christmas Day sermon and communion in college chapels, 6; 'tucking' freshmen, 37; Latin declamations in the hall, 121, 135; gentlemen-commoners admitted to the society of Fellows, 120, 142; 'speaking the narrare,' at Trinity, 191; on the election of President at St. John's Coll., 213, note; commemoration speech, etc. at Ch. Ch., 233; All Souls' Mallard Feast, 242-6; Queen's Coll. boar's head, 242; the 'gate bill,' 360-2. See CEREMONIES.

College exercises, totally unknown to Gibbon, 121; terminal, at Magdalen, 135-8; trite, dull, and uninstructive, 217.

College prizes, absence of, 214; Clinton gains, 233; Oakeley gains, 313.

College Porter, 198; in the Long Vacation, 280; at Univ. Coll., 283; 361.

College Visitors, 5, 355.

COLMAN, George, the Younger, reference to, in preface vi; account of, 168; dress when presented for matriculation, 168; involved in a money transaction, 170-2; trials of a *freshman*, 173; description of his scout and bedmaker, 174-6; a sleepless night, 176; distinguished members of Ch. Ch., 177-80; 'Poet Harding,' 180; Lord Wellesley's declama-

[16th cent. pp. 1-3; 17th, pp. 4-56; 18th, pp. 57-201; 212-27; 403-8; 19th, pp. 202-11; 228-402.]

tions, 180–1; sent to Aberdeen, 182. See TABLE OF CONTENTS.
Colquhoun, Archibald Campbell, of Ch. Ch., mentioned, 398.
Colquhoun, James Charles Henry de, Trinity Hall, Camb., 384.
Comedy presented to the University by gentlemen of Exeter Coll., 20.
Commemoration celebrated, 217; 222–4; Oakeley witnesses a, 304–6; Duke of Wellington at, 354; Heber recites his Newdigate at, 355.
Commemoration speech at Ch. Ch., 233.
Commoners, expenses of, at Hart Hall, 63–5; Colman's grievances on his *début*, 173; dress of, 184; coming out of chapel, 187; tables in Hall for, 190, 193; Dibdin has no vote as such, 213; none at New Coll., Magdalen, and Corpus, 347; 387, 388.
Common room, the, Gibbon admitted to, 120, 144; Vicesimus Knox wishes to return to, 159; — at Oriel Coll., 206–7, 213 note; Oakeley invited to the Senior —, 322; at Balliol, 344; men's characters discussed by Dons in, 371, 372; gentlemen-commoners have one of their own at Magdalen, 393.
Commons, Penton invited by the tutor to a, 50; rebellious members of Hart Hall put out of —, 58; — at Hart Hall, 65. See BATTELS.
'Common Sense,' the subject of the English Essay written by Daniel Wilson, 355.
Compton, Dr. ('brother to the Earl of Northumberland'), mentioned, 31.
Conopios, Nathaniel, coffee drinker, 19,
Constitutional Club, 76, 78.
Convocation, decree of, 27, 28; called on purpose for the creation of honorary doctors, 32; 84; proposal to confer a degree on Blanco White, 204; opposition to this proposal, 205, 206.
Convocation House, the, Evelyn visits, 23; paper to be read by Mr. Meadowcourt in, 83, 90; degrees conferred in, 164.
Conybeare, John Josias, Prof. of Poetry, contemporary and friend of Henry Fynes Clinton, 230.
Conybeare, Dr. John, dean of Ch. Ch., mentioned, 150.
Cooke, George Leigh, Fellow of Corpus, mentioned, 248, 250.
Cooke, John, Pres. of Corpus Christi Coll., mentioned, 247.

Cooper, Anthony Ashley. See SHAFTESBURY.
Copleston, Edward, mentioned, 218, 220; gains Latin Poem, and English Essay prizes, 222; called as umpire in the case of the Latin prize poem, 306; candidate for the Oriel Fellowship, 345.
Cork and Orrery, Hamilton, sixth Earl of, 150.
Cork and Orrery, Richard Edmund St. Lawrence Boyle, Earl of, as a volunteer coachman, 384.
Cornbury, Lord, mentioned, 25.
Cornish, Rev. George, mentioned, 252.
CORPUS CHRISTI college. See under COLLEGES.
Cotton, Richard Lynch, Prov. of Worcester Coll., friend of Blanco White, 208, 210; account of, 353.
Cotton, Sir Robert, letter from Laud to, 10; borrowed a Bede from St. John's Coll., 11.
Coursing, 36.
Courtenay, William Reginald. See under DEVON.
Cowley Marsh, cricket ground at, 347.
Cox, William H., Pemb. Coll., candidate for Oriel Fellowship, 345; Vice-Prin. of St. Mary Hall, 348.
Cracroft, Thomas, proctor in 1654, 21.
Crafford, Mr. John, mentioned, 20.
Cramer, John Anthony, tutor of Ch. Ch., 312, 314; Prin. of New Inn Hall, 348.
Crofts, 'Mr. —, and his great horses,' 5–6.
Cromwell, Clinton spends his vacation at, 234, 235.
Crotch, William, Prof. of Music, performing at Trin. Coll., 195–6.
Culet, i. e. *collecta*, 64, note.
Cumnor, mentioned, 368.
Curle, Walter, Bp. of Winchester, Laud's letter to, 4–5.
Curteis, Jeremiah, friend of George Colman, 178.
Curzon, David Francis, mentioned, 179.
Cust, Arthur Percival Purey; deserts the O.D.A. for a Queen's Coll. ball, 382; takes the part of Polonius in *Hamlet Travestie*, 385.
Customs. See under COLLEGE CUSTOMS.

Dashwood, Sir James, candidate in the 'great Oxfordshire election,' 120.
Daubeny, Giles Edwin, sad death of, 396.
'Dauncing and vaulting schole,' attended by Evelyn, 20.

[16th cent. pp. 1–3; 17th, pp. 4–56; 18th, pp. 57–201; 212–27; 403–8; 19th, pp. 202–11; 228–402.]

Davenport, Edward D., letter, 240-1.
Davis, under-cook at Magdalen, 398.
Davis, 'Windy' mentioned, 368.
Davy, John, Master of Balliol, described by Southey, 406.
Dean, the, of a college, 361, 362.
Declamations, Potenger addicted to the making of, 54, 165.
Defence of Atheism, by Shelley, 287.
Degree, Bodley takes his, 1; Hobbes takes his, 16; Evelyn witnesses the conferring of, 21; conferred on Evelyn, 32; Evelyn attends the conferring of, 33; Potenger takes his, 55, 56; method of disputation for, 74; exercises for, 90-6; Shenstone did not take his, 103; conferred on Whitefield a week after ordination, 112; the use of academical, 117; exercises for, 160-7; conferring of, on Blanco White, 204-5; 217; conferred at the *Encænia* of the Duke of Portland, 223; Clinton takes his, 232; improvement in Oakeley's position before he takes his, 322; Knatchbull-Hugessen takes his, 399.
Demies, of Magdalen, 388, 395, 396.
Denison, Edward, Bp. of Salisbury, attends Lloyd's Divinity lectures, 325.
Dennis, Samuel, Pres. of St. John's Coll., mentioned, 212-3.
Derby, Edward Geoffrey Smith Stanley, Lord, Ch. Ch., mentioned, 309.
Determination, 95, 164.
Devon, William Reginald Courtenay, Earl of, mentioned, 322.
DIBDIN, Thomas Frognall, account of, 212; goes with the rest of his college to do homage to Ch. Ch., 213; his studies, 214; his pleasures, 214-5; and reading, 215-7; assists in the establishment of a *Society for Scientific and Literary Disquisition*, 218; deputation waits on the Vice-Chan for his approval and permission, 218-9; which he refuses, 219; meetings of the society carried on privately, 220-1; title of 'Lunatics' given to its members, 221-2; *Encænias* of the Duke of Portland and the illumination in honour of Earl Howe, 222-5; takes his B.A. degree four years after quitting the University, and D.D. in 1825, 227. See TABLE OF CONTENTS.
Digby, Sir Kenelm, mentioned, 23.
Discessit, desired by Joseph Somaster of Hart Hall, 60.
Disputations, method of, at Oxford,

73, 91; opposing and responding in, 161.
D'Israeli's *Curiosities of Literature*, Dibdin's admiration of, 216.
Divinity School, the, Evelyn takes his wife to, 23; beadles parade to, 217.
Doctors, creation of, 21; do their exercises, 30; are entertained, 31, 32; creating, in Divinity, Law, and Physic, 33, 117, 166; march in state, 184; the 'sweeping semi-circle of Doctors of Divinity and Law,' 305.
Dodwell, William, referred to by Gibbon, 125.
'Dogging,' 96.
Doing austins, 164, see note.
Doing generals, 161, see note.
Doing quodlibets, 164.
Dons. See FELLOWS.
Dormer, Philip. See CHESTERFIELD.
Dowdeswell, Edward Christopher, Canon of Ch. Ch., 179, 352.
Dress of undergraduates, 168, 369.
Drinking King George's health (the case of Richard Meadowcourt), 71, 75, 77, 78, 81, 82, 85.
Drinking toasts, 193; to a chorus, 393.
Drummond, Henry Roger, mentioned, 179.
Duff, barber, 189.
Duncan, John Shute, Keeper of the Ashmolean Museum, friend of Blanco White, 202.
Duncan, Philip, antiquary, friend of Blanco White, 202.
Duns Scotus, 'beaten with stripes,' 222.
Du Pre, G. C., St. Mary Hall, candidate for Oriel Fellowship, 345.
Dyson, Rev. Francis, mentioned, 253.

Early-rising, Heber gets into a habit of, 242; still the custom at Oxford, 260; Hogg's habit of, 265; beneficial results of, 274.
Ebury, Robert Grosvenor, Lord, at Ch. Ch., mentioned, 309.
Eden, William. See AUCKLAND.
EDGEWORTH, Richard Lovell, account of, 152; attends the fencing school, 152; foul play at the fencing school, 153; absences from early chapel, 154; interview with the President on the subject, 154; attends assizes, 155. See TABLE OF CONTENTS.
Eldon, Lord, 'holder of loaves and the promiser of fishes,' 284.
Elizabethan revivalists, 366.
Ellerton, Edward, gentlemen-commoners

416　　INDEX.

claimed exemption from attending the lectures of, 392.
Elsfield, mentioned, 368.
Encænia. See COMMEMORATION.
English, Esther. See INGLIS.
Eton boys, courtesy shown to, 169; 397; must be happy at the University, 400.
Evangelical Party, the, at Ch. Ch., 329.
Eveleigh, Dr., mentioned, 128 note.
EVELYN, John, reference to, in preface, v; account of, 18; fellow-commoner of Balliol, 18; gift to the college library, 20; admitted to the dancing and vaulting school, 20; leaves Oxford, 20; visits Oxford, 21–5, 25–6, 29–33; procures the gift of the Arundel marbles to the University, 27; letters from the Vice-Chancellor, 28; receives degree of D.C.L., 32. See TABLE OF CONTENTS.
Evelyn, Richard, joins his brother at Balliol, 20.
Ewart, William, gains the Newdigate, 306, 320.
Examinations, 92–4, 163–4, 165; new system, with class lists, 232; mode of conducting, 238; impartiality in, 248; — at the end of four years, 285; Oakeley disappointed in the result of his final, 319; for a fellowship, 324; comparative advantages of paper and *viva voce*, 325; strictness of Balliol entrance, 333; standard of, 386. See GREATS; SMALLS; SCHOOLS; &c.
Examiners, appointed by the senior proctor, 93; the candidate chooses his own, 163; — discourage young men from applying to a wide range of books, 238, 285.
'Ex-college men,' 312.
Exercises. See under COLLEGE EXERCISES.
Exercises for degrees. See DEGREES.
EXETER college. See under COLLEGES.
Exhibitioners, four at Corpus, 248.
Expenses. See UNIVERSITY—Expenses.
Eynsham, mentioned, 368.

Falconer, Thomas, member of the *Society for Scientific and Literary Disquisition*, 219.
Fancy dress ball at Brasenose, 377.
Faringdon, mentioned, 404.
Fell, Dr., Dean of Ch. Ch., mentioned, 25, 32, 146.

Fellow-commoners, Evelyn, at Balliol, 18; at high table in Hall, 190.
Fellows: Bodley, of Merton, 1; Laud, of St. John's, 4, 8; urge Laud to stand for Proctorship, 9; of Magdalen, 119; Gibbon admitted to the society of, 120, 142–3, 144–5; respect paid to a senior, 159; disorder of, in leaving chapel, 187; table in Hall, 190; bowing to, 191; 192; 193; at Oriel in Blanco White's time, 206–7; voting for President, 213; medical, at Corpus, 247; twenty, at Corpus, 248; of University, 289; distinguished Balliol, 336; moral tone of, 342; of All Souls, 355, 360; changes among, 370–5; notable Magdalen, 391.
Fellowships: exam. at New Coll. for, 5; abuse of, 289; confined to some particular county or school, invariably ill-bestowed, 296; Oakeley resolves to read for, 322; candidates for the Oriel, 323, 345; examinations for, 324; temptation of a Balliol, 333; at Balliol the holder of a scholarship enjoys preference in an examination for a, 334; Tait elected to a Balliol, 335; requirements for an All Souls, 355; a freehold, 374.
Fell's Buildings. See COLLEGES—Ch. Ch.
Felpham, near Bognor, the living to which Cyril Jackson retires from Ch. Ch., 315.
Fencing school of Paniotti, 152–3.
Fiat, Peter, Exeter Coll., mentioned, 22.
Fine for being out of college after nine, 79, 361.
Fitzmaurice, William. See SHELBURNE.
Folly Bridge, a sail to Iffley from, 199.
Forster, George, Lincoln Coll., member of the *Society for Scientific and Literary Disquisition*, 220.
Foster, Joseph. See ALUMNI.
Fox, Charles James, 158.
Fox, Hon. Henry Edward. See under HOLLAND.
Fox, Henry Richard Vassall. See under HOLLAND.
French, Peter, mentioned, 21.
Freshmen, tucking, 37–8; forlorn animals, 173; the common lot of, 177; speaking the narrare, 192; distance between the head of a college and, 213; entertainment of, 307, 308; fall into a set, 317.
Froude, Rev. Richard Hurrell, candidate for the Oriel fellowship, 323, 345; attends Lloyd's Divinity lec-

tures, 325; differs in opinion from Ogilvie, 337.

Gahagan, Henry, mentioned, 232.
Gaisford, Thomas, companion of Henry Fynes Clinton, 236, 239; decides a question of pronunciation, 314; Oakeley's friendship with, 316; dean of Ch. Ch., 316, 352; 'learns manners,' 397.
Gardiner, Isaac, makes Henry Fynes Clinton his heir, 233-4, see note.
'Gate-bill,' 360-2.
Gaudies, 217.
Generals, doing, 161-2.
Gentleman-commoner, Richard Graves invited by, 98; dress of a, 114; admitted to the society of the Fellows, 120, 142, 144; not exempt from exercises, 136; Edgeworth at Corpus as, 152; under no restraint, 158; limited number at Corpus, 248; Balliol does not admit, as a privileged class, 342; at Ch. Ch., 352; doubt as to there being any standard of entrance examination for, 386; Knatchbull-Hugessen enters at Magdalen as, 387-9; of Magdalen, 393.
GIBBON, Edward, referred to, in preface, vi; matriculates at Magdalen, 113; his comparison of English and foreign universities, 113; description of his first introduction to the University, 114; quotation from Lowth, 115; condemnation of the schools of Oxford and Cambridge, 116; of professors, 117-8; description of Magd. Coll., 119; of the fellows, 120; lax discipline, 120; tutors, 121; neglectful behaviour, 122; writes an essay on *The Age of Sesostris* in the Vacation, 123; his second tutor, 123; absences from college, 123; conversion to the Church of Rome, 124-6; expulsion from Magdalen, 126; later, and modified, opinion of the University, 127-8, note; mentioned, 130, 148; Dibdin's affection for his works, 217. See TABLE OF CONTENTS.
Gibbons, Christopher, composer and organist, 24.
Gibson, James Thomas, Worcester Coll., member of the *Society for Scientific and Literary Disquisition*, 220.
Gilbert, Ashurst Turner, Prin. of B. N. C., 347; promoted to the see of Chichester, 378.

Gladstone, W. E., orator of the Union, 331.
Glasgow University, valuable piece of patronage enjoyed by, 334.
Gloucester, the Bell Inn at, home of George Whitefield, 104.
Godstow, the ruins of, 215.
Goethe's grandfather, library of, 240.
Gold tassels, 184 note.
Gower, George Granville, Earl, Clinton private tutor to, 232-3; mentioned, 233; quits the University, 235.
Granville, Lord, mentioned, 149.
Graves, Richard, Pemb. Coll., account of William Shenstone and his college, 97.
Grayson, Dr., Prin. of St Edmund Hall, 348.
'Greats,' mentioned, 378, 400.
Great Tom, mentioned, 84; 315.
Greenlaw, Dr., mentioned, 213.
Gregory, Dr., Dean of Ch. Ch., 150.
Grenville, William Wyndham, Lord, 178; elected Chancellor, 283.
Greswell, Richard, tutor of Worcester Coll., 353.
'Griffin's head,' 190, see note.
Griffith, James, Master of Univ. Coll., expels Shelley, 289-90; and Hogg, 291-3.
Griffiths, Dr. John, Warden of Wadham, 352.
Grosvenor, Robert. See under EBURY.

Hair-dressing, fashion of, 101, 168-9, 189.
Hall, college, Bodley reads a Greek lecture in Merton, 1; Evelyn sups in Balliol, 21; in Wadham, 22; — at Ch. Ch., 24; tucking freshmen in Exeter —, 37-8; Potenger reads in, 55; stated hours of, 113; 160; Colman dines at three o'clock in, 172, 176; at Ch. Ch., 174, note; at Trinity, 189-93; public examination in Corpus —, 249; Hogg meets Shelley in, 255; 263; Shelley dislikes the public dinner in, 270; mentioned, 396, 398.
Hall, Charles Henry, Dean of Ch. Ch., 179, 241, 301; imitator of Cyril Jackson, 311, 315; promoted to the deanery of Durham, 319.
Hall, Dr., mentioned, 31.
Hamilton, Rev. W. K., Vicar of St. Peter's-in-the-East, afterwards Bp. of Salisbury, 347.
Hammond, Dr. Henry, mentioned, 22.

[16th cent. pp. 1-3; 17th, pp. 4-56; 18th, pp. 57-201; 212-27; 403-8; 19th, pp. 202-11; 228-402.]

Hampden, Dr. R. D., Prin. of St. Mary Hall, 348, 352.
Hanbury, Arthur Allen Bateman, Ch. Ch., 398.
Harcourt, Venables Vernon, referred to in the censor's speech, 321.
Harding, poet, 180.
Harris, James. See under MALMESBURY.
Harris, James, M.P. for Christchurch, Hants, 157.
HART HALL. See under COLLEGES.
Hawkins, Edward, Provost of Oriel, good influence as tutor, 330.
Headington, an evening's ramble to, 227, 368; mentioned, 369.
Heathcote, Richard Edensor, mentioned, 232.
Hebdomadal Board, proposes to confer a degree on Blanco White, 204; condemns Newman's *Tract No. 90*, 352.
HEBER, Reginald, account of, 240; letter to E. D. Davenport concerning changes at Oxford, 240-1: letter to John Thornton respecting All Souls' Mallard Feast, 242-3; tells of early rising and a course of mathematics, 242 3; sees the Mallard Feast, 244; fellow of All Souls, 355. See TABLE OF CONTENTS.
Henley Regatta, the O. D. A. perform at, 379, 382.
Henley, Robert. See NORTHINGTON.
Henry, Dr. Robert, author of the *Hist. of Great Britain*, 216.
Henry, John West, Pemb. Coll., mentioned, 347.
HERTFORD COLLEGE. See under COLLEGES.
High Street, illumination of, in honour of Earl Howe's victory, 224; tramcars in, 367.
High Table, 190.
Hill, Rev. John, Vice-Prin. of St. Edmund Hall, promotes religion amongst the undergraduates, 348.
Hinksey, mentioned, 369.
HOBBES, Thomas, referred to in preface, vi; account of, 14; his tutor, 14; his studies, 14-16; takes his B.A. degree, 16; tutor in the Cavendish family, 16. See TABLE OF CONTENTS.
'Hobby-horse,' the, a 'light-built galley,' 199, 200.
HOGG, T. J., arrival at Oxford, 254; pleasure at the external appearance of Oxford, 254-5; his first meeting with Shelley, 255; discussion of German and Italian literature, 256; invites Shelley to his rooms, 256-7; discusses chemistry, etc., with him until one o'clock in the morning, 258-9; visits him at his rooms, 260-6; intimacy with Shelley, 264-6; pistol-shooting, 266-7; opinion of the Universities, 273-4; his reading, 279; spends long vacation at Oxford, 279-80; writes to the master and fellows concerning the expulsion of Shelley, 291; is summoned to attend the conclave, 291; is expelled, 292-3; departs from Oxford with Shelley, 294; anecdote of the University, 297-8; proceeds to London, 300.
Hole, Samuel Reynolds, of Brasenose, author of *Hints to Freshmen*, 377; and of *Hamlet Travestie*, 385.
Holland, Henry Edward Vassall Fox, fourth Baron, 203.
Holland, Henry Richard Vassall Fox, third Baron, offers Blanco White tutorship of his son, 203.
Holland House, Blanco White makes the acquaintance of Dr. Shuttleworth at, 202; settles at, as tutor, 204; Philip Nicholas Shuttleworth passes his youth at, 316.
Holt, Charles, Magdalen, sub-proctor in the case of Richard Meadowcourt, 76-8, 83.
Holt, the young Elizabethan revivalist, 366.
Holwell, William, 149.
Hook, Theodore, at Brasenose, 377.
Hooker, mentioned by Gibbon, 115.
Hooper, 'a dame,' who supplies gownsmen with boating craft, 200.
Horne, George, Pres. of Magd. Coll., Bp. of Norwich, 143, 145; Vice-Chan. at Colman's matriculation, 169.
Horseman, John, Corpus Christi Coll., member of the *Society of Scientific and Literary Disquisition*, 220.
Horses, keeping of, at Oxford, by Lord Shaftesbury, 35; the tutor's advice to Penton against keeping, at Oxford, 47.
'House,' the, 312, 379.
Howard, George William Frederick. See CARLISLE.
Howe, Earl, victory over the French, 222; illumination of Oxford in honour of, 224-5.
Howell, James, author of *Londinopolis*, 227.

Howley, William, Archbp. of Canterbury, Churton the domestic chaplain of, 306, 337.
Hugessen, E. K. See BRABOURNE.
Hughes, Thomas, Trin. Coll., *Tom Brown at Oxford*, vii; a celebrated 'coach,' 350-1.
Hume, Dibdin's *sofa* companion, 216.
Humphrey, Lawrence, Pres. of Magd. Coll., tutor to Thomas Bodley, 1.
Hunt, Joseph, Master of Balliol, 66.
Hunting, increase of, 241.
Hurdis, Rev. James, author of the *Vindication of Magdalen College*, 130. See TABLE OF CONTENTS.
Hussey, Mr., servitor of Lord Shaftesbury, 38.
Hussey, Robert, account of, 315; referred to in the censor's speech, 321; censor of Ch. Ch., 351.
Hutton, Henry Edward, 398.
Hyde, Dr. James, Prin. of Magd. Hall, Evelyn visits, 25; speech of, at the *Encænia*, 31.

Iffley, a sail in the *Hobby-horse* to, 199; the sacred antiquity of, 215; 368.
Illumination, in consequence of the victory of Earl Howe, 222, 224-5.
Impey, Elijah Barwell, friend of Clinton, mentioned, 232, 236.
Imposition, set for rebellious students at Hart Hall, 56, 57; written by the barber, 185 see note; 222.
Inchbald, performs at Trin. Coll., 197.
Inglis, or English, Esther, 23, note.
Inglis, Sir Robert, election of, 209; Ogilvie the leader of the High Church party at the time of the election of, 337.
Ingoldsby, Thomas, at Brasenose, 377.
Ingram, Dr., Pres. of Trin. Coll., author of *Memorials of Oxford*, 354.
Ion, Talfourd's tragedy of, 381-3.
Isis, the, boating on, 215, 227; the banks of, 282.
Islip, state of, 368.

Jackson, Cyril, Dean of Ch. Ch., receives the procession from St. John's Coll. on the election of their President, 213, note; confers with Dr. Wills on the subject of the establishment of the *Society for Scientific and Literary Disquisition*, 219; Clinton introduced to, 228; imitators of, 311-2; account of, 315; carelessness in the bestowal of studentships, servitorships, and choristerships, 320; mentioned, 127 note; 241.
Jackson, Rev. Magnus, Clinton's old master at Southwell, 229.
Jacobson, Mr., Vice-Prin. of Magd. Hall, 348.
Jago, Richard, 101-2.
James I, approves of Laud's election as President of St. John's Coll., 8.
James II, the question of the succession of, 51, 70.
Jelf, Mr., Ch. Ch., mentioned, 347, 352.
Jenkins, Sir Leoline, Prin. of Jesus Coll., 27.
Jenkinson, Charles. See LIVERPOOL.
Jenkyns, Richard, Vice-Chancellor, 204, note; Balliol under, 332-45, 353.
JESUS COLLEGE. See under COLLEGES.
Johnson, Frederick Pigot, a member of the O.D.A., 381.
Johnson, Dr. Samuel, remarks on Shenstone's employment at Oxford, 100; disapproves of servitorships, 101-2; mentioned, 366.
Jones, Christopher, Ch. Ch., friend of Clinton, mentioned, 236.
Jones, Sir Love Parry, mentioned, 232.
Jonge, Mr., performs at Trin. Coll., 196, 197.
Jowett, Benjamin, Master of Balliol, account of, 339, 340.
Juxon, William, mentioned, 11, note.

KEBBEL, Thomas Edward, author of *Old and New Oxford*, 366. See TABLE OF CONTENTS; PREF. viii. note.
KEBLE COLLEGE. See under COLLEGES.
Keble, Rev. John, author of the *Christian Year*, 252; enthusiastic attachment to Oxford, 303; and Tractarianism, 337; mentioned, 366.
Kendal, Dr., mentioned, 22.
Kennicott, Benjamin, a 'studious contemporary' of Gibbon, 144.
Kett, Henry, account of, 188.
King, William, Prin. of St. Mary Hall, account of, 150.
Kingsley, Charles, referred to in preface, vii.
Kitto, Mr., presented to the living of St. Martin's-in-the-Fields, 349.
KNATCHBULL-HUGESSEN, Right. Hon. Edward Hugessen. See under BRABOURNE.
Knatchbull, Reginald Bridges, at Balliol, 397.
'Knocking in,' 361, 393.

KNOX, Vicesimus, account of, 159; 'On the necessity of an attention to things as well as books,' 159; disgusted with life outside a college, 159; respect paid to a senior fellow, 159; 'On some parts of the discipline in our English Universities,' 160–7; exercises for degrees, 161–6. See TABLE OF CONTENTS.

Lady's Calling, 49.
Lamb, Thomas Davis, letter to, from Southey, 403.
Latham, George William, takes part in the tragedy of *Ion*, at Henley, 382.
Latin, colloquial use of, 54.
Latin sermon, 22.
Latin verses, Shelley composes, with singular facility, 281–2; Bull of Ch. Ch., composes, with ease, 313. See under UNIVERSITY PRIZES.
LAUD, William, Archbp. of Canterbury, referred to in preface, vi; account of, 4; letter to Walter Curle, Bp. of Winchester, respecting the study of Calvin's Institutions at New Coll., 4–5; letter to Richard Baylie, Vice-Chancellor, respecting 'Mr. Crofts and his great horses,' 5–6; extract from letter to Christopher Potter, Prov. of Queen's Coll., concerning Christmas Day sermon and communion in college chapels, 6; answer to the speech of Lord Say and Sele, 7–10; chosen President of St. John's, 8; letter to Sir Robert Cotton, 10–12; lends an ancient volume of Beda from St. John's Coll. library, 11; mentioned, 19, 23; the builder of part of the Bodleian library, 23. See TABLE OF CONTENTS.
Lausanne, Gibbon at, 134, 140.
Lawrence, Thomas, Master of Ball. Coll., mentioned, 19.
Lecturers, neglectful, 71; Lloyd, the very prince of, 325, 328–9; Bull and Short, at Ch. Ch., 326–7.
Lectures, at Hart Hall, 57; neglected, 71–2; attendance at, 91–2, 138–9, 141; one hour occupied by, 214; Shelley attends a mineralogy, 257; less difficult than lessons in a public school, 285; Lloyd's celebrated Divinity, 324–5; of Bull and Short, at Ch. Ch. 326–7; few, at Magdalen, 392; mentioned, 140, 280.
Lee, Jacob, Censor of Ch. Ch., 351.

Leigh, Cholmeley Austin, of Balliol, mentioned, 398.
Lennox, Hon. Charles Bateman Hanbury Kincaid, as a volunteer coachman, 384.
Letter from Wadham College to *Terrœ Filius*, 71.
LETTERS FROM OXFORD. See TABLE OF CONTENTS.
Liceat, 162, 165.
Liddell, Dean, as a junior tutor of Ch. Ch., 351.
Litton, Edward A., Oriel Coll., curate of St. Ebbe's, 354.
Liverpool, Charles Jenkinson, Earl of, consults Cyril Jackson upon Church-appointments, 315.
Lloyd, Dr., mentioned, 27.
Lloyd, Charles, Bp. of Oxford, tells an anecdote of Cyril Jackson, 320; his Divinity Lectures, 324–5, 326, 328–9.
Locke, John, expulsion of, from Ch. Ch., 115, 145.
Logic, 'this art of chopping—', 72–5; Shelley on, 278–9. See SYLLOGISMS.
London Review, the, Blanco White assists the starting of, 209; failure of, 210.
London, University of, 161; Dr. Arnold's letter on, 325.
Longley, Charles Thomas, Archbp. of Canterbury, tutor at Ch. Ch., 312; account of, 314.
Long Vacation, the, 58; an 'admirable and blessed institution,' 279; changes in the character of, 375.
Lowe, Robert. See SHERBROOK.
Lowth, Robert, Bp. of St. David's, 114, 118, 145.
Lowth, Robert, 179.
'Lunatics,' the, 221–2, 227.

Macbeth Travestie, acted by the O.D.A. at Henley, 379–81, 384.
Macbride, Dr. John David, Prin. of Magd. Hall, mentioned, 348.
Macdonald, Sir James, companion of R. L. Edgeworth, 152.
Mackenzie, Rev. Alexander, Ch. Ch., friend of Clinton, mentioned, 236.
Magdalen Bridge, widened for the convenience of tramcars, 367.
MAGDALEN COLLEGE. See under COLLEGES.
MAGDALEN HALL. See under COLLEGES.
Mallard Feast. See COLLEGES—All Souls.

INDEX.

421

MALMESBURY, James Harris, first Earl of, account of, 157; six months in London, 157; lax discipline at the University, 158; his tutor, 158; distinguished members of Merton Coll., 158. See TABLE OF CONTENTS.
Manciple, at Ch. Ch., 327; at St. Alban Hall, 347.
Manning, Dr., Archbp. of Westminster, 317; select preacher, 351.
Marcasites, 33, note.
Markham, Dr., Archbp. of York, improves the discipline at Ch. Ch., 127.
Marlowe, Michael, Dibdin's tutor, afterwards Pres. of St. John's Coll., 213, see note.
Marsh, Matthew, Clinton's tutor, 228.
Marsham, Charles, see under RUMNEY.
Marsham, Robert Bullock, Warden of Merton, 348, 387.
Master of Arts: Bodley proceeds, 1; young masters, at Exeter, 38; 'plainness and freedom' of, 51; Potenger performs the most difficult part of the exercises for the degree of, 56; exercises for the degree of, 138-9, 161, 163, 164-7; a kind of aristocracy among the, 206; Clinton takes his degree of, 234; at Commemoration, 305.
Maton, William George, founder of the *Society for Scientific and Literary Disquisition*, 218, 220.
Matriculation, Amhurst's account of, 68-70; Gibbon is excused his subscription to the Thirty-nine Articles at his, 124; imprudence of early, 130; of Eton and Westminster boys, 169.
Meadowcourt, Richard, Merton Coll., put into the black book, 71; drinking King George's health, 77-90; pleads the act of grace, 85, 89; takes his degree, 90.
'Men.' See UNDERGRADUATES.
Meredith, George, referred to in preface, vii.
MERTON COLLEGE. See under COLLEGES.
Methodists, 105, 106, 111.
Mewes, Dr., Pres. of St. John's Coll., 33.
Middleton, Charles, Earl of, 146.
Middleton, Dr., referred to by Gibbon, 124, 125, 126.
'Mitre' Inn, the, mentioned, 348.
Moberly, George, Bp. of Salisbury, attends Lloyd's Divinity lectures, 325; fellow of Balliol, 336, 337; inclined to Tractarianism, 338; candidate for the Oriel fellowship, 345.
Moderators, 73.
Moncreiff, James, member of the *Society for Scientific and Literary Disquisition*, 220.
Moncreiff, William, member of the *Society for Scientific and Literary Disquisition*, 220.
Morison, Dr., Botanic Professor, mentioned, 33.
Morley, George, Bp. of Winchester, mentioned, 53.
Moulding, John Bankes, Trin. Coll., account of, 192.
Moysey, Charles Abel, receives the second Bachelor's prize at Ch. Ch., 233.
Mozley, James Bowling, author of articles in the *Christian Remembrancer*, 391.
Murray, George William, acts in *Hamlet Travestie*, 385.
MY OXFORD DAYS, by the Right Hon. Edward Hugessen Knatchbull-Hugessen, M.P., 386-401.

Narrare, at Trin. Coll., 191-3, note.
'New buildings.' See COLLEGES—Magdalen.
Newcastle, Duke of, parliamentary intentions, 235.
NEW COLLEGE. See under COLLEGES.
Newdigate, the, by Ewart, of Ch. Ch., 306; Oakeley writes for, 310; gained by Ruskin, 352; by Heber, 355.
NEW INN HALL. See under COLLEGES.
Newman, Francis William, account of, 336, 337.
Newman, John Henry, connected with the 'No-popery' party, 210; enthusiastic attachment to Oxford, 303; attends Lloyd's divinity lectures, 325; vicar of St. Mary's, 347, 351; condemnation of the celebrated Tract of, 352; at Trinity, 354; mentioned, 366.
NEWTON, Richard, account of, 57; opposition of Exeter Coll. to the incorporation of Hart Hall, 57; rebellion among the Commoners of Hart Hall, 57; an attempt to obtain the complete evacuation of the Hall, 58; behaviour of Joseph Somaster, 59-60; Newton refuses an 'Instrument of leave' to Somaster, 60; Tutors at Hart Hall, 60 2; expenses at Hart Hall, 63-6; Somaster's scholarship

[16th cent. pp. 1-3; 17th, pp. 4-56; 18th, pp. 57-201; 212-27; 403-8; 19th, pp. 202-11; 228-402.]

at Balliol, unfairly gained, 67. See TABLE OF CONTENTS.
Newtoni Systema, Latin prize poem gained by W. R. Churton, 306.
Nicholson, Margaret, referred to, 289.
Nicholson, Nathaniel Alexander, acts in *Macbeth Travestie*, 380.
Nicoll, Alexander, friend of Blance White, 202.
Noblemen, Balliol does not admit the reception of, as a privileged class, 342; at Ch. Ch., 352.
Nomenclator, 184, note.
No-popery party, fury of, against Blanco White, 209, 210.
Norfolk, Henry, sixth Duke of, donor of the Arundel marbles, 26, 29.
North, Brownlow, Bp. of Winchester, 158.
Northington, Robert Henley, Lord, mentioned, 158.
Nowell, Thomas, D.D., Prin. of St. Mary Hall, 146.
Nuneham, a sail in the *Hobby-horse* to, 200; Dibdin mentions, 215; Queen and Prince Albert at, 354.

'Oak,' sporting the, 189; Shelley's admiration of, 275-7.
OAKELEY, Frederick, account of, 301; (*a*) Ch. Ch. under Dean Hall, 301-19; unhappy recollections of his undergraduate life, 302-4, 306-8; life with a private tutor before going to Oxford, 304; matriculates at Ch. Ch., 304; is taken to the Sheldonian Theatre at Commemoration, 304; opening of his residence at Ch. Ch., 306; sent home from college owing to want of space, 307; wine-parties, 307-8; 'gown and town rows,' 309; distinguished men at Ch. Ch., 309; writes for prizes, 310; college authorities at Ch. Ch., 311-7; gains a college prize, 313; falls in with a wrong set, 317-8; his rooms at Ch. Ch., 317; his pleasure in reading, 318-9; disappointing result of his examination, 319; (*b*) Ch. Ch. under Dean Smith, 319-31; careless bestowal of studentships, servitorships, and choristerships at Ch. Ch., 319-21; resolves upon reading for a fellowship, 322; gains Chancellor's prize for Latin essay, and later on for English essay, 323; candidate for fellowship at Oriel Coll., 323; attends Lloyd's Divinity lectures, 324-5, 328-9; moral and religious state of Ch. Ch., 329-30; establishment of the Union Debating Society, 330-1; (*c*) Balliol under Dr. Jenkyns, 332-45; scholarships on the foundation thrown open to competition, 334; election of Archibald Campbell Tait, 335; Oakeley placed on the foundation as fellow and college chaplain, 337; rise of Tractarianism, 337-8; distinguished additions to the society of Balliol, 339-40; Tractarianism at Balliol, 340-2; resignation of Mr. Ward, 340-2; moral tone of Balliol, 342-44; senior tutor of Balliol, 353. See TABLE OF CONTENTS.
Oakeley, Sir Herbert, mentioned, 316.
Oath of allegiance and supremacy, 69.
Oath of fidelity to the University, 69.
Ockham, 'beaten with stripes,' 222.
O. D. A., the, 377-85.
Ogilvie, Charles Atmore, friend of Blanco White, 208, 210; fellow of Balliol, 332; account of, 333; good influence on the college, 334, 344; opposed to Tractarianism, 337; Mr. Round sides with, 338.
OLD AND NEW OXFORD, 366-75.
Opponents, in the exercises for degrees, 73.
Opposing and responding, 73, 161.
Orator, Public, Bodley supplies the office of, 2; Dr. South's speech as, 30, 32.
Ordinaries (commonly called *Wall Lectures*), 165.
ORIEL COLLEGE. See under COLLEGES.
Ormond, James Butler, first Duke of, 32.
Ormond, Duke of, 70.
Owen, John, Dean of Ch. Ch., mentioned, 21.
Owen, the rebel, 70.
OXFORD: Evelyn visits, 21-5, 25-6, 29-33, 33-4; rule respecting the taking of orders in the diocese of, 146; incident during assizes at, 155; Shelley's opinion of the country near, 274; the chief inn at, 348; *Tournaments Holden at*, 356-65; *Old and New*, 366-76; — *Dramatic Amateurs*, 377-85; — *Days*, 386-401. See under UNIVERSITY, &c.
Oxfordshire election, 'Great,' 120, note.

Paddy, Sir William, benefactor of St. John's Coll., 11.
'Palestine,' the subject of the Newdigate, written by Heber, 355.

INDEX.   423

Palmer, William, tutor at Magd. Coll., 351, 391.
'Palmyra,' Newdigate poem (1822), Oakeley competes, 310.
Paniotti, master of the fencing school, 152-3.
Panting, Matthew, Master of Pemb. Coll., 104.
Paradise St., Dibdin's recollections of *No. 22*, 226.
Parkhurst, John, Master of Balliol, mentioned, 19.
Parliament at Oxford, 51.
Parret, Simon, benefaction of, 394, note.
Parsons, James, edits the Septuagint, calls on Blanco White, 203, 204.
Parsons, John, Master of Balliol, 332.
Patronage, acted by the O.D.A., 384.
Paul, Charles Kegan, acts in the *Thumping Legacy*, 384.
Pearson, the days of, mentioned, 239.
Peckwater Quadrangle. See COLLEGES—Christ Church.
Peel, Sir Robert, contest about, 209.
PEMBROKE COLLEGE. See under COLLEGES.
Pembroke, Philip, Earl of, mentioned, 38.
Pembroke, William, Earl of, much troubled at the disputes consequent on the election of proctors, 10.
PENTON, Stephen, referred to in preface, vi, vii ; his tutor, 39 ; enthusiasm and disappointment, 40; anger against Oxford, 40; debates what to do with his second son, 41 ; decides to take him to Oxford, 42 ; interviews the proctor, 42 ; the tutor, 43-50; becomes more satisfied with the University, 51. See TABLE OF CONTENTS.
Pett, Phineas, a canon of Ch. Ch., 179.
Philipps, Sir John, 111, 112.
Phipps, Constantinus, presented with D.C.L. degree, 71.
Physic Garden, the, Evelyn visits, 24, 26 ; 'Linnean Sibthorpe's gate' at, 201.
Pie, Sir Walter, mentioned, 25.
Pinke, Robert, Warden of New Coll., mentioned, 5.
Pitt, William, recovery of, declared hopeless, 235.
Plot, Robert, keeper of the Ashmolean, 33.
'Poet Harding,' 180.
Port, fiery Oxford, 172 ; 393 ; at £1 5s. per dozen, 213; at All Souls, 397.
Portland, William Henry Cavendish Bentinck, Duke of, 151 ; *Encænia* of, 222-3.
'Posting,' 96.
Postmasters, of Merton College, live at Beam Hall, 349, 387.
POTENGER, John, gains a scholarship at Corpus Christi, 53 ; his tutor, 54 ; his studies, 54 ; reading in the college hall, 55 ; takes his B.A. degree, 55 ; performs a portion of the exercises for M.A. degree, 56. See TABLE OF CONTENTS.
Potter, Christopher, Prov. of Queen's Coll., account of, 6.
Preston, R. M., takes part in the tragedy of *Ion*, 382.
Pricking *ager*, 263.
Prideaux, John, mentioned, 35, 38.
Proctors, Bodley and Bearblocke elected, 2 ; canvass for the place of, 7, 9-10 ; the Act at St. Mary's opened by the, 21 ; speeches of, 31 ; conversation with Penton, 42-3 ; forced to drink King George's health, 77, 81, 82 ; of the Court and of the University, 85 9 ; examiners appointed by, 93, 95 ; dress of, 184; set impositions, 185 ; *the Society for Scientific and Literary Disquisition* demand an interview with the Vice-Chancellor and —, 218 ; John Bull, senior, 305 ; mentioned, 160, 164, 166. See BLACK BOOK.
Professors, speeches of, 21 ; neglectful, 71-2 ; Gibbon's description of Oxford —, 117-8 ; vindication of, 133, 146-8 ; at a mineralogy lecture, 257 ; anecdote concerning the Oxford —, 297-8 ; 'deserve to be impaled alive,' 299 ; habitation of, 367.
Programma, 92.
Pusey, Edward Bouverie, Blanco White receives a letter from, 209 ; an undergraduate of Ch. Ch., 309 ; attends Lloyd's divinity lectures, 325 ; remarkable for very long sermons, 351 ; suspended for two years, 352, 353.
'Puseyism,' 338.
Pycroft, Rev. James, B.A., author of *Oxford Memories*, 371.

'Quads,' arm-chair races in the, 356-9, 394.
QUEEN'S COLLEGE. See under COLLEGES.
Quodlibets. See under *Doing quodlibets*.

Radcliffe library, 184.

[16th cent. pp. 1-3; 17th, pp. 4-56; 18th, pp. 57-201; 212-27; 403-8; 19th, pp. 202-11; 228-402.]

Radcliffe square, 242.
Randolph, Thomas, Pres. of Corpus Christi, account of, 153-4.
Reade, Charles, in a green coat with brass buttons, 369; at Magdalen during the Long Vacation, 375.
Reay, Stephen, Prof. of Arabic, and senior assistant librarian at the Bodleian, 348, 349.
Regent-Master of the Schools, 91, 162.
Residence, period of, at the University, 45, note; Gibbon's, 131-3; Shelley regrets the shortness of, 275.
Respondents, 73.
Responding, 161.
Rice, Rev. John Morland, a Fellow of Magdalen, 387.
Ricketts, Rev. W., Fellow of Merton, mentioned, 347.
Ridding, Charles Henry, takes part in arm-chair races, 395.
Riding-house, the, attendance of scholars, 6.
Riding-school, Lord Clarendon's bequest applied to the establishment of a, 128. See HORSES.
Roberson, George Thomas, or William Henry Moncrieff, Linc. Coll., a 'coach,' 350.
Robinson, Rev. Henry, D.D., author of *St. Alban Hall*, Oxford, 346; rooms at St. Alban Hall, 347; passes his final examination, 347. See TABLE OF CONTENTS.
Romney, Charles Marsham, Lord, mentioned, 158.
Roswell, John, Potenger's tutor, 54.
Round, James Hall, scholar of Balliol, 332, 333; opposed to Tractarianism, 338, 344.
Routh, Martin Joseph, Pres. of Magd. Coll., alluded to, 226; an Oxford celebrity, 353; account of, 389-91.
Rowe, William C., Balliol, candidate for Oriel Fellowship, 345.
Royal Oak, the, at Eynsham, 368.
Royal visitors, of 1814, 305; at Nuneham Courtenay, 354.
Rushworth's Collections, Dibdin's affection for, 216.
Ruskin, John, gentleman-commoner of Ch. Ch., 352.
Russell, John, scholar of Corpus Christi, 152.

ST. ALBAN HALL. See under COLLEGES.
St. Aldate's Church, 105.
St. Clement's, 367.
St. Ebbe's Church, mentioned, 353.

ST. EDMUND HALL. See under COLLEGES.
ST. JOHN'S College. See under COLLEGES.
St. Mary's Church, Evelyn matriculates in the vestry of, 18; Acts held at, 21, 26, 29; sermons at, 21, 31, 33, 407; behaviour of undergraduates at, 47; keeper of the galleries at, 64, note; clerk of, 64, note; prayers at, 95; Methodists go to, 105; Whitefield receives Sacrament at, 106; disputations held at, 164; beadles parade to, 217; illuminated in honour of Earl Howe's victory, 224; Latin epitaph at, 306; Newman, Vicar of, 347; mentioned, 366.
St. Peter's-in-the-East, coffee house in the parish of, 19, note; members of St. Alban Hall go to, 347.
Sala, George Augustus, a sketch by, 381.
Salisbury, Robert Arthur Talbot Gascoigne, Lord Cecil, third Marquis of, 398-9.
Sandby, Charles, mentioned, 179.
Sandford, a sail in the *Hobby-horse* to, 199-200, 368.
Saunders, Augustus Page, Dean of Peterborough, 321.
Savilian statutes concerning attendance at lectures, 91.
Say, Robert, Prov. of Oriel, 25.
Sayes Court, Evelyn's residence, 24, note.
Scagliola, 169.
Schemes, 95, 163.
Scholars, coming from chapel, 187; table in hall for, 190, 193; pledged by the newly elected President, 213, note; at Corpus, 248; at Univ., 296; mentioned, 387.
Scholarships, at Corpus, 248; open to public competition at Balliol, 334.
Schools, the, Evelyn goes to, 21; coursing in, 36, see note; Potenger does his public exercises in, 55, disputing for degrees in, 74, 161; examinations at, 92; deserted, 185; 'sitting in,' 378; Dr. Routh's book read in, 389. See EXAMINATION.
Sconced, 58.
Scotland, University of, 161.
Scott, Robert, Master of Balliol, account of, 339-40.
Scott, Sir William, tutor at Univ. Coll., 127, 147.
Scout, the, Colman's description of, 174-5; at Trinity, 186, 194; annoys Shelley, 260-1; Oakeley visited by,

INDEX. 425

318; Dons gain information concerning undergraduates from, 371.
Senior Fellow, respect paid to, 159.
Senior, Nassau William, accompanies Blanco White, 210; lectures of, 227.
Sermons. See under UNIVERSITY.
Servitor, visited in private, 101-2; George Whitefield admitted at Pembroke as, 104; duties of, 107; writes impositions for undergraduates, 185, 197.
Servitorships, at Ch. Ch., 319.
Severne, John Edmund, a volunteer coachman, 384.
Sewell, William, of Exeter Coll., distinguished college tutor, 351-2.
Seymer, John Gunning, St. Alban Hall, took a second class in the Schools, 349.
SHAFTESBURY, Anthony Ashley Cooper, first Earl of, of Lincoln's Inn, 35; keeps horses and servants at Oxford, 35; coursing, 36; attempt to alter the college beer, 37; abolition of 'tucking' freshmen at Exeter Coll., 37. See TABLE OF CONTENTS.
Shaftesbury, Anthony Ashley Cooper, Lord, at Ch. Ch., 309.
SHELBURNE, William Fitzmaurice, second Earl of, account of, 149; his tutor, 149; introduced to Lord Chesterfield and Lord Granville, 149; his reading, 150; attends Blackstone's lectures, 150; connected with the Anti-Westminsters, 150; low state of Christ Church intellectually, 151. See TABLE OF CONTENTS.
Sheldon, Dr. Gilbert, 26, 29.
Sheldonian Theatre, the, building of, 26; *Encænia* of, 29, 31; beadles parade to, 217; the *Encænia* of the Duke of Portland, 223; Oakeley at the, 304.
SHELLEY, Percy Bysshe, referred to in preface, vi; account of, 254; first meeting with Hogg at dinner, 255; enters into a discussion, 256; his discordant voice, 256-7; attends a lecture on mineralogy, 257-8; discourses on chemistry, 257, 258; his rooms at Univ. Coll., 260, 262; electrical experiments, 263; companionship with Hogg, 264-6; practice of pistol-shooting, 266-8; plays ducks and drakes during his country walks, 269; sails paper boats, 269-70; his opinion of the Universities, 273-4; affection for Oxford, 274; desires the old period of residence, 275; dilates on the blessing of the 'oak,' 275-7; his opinion of his instructors, 278; his reading, 279; Latin verse, 281-2; attached to the successful side in the election of Chancellor, 284; laments the political divisions of the University, 284; antipathy for a political career, 284-5; begins to print, 285; delight at a trick played at Oxford concerning English essay prize, 286; his pamphlet on Atheism, 287; *Posthumous Fragments of Margaret Nicholson*, 289; expelled from the University, 289-90; leaves Oxford, 294, 296. See TABLE OF CONTENTS.
SHENSTONE, William, at Pembroke Coll., 97, 99; intercourse with Richard Graves and Anthony Whistler, 99-100; writes the character of Mr. Graves, 100; his work, 100; personal appearance, 101; does not take a degree, 103; his house at Leasowes, 103. See TABLE OF CONTENTS.
Sherbrook, Lord, a popular 'coach,' 350.
Shippen, Robert, Prin. of Brasenose Coll., Vice-Chancellor, 86-9.
Short, Thomas Vowler, Bp. of St. Asaph, tutor of Ch. Ch., 312; account of, 314; lectures of, 326-7.
Shotover, 25, 33, 367.
Shuttleworth, Philip Nicholas, Warden of New Coll., friend of Blanco White, 202; of Oakeley, 316, 354.
Sibthorp, John, 147 note, 201.
Simeon, Mr., of Cambridge, promotes religion among the undergraduates, 348.
Sims, Mr., sells port at £1 5s. per doz., 213.
'Sitting in the Schools,' 378.
Skating on Ch. Ch. meadow, 189.
Skinner, John, probable writer of *Letters from Oxford*, account of, 183.
'Smalls,' 393, 399.
Smith, Adam, on professors, 118.
Smith, Samuel, Dean of Ch. Ch., 319.
Snell Exhibitions, the, at Balliol, 334.
Sneyd, Lewis, Warden of All Souls, description of, 354, 397.
Snowden, of University, mentioned, 398.
Society for Scientific and Literary Disquisition, 218.
Somaster, Joseph, of Hart Hall and Balliol, 59; desires a *discessit*, 60; expenses at Hart Hall, 63-5; scholarship at Balliol. 66.

Somaster, William, 62.
Sophs, description of, 161, note; exercises for the title and insignia of, 162; Colman among, 176.
South, Robert, Dr., Public Orator, 30.
SOUTHEY, Robert, letter of, to Thomas Davis Lamb, 403. See TABLE OF CONTENTS;—Appendix.
Southwell, Clinton educated at, 228, 229, 237.
Southwell, Marcus Richard, a volunteer coachman, 384.
Spanning farthings, 47, note.
Spencer, the name of, shouted at the *Illumination* in honour of Earl Howe's victory, 224.
Spencer, Lord Robert, 158.
Spencer, Mr. Robert, mentioned, 32, 33.
Sprat, Dr., mentioned, 31.
'Spreads,' 307, 308
Stanhope, Philip Henry, fifth Earl of, Oakeley meets, 322.
Stanley, Arthur Penrhyn, Dean of Westminster, at Balliol, 344.
Stanley, Edward Geoffrey Smith. See DERBY.
Stanley, Edward John Stanley, Lord, of Alderley, at Ch. Ch., 309.
Star Inn, the, 348.
Statutes. See under UNIVERSITY.
Stead, John, All Souls Coll., 80.
Steele, Sir Richard, quotation from his dedication to the Pope, 75.
Stepney, Sir John, 158.
Stillingfleet, the days of, mentioned, 239.
Stoddart, John, Ch. Ch., member of the *Society for Scientific and Literary Disquisition*, 219, 221.
Stodman, Mr., declares the antiquity of the All Souls Mallard Feast, 243.
Stokes, Master of the 'dauncing and vaulting schole,' 20.
Stone pulpit, Magdalen, 394, note.
Stow Wood, 368.
'Strings,' 74.
Studentships, choristerships, servitorships, the awarding of, at Ch. Ch., 319-21.
'Sugary' Thompson, an Oxford printseller, 381.
Supper-parties, at Pembroke, 97-8; at Merton, 158; at Trinity, 193-8; at Magdalen, 393.
Surtees (author of *Jorrocks*), 377.
Swiss education, 139.

Syllogisms, sets of, called 'strings,' 74; threadbare, 91, 93, 162, 278.
Symmons, John, contemporary and friend of Henry Fynes Clinton, 230, 232, 239.
Symons, Dr., Warden of Wadham, 354.

Tait, Archibald Campbell, Archbp. of Canterbury, candidate for a scholarship at Balliol, 335-6; becomes Archbishop, 347; opposes Newman's *Tract No. 90*, 336, 352.
Talfourd, Francis, of Ch. Ch., and the O.D.A., 379-85.
Talfourd, Sir Thomas Noon, author of *Ion*, 381-2.
'Taprobane,' Latin verse college prize poem, written by Oakeley, 313.
Temple, Frederick, Bp. of London, elected to a Snell Exhibition at Ball. Coll., 334.
Tennant, John Robert, of St. Alban Hall, 346.
Term-trotters, 165.
TERRÆ FILIUS (Nicholas Amhurst), reference to in preface, vi; account of, 68; admission and matriculation, 68; loyalty at Oxford, 70; letter from Wadham Coll. to the author of, concerning neglectful lecturers, 71; method of disputations, 73; account of Mr. Meadowcourt, his being put into the black book, and pleading the Act of Grace, 75-90; account of the method of acquiring university degrees, 90-6. See TABLE OF CONTENTS.
Testimonium, the granting of a, 93; ease in getting one signed, 163, 164.
Tests, abolition of, 370.
Thackeray, W. M., referred to in preface, vii.
Theatricals, 378-85. See COMEDY.
Themes, Whitefield's inability to perform his, 108.
Thicknesse, Mr. Jas., Fellow of Balliol, mentioned, 19.
'Thirds,' custom of paying, for furniture, 183, 262.
Thirty-nine articles, statute concerning 69, 124, 386.
Thompson, 'Sugary,' 381.
Thornton, John, schoolfellow of Bp. Heber, 298.
Tillotson, Dr., mentioned, 31.
Tilting, 358.
Toasts, 193; drinking to a chorus, 393.
Tom, of Christ Church, 84, 315.
Tookers, the, mentioned, 37.

[16th cent. pp. 1-3; 17th, pp. 4-56; 18th, pp. 57-201; 212-27; 403-*; 19th, pp. 202-11; 228-402.]

INDEX. 427

TOURNAMENTS HOLDEN AT OXFORD, 356-65. See TABLE OF CONTENTS.
'Town and Gown' disturbance, 309.
Tractarianism, Shuttleworth, Warden of New College, an enemy of, 317: the rise of, 337, 338; rapid progress of, 340.
Tracts, Oxford, 299; Newman's, 336, 352.
TRINITY COLLEGE. See under COLLEGES.
Tubney, shooting at, 375.
Tucker, Rev. John, mentioned, 252.
Tucking freshmen, 37-8.
Tutors, Hobbes', 14, 16; Penton's, 39-40; for Penton's son, 42, 43; the advice of, 44-9; invites Penton to a Commons, 49-50; charge of, 50; Potenger's, 54; pleased with Somaster, 59; for nothing, 60; charges of, 60-2; 63, note; Whitefield's, 107; should send their pupils to visit the sick, 112; Gibbon's, 121-3, 133, 139, 141; a narrow-minded, 149; Earl of Malmesbury's, 158; at Colman's matriculation, 169; at the Duke of Portland's *Encænia*, 222; changes in, 241; 248, note; at Corpus, 249; priggish, 277-8; depart during Vacation, 280; rumour ascribes the denouncing of Shelley, to a pert, meddling, 293; 'deserve to be impaled alive,' 299; Oakeley's private, 304; his college, 307; tutorial staff at Ch. Ch., 311; Longley a very popular, 314; seconds Oakeley's resolution to read for a fellowship, 322; tutorial lectures, 325; anecdote of, 326; college, 327; mathematical, at Balliol, 341; absence of donnish exclusiveness on the part of, 343; at St. Alban Hall, 347; 351; send for undergraduates, 361; houses of, 367; intercourse between undergraduates and, 371-5.
Twiss, Travers; only college tutor not in holy orders, 351.
Tyler, Miss, Southey writes a letter from the house of, 403.
Tyrrell, Sir Timothy, 25 note; 33.
Tyrwhitt, Sir Thomas, 178.

Unattached students, 370.
Undergraduates, 170; depart during Vacation, 280; Oakeley the sport of overbearing, 304; at the Sheldonian theatre, 305; Oakeley suffers from buoyant, 307; late at chapel, 311; idle career of, 319; improvement in Balliol, 333; and Tractarianism, 338; moral tone of, 342; at St. Alban Hall, 346, 349; at New College, 347; custom of, to sit in the 'quad,' 356; summoned to the Hall, 363; correct dress for, 369; change in the life of, 370; intercourse with younger tutors, 371; vanish during the Long Vacation, 375; sitting in the Schools, 378; not permitted to come to Oxford to read out of term, 390; dine in cap and gown, 391; Magdalen, 392; doings of, 393-4.
Union Debating Society, *The Attic Society* the germ of, 252; established, 330-1, 399.
Universities, English, use of arms banished from, 113; expenses at, 128 note; 141; held in high esteem, 160, 161, 299.
Universities, foreign, 113, 117, 242.
UNIVERSITY COLLEGE. See under COLLEGES.
UNIVERSITY, the, of Oxford, Bodley sent to, 1; decides to set up his staffe at the library door at, 2; orator, 2; public sermon of the, at Ch. Ch., 6; canvass for a proctor's place in. 7; the peace of, likely to be broken, 10; Hobbes sent to, 14; Evelyn goes to, 18; exceedingly regular under Laud, 19; gentlemen of Exeter College present a comedy to, 20; small benefit to Evelyn being at, 21; the Arundel marbles among the greatest treasures of 26, note; Evelyn procures Arundel marbles for, 27; acknowledges the obligation, 27; Decree from, to Evelyn, 28; letter from, to Mr. Howard, 29; exceeding all other universities, 29; large number of visitors at, 29; gift of the theatre to, 30; orator's speech, 30; intends conferring a degree on Evelyn, 32; Shaftesbury goes to, 35; Ch. Ch. the largest college in, 36; greatest conditions of *honour* and *trust* supplied from, 39; disturbances in Church and State slacken the discipline of, 40; Penton's sister's chaplain rails against, 40; fast to the monarchy, 41; improvement in, 42; country gentlemen's unfavourable account of, 42; residing the whole year at, 45, note; Penton becomes more satisfied with the government of, 51; carriage of, towards members of parliament, 51; Latin drops out of colloquial use at,

[16th cent. pp. 1-3; 17th, pp. 4-56; 18th. pp. 57-201; 212-27; 403-8; 19th, pp. 202-11; 228-402.]

54; ignorance of the rules of, 60; remuneration of tutors at, 61; Hart Hall as inexpensive as any House of learning in, 63; dues, 64; state of, 68-70; disputations in the public schools of, 74; the presence required at disputations, of students in, 74; the black book a register of the, 79; proctors of, 85; a proctor of the court afraid of disobliging the, 87; Mr. Meadowcourt denied the privilege of a member of, 89; meeting of the members of, 89; degrees, 90-6; sciences usually taught in, 100; Shenstone *amuses* himself with poetry at, 100; his personal adornment at, 101; takes no degree at, 103; it is judged proper for Whitefield to go to, 104; he finds the benefit of a holy life, when at, 105; his expenses at, 110; the place to prosecute his studies, 111; in his opinion the Heads of Universities should send their pupils to visit the sick, etc., 112; Gibbon matriculates at, 113; 130; 140; 143; his introduction to, 114; Bp. Lowth's description of, 114; Gibbon acknowledges no obligation to, 115; number of professors at, 117, 146; professors have given up teaching in, 118; sum of Gibbon's improvement at, 121; improvements in, 127, 299; no longer needs a riding-school, 128; vindication of, 130-48; Gibbon is plunged too early into the boisterous element of, 131; is incapable of self-management when sent to, 131; his residence in, 132; the term *Academical bigots* signifies the, 145; Gibbon expelled by, 146; botany not fashionable at, 147; injustice of Gibbon towards, 148; profitable hours spent by Edgeworth at, 153; James, Earl of Malmesbury at, 157; lax discipline at, 158; absurdities of the institutions of, 161; Dr. Fell supports the exercises of, 165, note; contemptible to its own members, 166; Colman matriculates at, 168; coming from one of the public schools to, 173; Blanco White establishes himself at, 202; feels mortified that he is not a member of, 204; notice of the proposition of the conferring of a degree on Blanco White, 204, note; he receives a degree of M.A. of, 206; want of sympathy with the governing party prevents Blanco White from settling in, 208; want of supporters among members of, 209; Sir R. Peel resigns his seat as member for, 209; senior members of the, opposed to Blanco White, 211; Dr. Whateley leaves, 211; Dibdin's affection for, 212; distressing somnolency of, 217; the laws of, 218; Copleston shields, 222; discipline of, 227; Clinton enters at, 228; examinations at, 238; study of Greek at, 239; Heber re-visits, 240; plan of tuition at, 249; Keble achieves the highest honours of, 252; theological studies deplorably low at, 253; Hogg's first impressions of, 254-5; Shelley and Hogg discuss, 273; great reforms needed at, 280; 'beardless politicians' at, 281: feuds at, 283-4; tuition at, 285; divided opinion of, concerning the case of W. Attfield, 286; abuse of the endowments of, 288-9; Shelley and Hogg leave the, 294; anecdote respecting, 297-8; Oakeley's want of congeniality with, 302; at Commemoration, 304; the authorities of, discourage the Union Debating Society, 331; with the rise of Tractarianism Mr. Ogilvie's influence decreases with, 337; Balliol the foremost college in, 353; authorities of, 360; approach to, 367; changes in 369; education, 370; theatricals at, 385; change at, 386; Knatchbull-Hugessen's happy recollections of, 400-1; Southey's journey to, 403. See ACADEMICAL DRESS; ALMA MATER; COFFEE HOUSES; EXAMINATIONS; HEBD. COUNCIL; LECTURES; MATRICULATION; PROCTORS; PROFESSORS; ST. MARY'S CHURCH; UNDERGRADUATES, &c.

AMUSEMENTS AT, riding, 6; dancing and vaulting, 20; bowling, 46, 50; fencing, 152-3; skating, 189; boating, 199-201, 214, 226, 347; hunting, 241; tournaments, 356-65; shooting, 368; theatricals, 377-85; archery, 390; arm-chair races, 395. See HORSES and HUNTING.

CEREMONIES, cap, ring and kiss, 21, 31; of *creating* '*Sophs*,' 162; of conferring a B.A. degree, 164.

CHANCELLOR of, 25; Duke of Ormond, 32-33; Lord Grenville, 178; Duke of Portland, 222; Duke of Wellington came as, 354; visitor at the Halls, 355.

EXPENSES at, Evelyn manages his own, 20; Lord Shaftesbury's, 35-6; the tutor's advice to Penton with

[15th cent. pp. 1-3; 17th, pp. 4-56; 18th, pp. 57-201; 212-27; 403-8; 19th, pp. 202-11; 228-402.]

regard to, 46, 48; Somaster's, at Hart Hall, 63-5; Whitefield's, at Pembroke, 104-5, 109-10, 112; students of Oxford and Cambridge provided at their own, or that of the founders, 113, 114; 128, note; Dibdin avoids amusements which entail, 226; 255; rather heavy at St. Alban Hall, 348; of gentlemen-commoners at Magdalen, 388; of matriculation, 407. See BATTELS; COMMONS.

PRIZES, Edward Copleston gains the Latin prize poem, and the English essay, 222, note; Coleridge gains the Latin verse prize, 247; Churton gains Latin poem, 306; Howard gains, 309-10; Newdigate gained by Ambrose Barber, 310; by James Shergold Boone, 321; Oakeley gains Latin essay and English essay prizes, 323.

SERMONS, at the, at Ch. Ch., 6; by Dr. French at St. Mary's, 21; Latin, 22; against Atheism, preached by Dr. Hall, 31; by a Fellow of Brasenose, 33; 217; Pusey remarkable for long, 351; Pusey suspended on account of, 352; much better attended formerly, 353; Southey goes to hear, 407. See ST. MARY'S CHURCH.

STATUTES, swearing to a volume of, 68-9; concerning the thirty-nine articles, 69, 124; referring to disputations, 74; fine imposed according to, for being out of college at a late hour, 79, 82; concerning the attendance of lectures, 91; concerning examinations, 92, 163; collectors, 96; respecting the attendance of undergraduates at assizes, 155 note; academical dress, 162; dress of undergraduates, 169; a sort of *caput mortuum*, 217; remodelling of, 221-2; concerning the age of competitors in examinations, 249.

VICE-CHANCELLOR of the, Laud's letters to, 5, 6; Dr. Baylie, when Evelyn matriculates, 18; speech of, at the Act, 21, 22; creation of doctors by, 21, note; invites Evelyn to dinner, 25; letters to Evelyn from, 27-8; at the *Encænia* of the new Theatre, 30-1; confers a degree on Evelyn, 32; does him great honour, 33; overcome, during *coursing*, 36, see note; 41; Richard Meadowcourt appeals to, 87-9; at examinations, 164; Colman before, 168-9; members of the *Society for Scientific and Literary Disquisition*, wait upon, 218-9; has no authority beyond the precincts of the University, 353; Southey before, 407.

Ussher, Dr. James, Archbp. of Armagh, 25.

Vacations, Gibbon's literary tastes revive during, 122, 140; Colman visits London during, 181; Clinton's, 232, 233; he begins the tragedy of 'Solyman' during,234; 235; short—deserve utter execration, 279-80: change in the character of, 375-6. See LONG VACATION.

'Vaulting Master,' the, 20, note.
Vicary, Mr., organist of Magd. Coll., mentioned, 351.
Vice-Chancellor. See under UNIVERSITY.
Vincent, William, Dean of Westminster, 228, 229.
VINDICATION OF MAGDALEN COLLEGE, 130-48. See TABLE OF CONTENTS.
Viner, Mr., his benefaction, 129.
Vinerian professorship, 128.
Visitors, Royal, 305, 354.
Vores, T., Wadham, candidate for Oriel Fellowship, 345.

WADHAM COLLEGE. See under COLLEGES.
Wainfleet, Bp. of Winchester, 119, 349.
Waldegrave, Samuel, All Souls, curate of St. Ebbe's, 354.
Waldegrave, Thomas, tutor to Gibbon, 121; leaves Oxford, 122, 139-41.
Walker, Obadiah, Master of Univ. Coll., 27, 34.
Wall, Rev. Henry, Vice-Prin. of St. Alban Hall, 346, 349.
Wallis, John, D.D., mentioned, 25, 31.
Wall-Lectures, 165, see note.
Ward, Seth, Pres. of Trin. Coll., mentioned, 21.
Ward, Rev. William George, Fellow of Balliol, 336; account of, 338; resigns his fellowship on account of his Tractarian opinions, 340-1.
Warren, Dawson, account of, 183; at college breakfast, 188; mode of spending an evening, 195; part owner of the *Hobby-horse*, 199.
Warton, Thomas, Prof. of poetry, 71, 148.
Water-drinkers, Richard Graves invited to a party of, 97, 99.

[16th cent. pp. 1-3; 17th, pp. 4-56; 18th, pp. 57-201; 212-27; 403-8; 19th, pp. 202-11; 228-402.]

Water Eaton, mentioned, 368.
Watkins, Thomas, mentioned, 174.
Webber, Charles, mentioned, 179.
Weipart's harp at the *Encænia*, 223.
Wellesley, Richard, Marquess, 178; declamatory practice of, 180; mentioned, 366.
Wellington, *Encænia* of the Duke of, 222, 354; autograph letter of, 389.
Wenman, Hon. Thomas Francis, 147.
Wenman, Viscount, candidate in the ' great Oxfordshire election,' 120.
Wesley, Charles, intercourse with Whitefield, 106, 107, 111.
Wesley, John, mentioned, 106, 111.
Westminster boys, the ruling party at Ch. Ch., 149, 150; courtesy shown to, in examinations, 169; distinguished, 321.
Whateley, Richard, Archbp. of Dublin, intimate with Blanco White, 208, 209, 211.
Whistler, Anthony, Pemb. Coll., 99.
Whitbread, Samuel, 178.
WHITE, Joseph Blanco, account of, 202; establishes himself at Oxford, 202; friends at Oxford, 202-3; tutor at Holland House, 203; Hebdomadal Board proposes to confer on him an M.A. degree by diploma, 204; opposition to this proposal, 204; finally carried by a majority, 204-5, see note; resides at Oxford, 206; admitted into Oriel Coll., 206; his ideal of a college, 207; unorthodoxy, 208; narrow means, supposed jealousy of the University in neglecting to give him employment, 209; sets up the *London Review*, 209; votes in the Peel contest, 209; his right of voting examined, 210; separation from the Church, 210. See TABLE OF CONTENTS.
White, Mr., in the case of Mr. Meadowcourt, of Merton, 77-80, 82-3, 88-9.
White, Dr., his Bampton lectures, 148 and note.
WHITEFIELD, George, referred to in preface, vi; Servitor at Pemb. Coll., 104; expenses at the University, 105; spiritual trials, 105; meets Charles Wesley, 106; joins the Methodists, 106; religious fervour, 105-9; his tutor, 107; falls ill, 109; is ordained, 111; labours at Oxford, 111. See TABLE OF CONTENTS.
Whitelock, William, Queen's Coll., member of the *Society for Scientific and Literary Disquisition*, 219.
Whiting, cook at Magdalen, 398.
Wilberforce, Robert Isaac, candidate for the Oriel fellowship, 323, 345; attends Lloyd's Divinity lectures, 325; mentioned, 351.
Wilkins, John, Warden of Wadham, mentioned, 22.
Wilkinson, Dr. John, Prin. of Magd. Hall, 16.
Williams, George, Sherardian Prof. of Botany, 247-8.
Williams, Dr. David, Warden of New Coll., 354.
Wills, John, Warden of Wadham, 212; receives the deputation of the members of the *Society for Scientific and Literary Disquisition*, 219.
Wilson, Daniel, Bp. of Calcutta, mentioned, 348, 355.
Wilson, St. John's Coll., condemns Newman's *Tract No. 90*, 352.
' Windy Davis,' mentioned, 368.
Wine-parties, 193, 307, 360. See PORT.
Wingfield, Rev. Edward John, at Ch. Ch., 313.
Winter, George Robert, takes part in *Macbeth Travestie*, 381.
Wolsey, Cardinal, gift to Ch. Ch. library, 24.
Woodcock, Henry, Canon of Ch. Ch., 352.
Wren, Christopher, 22, 25; designs Sheldonian Theatre, 26, 29.
Wychwood, mentioned, 368.
Wykeham, William of, mentioned, 349.
Wynnstay, the seat of Sir Watkin Williams Wynn, George Colman visits, 168, 181.
Wynter, Dr., St. John's Coll., suspends Dr. Pusey on account of a sermon, 352.
Wytham, mentioned, 368.

Yates, Edmund, referred to, 384.

[16th cent. pp. 1-3; 17th, pp. 4-56; 18th, pp. 57-201; 212-27; 403-8; 19th, pp. 202-11; 228-402.]

THE END.

Oxford Historical Society.

PUBLICATIONS.

1884.

1. **Register of the University of Oxford.** Vol. I. (1449–63; 1505–71), edited by the Rev. C. W. BOASE, M.A., pp. xxxviii + 364. (price to the public, without discount, and prepaid, 16s.)

2. **Remarks and Collections of Thomas Hearne.** Vol. I. (4 July 1705—19 March 1707), edited by C. E. DOBLE, M.A., pp. viii + 404. (16s.)

1884–85.

3. **The Early History of Oxford (727-1100), preceded by a sketch of the Mythical Origin of the City and University.** By JAMES PARKER, M.A. With three illustrations, pp. xxii + 420. (20s.)

1885.

4. **Memorials of Merton College, with biographical notices of the Wardens and Fellows.** By the Hon. GEO. C. BRODRICK, Warden of Merton College. With one illustration, pp. xx + 416. (16s., to members of Merton 12s.)

5. **Collectanea, 1st series**, edited by C. R. L. FLETCHER, M.A. (Contents :—*a.* Letters relating to Oxford in the XIVth Century, edited by H. H. Henson; *b.* Catalogue of the Library of Oriel College in the XIVth Century, edited by C. L. Shadwell; *c.* Daily ledger of John Dorne, bookseller in Oxford, 1520, edited by F. Madan; *d.* All Souls College *versus* Lady Jane Stafford, 1587, edited by C. R. L. Fletcher; *e.* Account Book of James Wilding, Undergraduate of Merton College, 1682–88, edited by E. G. Duff; *f.* Dr. Wallis's Letter against Maidwell, 1700, edited by T. W. Jackson.) With two illustrations, pp. viii + 358. (16s.)

1886.

6. **Magdalen College and King James II, 1686–88.** A series of documents collected and edited by the Rev. J. R. BLOXAM, D.D., with additions, pp. lii + 292. (16s., to members of Magdalen 12s.)

7. **Hearne's Collections,** as No. 2 above. Vol. II. (20 Mar. 1707—22 May 1710), pp. viii + 480. (16s.)

PUBLICATIONS (*continued*).

8. **Elizabethan Oxford.** Reprints of rare tracts. Edited by the Rev. C. PLUMMER, M.A. (Contents:—*a*. Nicolai Fierberti Oxoniensis Academiæ descriptio, 1602 : *b*. Leonard Hutton on the Antiquities of Oxford; *c*. Queen Elizabeth at Oxford, 1566 [pieces by J. Bereblock, Thomas Nele, Nich. Robinson, and Rich. Stephens, with appendixes] : *d*. Queen Elizabeth at Oxford, 1592, by Philip Stringer: *e*. Apollinis et Musarum Eidyllia per Joannem Sandford, 1592), pp. xxxii+316. (10*s*.)

1887.

9. **Letters of Richard Radcliffe and John James, of Queen's College, Oxford, 1749–83**: edited by MARGARET EVANS. pp. xxxvi+306. (15*s*., to members of Queen's 10*s*. 6*d*.)

10. **Register of the University of Oxford, vol. II (1571–1622), part 1. Introductions.** Edited by the Rev. ANDREW CLARK, M.A. pp. xxxii+468. (18*s*.)

1887–8.

11. **Do. part 2. Matriculations and Subscriptions.** Edited by the Rev. ANDREW CLARK, M.A. pp. xvi+424. (18*s*.)

1888.

12. **Do. part 3. Degrees.** Edited by the Rev. ANDREW CLARK, M.A. pp. viii+448. (17*s*.)

13. **Hearne's Collections**, as No. 2 above. Vol. III. (25 May 1710—December 14, 1712), pp. viii+516. (16*s*.)

1889.

14. **Register of the University of Oxford, vol. II, part 4. Index.** Edited by the Rev. ANDREW CLARK, M.A., pp. viii+468. (17*s*.)

15. **Wood's History of the City of Oxford.** *New Edition.* By the Rev. ANDREW CLARK, M.A. Vol. I. The City and Suburbs. With three Maps and several Diagrams. pp. xii+660. (25*s*. : to citizens of Oxford 20*s*. : the two Maps of old Oxford separately, not folded, 1*s*. 6*d*. : to citizens 1*s*.)

1890.

16. **Collectanea, 2nd series**, edited by Professor MONTAGU BURROWS. (Contents:—*a*. The Oxford Market, by O. Ogle ; *b*. The University of Oxford in the Twelfth Century, by T. E. Holland ; *c*. The Friars Preachers of the University, edited by H. Rashdall;

PUBLICATIONS (*continued*).

d. Notes on the Jews in Oxford, by A. Neubauer; *e.* Linacre's Catalogue of Grocyn's Books, followed by a Memoir of Grocyn, by the Editor; *f.* Table-Talk and Papers of Bishop Hough, 1703-1743, edited by W. D. Macray; *g.* Extracts from the 'Gentleman's Magazine' relating to Oxford, 1731-1800, by F. J. Haverfield. Appendix: Corrections and Additions to Collectanea, vol. I. (Day-book of John Dorne, Bookseller at Oxford, A.D. 1520, by F. Madan, including 'A Half-century of Notes' on Dorne, by Henry Bradshaw.) With one diagram, pp. xii + 518. (16*s.*)

17. **Wood's History of the City of Oxford**, as No. 15 above. Vol. II. Churches and Religious Houses. With Map and Diagram, pp. xii + 550. (20*s.*: to citizens of Oxford, 16*s.*: Map of Oxford in 1440, separately, not folded, 9*d.*; to citizens, 6*d.*)

1890-91.

18. **Oxford City Documents**, financial and judicial, 1268-1665. Selected and edited by J. E. THOROLD ROGERS, late Drummond Professor of Political Economy in the University of Oxford. pp. viii + 440 + 2 loose leaves. (12*s.*)

1891.

19. **The Life and Times of Anthony Wood, antiquary, of Oxford, 1632-1695, described by Himself.** Collected from his Diaries and other Papers, by the Rev. ANDREW CLARK, M.A. Vol. I: 1632-1663. With Illustrations. pp. xvi + 520. (20*s.*)

20. **The Grey Friars in Oxford.** Part I, A History of the Convent; Part II, Biographical Notices of the Friars, together with Appendices of original documents. By ANDREW G. LITTLE, M.A. pp. xvi + 372. (16*s.*)

1892.

21. **The Life and Times of Anthony Wood, antiquary, of Oxford, 1632-1695, described by Himself.** Collected from his Diaries and other Papers, by the Rev. ANDREW CLARK, M.A. Vol. II: 1664-1681. With Illustrations. pp. xxviii + 576. (20*s.*)

22. **Reminiscences of Oxford, by Oxford men, 1559-1850.** Selected and edited by LILIAN M. QUILLER COUCH. pp. xvi + 430. (17*s.*)

PUBLICATIONS *(continued)*.

Forthcoming Publications (subject to alteration).

1892-93.
23. **Calendar of Berkshire Wills, 1508-1652.**

1893.
24. **History of Kidlington, Yarnton and Begbrook.** By the Hon. Mrs. STAPLETON.

25. **History of Corpus Christi College, Oxford, with lists of its members.** By the Rev. the PRESIDENT OF THE COLLEGE.

The 3rd and 4th vols. of CLARK's edition of *Wood's Life and Times*, the 3rd vol. of the same Editor's *Wood's History of the City of Oxford*, the *Cartulary of St. Frideswide's* edited by the Rev. S. R. WIGRAM, the 4th vol. of *Hearne's Diaries* edited by C. E. DOBLE, Esq., the *Place Names of the diocese of Oxford*, and other volumes are in active preparation.

A full description of the Society's work and objects can be obtained by application to any of the Committee (Rev. C. W. BOASE, Exeter College; Rev. ANDREW CLARK, 30 Warnborough Road; P. LYTTELTON GELL, Esq., Headington Hill; FALCONER MADAN, Esq. (*Hon. Treasurer*), 90 Banbury Road; and C. L. SHADWELL, Esq., Frewin Hall, Oxford). The annual subscription is one guinea, and **the published volumes as a set can be obtained by new members at one-fourth the published price** (i.e. 10s. 6d. a year).

www.ingramcontent.com/pod-product-compliance
Lightning Source LLC
Chambersburg PA
CBHW022146300426
44115CB00006B/362